A HISTORY OF FINE ART IN INDIA & CEYLON

Wild duck, anonymous. Fol 10, Dara Shikoh's album. (Mughal school, Shah Jehan period. Mid-17th Century or earlier).

A HISTORY OF FINE ART IN INDIA & CEYLON

By

VINCENT A. SMITH

SECOND EDITION
Revised by
K. DE B. CODRINGTON

THIRD EDITION
Revised and Enlarged by
KARL KHANDALAVALA

D. B. TARAPOREVALA SONS & CO. PRIVATE LTD.
TREASURE HOUSE OF BOOKS
210, DR. DADABHAI NAOROJI ROAD, FORT, BOMBAY 1.

PRINTED IN INDIA

Distributed in Europe and British Commonwealth countries,
except India, Burma, Ceylon, and Pakistan,
by the Oxford University Press, London.

Published by Jal Hirji D. Taraporevala for D. B. Taraporevala Sons & Co. Private Ltd., Bombay, and Printed by Isaac N. Isaac at Vakil & Sons (Private) Ltd., Narandas Building, Sprott Road, 18, Ballard Estate, Bombay.

EDITOR'S NOTE TO THE THIRD REVISED AND ENLARGED EDITION

In the present edition of Vincent Smith's classic work the text of the Second Edition, pursuant to the arrangement with the publishers, remains unaltered. The editor however has added notes at the end of several chapters while several new illustrations have been included. Almost all the original illustrations have also been retained. It was felt that it would not be proper to interfere with Vincent Smith's viewpoint or appraisal of his subject matter as it appeared in the Second Edition for it is on the whole eminently fair despite the fact that there may be grounds for disagreement here and there. The book is a masterly exposition of a vast canvas and it is far from being out of date though written many years ago. This circumstance is a tribute to Vincent Smith's enlightened perception and feeling for Indian art. The present editor has limited his notes to the minimum so as to avoid undue increase in the text as well as much controversial matter of little interest to the general reader. The notes are only intended to draw attention to certain matters of essential importance. The legends to the illustrations do however indicate the present editor's preferences regarding provenance, schools, dates, etc.

KARL KHANDALAVALA

PUBLISHER'S NOTE

The original text of Vincent Smith and the footnotes by K. de B. Codrington to the Second Edition remain unaltered. Editorial changes where absolutely necessary have been placed in square brackets in the text. Additions to legends of illustrations appearing in the previous edition have also been placed in brackets.

EDITOR'S NOTE TO THE THIRD REVISED AND ENLARGED EDITION

[illegible] edition of Vincent Smith's classic work [illegible] text of the Second [illegible] in the arrangement with the [illegible] additions [illegible] several chapters [illegible] [illegible]

PUBLISHER'S NOTE

[illegible] of Vincent Smith and the footnotes by K. de B. Codrington [illegible] edition remain unaltered. Editorial changes [illegible] placed in square brackets in the text. Additions [illegible] appearing in the previous edition have also been placed in square brackets.

PREFACE TO THE SECOND EDITION

IT was left to Vincent Smith to summarize the results of the first century of historical and archaeological research in India, and his *Oxford History of India* and *Early History of India* are still authoritative works of reference. His *History of Indian Fine Art* was the outcome of his realization of the importance of the evidence of archaeology in Indian studies, and of his perception that the aesthetic nationalism preached by Mr. Havell and Dr. Coomaraswamy in their pioneer works was not acceptable without deeper research and a more accurate appreciation of the facts. It may be admitted that the criticism of art was never his chief care, although he had acquired an unrivalled experience of the great sites of India during his long period of service. His strength lay in his determination to set down on paper what was known and what was conjectured, and in such order that it might be easily grasped. Since then new discoveries have been made and new facts been brought to light. Opinions have consequently changed. For one thing Indian sculpture and painting have taken their place among the familiar arts: mediocre Mughal paintings are at a premium in the sale room; Ajanta and Ellora are made much of in the advertising schemes of the Indian railways; the literature of Indian art grows apace. Yet in spite of changes and the passage of years Vincent Smith's chronology of Early India remains a defensible whole, and we are no nearer to an exact knowledge of the Graeco-Buddhist art of Gandhara. In fact, an examination of the reports of recent discoveries would suggest that we are suffering from an over-abundance of new material which we are unable to handle.

Official research in India has many obstacles, the chief among which is, undoubtedly, conservation. Furthermore, until recently there has been no co-operation between the workers in the field and scholars in general. This period of isolation is passing. It was inevitable that the widening of research in the near east should raise questions concerning India, questions which must be answered. The problem is a hard one, but now that India has penetrated within the field of academic interest a more general and keener criticism will be brought to bear on Indian researches which must work for the good of all concerned. At the moment there is a distressing lack of attention to matters of classification. No corpus of Indian pottery exists, and very little information about the pottery of the classic Indian sites has been made accessible to scholars out of India. Apart from the many dark periods of Indian chronology no agreed period classification is in use, leading to much confusion, especially when an attempt is made to translate dynastic periods into geography. Furthermore, there is urgent need for a technical analysis of Gupta and medieval architecture after the manner of M. Jouveau-Dubreuil's excellent *Archeologie du Sud de l'Inde*.[1] In fact there is so much to be done that it is essential that any account of Indian history or art should confess the fact. In the present state of Indian knowledge to attempt the encyclopaedic is to mislead. At the moment a consecutive account, rather than a detailed account, is wanted.

1 A corpus of Indian Pottery and another of Indian Beads are being formed by the Indian Research Committee (Royal Anthropological Institute), 52 Upper Bedford Place, W. A short analysis of medieval pillars, mouldings, and motives is included in the editor's *Medieval India* (Ernest Benn, Ltd.) which is now in active preparation.

This, as has been said, was the great merit of the *History of Indian Fine Art*, and an attempt has been made to preserve it. The text of this revision is therefore not weighted down with recent references and theories, which, however, may be arrived at by means of the short bibliography provided. The greatest change is the unification of the dual accounts of the history of architecture and sculpture, which does away with a considerable amount of repetition. The plates and page illustrations have also been rearranged and a large number of new illustrations introduced. A great deal of aesthetic comment has, furthermore, been omitted, partly because it can quite well be left to the student himself, and partly because it was considered desirable to shorten the book as much as possible. Lastly, it must be stated that the matter dealing with Indian paintings is intended to be only general and introductory. In this subject much research is still necessary before 'schools' can be accurately distinguished from 'periods'.

The question of the period classification to be adopted was a difficult one. The dynastic periods in common use are seldom accurately datable, often of long duration, and always lead to geographical complications.[1] They are moreover archaeologically unreal. Three dynastic periods, however, may be preserved because they provide a sufficiently accurate chronology and because they happen to coincide with the evidence of the sculptures: these are the Mauryan, Kushan, and Gupta. It may be pointed out that our knowledge does not at present warrant our speaking of 'cultures' in India, if we use the word in its accredited archaeological sense. An accurate knowledge of Indian pottery would enable us to do so and would doubtless necessitate a completely new classification.

The present position with regard to the transliteration of place-names is complicated. Since the publication of the Index to the *Archaeological Survey Reports* there has been a tendency to Sanskritize place-names wholesale. It is only necessary here to point out that the central authority on Indian subjects, the *Imperial Gazetteer*, adopts a system based 'upon the usage now generally adopted', that is to say the system of the district gazetteers. These will always be the source-books of Indian studies, and the position is considerably confused by departing from their usage. As a whole, the place-names of India have acquired their present rendering at the hands of the early administrators and the compilers of route-books, not to speak of railway time-tables. In this edition the classes of consonants are not distinguished. In the first edition long vowels were marked 'where necessary as a guide to pronunciation'. They are here consistently omitted, and students in doubt are referred to the *Gazetteer* or the volumes given in the short bibliography.

I have to thank the Directors of the various Museums indicated in the list of illustrations, Mr. Ajit Ghose, and also the following, for permission to reproduce photographs:

The Archaeological Survey of India (Mysore, Madras, Western India, and Ceylon) for Plates 2, 3 B and C, 7 B, 15 B, 16, 17 B and C, 19 A-D, 20 B, 24 B, 31 A and B, 38 C, 41 D, 43, 44, 46 B and C, 58, 59, 60, 64, 66, 67, 68, 70 A, 71 A, 75 B, 76 A, 78, 79, 80, 81 C, 83, 88, 89, 90, 94, 96, 97, 98, 99, 100, 101, 102 B, 103, 104, 124 B, 136 C, 137, and 138; the Indian Office for Plates 4, 5, 6, 11, 12 A, 13 A, 22, 23, 39 C, 50, 51, 52 B and C, 65, 82, 84, 87, 91, and 93; the Council of the

[1] See Cousens, *Chalukyan Architecture*, a title which excludes the discussion of the Ellora Kailasa with its cognate building at Pattadkal. Also Coomaraswamy, *Hist. of Ind. Art*, use of 'Gupta' to include the Badami caves which are Chalukyan.

Royal Asiatic Society for Plates 57 B, and 77 B and C; the Council of the Royal Institute of British Architects for Plate 69 B; Professor A. A. Macdonell for Plates 10, 52 A, 85 A, 123 A, and 132; Dr. Führer for Plates 15 A and 21; Messrs. C. Whittingham and Griggs for Plates 27, 28, 29, 30 B, 31 C, 32, 33, 34 A and B, 35 A and B, 37, 38 D, 39 B, and 40 C; Dr. A. Nell for Plates 106, 107 B, 108 A and B, and 109 A; Dr. A. K. Coomaraswamy for Plates 102 A, 105, 110 A and B, 112 B, 113, and 165; Messrs. Klein and Peyerl, Madras, for Plate 69 A; Council of the Asiatic Society of Bengal for Plate 70 B; and Professor Grünwedel for Plate 120 C.[1]

I have especially to thank Mr. Laurence Binyon and Dr. Barnett for their kind assistance. I should also like to take this opportunity of stating my gratitude and offering my best wishes to my colleagues of the University of Cincinnati where the revision of this book was done, especially to the Dean of the Graduate School and the Dean of the College of Engineering and Science, to W. Semple, R. Robinson, B. A. G. Fuller, R. Casey, and H. Feis. I must acknowledge special gratitude to Miss Abbot, who was then in charge of the Art Library and is now on the staff of the Municipal Library. Her co-operation was of the greatest assistance to me.

K. DE B. C.

[1] [These references to photographs are to plates in the Second Edition].

PREFACE TO THE FIRST EDITION [illegible]

Royal Asiatic Society for Plate 5 [illegible] 73 [illegible] Institute of British Architects [illegible] Plate [illegible] Professor [illegible] 10, 32 [illegible] 123 and 182 [illegible] Plates [illegible] Whitcombe and Co. [illegible] Plates 27, 28, 29 [illegible] 8, 13, 35 [illegible] Dr. [illegible] Plate 106 [illegible] and 109 A; Dr. A. K. Coomaraswamy [illegible] Plates 107 A, 108 [illegible] 107 [illegible] Messrs. [illegible] Madras, for Plate [illegible] Society of Bengal for Plate 75 A, and [illegible] Plate 120 [illegible]

I have pleasure to thank Mr. Lawrence Binyon [illegible] kind assistance [illegible] and [illegible] necessary [illegible] this book was done, especially to the Dean [illegible] the Dean [illegible] College of Engineering and [illegible] Robinson [illegible] Fuller [illegible] and H. [illegible] special gratitude to Miss Abbott, who was then in charge of the [illegible] is now on the staff of the Municipal Library. Her [illegible] greatest assistance to me.

CONTENTS

LIST OF TEXT-FIGURES

LIST OF PLATES

COLOUR PLATES

MONOCHROME PLATES

Plate | *Facing page*

Colour Plates B and E are from N. C. Mehta's book *Studies in Indian Painting*.

INTRODUCTION

THE ART OF THE INDUS VALLEY CIVILIZATION

BY KARL KHANDALAVALA

The discovery of the most ancient civilization of India took place only about four decades ago. Till then there was nothing which could be ascribed to a period earlier than the Mauryas at the close of the 4th century B.C. Even their predecessors the Nandas and the Saisunagas were shadowy. From the mounds at Harappa, a site in the Montgomery district of the Punjab, now in the State of Pakistan, seals bearing a script which has still not been deciphered and incised mostly with animal figures, had been found from time to time. They indicated to scholars the possibility of a civilization much older than that of the 4th century B.C., but little else could be predicted. Even literary sources, such as the Vedic hymns of the Aryan tribes who entered India perhaps about 1500 B.C., the great epics, the Mahabharata and the Ramayana, and Buddhist, Jain and Brahmanical cannonical literature, gave a somewhat indeterminate picture of the civilization that prevailed from about 1500 B.C. to the time of the Mauryas. The usual exaggerations, the debatable meaning of words and phrases and the obvious inclusion of much later material into these texts made it difficult to visualize with any degree of certainty the architecture, art and civic life of the peoples who lived in those far off times. Archaeological discoveries also afforded little assistance in the solution of these matters. But the civilizations before the influx of the Vedic Aryans into India were enshrouded in total darkness. The Vedic hymns indicated the existence of peoples whom the Aryan invaders appeared to despise and some of whom may have lived in walled towns if certain phrases in the Hymns have been correctly understood. Such was the position till 1922 when the late R. D. Banerji of the Archaeological Survey of India, while excavating a site known as Mohenjodaro in Sind, now in the State of Pakistan, sensed that below the great mound there lay a very ancient civilization that might reveal a culture complex which hitherto had lain beyond the ken of scholars and archaeologists. The subsequent story is well known. Sir John Marshall, the then Director General of Archaeology, shrewdly realized that Banerji's surmise could unfold a new chapter in Indian history and accordingly extensive excavations at Mohenjodaro, Harappa, and other lesser sites were undertaken. These led to startling results and another horizon came to view.

After several decades of work the partition of India and Pakistan took place and it seemed that our knowledge of this ancient civilization had come to an unhappy halt. Then came the discovery in 1954 of Lothal in Kathiawar by S. R. Rao of the Archaeological Survey of India, throwing further light on this civilization and also bringing new problems in its wake.

The facts relating to the excavations of all these various sites have been extensively documented by the Archaeological Survey itself as well as by others and the details of these excavations need not detain us here. It need only be remarked that later day archaeologists feel that the stratigraphic data in these excavations are often very defective and consequently we are not on sure ground in arriving at chronological sequences.

There are two more handicaps in the way of a satisfactory chronology of many of the objects discovered. There have been disturbances of the layers of the mounds at all these sites by succeeding generations in search of building materials within easy reach, and secondly, the water-logged nature of the soil after a certain depth has made it impossible to determine the beginnings of these riverine city sites, the culture of which is termed the Indus Valley Civilization, as these cities grew up along the course of the Indus river. The discovery of Lothal in Kathiawar may not affect an established nomenclature, but it certainly calls for a review of the theory that the principal cities of this civilization were confined to the Indus Valley.

In accordance with archaeological practice the civilization is also termed the Harappan culture as Harappa was the first site discovered. Leaving aside minor excavations, the three great cities of this civilization so far brought to light are Harappa, Mohenjodaro and Lothal, together with a lesser site at Chanhudaro. It is not easy to determine the terminal dates for this civilization, but on the basis of Harappa-type seals and objects found in ancient Mesopotamian cities this civilization was flourishing from at least 2500 B.C. to the beginning of the 1st millennium B.C., even if in a degenerate form, as the recent excavations at Lothal and near-by sites seem to indicate. These recent excavations may also provide a link-up of the last phase of the Indus Civilization with later cultures in India though much spade work has yet to be done before arriving at conclusions.

It may seem surprising that despite the wealth of material which has been patiently unearthed from the mounds that were once the cities of the Indus Civilization, we are still faced with major problems which defy satisfactory solution. It is tantalizing that these great sites have revealed so much in terms of material objects and yet tell so little to answer all those queries that must come to mind in any effort to reconstruct the scene in its original historical, political, social and cultural background.

A salient feature of the Indus Civilization, as disclosed by the excavations, is that all the important settlements whether in Sind, the Punjab or Kathiawar were riverine because such a situation was essential to trading communities. That these settlements were for the most part peopled by commerce minded inhabitants is fairly certain. The hundreds of engraved seals which came to light at these sites (Plate 2A and B) led to a spate of theories as to their use, but the excavations at Lothal seem to indicate that their main use was as some form of merchandise marking on the cargoes which came to or left the wharfs of these riverside settlements, though what exactly were the purposes for the adoption of this practice is a matter of speculation. Some of these seals may also have had other commercial uses. Certain animals, including a mythical beast which looks like an unicorn, seem to have been stock types in the repertoire of the engravers and one or the other was selected by a trader for his seal. To this was added a combination of pictographs as required by the merchant to make his seal distinctive. These pictographs constitute the so-called Indus Valley script which has altogether defied decipherment. It may even been doubted if it is a language at all. Perhaps the lettering on the seals was no more than varying combinations of well-understood symbols so arranged as to differentiate the seal of one trader from that of another. Seals bearing only a script have also been found and this may suggest that the script was more important in a seal than the animal figures which appear to have resolved themselves into certain set representations with such natural variations as one would expect depending on the skill and powers of observation of the engraver. Of course, some of these seals may have been used as amulets and some may have had some religious or ritual significance. If the script is a language then the only hope of its decipherment is the discovery some day of a bi-lingual inscription.

The animal engravings on the seals are often of a very high order and evoke our admiration (Plate 2A and B). Seal engraving was a specialized craft in these trading settlements and the demand for this accessory of commerce often led to the making of seals with intaglios of real artistic merit. This is a phenomenon common in most craft production and is no indication that the inhabitants of the Indus Valley cities were particularly artistic. The seals are mostly of steatite and at Lothal sealings were also found which had been baked in a brick kiln near the wharf, no doubt to facilitate their use on the merchandise of the wharf warehouses. The hole in the seal was for tying it to the merchandise. Seals may also have been used on some kind of substance which dries rapidly, like we use seals on sealing wax.

The main settlements of Harappa, Mohenjodaro and Lothal are at considerable distances from one another and in all probability traded among themselves as well as with the lesser Indus Valley settlements, and also with foreign ports. This last factor would account for the presence of the Indus type seals in ancient Mesopotamian cities.

The discovery of this civilization is such a thrilling episode in Indian archaeology that sober appraisement sometimes tends to be at a discount, particularly when the artistic achievements of this civilization as a whole are sought to be evaluated.

There is no doubt that this was a developed urban civilization with well constructed dwellings, though drab in appearance and somewhat poky as in the manner of many small congested towns in India to this day. If one seeks to invest these cities with glamour, the picture becomes distorted. It is true that they had certain admirable features, such as, planned streets, a fairly efficient drainage system, quite unusual in those far off days, granaries, wharfs, and at Mohenjodaro, a great bath, perhaps for public use. But there is nothing to indicate any artistry in the Indus Valley dwellings, nor did the undoubted civic sense of the inhabitants ever seem to be infused with any desire for the adornment of their cities with any artistic structures. If an Indus Valley city could come momentarily to life it would certainly have a very quieting effect on any tendency to exaggerate the artistic achievements of these settlements.

The seals have already been referred to and the only other artistic achievements of these cities consist of a bronze figure (Plate 1A and B), two small portrait heads of a bearded deity, prince, king or dignitary (Plate 1D), a seated headless alabaster figure (Plate 1C), some attractive painted pottery, and a number of really fine animal studies in bronze, steatite and terracotta. In addition there are two torsos from Harappa (Plate 2C and D), and an assortment of rather attractive though unsophisticated jewellery. The sum total is not as impressive as one would have expected and the conclusion suggested thereby is that there was no emphasis in these cities on art as such, though certain forms of craft production did result, now and then, in turning out an object possessing aesthetic significance. One of the bearded portrait heads (Plate 1D) which is in steatite and about 7 inches high, seems to be a type which may have been derived from Western Asiatic sources. The upper lip is shaven and the eyes originally had shell inlay. The figure wears a garment with a trefoil pattern in relief. It was found at

Mohenjodaro. The other head, from the same site, has distinct similarities to the one just described, so far as the features and beard are concerned. Both heads are stylised yet compel attention.

It is more difficult to say much about the seated alabaster figure (Plate 1C) which is about 12 inches in height. It suggests that whatever sculptural art existed was formal and static. The two headless statuettes from Harappa (Plate 2C and D) have been the subject of controversy and it has been suggested that they do not belong to the Indus Valley culture, but are of a much later period. It is true that their plastic qualities are much in advance of the statutory from Mohenjodaro, but that is not a sufficient reason to ascribe them to a later age. Though the workmanship of the seals also varies greatly, that circumstance would not be enough to ascribe the finest examples to a period later than that of the Indus Valley culture. Again, in the case of the Harappa statuettes, the advanced modelling may be due to foreign influences. If the conclusion that these Indus settlements traded with foreign parts is correct, then the several Western Asiatic influences discernible in the Indus valley statuary and seals can be accounted for.

A quite remarkable find at Mohenjodaro is the bronze statuette of what is usually termed a dancing girl (Plate 1A and B). The significance of the figure must remain a matter of speculation, but here we have undeniably a work which indicates an attempt at something more than formal portraiture. Even if it is a ritual dancer cast in bronze for a ritualistic purpose, it has a sensitivity which entitles it to be considered as a genuine work of art. And the same is true of some of the bronze animal figures such as the splendid buffalo, a masterpiece of miniature animal sculpture, so powerful that one forgets its size. The purpose of these bronze miniature animal figures is again a matter of speculation for they are not in the category of the vast production of crude terracotta toys, mother goddesses, and such other figures which, despite their naivete, have no claim to be considered as any form of art.

There seems to have been a widespread worship of a mother goddess, but beyond that it would not be safe to hazard any conclusions as to the religion of the inhabitants of these settlements. The theory that the cross-legged seated figure surrounded by animals, which has been found on about three seals only, relates to an ancient form of Shiva worship is as speculative as most of the theories which prevail about this civilization. The Gilgamesh Enkidu myth of Mesopotamia does not seem to have been unknown in Mohenjodaro and its influence may have led to variations of the legend. Several seals, including the so-called Shiva, could be accounted for on that basis.

It is not easy to fit in the artistic achievements of the Indus Valley culture, such as they be, with the main trends of the development of Indian art from the Mauryan period onwards. The attempt has been made, but has never been convincing because the intervening gap is far too long and shrouded by the mists of time. The truth is that we are still not in a position to say who were the dwellers of these Indus Valley settlements. Were they of Dravidian origin or did they originally come, at intervals, from Western Asia, settling on Indian soil and intermingling with the original inhabitants whoever they may have been. This second surmise may be nearer the truth.

It has of late been suggested that the Indus Valley culture is that of the Vedic Aryans, but that theory seems to have even less to commend it than any other. How this ancient civilization faded away is yet another problem. Did it disappear due to the ravages of floods or did it disintegrate under the onslaught of the invading Aryans. The so-called fortifications at Mohenjodaro and Harappa may after all be no more than fort-like platforms to withstand floods. If this civilization continued in a degenerate form, as excavations near about Lothal seem to suggest, then what was the cause of its degeneration. We must await more material for an answer. For the time being we must needs confine the art of the Indus Valley civilization within its own span of time without seeking to link it up with the development of Indian art from the 4th century B.C. onwards.

Chapter One

INDIA AND ITS ART

Modern India.

IN discussing Indian studies I am forced to acknowledge considerable diffidence arising from a survey of the huge bulk of material to be dealt with. In the face of this objective complexity I find myself inclined to rely on evidence that is subjective and therefore more or less unscientific, in which personal experience and interpretation is increasingly stressed. In speaking of India, a country that in its wide extent offers more beauty to the eyes than any other in the world, a descriptive vein may well be excused, but the more graphic the form, the more dangerous does the method become. India is multiple; neither geographically, ethnologically, nor culturally can it be considered a unity (A 1). This being so, I am led to suspect that the India of many writers is more imagination than fact, existing rather in pictorial expression than in reality.

The appeal of the pictorial, rising from a craving for colour and movement, is general among the generations of the present, continually chaffing against narrowed horizons and an experience bounded by Economical Necessity. There is magic to be found anywhere between Cancer and Capricorn. There the demands of Necessity would seem to be more easily fulfilled and life to run more rhythmically, in the train of the tropic alternation of the seasons. There bread is to be gathered direct from the rich lap of the earth. There colour fills the day with its wealth, leaping to the eye, like the sudden glow of fruit and flower caught by the sunlight, or of kaleidoscopic crowds in narrow streets. To enter a tropic town is to enter, as in a dream, the life of a dead century.

Modern complexity is apparently to be regarded as successful and therefore not to be deterred by sentimental leanings towards the simplicities of Eden or Arcady. Yet the sentimental mood will have its way, not only in the West but in the East where the ready acceptance of change at the expense of tradition lies at the very root of the problem that is modern India. Modernism, supported by thorough-going educational propaganda, may overcome the great geographical and ethnological obstacles, and result in the crystallization of Indian nationality. The alternative offered seems to be a return to the past on an agricultural basis; Arcady in India under the good king Vikramaditya. The movement is not without parallels, and the pictorial and interpretational play a great part in its exposition; there is, indeed, something of the Pre-Raphaelite about it. The materialism of to-day is to be checked by Indian Spirituality. Arts and crafts are to flourish everywhere, centred upon the social organization of the village. India is to arise from the ashes of India.

Indian Art.

It might be claimed, therefore, that there could be no better time than the present for the republication of a survey of Indian Fine Arts, that the credit and loss of the exchange between the occidental and the oriental may be appraised. Indeed this nationalization of the subject has been set forth at length by certain authors. It is, however, in contradistinction to the spirit of true criticism and full appreciation. The opposition of Eastern spirituality to Western materialism is a generalization without support, while the postulation of a metaphysical basis for any art is equally as sterile, and in fact as inconsequential, as the postulation of the existence of eternal, immutable classical standards. Art cannot be localized, at least if the humanities upon which our culture is based have any meaning, and geographical differences should be no bar to appreciation, but rather an added attraction in these days, when for most of us our voyages of discovery do not exceed the bounds of the local time-table. It is, however, unfortunate that in the minds of many people the East has a certain romantic but quite indefinite lure about it, which accentuates the unusual and leads to the substitution of curiosity for appreciation.

Modern Art.

It is impossible for any one to deny the advance of modern science, with its consequent widening of horizons and enrichment of life. Yet aesthetically our advance from the station of our fathers is as great, and possibly greater, being more radically concerned with that personal interpretation of life which is Reason.

Modern painting and sculpture provide a definite line of advance and logical precepts to an extent that almost makes academicians of many of the younger school. This process is directly comparable to that of modern scientific method; modern art is indeed the result of methodical, aesthetic research. From the painting of Manet to that of Cezanne and the men of to-day, Matisse, Picasso, Stanley Spencer, Paul Nash, and many others, the story can only be told in terms of intellectual adventure and aesthetic discovery. The effect of the personal vision of the creators of modern art has been a widening of the circle of aesthetic interest and a revaluation of things unknown or unconsidered—Chinese painting and sculpture, Gothic sculpture, archaic Greek sculpture, Negro sculpture, the harmony of fine carpets, the virility of primitive design, and not least among these, Indian Art in all its branches.[1] In the face of these riches, once despised and rejected, the dogmas of the past generations with all their complacency, intolerance, and ignorance seem wilful in their restriction and impoverishment of life.

Appreciation of Indian Art.

So vital is this movement and so well founded that I would choose as the theme of a review of Indian Art aesthetic discovery rather than archaeological discovery, and for support I would rely upon the word of living artists[2] whose creative vision and fellow-craft appreciation provides the basis of a criticism of greater precision than archaeological chop-logic or the ulterior ends and confused categories of evidence of those who would carry the discussion beyond the proper field of art. I cannot believe it is necessary or even desirable to prelude the vision of a work of art with many words. Nor can I accept as sound criticism a discourse which shifts the foundations of a true understanding of art from the visual into the literary or historical or metaphysical. And I can but deplore the twisting awry of aesthetic criticism and appreciation to local and temporary ends, whatever the circumstances.

In 1897 Gauguin wrote: 'Ayez toujours devant vous les Persans, les Cambodgiens et un peu l'Egyptien.'[3] One wonders what he would have written if he had known of the frescoes at Ajanta with their magnificent surety of line and delicately rendered plasticity. The placing on exhibition of casts of Indian sculpture mainly of the late medieval period, in the Trocadero in Paris, may be taken as the first step towards the western appreciation of Indian Art.

[1] Fry, 'Oriental Art' (*Quart. Rev.*, Jan. 1910).
[2] Eric Gill, preface to *Visvakarma*; W. Rothenstein, preface to *Ancient India*.
[3] Rotonchamp, quoted on p. 165.

A.

B.

C.

D.

A, B. Front and rear views of bronze figurine of a girl. Ht. 9 cms. Indus Valley Civilisation, Mohenjodaro. 2500-1500 B.C. National Museum, New Delhi. C. Headless seated figure, from Mohenjodaro. D. Bearded figure in limestone wearing trefoil patterned garment, from Mohenjodaro.

PLATE 1

A. Seal with mythical horned animal and undeciphered script, from Lothal, Saurashtra. 2500-1500 B.C.

B. Seal with humped bull and undeciphered script, from Mohenjodaro. 2500-1500 B.C.

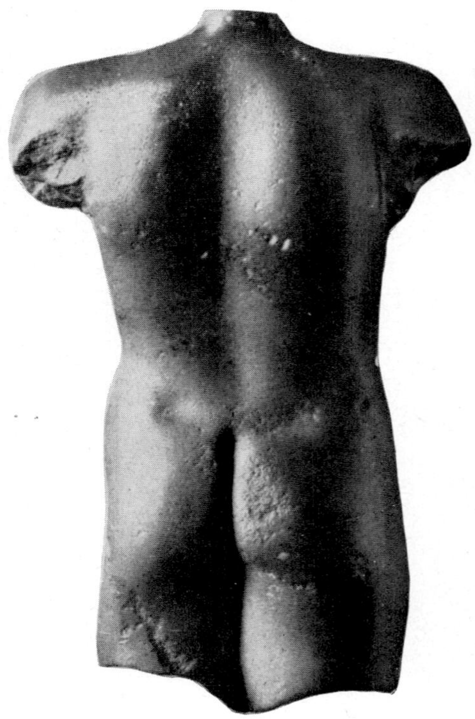

C, D. Front and back views of headless torso, from Harappa. 2500-1500 B.C.

PLATE 2

Until then Indian Art had been left to the archaeologists—not altogether without results. The work of Prinsep and Cunningham,[1] of Fergusson[2] and Burgess[3] is a well-laid foundation-stone for all future research.

In *The Times* of 28 February 1910 appeared the following declaration above the signatures of thirteen distinguished artists and critics:[4]

> 'We the undersigned artists, critics, and students of art . . . find in the best art of India a lofty and adequate expression of the religious emotion of the people and of their deepest thoughts on the subject of the divine. We recognize in the Buddha type of sacred figure one of the great artistic inspirations of the world. We hold that the existence of a distinct, a potent, and a living tradition of art is a possession of priceless value to the Indian people, and one which they, and all who admire and respect their achievements in this field, ought to guard with the utmost reverence and love. While opposed to the mechanical stereotyping of particular traditional forms, we consider that it is only in organic development from the national art of the past that the path of true progress is to be found. Confident that we here speak for a very large body of qualified European opinion, we wish to assure our brother craftsmen and students in India that the school of national art in that country, which is still showing its vitality and its capacity for the interpretation of Indian life and thought, will never fail to command our admiration and sympathy so long as it remains true to itself. We trust that, while not disdaining to accept whatever can be wholesomely assimilated from foreign sources, it will jealously preserve the individual character which is an outgrowth of the history and physical conditions of the country, as well as of those ancient and profound religious conceptions which are the glory of India and of all the Eastern world.'

The Criticism of Scholars.

This declaration was directly caused by a paper read before the Royal Society of Arts by Sir George Birdwood, the chronicler of Indian industrial arts.[5] As a matter of fact all that was then said had already appeared in print thirty years before, but the moment was not then ripe for the acceptance of the challenge. Birdwood can in no way be accused of lack of sympathy with Indian life or things Indian. A stylistic analysis of the crafts of modern India is illuminating with regard to one's attitude to the country itself, for one is forced to acknowledge the predominance of the Muhammadan and especially of the Persian culture of the Mughal court. Except in their everyday household form, pottery and metal-work are purely Muhammadan. Textiles, especially prints and brocades, are very largely Persian in design, although the Indian strength of imagination and purity of colour are evident. Certain forms of textiles are, however, purely Indian, the darn-stitch Phulkaris of the north-west and certain tied-and-dyed and warp-dyed forms. Only in jewellery has the Indian tradition been wholly preserved, in the seed-and-bead work of the villages as well as in the enamels of Jaipur. Birdwood's love of all this delicate and colourful though hybrid craftsmanship, and of the complex, changeful life of which it is a part, is expressed in many passages from his pen of very great beauty. The arts of Ancient and Medieval India were outside his field, and his criticism of them is not deeply considered and purely personal.

In his paper before the Royal Society of Arts he stated with regard to a certain Javanese seated Buddha that this 'senseless similitude, by its immemorial fixed pose, is nothing more than an uninspired brazen image, vacuously squinting down its nose to its thumbs, knees, and toes. A boiled suet pudding would serve equally well as a symbol of passionate purity and serenity of soul.' This

[1] *Arch. Survey Reports.*
[2] *History of Ind. Arch.*
[3] *Arch. Survey of West India.*
[4] The signatories are (1) Fred. Brown, (2) Walter Crane, (3) George Frampton, (4) Laurence Housman, (5) E. Lanteri, (6) W. R. Lethaby, (7) Halsey Ricardo, (8) T. W. Rolleston, (9) W. Rothenstein, (10) George W. Russel (A.E.), (11) W. Reynolds Stephens, (12) Charles Waldstein, and (13) Emery Walker.
[5] *J. R. Soc. of Arts,* 4 Feb. 1910. *Industrial Arts of India,* 1880.

attack, however, may be considered as being equally directed against the loose verbiage of those critics of Indian art to whom the ideal content of an object is of greater importance than its form, than against Indian art itself.

An earlier statement in the official handbook to the Indian Section of the Victoria and Albert Museum offers a more definite criticism.[1] 'The monstrous shapes of the Puranic deities are unsuitable for the higher forms of artistic representation: and this is possibly why sculpture and painting are *unknown*, as fine arts, in India. . . . How completely their figure-sculpture fails in true art is seen at once when they attempt to produce it on a natural and heroic scale, and it is only because their ivory and stone figures of men and animals are on so minute a scale that they excite admiration.' Here it must be noticed the subject under discussion is modern Indian ivory-carving.

In his *Handbook of Sculpture*, Professor Westmacott[2] dismissed Indian art in one paragraph, forming his judgement, apparently, from the steel engravings and lithographs of the two or three books that were all that was then accessible.

> 'There is no temptation to dwell at length on the sculpture of Hindustan. It affords no assistance in tracing the history of art, and its debased quality deprives it of all interest as a phase of Fine Art, the point of view from which it would have to be considered. It must be admitted, however, that the works existing have sufficient character to stamp their nationality, and although they possess no properties that can make them useful for the student, they offer very curious subjects of inquiry to the scholar and archaeologist. The sculptures found in various parts of India, at Ellora, Elephanta, and other places, are of a strictly symbolical or mythological character. They usually consist of monstrous combinations of human and brute forms, repulsive from their ugliness and outrageous defiance of rule and even possibility.'

In the opinion of Dr. Anderson, author of the catalogue of sculpture at the Indian Museum,[3] Calcutta, Indian sculptors 'have never risen . . . beyond the most feeble mediocrity', although he acclaims the Orissa temple-sculptures as 'extremely pleasing pieces of art'. A more guarded opinion is that of Sir. C. Purdon Clarke, who whilst giving Indian art a good place among the arts of the world, would not place it in the first rank, except for its 'eminent suitability to its country and people'.[4]

Such were the opinions current among scholars at the end of the last century, concerning an art already accepted by artists and acclaimed by its influence upon the work of such men as Rodin, Degas, and Maillol.

Interpretational Criticism.

The popularization of Indian art has been mainly the work of Dr. Coomaraswamy and Mr. E. B. Havell (A 2). To a certain extent their methods of exposition agree, the vein being interpretational, with a stressing of the literary. For Dr. Coomaraswamy 'all that India can offer to the world proceeds from her philosophy'[5], a state of 'mental concentration' (*yoga*)[6] on the part of the artist and the enactment of a certain amount of ritual being postulated as the source of the 'spirituality' of Indian art. The weakness of this attitude lies in its interweaving of distinct lines of criticism, form being dressed out in the purely literary with the consequent confusion of aesthetic appreciation with religious and other impulses. It is also historically ill-founded, for the sentiment and philosophy out of which the web is spun are the products of medieval[7] India, as an examination of the texts quoted will show (A 3); many of the southern

[1] Discussed by Havell, *Ideals of Indian Art*, p. xvii.
[2] Edinburgh, 1864, p. 51.
[3] Vol. i, p. 175 and vol. ii, p. 221.
[4] *J. I. A. & I.*, 1890, p. 526.
[5] 'What has India contributed to Human Welfare?', *Athenaeum*, 1915.
[6] *The Dance of Siva*, p. 21.
[7] *Post*, fifth century A.D.

Inscribed Asoka pillar, Lauriya - Nandangarh. (3rd Century B.C. Mauryan period).

PLATE 3

Capital of inscribed Asoka pillar at Sarnath. (3rd Century B.C. Mauryan period. Almost certainly the work of Asiatic-Greek craftsmen working under Asoka. Sarnath Museum).

(Copyright by Department of Archaeology, Government of India)

PLATE 4

A.

B.

Details from abacus of Sarnath pillar capital shown on Plate 4. 3rd Century B.C.
(Copyright by Department of Archaeology, Government of India)
PLATE 5

A.

B.

Details from abacus of Sarnath pillar capital shown on Plate 4. 3rd Century B.C.

PLATE 6

authorities quoted can only be classed as modern. The increasingly hieratic art of medieval and modern India, especially in the south, is doubtless closely knit with this literary tradition. But the literary tradition is not the source of the art, for iconography presupposes icons. The technical formulae of the *Sastras* resulted in a standardization of production in spite of which genius, which knows no bonds, asserted itself. The bronze *Nataraja* loaned by Lord Ampthill to South Kensington is supreme among a hundred examples of mere hack-work (A 4). The bones of the literary formulae too often remain bones; here they are clothed with life, and beauty of form is achieved. The miracle is a perennial one and world-wide; we marvel at the hand and eye that shaped this wonder. However, it is evident that many such images are not aesthetically worth the metal they are cast in (A 5). Their function as objects of worship is an entirely different matter. To insist on the necessity of burdening the mind with a host of symbolical and psychological adjuncts prior to appreciation is to obstruct the vision. Research literary or historical may aid vision, but cannot be substituted for it. Aesthetic vision is, of course, distinct from the practical vision of everyday life. Those who indulge in it are 'entirely absorbed in apprehending the relation of forms and colour to one another, as they cohere within the object'.[1] Intensity and detachment from the merely superficial and additional are essential to it. This rigid detachment may at any moment be broken by interest in all sorts of 'quasi-biological feelings' and irrelevant queries: but then the vision ceases to be critical and becomes merely curious.

India Past and Present.

A further element is apparent in the recent discussion of Indian art. Aesthetically we are not at all concerned with the sub-continent that is known as India or its peoples. But our curiosity must needs be strong as to its past and future. The pageantry of Indian history is as glorious as that of any country in the world. Artistically it falls into two main periods, the first of which, ending with the Muhammadan conquest, is an epic in itself. This period discloses the development of a great art. From the vividly pictorial, strictly popular sculpture of the Early Period, based on a living tradition, increased skill and wider vision lead to the classic art of the Gupta century. Henceforward it is evident that a literary tradition has come into being which may rightly be designated medieval. The art of the great cave-temples gives place to the art of the temple-cities of Bhuvanesvar and Khajuraho, where the literary tradition crystallizes into the iconographical forms of the *Sastras*. In the South an imposing architecture is found to survive up to the end of the seventeenth century, and the art of casting in bronze produces great works of art, few of which can, however, be dated in the last century (A 6). It is necessary to discriminate, and to acknowledge decadence and poor craftsmanship. Having taken its place among the arts of the world, Indian art belongs to the world. The future of art in India is another matter, chiefly concerning educationalists.

Traditions have died and the symbols that embodied them have died with them. Regret for the 'creed out-worn' is ineffectual. New traditions and new symbols are surely in the making. Proteus and Triton are become empty names, but the sea remains. Nothing is lost but a dream, or rather the means of expressing a dream.

Indian religious history must be unfolded against a background of primitive

[1] Fry, *Vision and Design*, p. 49.

The Complexity of Indian Religions.

savagery and sorcery. The Vedas, in spite of their antiquity, cannot be accepted as the sole source of religious thought in India, or as anything but a critical and highly selective representation of this unvoiced and necessarily formless background. This relationship between Brahmanism and the primitive, between the formulated philosophy of the schools and the worship and propitiation born of the vague fears and desires of savages, is present throughout the history of India, both religious and political. The *Atharva Veda* was not known to the early Buddhist writers but its practices and beliefs were, and they cannot be separated from the more altruistic and poetical polytheism of the less popular, more orthodox but not more ancient collections.[1] In the same way the powers and manifestations of the *Puranas* and Epics are not necessarily modern because they do not appear in the Veda; in a sense they are more ancient, being native to the soil. Vedic thaumaturgy and theosophy were never the faith of India. The countless Mother-Goddesses and village guardians of the South lie closer to the real heart of Indian religion, a numberless pantheon, superficially identified with Brahmanism but radically distinct and unchanged (A 7).

The Lesser Gods.

Among these lesser gods that keep their place on the fringes of the orthodox are to be found spirits of the Earth and of the Mountain; the Four Guardians of the Quarters with *Vessavana-Kuvera* at their head; *Gandharvas*, heavenly musicians; *Nagas*, the snake-people who have their world beneath the waters of streams and tanks, but who sometimes are identified with the Tree-Spirits; and *Garudas*, half men, half birds who by kind are the deadly foes of the *Nagas*. These diminished godlings must be regarded as the last remnant of a whole host of forgotten powers, once mighty and to be placated, each in its own place. Strange beings of another sphere, they could not wholly be passed over either by Brahman or Buddhist. *Vessavana-Kuvera* appears on one of the pillars of the Bharhut railing, as does also *Sirima Devata*. The latter also received acknowledgement at the hands of the compilers of the *Satapatha Brahmana* who are forced to invent a legend to account for her existence.[2] In the *Taittiriya Upanishad*[3] she is again fitly mentioned in company with the Moon and the Sun and the Earth. At Sanchi she is to be recognized exactly as she is still represented in painted and gilt marble at Jaipur, seated upon a lotus, lustrated by two elephants.

The Great Gathering.

In the *Maha Samaya Suttanta*[4] is described a great gathering of all the gods of the ten-thousand world systems to pay reverence to the Buddha in the Great Forest at *Kapilavatthu*. *Dhatarattha*, king of the East, *Virulhaka*, king of the South, *Virupakkha*, king of the West, and *Kuvera*, king of the North arrive with their *Yaksha* host and all their vassals. The *Nagas* come from *Nabhasa*, *Vesali*, *Tacchaka*, and *Yamuna*, among them *Eravana*. Their enemies the twice-born *Garudas*, too, are there and also the *Asuras*, dwellers in the ocean. Fire, Earth, Air, and Water are present, and the Vedic gods, and lastly the powers of *Mara* who bids creation rejoice at his own defeat at the Buddha's hands.

Another list of the same description, but possibly earlier, is to be found in the *Atanatiya*. Both lists are, patently, the outcome of a priestly attempt to bring these hundred and one strange spirits and godlings within the sphere of Buddhist teaching, by representing them as gathered in hosts at the Buddha's feet. The group of *Yakshas*, *Yakshinis*, and *Devatas* carved upon the stone pillars of the

[1] Macdonnell, *Sanscrit Literature*, p. 185 ; Rhys-Davids, *Buddhist India*, chap. xii. Also *Dialogues of the Buddha*, note to Ambattha Sutta, i. 3.

[2] xi. 4. 3.

[3] i. 4.

[4] Rhys-Davids, *Dialogues of the Buddha*, ii. 284.

Bull capital of Asokan pillar, from Rampurva. 3rd Century B.C. Mauryan period. Rashtrapati Bhawan, New Delhi.

PLATE 7

A. Elephant capital of Asokan pillar, from Sankisa. 3rd Century B.C. Mauryan period.

B. Lomas Rishi Cave, Barabar Hills. 3rd Century B.C. Mauryan period.

C. Asoka pillar at Bakhira, Muzaffarpur District. (3rd Century B.C. Mauryan period).

D. Lion capital of Asokan pillar, from Rampurva. (3rd Century B.C. Mauryan period.)

(Copyright by Department of Archaeology, Government of India)

PLATE 8

Stupa railing at Bharhut fulfil exactly the same function. They are manifestly earth-born and possess something of the delicate beauty of all forest creatures. They seem beneficent enough, but their manifestation here is admittedly chosen to serve Buddhist ends. Like all primitive powers they are exacting in their demands and when neglected or provoked their anger is implacable and cruel. They are adorned with earthly jewels to represent the treasures they have in their gift, but are to be more closely identified with the trees under which they stand and the forest flowers they hold.

This primitive cult of trees and tree-spirits has a long history. In the sculptures of the early period the Buddhas are represented only by symbols, among which are their distinctive trees. Gotama attained enlightenment seated beneath the *Asvattha* or pipal-tree[1] sacred from of old, for it was from pipal wood that the *soma* vessels were made and also the sacred fire-drill. In the *Atharva Veda* it is said that the gods of the third heaven are seated under the *Asvattha* and it may also be the 'tree with fair foliage' of the *Rig Veda* under which Yama and the blessed are said to pass their time.[2] In the *Upanishads* the Tree-spirits have definitely materialized. They, like all things, are subject to rebirth. If the spirit leaves the tree the tree withers and dies, but the spirit is immortal.[3] In the *Jatakas* these Tree-spirits play a great part, being worshipped with perfumes, flowers, and food. They dwell in many kinds of trees but the Banyan seems most popular. The scarlet-flowered silk-cotton tree[4] and the Sal tree as well as the Pipal retain their sanctity to-day. The goddess of the Sal is worshipped as giver of rain by the Oraons of Chota Nagpur,[5] and in South Mirzapur the Korwas place the shrine of *Dharti Mata* under its branches.[6] In the *Jatakas* more than once animal and even human sacrifices are spoken of in connexion with tree-worship.[7] To-day the slaughter of cocks and goats is added to the more usual offering of flowers and sweetmeats, in extreme cases of propitiation.[8]

The Mother-Goddesses.

The character and functions of these deities correspond closely to those of the Mother-Goddesses of Southern India. Among these are *Mariamma*, goddess of small-pox, *Kaliamma*, of beasts and forest demons, *Huliamma*, a tiger goddess, *Ghantalamma*, she who goes with bells, and *Mamillamma*, she who sits beneath the mango-tree.[9] However, it is usually made plain that these are but different names for the one great goddess. In Brahman hands this female pantheon appears as the *Ashta Sakti* or eight female powers. But a more primitive group is that of the *Sapta Kannigais* or seven virgins, tutelary deities of tanks. In Mysore, too, is found a similar group of seven sister-goddesses, vaguely identified with the Sivaite mythology. However, they and all the Mother-Goddesses are distinguished from the true gods of Brahmanism by the fact that they are acknowledged to be local in their influence warding off or inflicting calamities of various kinds, but strictly limited in their sphere of action. Still more limited are the powers of tanks, trees, and groves which periodically are alternately propitiated and exorcized, but are, as a whole, unsubstantial in personality and short lived.

It is against this complex background of creed and culture that Indian philosophy

1 The oldest accounts make no mention of the tree under which the enlightenment took place. Rhys-Davids, *Buddhist India*, p. 230.

2 Zimmer, *Altindisches Leben*, p. 58; Macdonnell, *Sans. Lit.*, p. 146.

3 Chand, vi. 11 ; Kathaka, v. 7.

4 Sleeman, *Rambles and Recollections* (1915), p. 385.

5 Dalton, *Descriptive Ethn.*, p. 201.

6 Crooke, *Popular Religion*, i. 32.

7 Nos. 472, 488.

8 Marriages of fruit-bearing trees, and between women and trees, are an extension of this subject : the mango, sacred basil, and jasmin being commonly chosen.

9 Whitehead, *Village Gods*, p. 23.

Indian Philosophy.

and Indian art, and all things Indian, must be viewed. Here lies the origin of the lovely treatment of flower and fruit at the hands of Indian sculptors and painters, and also of the imagination that kindled their vision and gave such dynamic power to their designs (A 8).

Indian philosophy begins with Vedic speculations, or rather questionings as to existence and the creation. The unformulated philosophy of the *Upanishads* sprang from these and from it the pantheistic *Vedanta* system was evolved. As a foil to this existed from early times the atheistic *Sankhya* system, upon the reasoning of which Buddhism and Jainism were founded. At the root of everything lies the acceptance of metensomatosis[1] and a cycle of existences [*samsara*], modified only by *karma*, past action, called *adrishta*, the unseen. At the root is ignorance, *avidya*. From ignorance comes desire, which leads to action, so the wheel revolves within the wheel. The Vedanta doctrine derived from the *Upanishads* taught the absolute identity of the individual soul with the spirit of the universe—'That is the Eternal in which space is woven and which is interwoven with it. . . . There is no other seer, no other hearer, no other thinker, no other knower. . . .'[2] From this identification of the mortal, limited self with the eternal and universal sum of all things arose[3] the idea of the illusion [*maya*] of the world of sensual experience. Only when the illusion of experience ceases, as in dreamless sleep, can the lesser self reunite with the universal self. This implied duality is in fact itself an illusion. Desire and action are inherent in such an illusion and the consequence is *samsara*. But Knowledge disperses the Illusion. 'Whoever knows this: "I am Brahma", becomes the All. Even the gods are not able to prevent him from becoming it. For he becomes their Self.'[4]

The *Sankhya* system is atheistic and dualistic, admitting matter and the individual soul as eternal but essentially different. In the absoluteness of this division lies release. The soul being removed from all matter, consciousness must cease, and the bondage to pain, in which term pleasure is included, be ended.

Buddhism.

Both Buddhism and Jainism presuppose the existence of the *Sankhya* philosophy. But it is evident that the sixth century B.C. when both Gautama and Vardhamana lived and taught was a period of extensive mental activity of an extremely sophisticated kind (A 9). The *Brahma-Jala Sutta* mentions Eternalists, Non-Eternalists, Semi-Eternalists, Fortuitous originists, and Survivalists, and also certain recluses and Brahmans who as dialecticians are typified as *Eel wriglers*. Buddhism is as much in revolt against this mental complexity as against the ritual complexity of the Brahman priest-craft. With regard to generalities its position is Agnostic. The Three Marks of Impermanence, Pain, and Lack of Individuality must be considered as a practical summary of the characteristics of life. Upon these the doctrine of the Four Noble Truths, the essence of Buddhism, is founded:—Suffering exists; ignorance and desire are its causes; release is possible; the means are the Eight Points of Doctrine=right knowledge, right aspiration, right speech, right conduct, right living, right endeavour, right mindfulness, and right meditation. Throughout the teaching uncertain, empirical opinion [*ditthi*] is set apart from true wisdom [*panna*]. Above all, the cultivation and regulation of the will is stressed in an entirely new way.[5]

Lastly, as against the changing, foundationless illusions of the unregulated

[1] It appeared during the period of the *Upanishads*.
[2] *Brihadaranyaka Upanishad*, III. viii: trans. by Macdonnell
[3] *Svetasvatara Up.*, IV. 10
[4] *Brihadaranyaka Up.*, I. iv. 6, trans. Macdonnell.
[5] Rhys-Davids, *Buddhist Dialogues*, i. xxvi.

A

B

A. Yakshi from Didarganj, near Patna. B. Yaksha from Patna. Probable date, 240-185 B.C. Mauryan period. Both bear the characteristic Mauryan polish. The theory that these figures belong to the late 1st Century B.C. cannot be seriously considered.

(Copyright by Department of Archaeology, Government of India)

PLATE 9

A. Fragment of carved stone disc, from Rupar. Probable date, 240-185 B.C. Mauryan period.

B. Male head, from Sarnath. Probable date, 240-185 B.C. Mauryan period. Sarnath Museum.

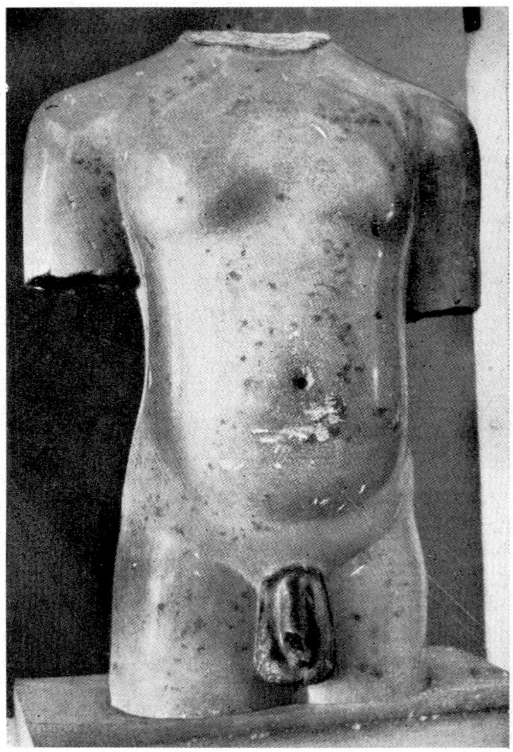

C. Nude headless torso of Jain Tirthankara, from Lohanipur, near Patna. Probable date, 240-185 B.C. Mauryan period. Bears Mauryan polish. Patna Museum.

PLATE 10

personal life in a universe that can only be described in terms of change, the Buddhist Doctrine [*Dharma*] is held out as being well-founded in time or rather in human experience. It is described as an ancient path well-trodden, a claim that paves the way to the conception of not one Buddha but many Buddhas. At Bharhut and Sanchi the seven Buddhas of the canon are all found, symbolized by their respective trees.

Jainism.

This doctrine of wise renunciation was preached by Gautama, a prince of the Sakya clan, who renounced his worldly heritage in pursuit of truth. Much of the adverse criticism which Buddhism has been subjected to has been due to a misunderstanding of *Nirvana*, the goal of all Indian speculation. Buddhism has had a complex history. Divided into two main sects, that of the Lesser and that of the Greater Vehicle, and changed beyond recognition, it exists no longer in the land of its origin. The Jain faith preached by Vardhamana, a contemporary and therefore rival of Gautama,[1] still persists in India. He, too, was of the *Kshatriya* race, and renouncing his birth-right, eventually attained Wisdom, appearing as the leader of the Nirgrantha ascetics. According to Jain tradition Vardhamana, or *Mahavira*, as he came to be known, was the twenty-fourth of a series of *Jinas* or conquerors of the world. Like Buddhism the Jain faith opposes the exclusiveness of Brahmanism by a claim to universality. Like Buddhism it is founded upon the teaching and achievement of Right Faith, Right Knowledge, and Right Action. Unlike Buddhism asceticism[2] is greatly stressed even to the point of voluntary death by the refusal of nourishment on the part of those who have attained the highest knowledge, the *Kevalin*. From an early date two Jain sects have existed, the *Digambara*, who regard nudity as indispensable to holiness, and the *Svetambara* or 'white-clothed', who do not. Besides these two bodies of ascetics, the Faith is extended to a large body of laity, who are represented in the history of Indian art, by many sculptures dedicated in the Kushan era, and by the magnificent medieval temples at Mount Abu, Girnar, and Satrunjaya (A 10). Like the Buddhists the Jains founded many monasteries. The worship of *stupas* was also included in their rites.

Hinduism.

The cult of the *Upanishads* and its forest-dwelling adherents is described in the *Agganna Suttanta*.[3]

> 'They making leaf-huts in woodland spots, meditated therein. Extinct for them the burning coal, vanished the smoke, fallen lies the pestle and mortar ; gathering of an evening for the evening meal, they go down into the village and town and royal city, seeking food. When they have gotten food back again in their leaf-huts they meditate.'

But from forest-life and meditation many sank to a mendicant life on the outskirts of the towns and to being mere repeaters of the sacred books.[4] Such were the Brahmans of the Buddha's day.

Modern Hinduism is divided into two main cults, *Vaishnavism* and *Saivism*. From the point of view of Indian art the early period is almost entirely Buddhist, while the Gupta period, and the succeeding medieval period are Brahmanical, the sculpture of the latter period being radically based upon Brahmanical iconography (A 11).

Rudra, the storm-god of the Vedas, is made known by many epithets. He

[1] See Buhler, *Indian Sect of the Jainas*.
[2] *Dialogues of the Buddha*, Pt. I, p. 218. See *Kassapa-Sihanada Sutta* for the Buddhist view.
[3] *Dialogues of the Buddha*, Pt. III, p. 88
[4] Comment: 'compiling the three Vedas and teaching others to repeat them.' See Jataka, No. 94; 'Beside no fire, but all afire within, Naked the hermit wrestles for the Truth.'

is called *Girisa*, 'lying on a mountain', *Kapardin*, 'wearer of tangled locks', and *Pasupatih*, 'lord of cattle'. When appeased he is known as *Sambhu* or *Samkara*, 'the benevolent', and as *Siva*, 'the auspicious', but he remains lord of the powers of the universe and is to be feared as well as loved. Yet the element of *bhakti*, of personal adoration and willing self-surrender to the deity is not wanting in the worship of the Great Lord as unfolded in the later Upanishads.[1]

In a lesser aspect Siva is lord of spirits [*bhutas*] and his rites are connected with snake-worship. In his worship the central object is the phallus [*linga*]. The *Siva-linga* does not seem to have been known to Patanjali, nor does it appear on the coins of Wema-Kadphises on the reverse of which the god is represented, holding the trident, with the bull, *Nandi*, in the background. In the *Mahabharata*, Siva is represented as dwelling in the Himalaya with his hosts. His vehicle is the bull and his consort is variously known as *Uma*, *Parvati*, *Durga*, and *Kali*. Having completed the creation, he turned *yogi* and the phallus became his emblem.

The earliest *lingas* existing do not ante-date the Kushan period (A 12). They are of the kind known as *Mukha-lingas* with one or more faces at the top of the member. One of the earliest iconographical representations of the god is the *Dakshinamurti* in relief on one side of the Vishnu Temple at Deogarh (Plate 64A) which may be dated in the second half of the fifth century A.D. (A 13).

The earliest historical records of Vaishnavism are the Besnagar *Heliodora* inscription and the Ghosundi inscription, both of the second century B.C. The former testifies to the erection of a *Garuda* pillar to *Vasudeva*, god of gods (Plate 12A). *Heliodora*, who was the son of *Diya* and a native of Taxila, was ambassador from the *Yavana Amtalikita* [Antialkidas?] to *Bhagabhadra*. He calls himself *Bhagavata*. The Ghosundi inscription witnesses to the erection of a hall of worship to *Samkarshana* and *Vasudeva*.

Vishnu is a Vedic deity and although he is represented by but few hymns, his personality is vividly portrayed. He measures all things with his three wide strides, the third passing beyond human discernment to the high places of the diety.[2] This conception of the third step of Vishnu as the highest heaven and goal of all things, had obviously much to do with his elevation as Supreme Being. In the *Mahabharata* this Supreme Being is addressed as *Narayana*, *Vasudeva*, and *Vishnu*.

Later Vishnu found a more intimate place in popular worship by means of his ten incarnations [*Avataras*].

The earliest iconographical presentations of the god are two standing, four-armed figures, one on either side of the door-guardians of the Chandragupta Cave at Udayagiri [A.D. 401] (A 14).

Hindu architecture.

Unlike Buddhism and Jainism, the Hindu sects are not organized into definite congregations. Whatever the shrine be, one of the magnificent temples of Bhuvanesvar or Khajuraho, or a red daubed stone by the roadside, the worship is individual. For certain ceremonial purposes the aid of priests is sought, and all the larger temples have their hosts of attendants. But there is never a congregation worshipping in unison. Architecturally speaking, the Hindu shrine is the dwelling-place of the god, although various pavilions or porches dedicated to the preparation of the offerings or to music and dancing stand before it (A 15).

The earliest structural Hindu shrines existing are the flat-roofed Gupta temples, square in plan with a verandah supported by four pillars,[3] the doorway being

[1] *Svetasvetara Upanishad.*   [2] R. V., i. 155. 5.   [3] As at Sanchi and Tigowa.

A. Terracotta. Probably Mauryan period. Patna Museum.

B. Front and back views of colossal female statue (a Yakshi), from Besnagar. Probable date, 185-150 B.C. Sunga period. Indian Museum, Calcutta.

C. Colossal Yaksha statue, from Parkham, near Mathura Probable date, 185-150 B.C. Sunga period. Mathura Museum.

(*Copyright by Department of Archaeology, Government of India*)

PLATE 11

A. The Heliodoros Pillar, Besnagar. (Late 2nd Century B.C. Sunga period).

B. Inner view of eastern gateway, Bharhut. (*c.* 150 B.C. Sunga period. Indian Museum, Calcutta).

PLATE 12

elaborately carved. At Ajanta the cell in the centre of the back wall of the oblong, many pillared caves, is cut on exactly the same plan, the doorways corresponding very closely. The introduction of the *linga* shrine at Badami and Ellora eventually altered the plan radically by placing the shrine in the body of the hall as at Elephanta. The great medieval temples consist of high-towered shrines, each with its entrance-pavilions.

Indian iconography.

As portrayed in the *Brahma-Jala Sutta,* primitive Buddhism gave no place to aesthetics, for music, song, and the dance are classed with sorcery and cock-fighting as minor examples of foolishness, unprofitable to the wise. *Manu* and *Chanakya* also adopt this slighting attitude towards the arts. However, that is of little account, and Bharhut and Sanchi are not less fine because they are not supported by the argumentative analysis of the schoolmen. The art of the Early Period is a spontaneous growth, endued with native virility. Essentially narrative, it is vividly perceptive. The history of Indian art must be written in terms of the action of a literary, metaphysical mode of thought upon this naive, story-telling art, resulting in the formation of an immense and intricate iconography. Around this iconography has grown a still more abstruse, secondary literature, in which the least variation of detail is seized upon to sanction the subdivision and endless multiplication of types of icons.

Images are roughly divided into two classes, the fixed and the movable [*Achala* and *Chala*]. They are likewise roughly described as standing [*Sthanaka*], sitting [*Asana*] or reclining [*Sayana*]. Also they may further be described in terms of the nature of the manifestation: as terrible [*Ugra*] as is Vishnu in his Man-Lion incarnation, or pacific [*Santa*]. The images of Vishnu are further classified according to their natures as *Yoga*, *Bhoga*, and *Vira*, to be worshipped respectively according to the personal desires of the worshipper.

This classification of gods and devotees according to their innate natures refers directly to the classification by natures of the *Sankhya* philosophy, primeval matter being distinguished by the three properties [*Gunas*] of Light [*Sattva*], Might [*Rajas*], and Darkness [*Tamas*]. It is clear that the needs of the worshipper specify the type of the image worshipped. Complex manifestations, whose many attributes are symbolized by their many hands are considered *Tamasic* in character, and their worshippers of little understanding. To the wise images of all kinds are equally superfluous.

Indian aesthetics.

Indian aesthetics must be regarded as being of late date, a supplement to the iconographical literature of the medieval period. Much of the *Agamas* is of great iconographical interest, but these late literary canons have no aesthetic light to shed, although they do indicate something of the religous, hieratical atmosphere which deadened artistic creation in the last period of medieval decadence.[1] Indian aesthetics are based upon the conception of aesthetic value in terms of personal response or reproduction. This value is known as *Rasa*, and when it is present the object is said to have *Rasa* [*Rasavant*] and the person to be *Rasika* or appreciative. Rasa produces various moods in the *Rasika* varying in kind according to the initial stimulus; from these moods emotions spring. The mechanics of this system is worked out in detail in the *Dhanamjaya Dasarupa* and the *Visvanatha Sahitya Darpana.* The whole system is based upon and illustrated by literature, and cannot be applied directly to sculpture and painting.[2]

[1] Rao, *Hindu Iconography*, Pt. I, vol. i, p. 31.

[2] See Coomaraswamy, *Dance of Siva*, p. 30.

NOTES TO CHAPTER ONE

(A 1) It is now recognized that a certain unity did exist in art forms in many parts of the country. For instance, the sculpture of Mathura during the 1st and 2nd centuries A.D. under Kushan rule has obvious affinities with some of the sculpture of the Deccan cave monasteries and Krishna Valley stupas built during the same period either under the Satavahana Kings or the Kshaharata Satraps. The reasons for such affinities can only be understood against the background of the spread of Buddhism. It originated in the North-East and slowly spread all over the country due to the circumstance that the Mauryan Emperor Asoka made it a state religion, though this proposition has been disputed. Once Buddhism was established all over the country, the Buddhist monks travelled from north to south and south to north in the course of their proselytizing activities. The various establishments of monks in different parts of the country did not function in isolation. In such circumstances it was natural that architectural and sculptural concepts formulated and developed in the original homeland of Buddhism should also come to be adopted, with local variations, by the Buddhist settlements further afield such as those of the Krishna Valley in the Deccan. It would be a grave mistake to imagine that Buddhist monastic and stupa architecture developed in a haphazard manner dependent on the fancies of individual architects. All architectural activities were carefully regulated and followed prescribed plans. So also the embellishment of stupas, railings, chaityas and monastic dwellings followed certain well accepted principles though variations in carrying out the actual work were bound to result due to local conditions and other circumstances. It is certain that foremen (*avesanis*), masons and sculptors coming from one part of the country did not confine themselves to the districts of their domicile. Many of them must have also worked in other parts of the country, distant from their home provinces. So also, it is probable that supervisor monks (*navakarmikas*) who were in charge of the construction of Buddhist establishments in northern or central India also supervised, at least in part, certain of the building activities in the Deccan and other places. Moreover, it appears that foreign artisans, working in a common tradition, gave their services from time to time to monastic establishments in all parts of the country and this factor also had an unifying effect on art motifs. This unity in art forms is not confined to any one phase in the development of Indian art, though the reasons for this unity vary to a greater or lesser extent, in different periods. This unity is also to be observed in Hindu and Jain art. Though it is convenient for the purpose of classification to talk of Buddhist, Hindu and Jain Art, the principles underlying their concepts of sculpture were in the main similar. At the same time it would not be correct to say that there were no visual differences in the plastic output of these three great religions. Each developed its own iconography. But there can be no doubt that guild sculptors used to work alike on Buddhist, Hindu and Jain architectural projects, meeting the special requirements of each sect. There is, as a rule, a warmth in Buddhist sculpture and a dynamic quality in Hindu sculpture both of which are lacking in Jain art. The rather cold and mechanical sculptural output of this religion, particularly after the Gupta Age, is in some measure due to its outlook on life and the importance it gave to asceticism.

(A 2) These were the great pioneers but since their time there has been a vast amount of research and many of their conclusions require modification or explanation. Several of Vincent Smith's own conclusions also require revision but it has not been thought fit to burden the present volume with controversial matter.

(A 3) This viewpoint would not find wide acceptance today because we know that the sentiment and philosophy underlying Indian art motifs and forms can be traced to periods several centuries before the Christian era.

(A 4) The Ampthill Nataraja cannot be regarded as a masterpiece though undoubtedly superior to mere hack-work. Today we know of Pallava and Chola Natarajas incomparably finer than the Ampthill Nataraja which it has not been thought necessary to illustrate.

(A 5) This statement has no application to the output of the Pallava and Chola periods when a uniformly high standard of work was maintained. The deterioration is seen in the Vijayanagar and post-Vijayanagar images.

(A 6) Nowadays, numerous modern copper images, many of them of considerable size, are being produced in South India and Mysore. They are usually very ornate. Some are not unattractive, but all proclaim the decadence into which this art has fallen. Unfortunately, this revival of casting copper images has brought the art of faking in its wake. One such group of faked images, in which the fingers taper to thin sharp points, and which invariably have a depression in the middle of the forehead, came into the market a few years ago. They were passed off as examples of an hitherto unknown provincial school alleged to have come to light for the first time. Unwary foreigners and even several collectors who acquired many of these images were deceived. The present editor exposed this racket and in consequence no respectable museum countenanced their purchase. Since this exposure they have disappeared from the market and now the fakes which are produced are made to resemble the old images. The stunt of a new provincial school having suddenly come to light has been abandoned.

When the Buddhists sought to propagate their faith amongst the people they were quick to realize that it was essential not to suggest any antagonism between the Buddhist doctrine and the tree and water cosmology which had through countless years crystallized into the worship of tree and forest godlings, known as Yakshas, and serpent-hooded river deities known as Nagas. These godlings were always conceived in anthropomorphic form. The Buddhist gospellers astutely brought the Yakshas and Nagas into the Buddhist fold as good and devout worshippers of the Buddha. At the same time they gave them considerable importance not only in the legends relating to the Buddha but also in sculptural representations of these legends and in scenes relating to the worship of the Buddha. The prominence given to Yakshas can be seen for instance in the Bharhut railing of the 2nd century B.C., now in the Indian Museum, Calcutta (Pl. 13A,B, C.) as well as in the famous railing and gateways at Sanchi (Pl. 19). Another well-known instance is the Nagaraja group outside the Chaitya Cave No. IX at Ajanta belonging to the 6th century A.D. (Pl. 67B). The Buddhists thus succeeded in making the masses receptive to Buddhism without interfering with the Yaksha and Naga cults which they realized could never be rooted out. (A 7)

The study of art motifs indicates that their origin can often be traced to the imagery one finds expressed in the hymns of the Rig Veda, to the beliefs of ancient forgotten peoples which still manifest themselves in village life, to hoary Western Asiatic sources and to the vast bewildering mythology which today may be localized, but once seems to have been a common heritage of many races and many countries. (A 8)

The Buddha and Vardhamana had to contend with the views of several well-known teachers of those times. There were powerful sects such as the Ajivikas, who did not subscribe to the philosophy of Buddhism and Jainism. It was an age that gave birth to a remarkable galaxy of preachers and thinkers and it was long after the death of Buddha and Vardhamana that Buddhism and Jainism emerged as the greatest faiths along with Brahamanism. (A 9)

The temples at Girnar and Satrunjaya, owing to later additions and repairs, have lost most of their pristine qualities. That is not quite the case with the Mount Abu shrines, where despite renovations original work of excellence can be seen particularly in the Tejapala shrine of 1232 A.D. The renovations and additions in the earlier Vimalavasahi temple of 1031 A.D. are mostly more than a century later and little of the original sculpture can be traced today with any certainty. (A 10)

The Gupta period, for the purpose of a proper classification on a stylistic basis, must be extended somewhat beyond the rule of the Imperial Guptas which ended *circa* 550 A.D. Accordingly, the period 320-600 A.D. should be regarded as the age of the Guptas so far as the chronology of Indian art is concerned. The period immediately following the Gupta Age has been included in the medieval period by several writers including Vincent Smith. But it appears to the editor to be a grave error to do so. The period 600-800 A.D. should always be referred to as the 'post-Gupta' period, while the term 'medieval' should be applied to the work of *circa* 800 A.D. onwards. It is not a matter merely of nomenclature. The difference is so vital that the failure to comprehend the distinction would seriously affect a proper perspective of Indian art and Indian sculpture in particular. In the post-Gupta period not only is the Gupta tradition continued in matters of form and detail but the art of sculpture largely retains its qualities as pure sculpture. In the medieval period, however, it increasingly becomes architectonic in character apart from the fact that it loses the essential plastic qualities of great sculpture and tends towards over-elaboration and pronounced sensuality. (A 11)

Most critics regard the Bhita Linga and the Gudimallam Linga as much earlier than the Kushan period and assign them to about the 1st century B.C. See Gopinath Rao, *Elements of Hindu Iconography*, 1914-16, Vol. 2, Pt. 1, Pls. 1 and 2. (A 12)

Though the attempt to trace the worship of Shiva to the Indus Valley civilization is not very convincing, Shiva images belonging to the Kushan period (1st and 2nd century A.D.) are known, as for instance, the Shiva head in the Mathura Museum (No. 2085) where the third eye on the forehead is seen. It belongs most probably to the 2nd century A.D. The Deogarh relief (Pl. 64A) belongs to the late 6th and not to the 5th century A.D. It is really a representation of Nar-Narayan. (A 13)

(A 14) For still earlier Vishnu images, belonging to the Kushan period (1st and 2nd century A.D.), see the examples in the Mathura Museum listed in the *Journal of the United Provinces Historical Society*, Vol. XVIII, Pls. 1-2, pp. 105-107.

(A 15) At the same time it must be remembered that the temple, particularly in South India, was the centre of all community activities. Here the local inhabitants would listen to religious discourses, recitations of the *Ramayana*, witness dance performances, arrive at decisions of civic importance and meet one another in general. The life of a South Indian village centred round the temple.

A

B

C

D

A. Sundarsana Yakshi, Bharhut. B. Chulakoka Yakshi, Bharhut. C. Yakshi, Bharhut. (All three datable *c.* 150 B.C. Sunga period. Indian Museum, Calcutta).
D. Acrobats, Bharhut. *c.* 150 B.C. Allahabad Museum. Courtesy, Shri Pramod Chandra.

PLATE 13

A. Bharhut, medallion. (Humorous scene of monkeys extracting a tooth. Unidentified Jataka story).

c. 150 B.C. Sunga period. Indian Museum, Calcutta.

(Copyright by Department of Archaeology, Government of India)

B.

C.

B. Bharhut, medallion. (Monkeys leading a captive elephant. Unidentified Jataka story.) C. Maya's Dream, Bharhut.

PLATE 14

Chapter Two

THE MAURYAN PERIOD

A SHORT time after the death of Alexander in 323 B.C. the throne of Magadha or Bihar, then the premier kingdom of Northern India, was seized by Chandragupta, surnamed The Maurya, known as Sandrokottos to Greek authors. In the course of a victorious reign of twenty-four years this able prince caused his influence to be felt over all India, at least as far south as the river Narbada, and acquired from Seleukos Nikator, first his enemy and then his ally, the valuable provinces lying between the Indus and the Hindu Kush mountains which now constitute the major part of the kingdom of Afghanistan.

The Mauryan Dynasty.

Chandragupta was succeeded by his son Bindusara, who, in or about 273 B.C., transmitted the imperial sceptre to his son, Asoka, the third and most renowned sovereign of the Maurya dynasty. For forty-one years (273-232 B.C.) Asoka ruled his immense empire with great power and might, maintaining friendly relations with his neighbours, the Tamil states of the extreme south and also with the island kingdom of Ceylon and the more remote Greek monarchies of Macedonia, Epirus, Western Asia, Egypt and Cyrene.

Early in life the emperor became a religious convert and as the years rolled on his zeal increased. Finally, his energies and riches were devoted almost entirely to the work of honouring and propagating the teaching of Gautama Buddha. With one exception he abstained from wars of conquest and was thus free to concentrate his attention upon the task to which his life was consecrated.

Asoka's patronage of Buddhism.

The imperial palace at Pataliputra, the modern Patna, the capital of Chandragupta Maurya is described by Greek and Roman authors as excelling in splendour the royal residences of Susa and Ekbatana. Although no vestige of such a building has survived, with the possible exception of some brick foundations, there is no reason to doubt the statements of the historians (A 1). The result of much excavation seems to support the literary evidence that Indian architects before the time of Asoka built their superstructures chiefly of timber, using sun-dried brick almost exclusively for foundations and plinths. No deficiency in dignity or grandeur was involved in the use of the more perishable material; on the contrary, the employment of timber enables wide spaces to be roofed with ease which could not be spanned with masonry, especially when, as in India, the radiating arch was not ordinarily employed for structural purposes.

Early wooden architecture.

Excavations of widely spread sites dating from the Maurya to the Gupta periods, and even later, emphasize the fact that timber and unburnt brick were the standard architectural materials of ancient India, mud being used as it still is, for ordinary, domestic work. However, Asoka is credited by the literary sources with the use of masonry in the many building activities reported of him. It is on record that during his reign of about forty-one years he replaced the wooden walls and buildings of his capital by more substantial work and caused hundreds of fine edifices in both brick and stone to be erected throughout the empire. So astonishing was his activity as a builder that people in after ages could not believe his constructions to be the work of human agency, and felt constrained to regard them as wrought by familiar spirits forced to obey the behests of the imperial magician (A 2). Few sites can, however, be definitely ascribed to the Asokan or even to the Mauryan period. No building with any pretensions to be

Stone buildings.

considered an example of architecture can be assigned to any earlier period than this, with which the history of Indian architecture as of the other arts begins.

Beginnings of Indian art. The Mauryan emperors must surely have built palaces, public offices, and temples suitable to the dignity of a powerful empire and proportionate to the wealth of rich provinces, but of such structures not a trace seems to survive. The best explanation of this fact is the hypothesis that the early works of Indian architecture and art were mainly constructed of timber and other perishable materials, ill-fitted to withstand the ravenous tooth of time. Whatever the true explanation of this may be the fact remains that the history of Indian art begins with Asoka. 'But', as Professor Percy Gardner observes, 'there can be no doubt that Indian art had an earlier history. The art of Asoka is a mature art: in some respects more mature than the Greek art of the time, though, of course far inferior to it, at least in our eyes.'[1]

Its origins. We can affirm with certainty that the forms of Asokan architecture and plastic decoration were descended from wooden prototypes, and may also discern traces of the influence of lost works in metal, ivory, terracotta, and painting. The pictorial character of the ancient Indian reliefs, *histoires sans paroles*, is obvious, and the affinity of much of the decorative work with the jeweller's art is equally plain. The sculpture on a pier of the southern gate at Sanchi was actually executed by the ivory-carvers of the neighbouring town of Vedisa (Bhilsa).[2] We may, moreover, feel some confidence in affirming that the sudden adoption of stone as the material for both architecture and sculpture was in a large measure the result of foreign, perhaps Persian, example. The fuller consideration of the foreign influences affecting Indian art will be more conveniently deferred and made the subject of a separate chapter.

Personal initiative of Asoka. Whatever the foreign elements of ancient Indian art may have been, great weight must be allowed for the personal initiative of Asoka, a man of marked originality of mind, capable of forming large designs and executing them with imperial thoroughness. The direction taken by Indian art was like the diffusion of Buddhism, determined in its main lines by the will of a resolute and intelligent autocrat.

Early art nearly all Buddhist. Like most of the extant works of early Indian art, the Mauryan columns and caves (Plate 8B) were executed in honour of Buddhism (A 3), which became the state religion in the empire of Asoka and is said to have been introduced during his reign into independent Ceylon. Although we know that both Jainism and Brahmanical Hinduism continued to attract multitudes of adherents during the Mauryan period, hardly any material remains of works dedicated to the service of those religions have survived (A 4).

Inscriptions, columns, and sculpture. The monuments which can with certainty be dated in Asoka's reign are not very numerous, but it is not improbable that more may be discovered. His buildings having perished, our direct knowledge of the art strictly contemporary with him is derived from his inscriptions, the carving and sculptures on his monolithic columns, certain caves, and a few fragments of pottery excavated at Mauryan level.[3] The inscriptions are worthy of being mentioned among the Fine Arts

[1] *Trans. 3rd Inter. Congress for the Hist. of Religions* (Oxford, 1908), vol. ii, p. 81.

[2] *Ep. Ind.*, ii. 92, 378, insr. § 200 of Stupa L: C. 189: Buhler.

[3] With regard to archaeological method in India it is to be regretted that the evidence of the pottery of the various sites and levels has not been given more prominence. Nor is it always clear where such lesser finds are deposited for research purposes.

A.

B.

A. Worship of stupa by earthly and aerial beings, Bharhut.
B. Jataka scenes on coping, Bharhut. *c.* 150 B.C. Sunga period. Indian Museum, Calcutta.

A.

B

(*Copyright by Department of Archaeology, Government of India*)

C.

D.

E.

Reliefs from the (stupa) railing, Bodh-Gaya. (1st Cent. B.C. Late Sunga period).
(Photos: Indian Museum, Calcutta)
PLATE 16

A

B

Reliefs from the (stupa) railing, Bodh-Gaya. (1st Cent. B.C. Late Sunga period).
(Copyright by Department of Archaeology, Government of India)

PLATE 17

A. Stupa No. 1, with railings and gateways, Sanchi. 1st Cent. B.C.
(Copyright by Department of Archaeology, Government of India)

B. Detail of gateway, Stupa No. 1, Sanchi. 1st Cent. B.C.
(Photo : A. L. Syed)

PLATE 18

on account of their beautiful execution, for nearly all are models of careful and accurate stone cutting. The most faultless example is the brief record on the Rummindei Pillar, which is as perfect as on the day it was incised.[1] The craft of the skilled mason and stone-cutter, so closely akin to fine art, reached perfection in the days of Asoka, as appears from every detail of their work, and especially from an examination of the beautifully polished surface of the monoliths and the interiors of the cave-dwellings dedicated by him and his grandson, Dasaratha, in the hills of Bihar.

Monolithic pillars of Asoka.

Isolated pillars, or columns, usually associated with other buildings, and frequently surmounted by a human figure, animal sculpture, or sacred symbol have been erected in India at all times by adherents of all the three leading Indian religions. The oldest are the monolithic pillars of Asoka (A 5), who set up at least thirty of these monuments, of which many survive in a more or less perfect state.[2] Ten of these bear his inscriptions. The Lauriya-Nandangarh monument, inscribed with the first six Pillar Edicts, and practically uninjured, is shown on Plate 3. The shaft of polished sandstone, 32 feet 9½ inches in height, diminishes from a base diameter of 35½ inches to a diameter of only 22½ inches at the top—proportions which render it the most graceful of all the Asoka columns. The uninscribed pillar at Bakhira (Plate 8C) in the Muzaffarpur District, in perfect preservation, and presumably of earlier date, is more massive and consequently less elegant (A 6). The fabrication, conveyance, and erection of monoliths of such enormous size—the heaviest weighing about fifty tons—are proofs that the engineers and stone-cutters of Asoka's age were not inferior in skill and resource to those of any time or country.

The capitals of these pillars provide excellent evidence of the state of the art of sculpture, both in relief and in the round, during the period between the year 250 B.C. and the end of the reign of the great emperor in 232 B.C.

Sculptured capitals.

The capital of each pillar, like the shaft, was monolithic, comprising three principal members, namely, a Persepolitan bell, abacus, and crowning sculpture in the round. The junction between the shaft and the abacus was marked by a necking, the edge of the abacus was decorated with bas-relief designs, and the crowning sculpture was occasionally a sacred symbol, such as a wheel, or more commonly a symbolical animal, or group of animals. Sometimes the inanimate and animal symbols were combined.

Forms of abacus.

Within the limits thus determined the artists enjoyed considerable latitude, and in consequence the surviving capitals vary widely in detail. The abacus might be either rectangular or circular so as to suit the form of the sculpture above. The edge of the abacus of the beautiful Lauriya-Nandangarh pillar is decorated by a row of flying sacred geese in quite low relief. The abaci of the pillars at Allahabad and Sankisa (Plate 8A) and the bull pillar at Rampurva (Plate 7) exhibit elegant designs composed of the lotus and palmette or honeysuckle. Whatever the device selected, it is invariably well executed, and 'chiselled with that extraordinary precision and accuracy' which characterize the workmanship of the Maurya age, and have never been surpassed in Athens or elsewhere.[3]

Animal symbolism.

The topmost sculpture in the round was most often one or other of four animals —namely, the elephant, the horse, the bull, and the lion (A 7). All these animals,

[1] *Asoka, the Buddhist Emperor of India*, VI. ii.

[2] See the author's paper on the subject. *Z. D. M. G.* for 1911.

[3] Sir John Marshall, in *Ann. Rep. A. S.*, India, 1906-7, p. 89.

except the horse, are actually found on the round on extant capitals, and it is recorded that a horse once crowned the pillar at Rummindei, the Lumbini garden. On the sides of the abacus of the Sarnath capital (Plate 4) all the four creatures are carved in bas-relief[1] (Plates 5, 6).

The elephant of the Sankisa capital (Plate 8A) is well modelled, but unhappily has been badly mutilated. The two pillars at Rampurva bear respectively the bull and lion[2] (Plates 7, 8D).

The Sarnath capital.

The magnificent Sarnath capital discovered in 1905, unquestionably the best extant specimen of Asokan sculpture, was executed late in the reign between 242 and 232 B.C. (A 8). The column was erected to mark the spot where Gautama Buddha first 'turned the wheel of law', or in plain English, publicly preached his doctrine.[3] The symbolism of the figures, whether in the round or in relief, refers to the commemoration of that event for the benefit of the Church Universal. The four lions standing back to back on the abacus once supported a stone wheel, 2 feet 9 inches in diameter, of which only fragments remain.[4]

It would be difficult to find in any country an example of ancient animal sculpture superior or even equal to this beautiful work of art, which successfully combines realistic modelling with idealistic dignity, and is finished in every detail with perfect accuracy. The bas-reliefs on the abacus are as good in their way as the noble lions in the round. The design, while obviously reminiscent of Assyrian and Persian prototypes, is modified by Indian sentiment, the bas-reliefs being purely Indian. Sir John Marshall's conjecture that the composition may be the work of an Asiatic Greek is not supported by the style of the relief figures. The ability of an Asiatic Greek to represent Indian animals so well may be doubted (A 9).

Sanchi edict-pillar capital.

The only rival to the artistic supremacy of the Sarnath capital is the replica which once crowned the detached pillar at Sanchi engraved with a copy of the Sarnath edict denouncing schism. The Sanchi capital is decidedly inferior to that at Sarnath, but it is possible that both works may proceed from the hands of a single artist[5] (A 10). A century or so later, when an inferior sculptor attempted to model similar lions on the pillars of the southern gateway at Sanchi, he failed utterly, and his failure supports the theory that the Sarnath capital must have been wrought by a foreigner. Certainly no later sculpture in India attained such high excellence.

The Bakhira pillar.

The perfection of the Sanchi and Sarnath lions on the edict-pillars must have been the result of much progressive effort. The uninscribed pillar at Bakhira (Plate 8C) seems to be one of the earlier experiments of Asoka's artists (A 11). The clumsy proportions of the shaft contrast unfavourably with the graceful design of the Lauriya-Nandangarh column (*ante*, Plate 3), which bears a copy of the Pillar Edicts, and may be dated in 242 or 241 B.C., while the seated lion

[1] These animals may symbolize the four corners of the world, which explanation of the symbolism was suggested by the discovery of rude symbolical bronze figures of the four animals in Ceylon. See Vincent Smith : 'The Monolithic Pillars of Asoka', in *Z. D. M. G.*, 1911. The lion was also regarded as a symbol of Buddha himself.

[2] *J. R. A. S.*, 1908, p. 1085, Pl. I.

[3] The wheel is one of the earliest Buddhist symbols and with the Tree and the *Stupa* appears everywhere at Bharhut and Sanchi. Foucher associates these three symbols which obviously represent the First Sermon in the Deer Park. the Enlightenment at Bodh-Gaya, and the Death at Kusinagara with a fourth, the Goddess Sri and the *Bhadra-Ghata* (vase with lotuses), representing the birth at Kapilavastu. *Beginnings of Buddhist Art*, p. 70, note 88.

[4] Discovered by Mr. F. O. Oertel and described by him in *Ann. Rep. A. S.*, India, 1904-5, pp. 68-70, Pl. XX. His account of the excavations has been reprinted in a separate volume entitled *Buddhist Ruins of Sarnath, near Benares*, 1904-5.

[5] Maisey, *Sanchi and its Remains*, Pl. XIX, 2 ; Codrington, *Ancient India*, Pl. I.

East gate, front view, Sanchi. 1st Cent. B.C.
(Photo: A. L. Syed)

A. Detail from Stupa No. II, Sanchi. Mid-2nd Cent. B.C. Sunga period.

(*Copyright by Department of Archaeology, Government of India*)

B. Detail from North Gate, Stupa No. 1, Sanchi. Worship of the Bo tree symbolising the Buddha. 1st Cent. B.C.

(Photo : A. L. Syed)

PLATE 20

on the summit is by no means equal to the animals on the edict-pillars of Sarnath and Sanchi erected between 242 and 232 B.C. I am disposed to think that the Bakhira column was set up soon after 257 B.C., the date of the earliest Rock Edicts. It must also be noted that at Rampurva there are two pillars only one of which is inscribed. In the Sahasram inscription it is clearly stated that edicts are to be inscribed on rocks, or on pillars wherever a stone pillar is standing, which suggests that some of these pillars may considerably antedate Asoka's reign, although their technique is obviously one with the inscriptions and caves, and they are clearly Mauryan'[1] (A 12).

NOTES TO CHAPTER TWO

With the downfall of the great Persian Empire at the hands of Alexander, it appears that Western Asiatic builders and craftsmen, Persians and colonial Greeks, many of them settled in Persia, found their way to India and took service under the Mauryas. Though Persia was defeated, the ancient world continued to associate Imperial pomp and power with everything Persian. It is not therefore surprising that Chandragupta Maurya, with his design for Imperial greatness, should seek to emulate the splendid architecture of the Persian Kings. That he successfully did so we gather from the pages of Megasthenes, the ambassador of Seleukos Nikator to the Mauryan court. It is unlikely that Megasthenes would compare the Mauryan palace to those of Susa and Ekbatana unless it was a splendid structure, as we now know it was, in stone and wood. In fact, the very reference to the Persian palaces indicates the spirit of the times and the atmosphere at the Mauryan court, namely, a keen desire to emulate or even surpass the architectural achievement of Persia. It is fairly certain that the Indian builder prior thereto was not accustomed to the construction of great stone structures or even structures of wood resting on colossal stone pillars. It is thus evident that the sudden change to residences emulating those of Susa and Ekbatana could not be achieved by indigenous workmen without the active assistance and supervision of Persian and colonial Greek architects and craftsmen. The excavations at the ancient capital of Pataliputra have brought to light part of a polished pillar, fragments of polished stone, a fragment of gilded vine and have revealed a plan of a great stone-pillared hall based on Achaemenid architecture. This no doubt was the great palace referred to by Megasthenes; though it may have been added to by Asoka who it is said had many buildings constructed in brick and stone. A 1

This is the usual exaggeration common to literary forms of expression in all periods. A 2

One of the caves in the Barabar hills donated by Asoka was for the use of the Ajivikas, who were a religious sect of importance. This fact indicates that Asoka was not a bigot. A 3

The two torsos from Loharipur near Patna, and now in the Patna Museum, represent Jain Jinas. One of them (Pl. 10C) bears the famous Mauryan polish never seen save in the Mauryan period. A 4

The theory that some of the pillars predate Asoka has not much to commend it, even though a number of them are not inscribed with the edicts. A 5

It is not certain whether the Bakhira pillar is an early example or a later one of inferior workmanship executed without the supervision of skilled foreign stone cutters. A 6

A variety of explanations have been given by scholars for the symbolism of the Asokan animal capitals. The most likely explanation, however, is that they represent the guardians of the four quarters of the universe. Though they are not appropriately distributed according to the cardinal points, the underlying intention of these capitals seems only to have been to emphasize that Asoka had spread the faith in all directions. A 7

This circumstance indicates that right from the time of Chandragupta Maurya to late in the reign of Asoka, the Imperial Mauryan policy was to take into the royal service the finest available foreign stone cutters and sculptors. Foreign masters had numerous Indian craftsmen under them constantly learning the new art of fashioning colossal polished pillars and colossal capitals in stone. There can be no manner of doubt that the Sarnath capital (Pl. 4) including the reliefs on the abacus (Plates 5, 6) is the handiwork of a stone carver, Persian or colonial Greek, bred in the Achaemenid tradition. None of the animals in relief on the abacus display any pronounced Indian feeling. The horse (Pl. 5A) is frankly Hellenistic, while the bull (Pl. 6B) is quite unlike the Rampurva bull (Pl. 7) which is admittedly Indian in feeling. The bull on the Sarnath pillar approximates in construction to A 8

[1] *Camb. Hist. of India*, p. 501.

Western Asiatic bulls. The elephant (Pl. 5B) also is not the work of Indian craftsmen. One has only to compare it to the unfinished Dhauli rock elephant to realise the difference. But though the Sarnath capital is the work of foreign craftsmen the influence of Asoka dominates the conception of all the pillars and their animal sculptures. The Rampurva single lion capital in the Indian Museum (Pl. 8D) is also of foreign workmanship. It is not spectacular like the Sarnath capital, and the face of the lion is damaged, yet for sheer plastic values it is the finest of all the Asokan lions. The Rampurva bull capital (Pl. 7) is equally magnificent. The bull is characteristically Indian in feeling, but the workmanship is of such high excellence that the probabilities are that it is by a foreign craftsman, who, perhaps by long residence, was able to conceive the bull, evidently belonging to a *deshi* breed, with that sensitiveness and insight which the Indian sculptor usually brought to his portrayals of animal life. Some writers have criticized the proportions of the Rampurva bull, but such criticism may be dismissed as meriting no serious consideration. The high polish which is seen on almost all Mauryan sculpture is a technique derived from Achaemenid Persia. The secret of this polish when carried to India was evidently not preserved for many generations. It is never seen save in Mauryan art. Though we have a number of Sunga sculptures in the same Chunar sandstone as used by the Mauryan stone cutters, not a single Sunga sculpture bears this high polish or any polish at all. Nor is it seen in any other period of Indian art. Certain medieval sculptures do bear a high polish but no one would confuse that with the Mauryan polish.

These animal pillar-capitals represent the court art of the time of Asoka. But there is also another form of sculpture, more popular in conception, belonging to the Mauryan period. This group consists of Yaksha and Yakshi figures, Jain Tirthankaras, portrait heads, some miscellaneous sculptures and carved discs. Though the specimens which have survived are very limited in number there can be no doubt that many more such sculptures must have been commissioned. The best known of the group is the famous Yakshi from Didarganj (Pl. 9A) near ancient Pataliputra, the capital of the Mauryas. It is a large figure which has all the massiveness and solidity so characteristic of the Asokan pillar capitals, smooth ample surfaces and the 'grand manner' in the sculpturing of form. In addition it bears the characteristic high polish of Mauryan art. Two massive Yakshas from Patna (Pl. 9B) also bearing the high polish are more or less contemporary with the Yakshi. From Lohanipur, also near ancient Pataliputra (the modern Patna), come two nude headless torsos. One of them bears the Mauryan polish (Pl. 10C). There can be little doubt that they are Jain Tirthankaras. In plastic qualities they are in keeping with what one would expect during the Mauryan period. They are thus the earliest known Jain sculptures and hence of great significance. It is apparent that the indigenous sculptors who created the Didarganj Yakshi, the Patna Yakshas and Lohanipur torsos, though not trained in the court art of Asoka, were inspired by that bigness of concept and simplicity in rendering of surfaces which they saw in the great pillar capitals. Though in subject matter the Yaksha-Yakshi figures and the animal capitals are worlds apart, those who are sensitive to form will not fail to sense that Asokan court art was the inspiration behind the Mauryan images referred to above. A few fragments from Sarnath, include two powerful heads (Pl. 10B), one of which, not reproduced, bears the Mauryan polish. Of the small carved discs the most remarkable is that recently found at Rupar in the Mauryan level (Pl. 10A). One cannot fail to observe the resemblance in the features of the male head (Pl. 10B) from Sarnath (side face view) and those of the seated figure in the Rupar disc. Some European critics — and they have been followed by some Indian writers — have opined that the Didarganj Yakshi, the Patna Yakshas, the Lohanipur torsos and the Sarnath heads are all products of the mid or late 1st century B.C. The paleography of certain inscriptions on the two Patna Yakshas, cut on the scarfs of each statue obviously at a later date, has been pressed into service to support this theory as also stylistic comparisons between the Didarganj Yakshi and the early Kushan period female figures from Mathura. It is not however profitable to enter into this barren controversy. The theory that these sculptures belong to the 1st century B.C. cannot gain in stature by reason of the fact that a scholar of the eminence of Sir John Marshall has propounded it. The unstable basis of this theory becomes evident when we find that some of its supporters, in order to surmount the problem of the Mauryan polish, apart from other difficulties, have deluded themselves into seeing some sort of polish on the carvings at Sanchi and on the Parkham Yaksha of Mathura though not a vestige of Mauryan polish exists on any of these sculptures. It may reasonably be concluded that all sculptures bearing the Mauryan polish belong to the Mauryan period and therefore cannot be later than *circa* 185 B.C. The available evidence and the probabilities support that view.

One cannot leave the problem of Mauryan sculpture without reference to the terracottas which have been found in the vicinity of Patna, and which have often been ascribed to the Mauryan period (Pl. 11A). The entire question of dating terracottas is a very knotty problem. One need not doubt the existence of an extensive terracotta art during Mauryan times, but it is not always easy to decide whether a particular piece belongs to the Mauryan period or should be ascribed to the Sunga period.

False notions of national pride have obscured the vision of certain writers when dealing with the question of the Asokan capitals which are mostly the handiwork of foreign craftsmen. In this connection it is of interest to note that the technical excellence seen in the court art of Asoka is absent in Sunga art. Sculptured representations of Asokan pillars in Sunga and post-Sunga art are very inferior copies of the splendid originals. This fact goes to indicate that when the foreign craftsmen and their descendants were no longer available, Sunga and post-Sunga art, though fascinating in content, could not produce anything which had the technical excellence of Asokan court art.

See note A 8. A 9

This can hardly be the case. The Sanchi capital lacks the marked perfection of the Sarnath capital. A 10

See note A 6. A 11

The absence of inscriptions on several pillars has led some writers to conjecture that some of A 12
the pillars are pre-Asokan. But it is clear that they are all connected with the propagation of the Buddhist faith and hence this conjecture has little to recommend it. None of Asoka's predecessors had any known leanings towards Buddhism.

Chapter Three

THE EARLY PERIOD

Part I. ARCHITECTURE

Early architecture.

AFTER the death of Asoka the empire broke to pieces, but his Maurya descendants continued to rule the home provinces for about half a century, at the end of which they were superseded by the Sunga kings who governed parts of Northern India until the beginning of the first century B.C. (A 1). However, the style of architecture, decoration, and sculpture which perhaps first assumed a permanent form under the patronage of Asoka continued in use up to about the close of the first century of the Christian era, forming a distinct and definite period in the history of Indian art.

Although Buddhism at this period, approximately extending from 273 B.C. to A.D. 100, was by no means the only religion in India, it enjoyed a dominant position as the result of the great Buddhist emperor's propaganda, and the monuments remaining, therefore, are almost all Buddhist, though few are as early as the reign of Asoka. The huge mass of solid brick masonry known as the great *stupa* of Sanchi (Pl. 18A), later encased with stone, may belong to his reign, as well as several other similar structures, but most of the buildings that now survive are of a later date.

Architectural forms.

The ancient civil buildings having all perished utterly, except the tangle of superimposed foundations that is all that the spade lays bare at most of the early sites, the story of Indian architecture must therefore be reconstructed from the somewhat one-sided evidence of the temples and shrines, and the bas-reliefs that adorn them. The most characteristic early architectural compositions were *stupas*, with their appurtenant railings and gateways, monasteries, and churches, the '*chaitya*-halls' of Fergusson. The monasteries and churches include both rock-cut and structural examples. Isolated pillars also were frequently set up.

Stupas, Dagaba, or 'topes'.

Stupas or 'topes', the Dagabas of Ceylon—solid cupolas of brick or stone masonry—were constructed either for the safe custody of relics hidden in a chamber near the base, or to mark a spot associated with an event sacred in Buddhist or Jain legend. Until a few years ago the *stupa* was universally believed to be peculiarly Buddhist, but it is now a matter of common knowledge that the ancient Jains built *stupas* identical in form and accessories with those of the rival religion. However, no specimen of a Jain *stupa* is standing, and our attention may be confined to the Buddhist series.[1] The earliest *stupas* were of unburnt bricks like the Bharhut *stupa*. The great *stupa* at Sanchi was originally of this type, a casing of roughly trimmed masonry and a ramp forming an upper procession-path being added later. This *Stupa* as it appeared before restoration is shown in Plate 4.[2] As time went on, the originally hemispherical dome was raised on a high drum or tier of drums, and so by a series of gradual amplifications the ancient model was transformed first into a lofty tower after the kind of Kanishka's *Stupa* at Peshawar, described by Hiuen Tsiang, and ultimately into the Chinese pagoda.

Plain *stupas* and railings.

The most ancient *stupas* were very plain. They were usually surrounded by a stone railing, sometimes square in plan, but more often circular, marking off

[1] See the bas-relief of a Jain *stupa* from Mathura, Pl. 31B.
[2] [This plate has been replaced in the Third Edition by a newer photograph, Pl. 18A].

A

B

C

A. Detail of mythical beasts from Stupa No. 1, Sanchi. 1st Cent. B.C. B. Detail of man fighting lion, Sanchi. C. Detail from North Gate, Stupa No. 1, Sanchi. Jataka story of monkeys offering honey to the Buddha, symbolised by the Bo tree. 1st Cent. B.C. Sunga period. (Photo: A. L. Syed).

PLATE 21

A

B

East Gateway, Sanchi. (Details from Stupa No. 1. 1st Cent. B.C.).

(Photos: A. L. Syed)

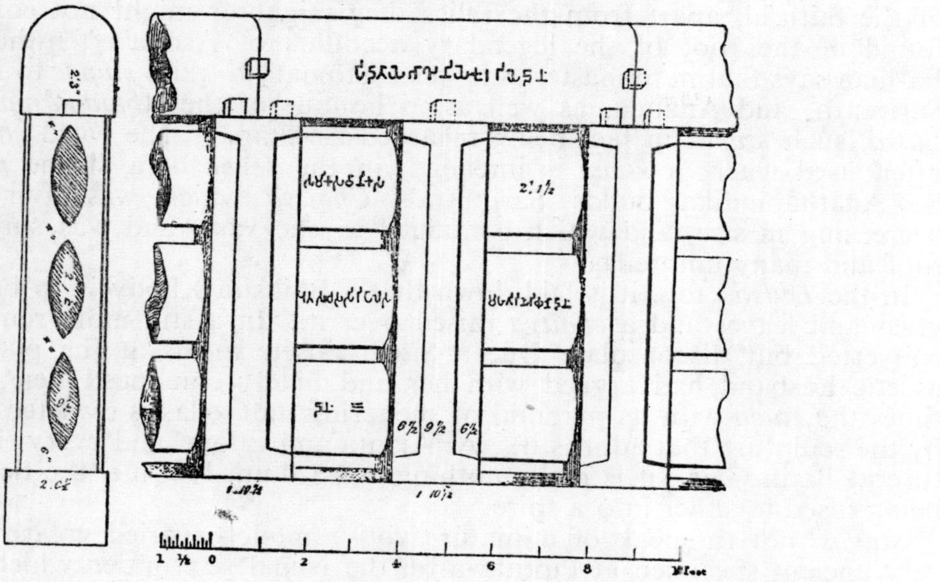

Sanchi railing.

a procession-path for the use of worshippers and serving as a defence against evil spirits. The earliest examples of such railings, at Sanchi, are unadorned copies of wooden post-and-rail fences. The bars of the railing were usually lenticular in section, inserted in the posts as shown in the diagram. At Besnagar another form of ancient railing has been unearthed, consisting of oblong slabs held by grooved uprights.[1]

Bharhut and Sanchi represent two sequent stages in the development of the *stupa* of the Early (post-Mauryan) Period. They and their appurtenances had become more ornate. Sculpture was freely applied to every member of the railing—to the posts, rails, and coping. Late in the second century of the Christian era at Amaravati the railing was transformed into a screen covered with stone pictures in comparatively low relief[2] but with the richest effect. The openings giving access to the procession-path inside the railing were dignified by the creation of lofty gateways (*torana*) copied from wooden models, and covered with a profusion of sculpture. The best examples of such gateways are those at Sanchi (Plate 19).

The origin of the *stupa* lies in primitive burial ceremonies for they are primarily tombs[3] like the 'iron-age' cairns of the south and such tumuli as those excavated by Bloch near Nandangarh in the Champaran District.[4] Originally mounds of earth, the earliest *stupas* existing are of unbaked brick, hemispherical in shape. Although their first object was the enshrinement of sacred relics, in later times they acquired a symbolical value and many cenotaphs were built, the dedication of miniature *stupas* of stone or clay being customary at the great shrines. This idea of the symbolic value of *stupas* and the merit of *stupa*-building, on the part

[1] *A. S. I.*, 1913-14.

[2] The same development applies to the railings of rock-cut Viharas as seen in the Gautamiputra Cave (No. 3) at Nasik.

[3] The use of the *stupa* as the symbol of the *Parinirvana* indicates this.

[4] *Ann. Rep. A. S.*, East Circle, 1908-9, p. 3.

of the faithful, apart from the relics they might or might not contain, is to be found at the root of the legendary accounts of Asoka's ten-thousand *stupas*. Fa-hian says that in monasteries it was customary to raise *stupas* to Mudgalaputra, Sariputra, and Ananda, as well as in honour of the *Abhidharma*, *Vinaya*, and *Sutra*, such *stupas* in fact being regarded as altars.[1] The word *chaitya* is indeed often used where a *stupa* is intended, in the sense of a shrine or holy place. So Anathapindika builds Sariputra's *Chaitya* which was four stories high, decreasing in size, and which contained a relic vase, and was surmounted by a roof and many umbrellas.[2]

In the *Dulva*,[3] too, it is laid down that a Bhikshu's body is to be covered with grass and leaves and a *chaitya* raised over it. In a still more remote sense, the converted but disconsolate Queen Sivali raised *stupas* at the places where her ascetic husband had argued with her and finally convinced her.[4] In medieval times the *stupa* with its pyramid of sheltering umbrellas is dwarfed in importance by the sculpture that adorns it. At Ajanta and Ellora[5] and everywhere, in miniature at Bodh-Gaya, it is really nothing but a domed shrine, the tier of umbrellas being fused together into a spire.[6]

Size of *stupas*.

Stupas, not to speak of miniature votive models, varied greatly in size. The very ancient specimen at Piprahwa on the Nepalese frontier, which may possibly be earlier than Asoka, has a diameter of 116 feet at ground level, and stands only about 22 feet high. The diameter of the great Sanchi monument at the plinth is 121½ feet, the height about 77½ feet, and the stone railing is a massive structure 11 feet high. Several monuments in Northern India, some of which were acribed to Asoka, are recorded to have attained a height of from 200 to 400 feet; and to this day the summit of the *Jetavanarama Dagaba* in Ceylon towers 251 feet above the level of the ground. The larger monuments afforded infinite scope to the decorative artist.

Indian wooden architecture.

On the Bharhut bas-reliefs two types of buildings are to be found. The first is domed and round in plan. The second is barrel-roofed and sometimes three stories high. This second type is the origin of the barrel-roofed *chaitya*-caves where the details of the octagonal pillars, the balcony railings and the arched doorways and windows are faithfully portrayed. At Sanchi the same types appear and also at Amaravati and Mathura. Shrines are shown in three instances and are all of one type. At Bharhut the Shrine of the Head-dress Relic, is circular in plan, closed in by a low railing but otherwise open on all sides. It has the usual ogee doorway, the arch of which is ornamented, above its beam-heads, with little rosettes. The semicircular part of the opening is filled in with the usual framework which served as a weather screen. The roof is dome-shaped and has a pointed finial. It is divided into two by a narrow clerestory opening which comes between the dome and the curved eave. In the centre on a stone platform technically known as a 'throne'[7] is a cushion bearing the sacred relic. The throne is ornamented with pendent garlands and is marked with the impressions of the right hands of devotees, a custom still common in India.

[1] Beal, i. xxxviii.
[2] Rockhill, *Life of Buddha*, p. iii.
[3] xi. 53.
[4] *Mahajanaka Jataka*.
[5] *Visvakarma Cave*.
[6] Vincent Smith, because of the cenotaphs and of the domical shape of these structures, considers them to have no connexion with the tumuli. He put forward the suggestion that the brick *stupa* was derived from 'the curved roof of bamboos built over a primitive circular hut-shrine constructed of perishable materials' and quotes the Toda hut. At the same time he refers to similar Phoenician tombs at Anvinth (Perrot and Chipiez, *Hist. de l'Art, Phénicie*, Figs. 94, 95).
[7] *Asana*.

A

B

A. Details from East Gateway, Sanchi, and B. details from South Gateway, Sanchi. (Stupa No. 1, 1st Cent. B.C.)

Portion of frieze in Rani Gumpha Cave, Udayagiri, Orissa. (*c.* 100 B.C.)

(*Copyright by Department of Archaeology, Government of India*)

PLATE 24

A. Chaitya at Bhaja Caves, near Poona. 150-100 B.C. Satavahana period.
(Copyright : Photoflash)

B, C. Reliefs of Indra (*left*) and of Surya (*right*) from the Vihara at Bhaja. Identification problematic. 150-100 B.C. Satavahana period.
(Photos : A. L. Syed)

PLATE 25

A. Chaitya Cave, Nasik. (1st Cent. B.C. Satavahana period).

(*Copyright by Department of Archaeology, Government of India*)

B. Chaitya Cave, Karle, near Poona. (A.D. 40-100. Satavahana period).

PLATE 26

The first scene of the conversion of Kasyapa of Uruvilva on the middle of the inner side of the left-hand pillar of the East gateway at Sanchi shows another shrine of this type (Plate 23A).[1] This is the Shrine of the Black Snake which the Buddha eventually caught in his begging-bowl. Here the dome is broken by eight windows and is surrounded by a balcony railing.

The famous shrine which Asoka built around the Bodhi-tree appears at Bharhut, Sanchi, Mathura, and Amaravati. At Bharhut it is sculptured on the Prasenajit pillar[2] and seems to consist of a barrel-roofed colonnade, circular in plan entirely surrounding the tree. The upper story is provided with many windows and a balcony railing. At Sanchi this same building is accurately reproduced on the front of the left pillar, and again on the outside of the lower architrave, of the East gateway, where it is the centre of a huge host of pilgrims. At Mathura it also appears on an architrave of Kushan date[3] and again in a slightly amplified form at Amaravati.[4] Here other buildings have arisen around it and to one side is a gateway (*torana*). These gateways were apparently used everywhere, for secular purposes as well as ecclesiastical, for on the middle architrave of the East gateway at Sanchi, one appears as the entrance to a town through which a procession is passing beneath crowded windows and balconies.

The use of stone pillars.

A survey of such scenes where buildings of two and three stories abound accords with the colourful descriptions of the splendours of such towns of ancient India as Vaisali[5] or Pataliputra. Buildings of seven stories in height are even spoken of (*Satta-Bhumaka-Pasada*). Among the most famous of these piles was the *Kutagara-Vihara* at Vaisali, which Buddhaghosa describes as a storied building raised on pillars with a pinnacle, and like the chariot of the gods.[6]

Civil architecture is described in the *Jatakas* on almost as lavish a scale. The large houses had wide gateways leading into an inner courtyard with rooms opening into it on ground level. There were granaries and store-rooms and a treasury, but the flat roof, as at all times in the East, played a great part in the life of the house, at least during the day, being probably roofed-in to form an open-sided, airy pavilion.

Plaster (*chunam*) was used everywhere to adorn these buildings, and as a base for painting. *Yaksha* figures were painted as door-guardians and certain decorative motives are also mentioned: wreath-work, five-ribbon work, Dragon's teeth work, and creeper-work.[7]

As has been said, nothing of these splendours has come down to us in any of the various sites that have been excavated. It is obvious, however, that the greater part of these structures was of wood and therefore perishable, as, indeed, layers of ashes testify in many places. It is noticeable that the pillars of the upper stories of the buildings depicted on the bas-reliefs are octagonal, usually without capital or base. The pillars on the ground floor are octagonal also but have heavy bells surmounted by animal-capitals or brackets, which suggests that the lower pillars were possibly of stone. On the right jamb of the East gateway at Sanchi are represented six superimposed stories, said by Grünwedel to represent the six *Devalokas*. The pillars of these structures are grouped in pairs, the lowest of each having bell-capitals, the upper being plain and leading up to the barrel-roof.

[1] Burgess and Grünwedel, *Buddhist Art in India*, p. 62.
[2] Cunningham, *Bharhut*, vi, xii, and xxx.
[3] Plate XIIA and XIIIB.
[4] List of Negatives Ind. Off., § 2163, Serial 798.
[5] Fausboll, *Dhammapada*, p. 390 ; Lefman, *Lalitavistara*, p. 21; Rockhill, *Life of the Buddha*, p. 63 ; For the site : Vincent Smith, *J. A. R. S.*, 1902, p. 267 n. ; Marshall, *Ann. Rep. A. S.*, I, 1903-4, p. 74.
[6] See Law, *Ksatriya Tribes*, p. 43.
[7] *Vinaya Texts*, 3-170.

There is a considerable difference between the proportions of the upper and lower pillars, which again suggests a difference in material.[1]

Buddhist monasteries.

Although monastic institutions in India were not confined to the Buddhists, the Buddhist *Sangha* attained a height of power and a detail of organization to which the Jain and Brahmanical communities never aspired; and in consequence, the buildings dedicated to the use of the Order were frequently designed on a scale of the utmost magnificence. The central and all important building of the early monasteries seems to have been the *Sabha* or hall of meeting of the community. Gateways, store-houses, kitchens, and well-houses are mentioned, but the actual cells of the monks were apparently a group of separate buildings. These, it seems, were built by the brethren themselves, among whom were many skilled architects.[2] In the *Jatakas* it is said, however, that only the senior brethren had their own chambers, while the juniors slept in the Hall. Later the Buddha ordained that novices should be lodged with their supervisors for three days and then sent to their own place.[3] The forest-dweller's leafy hut is often portrayed in the early sculpture and many of the lesser dwellings of the monastery were probably of this type. The meeting-hall or service-hall must have been a common type of building in ancient India, for the Buddhist *Sangha* was by no means an innovation and can be directly compared to the hundred and one political and social corporations of the time. Every village, profession, and craft was organized into guilds which had their appointed places of meeting.[4] The Mote-hall of the Licchavis (*Santhagara*) must have been a building of the same kind as the Assembly-hall of the Buddhists.

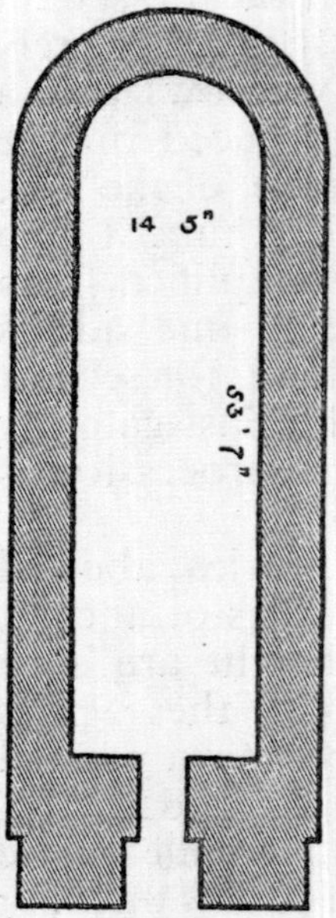

Monasteries of later times.

Before the period of the rock-cut halls and cells like those at Bhaja and Bedsa, in Gandhara and in medieval India generally, the monasteries took up a quadrangular form, the cells being built so that they faced inwards on the four sides of a courtyard.

When such a quadrangle became multiple, through the addition of chapels, *stupas*, refectories, halls, churches, store-houses, and other buildings, the greater monasteries covered an enormous area, and offered to the architect, sculptor, and painter endless opportunities for the display of art in every form.

[1] See Rhys-Davids, *Buddhist India*, p. 66. Stone pillars and stone staircases are mentioned in the *Jatakas* and a stone palace in Fairyland (6.269). Vincent Smith develops Fergusson's idea of likening *stupas* to the early circular shrines, but he obviously is considering the medieval *stupas* of Ajanta and Ellora, which he goes on to discuss. There the sanctity of the relic has long been confused with the *stupa* itself as a symbol which again has been subjugated in ceremonial importance by the Buddha figures sculptured upon it. *Hist. of Ind. Arch.*, VI, i, p. 66.

Simpson developed the idea of the bamboo origin of all Indian architectural forms, citing the Toda hut. The early shrines and halls are, of course, wooden in construction and not lithic, but it is a hewn wood construction of joint and tenon. The origin of the form of the 'Indo-Aryan' steeple (*sikhara*) cannot be traced to this ancient art, still less to bamboos. It lies in the nature of the material accessible to the hand of the medieval builders, finely burnt brick and well-trimmed stone. It is a logical development of the Indian corbelling methods. *J.R.I.B.A.*, VI, vii, p. 225.

[2] Cowell, *Jat.*, § 6.

[3] Cowell, *Jat.*, § 16.

[4] Omitting the family council (*Kula*) and the probably later organizations of castes, among them were the *Gana*, *Puga*, *Vrata*, and *Sreni* of Sanksrit literature. The *Sangha* being the generic term, the *Gana* is specifically tribal, the *Puga* is based on common interests, financial or social, the *Vrata* is an organization of labour outside the crafts, while the *Sreni* is essentially a craft or professional guild. The *Setthi* of Buddhist literature was a prominent member of these corporations whose officers (*Seniyo*) were the *Pamukha* (president) and the *Jetthakas* (aldermen). Political confederations such as that of the Licchavis are of the same origin, which is in fact the source of the whole system of political and social life in Northern India. Bhandarkar, *Carmichael Lectures*, 1918, p. 181; Mookerji, *Local Government*, p. 36 et. seq

A. Mithuna couples, wrongly identified as donors, facade of Karle Chaitya. A.D. 40-100. Satavahana period. Note that the lower, middle and upper panels belong to the Deccan Gupta school of *c.* 600 A.D.

B. Mithuna couple and elephants, facade of Karle Chaitya. A.D. 40-100. Satavahana period. Note that the upper panel is in Deccan Gupta school of *c.* 600 A.D.

PLATE 27

A.

B.

Mithuna couples from facade of Karle Chaitya. A.D. 40-100. Satavahana period.
(*Copyright by Department of Archaeology, Government of India*)
PLATE 28

Although no very early monastery has survived in a condition at all complete, the ground-plans of many such establishments have been clearly traced, and in Gandhara considerable remains of superstructures crowded with statuary have been disclosed. Recorded descriptions and extant remains amply attest the splendour of the more important monasteries, each of which was a centre of secular as well as of religious education, and also a school of art in which men were trained in all the crafts needed for the adornment of the holy places.

Cave-temples. Something of this great school of art is preserved for us in the great rock-cut halls and dwelling-caves of Western India. Here, at Bhaja (Plate 25A), Kondane, Pitalkhora, Bedsa, Ajanta, Nasik (Plate 26A), Karli (Plate 26B), and Kanheri, have been hewn out of the very heart of the rock full-scale reproductions of the ancient Assembly-halls in all the detail of their wooden construction. In general plan they correspond with the barrel-roofed buildings of the early sculpture. They are apsidal with side aisles on either hand and are lit by the great horse-shoe window at one end. A survey of this series of caves lays bare a stylistic advance from purely wooden imitation to definitely lithic forms. At Bhaja the plain octagonal pillars rake inwards considerably; the screen that closed the lower part of the great window was actually of timber morticed into the rock as are the carefully inset roof beams. There is no decoration except bands of railing-pattern and tiers of miniature '*chaitya*-windows', derived from the piled-up stories of the wooden originals. These details apply to the caves at Kondane, Pitalkhora and to the earliest at Ajanta (Cave X). Later the wooden screen is reproduced in stone and bell-capitals and bases, and tiered-up abaci with heavy animal upper-capitals appear, while at Nasik, Karli (Plates 27, 28 & 29) and Kanheri (Plate 30A and B), sculpture is freely used. This sculpture is all obviously post-Sanchi. At Karli and Kanheri highly decorated railings of the Amaravati kind are found and also guardian figures which closely correspond to the middle phase of Kushan sculpture, found at Mathura. The epigraphical evidence coincides with the artistic evidence, dating the last of these early caves (Karli and Kanheri) in the second century A.D. (A 2). The facade of Bhaja is so exactly like the bas-relief representations of the wooden original at Bharhut and Bodh-Gaya that the earliest of the series may be accepted as second century B.C. (A 3).

The Lomas Rishi Cave (Plate 8B) in the Barabar hills belongs to a group of small rock-cut cells some of which were dedicated in the reigns of Asoka and Dasaratha, his grandson. Like the other caves its interior walls have received the fine polish which is so typical of Mauryan work. The original work seems to have been discontinued owing to a flaw in the rock. The facade must [may] have been a later addition, for it is akin to the work at Bharhut. It, however, offers a good example of the close imitation of wooden construction.[1]

Structural churches. At Ter, the ancient Tagara, in the Sholapur District, Bombay Presidency,[2] there is an example of a structural *chaitya*-hall which has escaped destruction by being converted into a Brahmanical temple.[3] It is a long chamber, constructed of brick, 26 feet in length and 12 feet in width on the inside, with walls $3\frac{1}{2}$ feet thick, an apsidal end, and a waggon-vaulted ridge roof. The bricks, laid in mud cement, with exceedingly fine joints, are of huge size, measuring $17 \times 9 \times 3$ inches.

[1] *Ann. Rep. A. S.*, i, 1902-3, p. 197.
[2] [Now in Maharashtra State].
[3] G. O. Madras Pub. 382, 30, April 1889.

They are finely burnt. The building is medieval and probably belongs to the eighth century.[1]

Part II. SCULPTURE

Early sculpture.

The art of the times dealt with in this chapter is characterized by frank naturalism. It is thoroughly human, a mirror of the social and religious life of ancient India, apparently a much pleasanter and merrier life than that of the India of later ages, when the Brahmans had reasserted their superiority and imposed their ideas upon art and upon every branch of Hindu civilization. The early sculptures, while full of the creatures of gay fancy, are free from the gloom and horror of the conceptions of the medieval artists. The Buddhism with which nearly all of them are concerned was, as already observed, the popular creed of men and women living a natural life in the world, seeking happiness, and able to enjoy themselves. The recent critics of the 'nationalist' school, in their anxiety to secure adequate recognition for the merits of the medieval Brahmanical art, sometimes appear to believe that it alone truly expresses Indian thought. It is well to remember that for several centuries Indian thought was content to find its artistic utterance in a fashion much less sophisticated.

There has, also, been a tendency to apply certain literary standards, which are in essence medieval, to the work of the Early Period, and in fact, to all Indian art, wholesale. The various members, mouldings, and motives dealt with in the *Silpa Sastras* cannot be found outside the buildings of the medieval period. With regard to the passages dealing with the sculpture the same thing applies. The Sastras are in fact technical memoranda based on a literary tradition, which may be taken to have crystallized out from the great literary activity of the Gupta period. Their import is very great with regard to the iconography of medieval and modern India. They can only be applied with great circumspection to the earlier art, the inspiration of which is oral and living.[2]

Its relation to the Asokan.

The study of the existing monuments of Asoka, scanty as they are, leaves one with a clear impression of a definite and distinct school of sculpture,[3] with great stylistic and architectonic qualities and certain characteristics which distinguish it from the sculpture of the Early Period and from all other periods of Indian art. Firstly, finely stylized as these works are they are essentially naturalistic. Secondly, columns, capitals, and caves all have a highly finished, polished surface which is unique and unmistakable. Certain sculptures, however, exist which possess this distinguishing finish and yet as sculptures are to be classed with the work of Bharhut and Sanchi. These may be treated as a link between the two schools. Anyhow the Mauryan period, which is historically exact, provides a lower limit for the dating of the work of the Early Period.

The Parkham Yaksha.

Among these sculptures, which are mostly of colossal size, is a mutilated standing statue of a male, perhaps representing the *Yaksha* demi-god *Kuvera*, god of wealth, found at Parkham (Plate 11C) in the Mathura District, and now

[1] The apsidal plan also survived in medieval stone construction, as is shown at Sanchi and Pattadkal. [Douglas Barrett in his *Ter*, 1960, has suggested 2nd to 5th century A.D. for the Ter Chaitya—K. K.]

[2] Havell compares the development of *Puranic* (medieval) art to the use made by the great masters of modern music of popular folk-music. He claims that medieval art is the 'expression of the Indian consciousness at the height of its greatest intellectual, literary, and artistic activity'. One feels that here there has been some confusion of purely artistic appreciation with the literary.

[3] In many senses un-Indian, although the exact extent of its un-Indian qualities and their origin is very hard to state.

in the Mathura Museum.[1] The material is polished grey sandstone similar to that used for the Asoka pillars (A 4). The height, including pedestal, is 8 feet 8 inches, and the breadth across the shoulders is 2 feet 8 inches. The excessively massive body, which possesses considerable grandeur, is clothed in a waist-cloth (*dhoti*) held around the loins by means of a flat girdle tied in a knot in front. A second flat girdle is bound round the chest. The ornaments are a necklace and a torque from which four tassels hang down on the back. Some praise may be given to the treatment of the drapery.

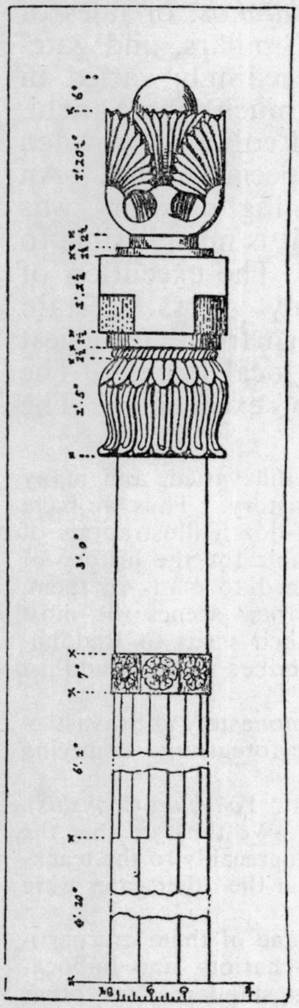

Fan-palm capital, Besnagar.

This is probably the earliest example of 'early' sculpture as distinct from the Mauryan. In treatment and detail it is clearly a forerunner of the sculpture of Bharhut and has nothing in common with the art of the Mauryan capitals.

Besnagar sculptures.

Several other colossal sculptures, which do not possess the distinctive Mauryan polish, emphasize this development. An uninscribed statue of a female (Plate 11 B), 6 feet 7 inches in height, found near Besnagar adjoining Bhilsa in the Gwalior State, Central India, a locality associated by tradition with Asoka, is to be classed among these on account of the style and costume. The figure wears the heavy head-dress as found at Bharhut and Sanchi and also the linked belt of beaded strands and the double breast chain. The finely pleated waist-cloth is held at the hips by a belt with a looped clasp and its folds are treated in fashion that is reminiscent of the Sanchi bracket-figures rather than the Bharhut *devatas*. The modelling is naturalistic, but the sculpture has suffered severely from violence and exposure (A 5).

There is a second colossal female at Besnagar, 7 feet high, locally known as the *Telin* or Oil-woman, which has been described by Cunningham. He also mentions the existence in his time of a polished sandstone elephant and rider.

The *stupa* of Bharhut.

In 1873 Cunningham discovered at Bharhut, about midway between Allahabad and Jabalpur, the remains of a Buddhist *stupa*, surrounded by a stone railing adorned with sculptures of surprising richness and interest (Plates 12B, 13, 14, 15). The *stupa* had then been almost wholly carried off by greedy villagers in search of bricks, who treated the sculptures with equal ruthlessness, and were prevented from destroying them only by the great weight of the stones. During the following years to 1876, Cunningham and his assistant uncovered the ruins and saved a large number of the sculptured stones by sending them to Calcutta, where they now form one of the chief treasures of the Indian Museum. Everything left on the site was taken away by the country people and converted to base uses.[2] (A 6).

The railing.

The railing, constructed after the usual pattern, in a highly developed form,

[1] For the inscription see *J. B. O. Res. Soc.*, vol. v, Part IV, Dec. 1919, where this sculpture and the Patna sculptures are said to be contemporary portraits of kings of Magadha in the fifth century B.C.

[2] Anderson, *Catalogue*. Part I, pp. xiii-xx, 1-120.

was extremely massive, the pillars being 7 feet 1 inch in height, and each of the coping stones about the same in length. The sculptures of the coping (Plate 15B) were devoted mainly to the representation of incidents in the *Jatakas*, or tales of the previous births of the Buddha. The carvings on the rails, pillars, and gateways (Plate 12B), all treating of Buddhist legends, were exceedingly varied in subject and treatment. The structure must have been very much like Sanchi. The composite pillar of the gateway, made up of four clustered columns crowned by a modified Persepolitan capital (Pl. 12B) is worthy of special notice. An inscription records that the Eastern gateway with the adjoining masonry was erected during the rule of the Sunga dynasty (185-75 B.C.), but it is not possible to determine the date of the monument with greater precision.[1] The execution of work so costly and elaborate must have extended over many years. Certain masons' marks in the *Kharoshthi* character of the north-western frontier suggest that perhaps foreign artists were called in to teach and assist local talent.[2] The railing exhibits a great mass of sculptures of a high order of excellence. The subjects and style are described by Cunningham as follows:

Subjects and style of the sculptures.

'The subjects represented in the Bharhut sculptures are both numerous and varied, and many of them are of the highest interest and importance for the study of Indian history. Thus we have more than a score of illustrations of the legendary Jatakas, and some half-dozen illustrations of historical scenes connected with the life of Buddha, which are quite invaluable for the history of Buddhism. Their value is chiefly due to the inscribed labels that are attached to many of them, and which make their identification absolutely certain. Amongst the historical scenes the most interesting are the processions of the Rajas Ajatasatru and Prasenajita on their visits to Buddha; the former on his elephant, the latter in his chariot, exactly as they are described in the Buddhist chronicles.

'Another invaluable sculpture is the representation of the famous Jetavana monastery at Sravasti—with its mango tree and temples, and the rich banker Anathapindika in the foreground emptying a cartful of gold pieces to pave the surface of the garden.

'Of large figures there are upwards of thirty alto-relievo statues of *Yakshas* and *Yakshinis* (*Yakshis*), *Devatas*, and *Naga Rajas*, one half of which are inscribed with their names. We thus see that the guardianship of the north gate was entrusted to *Kuvera*, King of the *Yakshas*, agreeably to the teaching of the Buddhist and Brahmanical cosmogonies. And similarly we find that the other gates were confided to *Devas* and the *Nagas*.

'The representations of animals and trees are also very numerous, and some of them are particularly spirited and characteristic. Of other objects there are boats, horse-chariots, and bullock-carts, besides several kinds of musical instruments, and a great variety of flags, standards, and other symbols of royalty.

'About one half of the full medallions of the rail-bars and the whole of the half-medallions of the pillars are filled with flowered ornaments of singular beauty and delicacy of execution.'[3]

The medallions on the rail-bars and the half-medallions on the pillars are filled with a wonderful variety of bas-relief subjects (Pls. 12B, 14). The comic monkey scenes collected in Cunningham's Plate XXXIII display a lively sense of humour, freedom of fancy, and clever drawing. They must, of course, like all the early bas-reliefs, be judged as pictures drawn on stone, rather than as sculpture. The rollicking humour and liberty of fancy unchecked by rigid canons, while alien to the transcendental philosophy and ascetic ideals of the Brahmans, are thoroughly in accordance with the spirit of Buddhism, which, as a practical religion, does not stress the spiritual to the extinction of human and

[1] *Ind. Art.*, vol. xxi, p. 227, also vol. x, p. 118 n., vol. xi, p. 25 n., vol. xiv, p. 137 n.

[2] Whatever its origin, the use of Kharoshti was not necessarily confined to the north-west. Asoka's inscriptions were inscribed in both scripts and the Maski inscription is signed in Kharoshti. It is posible that the scribes of the day were skilled in both scripts. Lack of evidence must at any rate qualify any statement.

[3] Cunningham, *The Stupa of Bharhut* (1879), p. [illegible]8.

A. Pillars with elephant and rider capitals, Karle Chaitya. A.D. 40-100. Satavahana period.

B. Mithuna couple, facade of Karle Chaitya. A.D. 40-100. Satavahana period (Photo : A. L. Syed)

PLATE 29

A. Mithuna couples from facade of Kanheri Chaitya. 2nd half of 2nd Cent A.D. Satavahana period.

(*Copyright by Department of Archaeology, Government of India*)

C. Miniature bronze elephant with riders, from Brahmapuri, Kolhapur. 2nd half of 2nd Cent. A.D. Satavahana period.

B. Male figure from Kanheri Chaitya. 2nd half of 2nd Cent. A.D. Satavahana period.

animal happiness. Everything seems to indicate that India was a much happier land in the days when Buddhism flourished than it has ever been since. The first medallion selected for illustration is a very funny picture of a tooth being extracted from a man's jaw by an elephant pulling a gigantic forceps, and the second is nearly equally humorous. The stories alluded to are presumably of the *Jataka* class (Plate 14A) (A 7). The spontaneity of the work vouches for the popularity of the tradition, stories that must have been on every child's lips.

Coping.

Pl. 15B gives a characteristic and well-preserved specimen of the bas-reliefs on the coping. The large fruit is that of the jack (*Artocarpus integrifolia*), and the deer are the spotted hog-deer kind (*Axis porcinus*). The artists who could design and execute such pictures in hard sandstone had no small skill. Mr. Havell observes that the technique is that of the wood-carver. The *Chulakoka* (Cunningham, Plate XXIII, 3) sculpture is especially interesting as the earliest extant example of the woman and tree motive (Plate 13B).[1] One of the best statues is that of the *Yakshi Sudarsana* (Pl. 13A) which exhibits a good knowledge of the human form and marked skill in the modelling of the hips in a difficult position.[2]

The large alto-relievo images of minor deities on the pillars (Plate 13A, B and C) vary much in execution.

Sculptured railing at Besnagar.

Besnagar offers an excellent example of a sculptured railing of the same type and style as Bharhut.[3] The coping-stone is adorned with a frieze representing a religious procession, with elephants, horses, &c., divided into compartments by the graceful sinuosities of a lotus stem. The pillars exhibited various scenes in panels and on the cross rails elegant lotuses are carved.

Sculptured railing at Bodh-Gaya.

A better-known example is the often described railing at Bodh-Gaya, which used to be called 'the Asoka railing', but is stylistically later than Bharhut, though earlier than Sanchi. Thirty pieces have been found, evidently belonging to two distinct structures, some pieces being of granite and others of sandstone. All are similar in style, irrespective of material.

Most of the subjects are treated in low relief. Those on the coping are purely fanciful; those on the panels and medallions include weird centaurs, winged beasts, domestic animals, sacred trees, and sundry scenes of human life, all no doubt significant and readily intelligible to ancient Buddhists versed in the legends of their scriptures and traditions, but now difficult of interpretation. Most of the more interesting sculptures have been published more than once; a few are here reproduced from photographs. They are simply pictures in stone, and should be criticized as drawings slightly in relief rather than from the point of view of a sculptor. They exhibit a lively fancy, considerable skill in drawing, and much neatness of execution; both conception and execution are purely Indian.

Specimens of Bodh-Gaya sculptures.

In Plate 9 [of previous edition] is shown a part of an animal frieze on the coping, very similar to what we shall meet later at Amaravati. Fig. A gives an interesting picture of an early Buddhist chapel enshrining the symbol of the preaching of the Law.[4] Images of Buddha still do not occur. The facade, with its curved roof, exactly illustrates the origin of the architecture of the western cave-temples, and their wooden prototypes. A frieze on the coping pictures queer fish-tailed

[1] Repeated several times at Bharhut.

[2] Vincent Smith comments on the narrow waist and exaggerated hips which 'disfigure' so many Indian sculptures.

[3] Cunningham, *A. S. Rep.*, vol. x, p. 38, Pl. XIII.

[4] [The plate substituted in the Third Edition does not show this animal frieze or chapel—K. K.].

monsters, which recall many forms in Hellenistic art familiar in variant shapes to Asiatic art from very remote times (Pl. 16D).[1]

The series of illustrations may be closed by two purely naturalistic pictures —an excellent buffalo (Pl. 17B), and a husband and wife seated together (Pl. 16E). The treatment of the lotus is excellent. It is the most characteristic and universal of all Indian art motives. Infinite variety in the treatment of the conventionalized flower is exhibited in the minute details both at Bodh-Gaya and elsewhere.[2]

Plate 16A is equally instructive concerning the practice of the early Buddhist cult. This sacred tree, surrounded by a plain railing, square in plan, is an example of the many shrines of Chaityas of ancient India, another example being the Deer-and-Lions-Lying-down-together Chaitya of the Bharhut coping-stone: the latter is of special interest for it does not seem to be Buddhist in origin and may represent the survival of a pre-Buddhist cult.[3]

The remaining figures illustrate various fantastical hybrid creatures (Plate 16C), winged lions and oxen, a centaur (Plate 17A), a horse-headed female or *kinnara* (Plate 16B), and a frieze of the fish-tailed monsters common at Mathura and in Gandhara. These are human-bodied and appear to be half-*naga*, half-*makara*. These strange beasts have a debatable origin. The Naga or snake-godling is usually represented with his snake-hood, but in the *Jatakas* appears to be able to cast off this stigma and is then only to be known by his red-eyes. These lesser divinities are by birth Indian and native in the earliest folklore and sculpture. The *makara*, too, whose scrolled tail is used so magnificently to form the volutes of the architraves of *toranas* at Bharhut, Sanchi, and Mathura, is also well founded traditionally. These with the *kinnaris* or half-bird musicians and the horse-headed *kinnaras* may be classed together as *gandharvas* or lesser heavenly beings.[4] They are as types paralleled with several other motives of early Indian art in the sculpture of West Asia, Assyria, and Persia. The bell and frieze design of the Bharhut cope-stone and its upper pyramid and lotus band are among these, and also, the bell capital surmounted by animal groups. Whatever the distant sources of these motives may be, their treatment at Bharhut, Bodh-Gaya, and Sanchi, is wholly Indian. As has been said many of them spring directly from the soil.

The remains at Sanchi.

The Bharhut sculptures, having escaped the destructive zeal of Muhammadan iconoclasts by reason of their situation in an out-of-the-way region, lay safely hidden under a thick veil of jungle until a century ago, when the establishment of general peace and the spread of cultivation stimulated the local rustics to construct substantial houses from the spoils of the old monuments for which they cared nothing. The extensive group of early Buddhist buildings at and near Sanchi in the Bhopal State similarly evaded demolition because it lay out of the path of the armies of Islam. Although the monuments of Sanchi have not suffered as much as those of Bharhut from the ravages of the village builder, they have not wholly escaped injury. During the first half of the nineteenth century much damage was done by the ill-advised curiosity of amateur archaeologists. Now, however, the authorities concerned are fully alive to their responsibility, and

[1] Vincent Smith accepts the West Asiatic origin of these motives, but they have close parallels in Indian legend : the *Makara* is undoubtedly indigenous.

[2] For numerous drawings of the sculptures on the Bodh-Gaya railing see Cunningham, *A. S. Rep.*, vol. i, Pls. VIII-XI; vol. iii, Pls. XXVI-XXX; and Mahabodhi; also Rajendralala Mitra, *Buddha Gaya*.

[3] Codrington, *Ancient India*, p. 31.

[4] Burgess and Grünwedel, *Buddhist Art in India*, p. 47.

A. Part of frieze on *torana* beam, Mathura. (1st Cent. B.C. Pre-Kushan period).
(*By Courtesy of Dr. Führer*)

B. Tablet with relief sculpture of a jain *stupa*.
(Mathura. 1st Cent. A.D. Early Kushan period).

(*Copyright by Archaelogical Museum, Mathura*)

PLATE 31

A

D

C

B

A. Naga statue, with inscription of Huvishka's reign, from Chhargaon. Mathura Museum. (A.D. 117. Kushan period).

B, D. Fragments in Bharhut style. Mathura Museum. (Late 1st Cent. B.C. Satrap period).
(*Copyright by Archaeological Museum, Mathura*)

C. Yakshi on dwarf. Mathura Museum. (1st-2nd Cent. A.D. Kushan period).

PLATE 32

A. Pali Khera block, front group. Mathura Museum. (Bacchanalian scene. 1st-2nd Cent. A.D. Kushan period).

B. Kuvera. Mathura Museum. (Medieval period).

C. Bodhisattva, from Mathura, Indian Museum. (2nd Cent. A.D. Kushan period).

D. Standing Bodhisattva, from Mahuli, near Mathura. 2nd. Cent. A.D. Kushan period.

A. Two Yakshis. Indian Museum. (2nd Cent. A.D. Kushan period).

C. A Bodhisattva, from Katra. Mathura Museum. (2nd Cent. A.D. Kushan period).

(Copyright by Department of Archaeology, Government of India)

B. Female, half back view. Mathura Museum. (1st-2nd Cent. A.D. Kushan period).

D. Colossal head of the Buddha. 3rd Cent. A.D. Kushan-Gupta transition period.

PLATE 34

everything possible is being done to conserve the local memorials of India's ancient greatness. Sanchi to-day is a triumph of archaeological restoration.

Chronology.

The importance of Sanchi in the history of Indian art rests chiefly upon the four wonderful gateways forming the entrances to the procession path between the *stupa* (Plates 18 and 19) and the surrounding railing. A key to the chronology of the site is provided by the Asoka column which stands to the right of the South gateway. The Mauryan level is marked by a floor of pounded earth and clay. Three other levels or floors appear over it, the topmost being lime-plastered. Above all is the pavement of large slabs contemporary with the *stupa* railing. This is a perfectly plain copy of a wooden post and rail fence and may be dated in the latter half of the second century B.C., since there is 4 feet between the upper pavement and the Mauryan level, which could hardly have accumulated in less than a century.

The four gateways, 50 B.C.-A.D. I.

The four gateways, which are additions to the original railing, fall artistically into pairs, the East and West gates, showing a slight development in modelling and the use of light and shade. A little more than fifty years may have elapsed between their execution, the end of the first century B.C. being accepted as a general date for all four. The Southern gateway was prostrate when visited by Captain Fell in 1819. The Western gate collapsed between 1860 and 1880, but the Northern and Eastern gates have never fallen. All have undergone thorough repairs during recent years under the able direction of Sir John Marshall, the Director-General of Archaeology in India. Sanchi has taken on a new lease of life and beauty in his hands, the more important remains of this huge site being carefully and exactly restored and preserved.

Construction of the gateways.

The Sanchi gateways, or *toranas*, stand 34 feet high, and are all substantially alike, while differing much in detail:

'Two massive square pillars, one on either side, 14 feet high, forming as it were the gate-posts, support an ornamental superstructure of three slightly arched stone beams or architraves placed horizontally, one above the other, with spaces between them. The topmost beam of each gate was surmounted by the sacred wheel flanked by attendants and the *trisula* emblem.

'The faces, back and front, of the beams and pillars are crowded with panels of sculpture in bas-relief representing scenes in the life of Buddha, domestic and silvan scenes, processions, sieges, adoration of trees and topes, and groups of ordinary and extraordinary animals, among which are winged bulls and lions of a Persepolitan type and horned animals with human faces.'[1]

Extent of sculptures.

Plate 19, representing the Eastern gateway, will enable the reader to appreciate the wealth of ornament lavished on the four monuments. The same gateway may be further studied by the aid of full-sized casts supplied to the Victoria and Albert Museum, South Kensington, and other institutions, some of which, however, do not exhibit the casts. Numerous illustrations, more or less accurate and satisfactory, will be found in the works of Fergusson, Maisey, Cunningham, and other writers on Indian archaeology, the best of all being the official handbook issued by the Archaeological Survey.[2] In January and February 1901, Mr. H. Cousens succeeded in photographing the whole mass of sculptures on 225 negatives to a uniform scale of one-eighth, but so far little use has been made of the huge supply of material thus accumulated. The preparation of a full descriptive and critical monograph would be an arduous undertaking, and the work would probably fill several large quartos (A 8).

[1] Cousens, *Progr. Rep. A. S.*, *Western India*, for year ending 30 June 1900, para. 9.

[2] Guide to Sanchi, also see *A. S. Report*, 1913-14, and Foucher, *Beginnings of Buddhist Art*.

Capitals of the southern gate-posts.

All critics are agreed that the gateways were built in pairs and that the southern gateway is one of the earliest of the four. The capitals of its gate-posts are formed by four lions seated back to back, 'indifferently carved', and of the same type as those on Asoka's inscribed pillar already noticed (*ante*). The marked decline in skill demonstrated by the contrast between the lions on the gate-post and those on the inscribed pillar is surprising considering the shortness of the interval of time, about a century (A 9), between the two compositions, or rather the essential difference between the Mauryan and the ancient Indian school. The difference is most easily verified by comparing the treatment of the lions' paws on the gate-post capital (Maisey, Plate XIX) and of the same members on the capital of the inscribed pillar, or the similar Sarnath pillar. The paws of the early Asokan sculptures are correctly modelled with four large front claws and one small hind claw, the muscles also being realistically reproduced. In the later work five large claws, all in front, are given to the paws, and the muscles are indicated by some straight channels running up and down in a purely abstract manner.[1]

Other capitals.

The capitals of the gate-posts of the northern gateway exhibit four elephants standing back to back, and carrying riders. Those of the eastern gateway (Plate 19) are similar. On the capitals of the latest gateway, the western, four hideous dwarfs, clumsily sculptured, take the place of the elephants or lions (Plate 18B).[2] [Similar dwarfs are seen on the gateway of Stupa No. 3].

Subjects all Buddhist.

All the Sanchi sculptures, like the Ajanta paintings, deal with Buddhist subjects. If a composition seems in our eyes to be purely secular, that is only because we do not understand its meaning. Genre pictures, whether in paint or bas-relief, do not exist in the ancient art of India. The main object of the artist was to illustrate his Bible, and if, perchance, the illustration could be made into a pretty picture, so much the better; but anyhow, the sacred story must be told.

Worship by the whole creation.

In addition to his desire to tell edifying stories in a manner readily intelligible to the eyes of the faithful, the old artist clearly was dominated by the feeling that he was bound to impress on all beholders the lesson that the dead Teacher, the last and greatest of the long line of Buddhas, had won and continually received the willing homage of the whole creation — of men, women, and children, of the host of heaven, the water-sprites, and the demons — nay, even of the monsters of romance and the dumb animals. And so, in all the ancient Buddhist art, whether at Sanchi or elsewhere, weird winged figures hovering in the air, snake-headed or fish-tailed monsters emerging from their caverns or haunting the deep, offer their silent homage to the Lord of all, and the monkeys bow down in adoration before the Master who had turned the wheel of the Law and set it rolling through the world. The early artists did not dare to portray his bodily form, which had forever vanished, being content to attest his spiritual presence by silent symbols — the footprints, the empty chair, and so forth.[3] But, whether the Master was imaged or symbolized, the notion of his adoration by all creation was continually present in the minds of the artists and influenced their selection of decorative

[1] Vincent Smith quotes Coomaraswamy's *Aims of Indian Art*, p. 14, and states his preference for the naturalistic Asokan lions.

[2] These dwarfs have already appeared as Atlantes at Bharhut.

[3] 'The outward form, Brethren, of him who has won the truth (*Tathagata*) stands before you, but that which binds it to rebirth is cut in twain. So long as his body shall last, so long do gods and men behold him. On the dissolution of the body, beyond the end of his life, neither gods nor men shall see him' (*Brahmajala Sutta*, transl. Rhys-Davids, *Dialogues of the Buddha*, p. 54). The absence of images of Buddha from early Indian art does not imply that images of the Hindu gods were then unknown. It has been claimed that they were in use as early as the fourth century B.C. [*Ind. Ant*. xxxviii (1909), pp. 145-9]. Rao, *Hindu Iconography*, Introd., vol. i, Pt. I,

A. Nude female on Jain railing pillar, Mathura.

B. Medallion, Mathura.

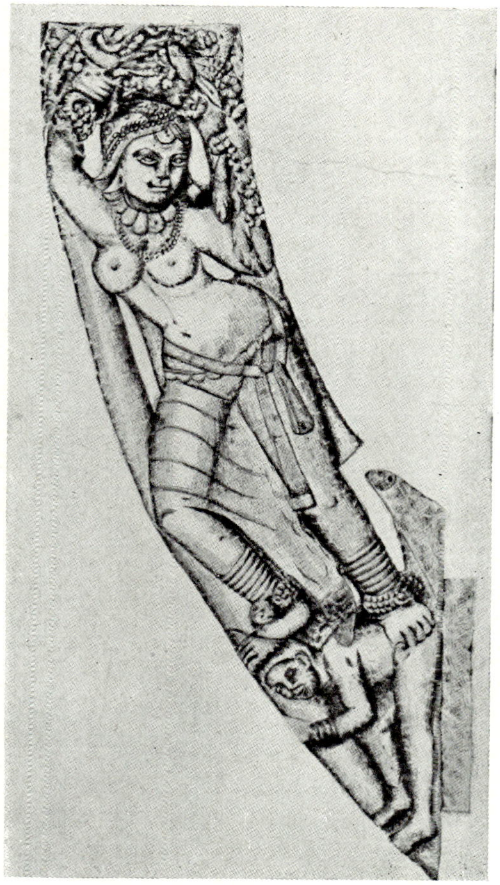

C. Bracket figure, Mathura.

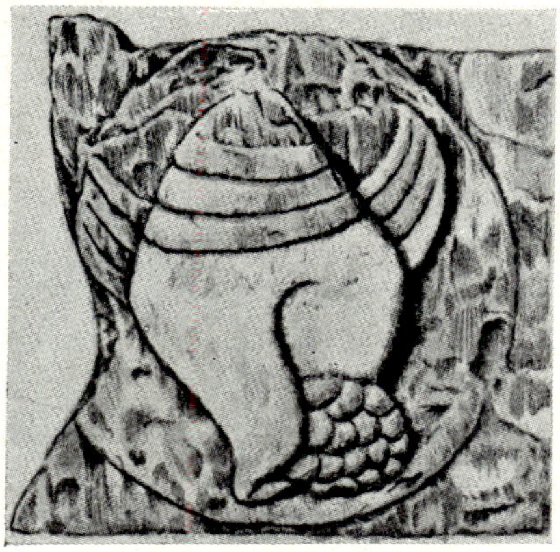

D. Medallion, Mathura.

E. Medallion, Mathura.

F. Medallion, Mathura.

These details illustrate the period from late 1st Cent. B.C. to 1st Cent. A.D.
(*From Jain Stupa of Mathura*).

PLATE 35

A. Female with right arm bent. Mathura Museum.

B. Female with right leg bent. Mathura Museum.

C. Soldier. Mathura Museum.

D. Female and child. Mathura Museum.

E. Lion and rider. Indian Museum.

(1st-2nd Century A.D., Kushan period)

PLATE 36

motives. Although concerned in the main with thoughts of religion and worship they were not unmindful of beauty, which they often succeeded in attaining in no small degree.

In the early works, like those of Sanchi and Bharhut, the absence of images of Buddha has the advantage of saving the stone pictures from the formal symmetrical arrangements grouped round the central figure which often weary by their monotonous iteration in Gandhara and at Amaravati.

In a general way, the style of the Sanchi reliefs resembles that of those at Bharhut, compensation may be found in the elegant bracket figures, practically statues in the round, which are a specially pleasing feature of Sanchi art. A good example of such a figure is shown in Plate 19. It is a form of the Woman and Tree motive. The beautiful decorative details of the pillar are worthy of careful study (Plate 23A and B). No nation has surpassed the Indians in the variety and delicacy of the floral designs enriching their sculptures and pictures. Bracket figure, &c.

Plates 20, 21, 22, 23 may be taken as being typical of the Sanchi reliefs. Plate 23A is from the inside of the left pillar of the East Gate.[1] At the bottom stands the *Yaksha* guardian of the door in princely dress. His fellow stands opposite him on the other pillar. They are comparable with the Bharhut *Yakshas*, but the treatment of figure and ornament is considerably more rhythmic. The tree in the background is a *Bignonia* and the *devata* holds one of its blossoms in his right hand. The upper panel of Plate 23A represents the Buddha's victory over the black snake and the conversion of Kasyapa at Uruvilva. The snake and the flames of the conflict and the astonished Brahmans, some of whom are attempting to fetch water, are all shown, but the figure of the triumphant Buddha is left to the imagination. Below this scene the story of the conversion of Kasyapa is continued and the incident of Buddha and the Brahman sacrifice is shown. Wood is being split and the preparations made, but the fire springs up and dies at the Buddha's command. On the front of the same pillar the final incident of the Buddha walking on the waters is told and the sequent visit to Rajagriha, King Bimbisara being depicted as arriving at the gate of the city in his two-horsed chariot. In one panel of Plate 23A is the *Bodhi-tree Shrine* already discussed. Reliefs on the East gateway.

Surveying the work of the Early Period (second century B.C.–early first century A.D.) one recognizes certain distinctive common elements : the absence of the Buddha figure; its replacement by certain simple symbols; and the popular quality of the work, the living oral tradition of which is indicated by the predominance of Jaṭaka scenes even over the scriptural;[2] the native technique which treats each story as a pictorial entity contained in a single panel or medallion, the figures of the protagonist being repeated twice and three times according to the demand of the drama to be unfolded. At Sanchi, while the method of exposition and the bulk of the decorative motives are the same as at Bharhut, the canonical is very definitely to the fore, and the technique has advanced considerably. At Mathura and many other sites in India sculptures have been found which belong to the Early Period. With regard to these it is advisable to take Bharhut and Sanchi as types of sub-periods and so arrive at the classification Early Period I and Early Period II. Other early sculptures.

From Mathura come the reliefs shown in Plate 32B and D. These fragments are respectively 1 foot 3 inches and 1 foot 4 inches in height. The turbans and Early sculpture at Mathura.

[1] For a detailed discussion of all these reliefs see Foucher, *Beginnings of Buddhist Art.*, p. 97, vols. viii and ix.

[2] At Bharhut, eight *Jatakas* have been recognized, at Sanchi only five.

jewellery and the general treatment of form and features are distinctly of the Bharhut kind. Plate 31A is also of this period and is interesting because of its garland-bearers[1] and its three-tiered *stupa*.

Sculptures on the cave-temples.

The sculpture in the most ancient cave-temples of Western India, at Bhaja and Bedsa (Poona District), Pitalkhora (Khandesh District), and Kondane (Kolaba District), offers little of aesthetic interest (A 10). The small five-celled hermitage at Bhaja is perhaps the oldest. The cornice is supported by male figures used as carytids, wearing waist-cloths, large turbans, and much jewellery. The statues of the armed door-keepers are similarly clothed. They must be compared to [early] Sanchi rather than to Bharhut. The 'horses and elephants bearing men and women of bold execution' of the Bedsa capitals are likewise post-Bharhut. The sculpture at Karli, Kanheri, and Nasik is all later than Sanchi and must be compared to Kushan types among which close similitudes are to be found.

Jain bas-reliefs in Orissa.

The sandstone hills known as Khandagiri, Udayagiri, and Nilagiri, situated in the Puri District, Orissa, a few miles from the Bhuvanesvar temples, are honey-combed with Jain caves of various dates, probably covering a considerable period. The local worship appears to have been devoted chiefly to the Tirthankara Parsvanath. The elaborate, but ugly and semibarbaric sculptures in the *Rani Gumpha*, or Queen's Cave (Plate 24), are interpreted as representing a procession in honour of Parsvanath. This work is unskilled rather than primitive and is probably post-Sanchi.[2]

Female statue.

At the Jayavijaya Cave on Udayagiri a female statue about 6 feet high, and almost in the round, seems to be of early date and to possess considerable merit. The goddess, or whoever the personage may be, is represented as leaning her weight on the right leg, the left foot being bent in behind the right, so that only the toes touch the ground. In her right hand she holds up an object, presumably a flower, while the left forearm is bent horizontally across her waist. She apparently wears drawers, and is nude above the waist, in accordance with the fashion of ancient India, maintained in the south until recent days. The head-dress is a peculiar ribbed cap with long lappets. The features have been destroyed. The form is naturalistic and the pose easy.

[1] *Suparnas* and *Kinnaras*.

[2] Sixty-six caves, viz. 44 on Udayagiri, 19 on Khandagiri, and 3 on Nilagiri. The inscription of King Kharavela in the *Hathi Gumpha*, or Elephant Cave, is of the second century B.C., but not precisely dated, as formerly supposed (Fleet, *J. R. A. S.*, 1910, p. 242). See Imp. Gaz. (1908), s.v. Khandagiri, *Ann. Rep. A. S., India*, 1902-3, pp. 40-2. The best account of the caves is that by Babu Monmohan Chakravarti in Gaz. Puri District (1908). See also Fergusson, *Hist. of India and Eastern Architecture*, 2nd ed. (1910), vol. ii, pp. 9-18.

NOTES TO CHAPTER THREE

Sunga rule extended from circa 185 B.C. to 75 B.C. A 1

The date of the Karle Chaitya can be fixed with reasonable certainty between 40 and 100 A.D. A 2
Thus it took about 60 years for completion (*Lalit Kalā*, Nos. 3 & 4).

The sculpture at Bhaja (Pl. 25B and C) also belongs to the 2nd century B.C. A 3

The Parkham Yaksha though made in Chunar stone and smoothly finished has no trace of the A 4
Mauryan polish on it. It belongs to the early Sunga period and can be dated approximately to the period 150-175 B.C.

A number of colossal Yaksha and Yakshi sculptures are now known. They have been found in A 5
different parts of the country. They all appear to belong to the 2nd and 1st centuries B.C.

A few sculptures from Bharhut did remain at the site and are now housed in the Allahabad A 6
Museum (Pl. 13D) while a few fragments are in the Prince of Wales Museum. Plate 13D represents a group of acrobats.

Most of the panels have been indentified with Jataka stories or incidents from the life A 7
of Buddha.

A magnificent publication on Sanchi by Sir John Marshall, in three volumes, has now been issued. A 8
The scenes have been identified therein by M. Foucher.

The interval of time is a period of two centuries. Of course there is earlier and later work at A 9
Sanchi. The earlier style is typified by Pl. 20A and Pl. 21B, probably late 2nd century B.C.

Though the early sculpture of the Western India cave temples is nowhere so prolific as at Bharhut, A 10
Sanchi, Mathura and Amaravati, it is of high importance in the study of early Indian sculpture and particularly in the study of the plastic art of the Krishna Valley during Satavahana rule. The earliest reliefs are those at Bhaja (Pl. 25B and C) usually identified as Indra and Surya though this identification has been doubted. The sculpture at Bhaja can in several respects be likened to Sunga art such as Pl. 20A of the early period of Sanchi, and may be dated round about 100 B.C. or even earlier. Its eastern counterpart can be seen in the slightly latter sculpture of Jagyapetta where one finds similar elongation of figures and low relief. The sculptures of the Karle Chaitya belong to the period 40 A.D. to 100 A.D. and the Mithuna couples on its facade are amongst the finest creations of Indian art. An exact chronology of the early sculpture of the Western Caves has yet to be worked out, but in general they cover the period *circa* 100 B.C. (Bhaja) to the second half of the 2nd century A.D. (Kanheri). Recently some very fine early sculptures have been brought to light at Pitalkhcra, not far from Ajanta.

Chapter Four

MATHURA AND AMARAVATI

Part I. THE KUSHAN PERIOD (A 1)

The Kushan dynasty.

MATHURA is the chief find-spot of Kushan sculpture and, since it is linked directly to Bharhut and Sanchi by many works from its studios which clearly belong to the Early Period of Indian sculpture, it is advisable to discuss the Kushan sculpture of this site by itself, apart from Gandharan art and questions of foreign influence.

The chronology of the Kushan dynasty is still unsettled, and decisive proof is lacking of any one of the many rival theories on the subject. Six sovereigns of the dynasty are of importance for the history of India and of Indian art. The first two are most conveniently cited as Kadphises I and II. The next four kings, Kanishka, Vasishka, Huvishka, and Vasudeva I, certainly reigned in that order for a century in round numbers.[1] As a working hypothesis I revert to Professor Oldenberg's old theory, and assume that Kanishka (Plate 39A) came to the throne in A.D. 78 (A 2). Thus the first and second centuries after Christ are approximately filled by the rule of the leading kings of the dynasty.[2]

Mathura.

In the early centuries of the Christian era Mathura on the Jumna, a city of immemorial antiquity, and prosperous to this day in spite of many disasters, was sacred in the eyes of the adherents of all the three indigenous Indian religions — Jainism, Buddhism, and Brahmanical Hinduism. The abundant supply of excellent red sandstone at Rupbas and other quarries in the neighbourhood favoured the development of an active school of sculptors, whose workshops supplied all parts of Northern India with idols, much as Jaipur does now. The craftsmen, of course, were prepared to supply whatever was wanted by their patrons of any religion. The character of the local stone is so distinct that the products of the Mathura studios are easily recognized wherever they may be found.[3] Wealthy worshippers did not hesitate to undertake the cost of transporting heavy, even colossal, statues for hundreds of miles.

Sarnath.

Sarnath, like Mathura, was holy ground to the Jains as well as the Buddhists, and is connected with Mathura and declared a Kushan site of importance by finds of fine sculptures of red Mathura sandstone inscribed in the Kushan era (A 3). Its richly adorned buildings, crowded with sculpture, were involved in common ruin by the violence of the fierce hosts of Islam at the close of the twelfth century. The Brahmanical Hindus lavished their devotion on the neighbouring city of Benares, and shared the misfortunes of their rivals. The sculptors of Sarnath ordinarily used the excellent pale sandstone from the quarries of Chunar in the Mirzapur District, which had supplied the blocks for Asoka's pillars. But, as already observed, wealthy donors sometimes preferred to import red sandstone images from Mathura. During the last few years much progress has been made in unearthing the buried treasures of Sarnath, but much more remains to be found.

[1] Inscribed pillar of Maharaja Shahi Vasishka, dated in 24th year (Mathura Museum, Q. 13, *Catal.*, p. 189). In India the reigns of Kanishka, Vasishka, and Huvishka overlap. Probably Vasishka reigned in India only, and Huvishka succeeded to the whole empire on Kanishka's death about A.D. 123.

[2] Vincent Smith puts forward a dynastic chronology of Indian Art. His Sunga Period (Sanchi) is thus followed by the Kushan Period, which he applies to everything up to the Guptas (*c.* A.D. 320), including Amaravati. It is better to avoid such pseudo-dynastic classifications which are literary in origin and arbitrary in application.

[3] Vindhyan sandstone, however, often has a red tinge: mistakes have occurred where the evidence of the stone has been set above that of the style, especially with regard to medieval sculptures.

A. *Torana* arch, Mathura. (1st Cent. A.D. Kushan period).
(*By Courtesy of Dr. Führer*)

B. Detail of couple on a pillar, Mathura. 2nd Cent. A.D. Kushan period.
Mathura Museum

PLATE 37

Bacchanalian scene on pedestal of bowl, from Mahuli, near Mathura. 2nd Cent. A.D. Kushan period.

Several statues of Bodhisattvas, executed in the round on a large scale, are almost identical with the Mathura specimen reproduced above (Plate 33C), and one of these is dated in the third year of the reign of Kanishka, which may be regarded provisionally as equivalent to A.D. 80. The Kushan age of such works is thus definitely determined. Halos, when present, are plain, not highly decorated as in the Gupta period (A 4).

A finely executed bas-relief, which once decorated a doorway and exhibits artistic lotus and vine patterns, besides a picture of an elephant worshipping a *stupa*, is quite in the Mathura style, and may be assigned with some confidence to the first century of the Christian era.[1] The style of the Sarnath works is so closely related to that of Mathura that illustrations may be dispensed with.

Relief of a Jain *stupa*.

As at Bharhut and Sanchi the earlier sculptures at Mathura are derived from *stupas*. Many of them are pre-Kushan and may be directly compared to Bharhut and Sanchi as belonging to the early period. The *Lonasobhika* votive-tablet (A 5) shown in Plate 31B may be taken as illustrating the Mathura *stupas*, of which none have escaped the hand of the iconoclast. It must be referred to Kushan times, however, being distinguished from the latest work of the Early School (Sanchi) by its three superimposed tiers, the form of its corner pillars, and the stylized representation of the octagonal railing pillars, as well as by the freer treatment of the flying spirit-host.

This 'tablet of homage', with a relief sculpture of a Jain *stupa* (2 feet 4 inches high, 1 foot 9¾ inches wide), now in the Mathura Museum, was found embedded in a wall near the Holi gate, but is said to have come from a field near the village of Maholi. It was dedicated by a certain courtesan named *Lonasobhika* to the *Arahat Vardhamana* or *Mahavira*, and gives a good picture of an ancient Jain *stupa*, which was constructed and decorated on exactly the same lines as the Buddhist edifices of a similar kind. In this case the building depicted stood on a high plinth, and was approached by nine steps, leading to a *torana* gateway of the Sanchi type, with a garland hanging from it. The *stupa* was surrounded by a plain railing, and two similar railings were carried round the drum. The posturing females are unmistakably nude. The side columns are of the so-called Persepolitan type and bear the Wheel and Lion.[2]

Early sculpture at Mathura.

Not only are certain of the Mathura sculptures (Plates 31A, 32B and D, 34C) definitely comparable to Bharhut and Sanchi, but it is evident that the tradition was never broken, Kushan sculpture springing directly from the older school. As has been said, most of these sculptures had as their function the adornment of Jain or Buddhist *stupas* and consist chiefly of railing pillars and medallions. Many of the ancient motives are preserved such as the bull of Plate 35E and the fish-elephant (*Makara*) of Plate 35F. The bracket figure in Plate 35C is a development of the 'Woman and Tree' motive used for the same structural purpose as at Sanchi. Here the rendering is a little more schematic and architectural but much of the bold sinuous freedom of the East Gateway nymphs is preserved. The work of this period shows an increasing schematic and patterned quality (Plate 35D) well illustrated in the knotted foliage of Plate 35B. This delicate abstract treatment of foliage, suggesting the half unfurled leaves of the vine, was afterwards used with great effect in the doorways of Gupta shrines.

Sculptures on railings.

The excavations at Mathura have yielded numerous specimens of pillars of

[1] See *Ann. Rep. A. S., India*, pp. 59-104.

[2] The palaeographical dates quoted in V. Smith's *Jain Stupa* cannot be accepted.

stone railings associated with *stupas*, both Jain and Buddhist. Most of the Buddhist ones were found on the site of Huvishka's monastery in the Old Jail or Jamalpur mound, now entirely removed. The Jain specimens came from the Kankali mound, which included the remains of an early *stupa* and two temples. The pillars have high-relief statuettes, usually of females (Plates 32C, 34B, 36A, B and D, 39C), on the front, and other panelled scenes one above the other, or floral patterns on the back.

Plate 35A represents a Jain railing pillar on which is carved a *Yakshi* in the conventional Woman and Tree pose. Her beaded belt, heavy ear-rings and anklets are interesting and typical of the period. The sword she holds is of the ancient Indian kind which was still in use in Mughal and Maharatta days. Such rather immodest females adorning many of the pillars were supposed by Cunningham to be dancing-girls, an opinion certainly erroneous. They appear rather, as argued by Dr. Vogel, to belong to the *Yakshi* class, like the similar figures of the Bharhut railing. Some of the figures seem to be naked, but in others the apparent nudity is merely an artistic convention, the female drapery being treated schematically by flowing incised lines. This treatment of drapery persists throughout Indian art, and is radically different from the deeply undercut naturalistic drapery of certain Gandharan work.[1]

Plate 32C represents a variant of the common Woman and Tree motive. The female stands on a prostrate dwarf, a male *Yaksha*. The pose, as in many other cases, is easy and graceful. A sculpture in Calcutta shows two females together, under a tree (Plate 34A). A pillar in the Mathura Museum (Plate 34B) presents a half-back view of a female. The unusual attitudes shown in Plate 36A and B are treated much more skilfully, the first being obviously a dancing pose. The male figure, seemingly of a soldier, in Plate 36C is quite exceptional and effectively designed. A well-executed sculpture in the Indian Museum (Plate 36E) represents a youth riding a conventional lion.[2]

There is a dearth of photographs of the magnificent sculptures in the Mathura Museum and an illustrated catalogue is urgently needed.

A Bodhisattva.

A seated Bodhisattva (Plate 34C) in the Mathura Museum (A 6), bearing a dedicatory inscription, 'for the welfare and happiness of all beings', is of special interest as exhibiting the saint seated in the traditional *yogi* attitude, which became general subsequently, with his right shoulder bare, and the right hand raised in *Abhaya Mudra*.[3] The drapery is excessively formal in its folds, though the modelling of the figure is very suavely accomplished. The two flying spirits are early examples of a motive common in the sculpture and painting of later periods. The formal portrayal of their scarves and the knotted waist-clothes of the other two attendant figures is typical of Kushan work. The *ushnisha* or skull-protuberance is simply represented in a unique manner which must be accepted as the primitive form of this divine sign of Buddhahood, afterwards influenced by Gandharan forms. The figure is called a Bodhisattva in the inscription, although he is seated underneath the *Bodhi-tree* and wears the orthodox costume of the Buddha. The tree is the Pipal [*ficus religiosa*], the proper tree of Gautama.

[1] Marshall, *Taxila*, Pl. XXII.

[2] Dr. Vogel describes a mutilated statue (height 3 feet 10 inches or 1 metre 17) of a male deity standing with his left hand resting on his hip (Mathura Museum, E. 12, Catal., p. 108), which evidently had three heads, of which that on the proper right has been lost. The style indicates that the image belongs to the Kushan period. 'It is of interest as the only polycephalic image which can be attributed to that epoch.'

[3] In the Kushan period the hand in this *Mudra* is left *en bloc* with the shoulder. The *Abhaya* is the usual *Mudra*, both at Mathura and Amaravati.

A. Headless statue of Emperor Kanishka. 2nd Cent. A.D. Kushan period. Mathura Museum.

B. Yakshi-pedestal of bowl, from Mathura. 1st-2nd Cent. A.D. Kushan period. Bharat Kaḷa Bhavan, Banaras.

C. Yakshi with bird-cage, from Mathura. 2nd Cent. A.D. Kushan period. Indian Museum, Calcutta.

PLATE 39

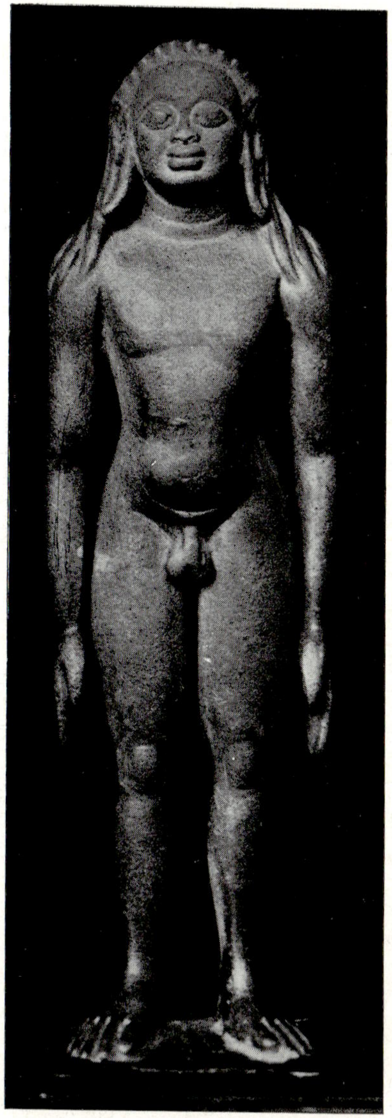

A.

B.

C.

A. Bronze figure of Jain Tirthankara, from Chausa. 1st-2nd Cent. A.D. Kushan period. Patna Museum. B. Bronze figure of Jain Tirthankara, from Chausa. Late 3rd Cent. A.D. Kushan-Gupta transition period. Patna Museum. C. Bronze male figure wearing turban, from Rupar. 1st-2nd Cent. A.D. Kushan period.

PLATE 40

A. Slab with representation of a *stupa*, &c. from the base of the great *stupa*, Amaravati. (2nd Cent. A.D. Satavahana period).

(*Copyright by the Department of Archaeology, Government of India*)

B. Undulating roll motive on coping of rail, Amaravati. (2nd Cent. A.D. Satavahana period. Madras Museum).

(*Copyright by Government Museum, Madras*)

PLATE 41

A. Basal medallion, Amaravati.

(Copyright by Department of Archaeology, Government of India)

B. Man and boy, Amaravati. (1st Cent. B.C. Satavahana period).

(Copyright by Government Museum, Madras)

C. Marble Buddhas, Amaravati. (2nd Cent. A.D. Satavahana period).

PLATE 42

This sculpture closely corresponds to the Anyor Buddha [Mathura Museum, No. A 2], and is typical of the middle Kushan period to which the bulk of Mathura sculpture belongs.

The standing Buddha of the Mathura school found at Sarnath, mentioned above, is the earliest dated Buddha-figure, being inscribed in the Kushan third year. It may be compared to a Bodhisattva in the Indian Museum, Calcutta (Plate 33C). In the Sarnath sculpture the *ushnisha* seems to have been inset in the head by means of a tenon or mortice. It is interesting to note how naïvely this divine excrescence is treated by the sculptors who first dared to portray the Buddha in stone; quite different is the sophisticated attempt at disguisement of the Graeco-Buddhist tradition. The treatment of drapery and jewellery in these Kushan Buddhas and Bodhisattvas (Plate 33D) is purely Indian. However, a distinct type of Buddha-figure is to be found at Mathura, which approaches the Gandharan image in its treatment of the clothing and its drapery. Most of these figures appear to belong to the later reigns of the dynasty. They have a certain clumsiness about them that suggests foreign influence (A 7).

Western influence.

Among the Mathura sculptures of the Kushan period is a rather anomalous group which is usually considered to be the result of foreign influence. The technique of these sculptures is one with that of the purely Indian sculptures already discussed. The treatment of the figure is easy and naturalistic, although somewhat heavy and lacking in rhythm when compared to Bharhut and Sanchi. The drapery is somewhat markedly less stylistic than that of the early Buddhas and Bodhisattvas. The foliage backgrounds are also absolutely according to the Indian tradition. However, the subjects of this group of sculptures do not seem to be either Jain or Buddhist.

Herakles and the Nemean Lion.

The much discussed group, usually described as 'Herakles and the Nemean Lion', was discovered by Cunningham serving a lowly purpose as the side of a cattle-trough and is now in the Indian Museum, Calcutta. It is 2 feet 5 inches high. The hero grasps the beast with his left arm and presumably threatened it with a club in the missing left hand. He is nude, except for a skin hung behind his back, and fastened by the paws round the neck. The lion with stylized mane is typically Indian, like the lions supporting Kushan thrones. The naturalistic, full modelling of the figure has been considered to be the result of Greek reminiscences.[1]

The Herakles-and-Lion motive is of great antiquity, going back to Assyrian art, which represented Gistubar, the 'Assyrian Hercules', clubbing and strangling a lion in the same way.[2] This Indian version is usually dubbed Hellenistic with an airy indication of Western Asia as the source of the foreign influence.

Bacchanalian images.

A certain group of sculptures from Mathura (A 8) or its neighbourhood (Plates 33A, 38), all dealing with strong drink and intoxication, which may be classed together as 'Bacchanalian', have excited much interest and discussion, in spite of which their interpretation is still far from clear. The supposed Greek character of these sculptures, when first discovered, was much exaggerated by the early commentators. As with the Herakles and most examples of Western influence in Indian art this 'Greek character' is difficult to define.[3]

[1] The group is M. 17, I. M., Calcutta: Anderson, *Catal.*, Pt. I, p. 190. See Cunningham, *A. S. Rep.*, vol. xvii, p. 139, Pl. XXX. Vincent Smith refers to the bronze figure, 2½ feet high, from Quetta, Baluchistan: *J. A. S. B.*, Pt. I, vol. lvi, p. 163, Pl. X.

[2] Bonomi, *Nineveh and its Palaces*, 2nd. ed., P. 136, Fig. 36; Maspero, *Ancient Egypt and Assyria* (trans. 1892), p. 302, Fig. 152.

[3] V. Smith says that many of these groups have 'nothing Hellenistic about them'. Like the Gandharan sculptures their subjects are clearly Indian though neither Buddhist, Hindu, nor Jain.

Silenus. The block discovered in 1836 by Colonel Stacy at Mathura and now marked M. I in the Indian Museum, Calcutta, was at first supposed to represent Silenus, and so became known as the 'Stacy Silenus'. But everybody now acknowledges that the subject is Indian, whether the sculptor was influenced by the Silenus model or not. The stone is 3 feet 8 inches high, 3 feet broad, and 1 foot 4 inches thick, with a circular basin on the top 16 inches in diameter and 8 in depth, seemingly intended to serve as the socket for a column. Both this block and its replica, to be described presently, were carved on back as well as front, and were evidently designed to be viewed from both directions. Apparently they were the bases of columns, which stood at an entrance, or entrances. But the difference of dimensions suggests that the two blocks may have belonged to distinct buildings.

The front group comprises four persons in two pairs, each consisting of a man and woman standing under an *asoka* tree in flower. The stout man on the right has his left arm round the waist of his female companion, who holds his right hand in hers, thus giving him the support rendered necessary by his intoxicated condition, due to the liquor, pots of which stand on the ground. The couple on the left stand facing, in attitudes apparently indifferent, but their countenances have been destroyed, so that their expression is lost. Traces of chaplets may be discerned on the heads of all.

The reeling man wears nothing except a pair of short bathing-drawers, and a scarf or cloak hanging behind his back and fastened round his neck by a knot. The slighter and perfectly sober man on the left is decently dressed in long drawers extending to his ankles, and a close-fitting tunic reaching below his knees. Both of the women are clad in a short tunic coming down a little below the waist, and possibly also in a long skirt. Each holds a piece of loose drapery, worn as a scarf, across her legs. The woman on the left has it thrown over her left arm in the fashion adopted by some of the Gandhara Bodhisattvas. Both women are adorned with heavy Indian anklets, armlets, and collars.

The reverse group, much mutilated, comprises five figures, of whom the principal is a fat elderly man sitting on a stone seat with his left leg tucked up, and so drunk that he has to be supported on his left side by a man and a boy, and on his right by a woman dressed like the females in the front group. The drunkard does not wear drawers like the merry fellow in that composition, but has a waistcloth loosely fastened. In style both reliefs are similar, the modelling being life-like, and the action clearly expressed.

The Pali Khera block. The companion block of nearly the same dimensions, but somehwat larger, was discovered many years later by the late Mr. F. S. Growse at Pali Khera, a suburb of modern Mathura included within the limits of the ancient city. The reverse group, exhibiting the effects of deep potations, being almost identical with the reverse of the Stacy block, need not be further described. The front group, however, differs from its companion. Five figures under an *asoka* tree again appear. The principal is a fat man, seemingly nude, seated with his left leg tucked up, on a low heap of stones laid in courses, in the conventional manner usually used to indicate mountain-heights. He is drinking from a noggin, apparently of wood, which a male attendant is ready to replenish. The proceedings are watched by another man, a woman, and a small boy (Plate 33A).

Bacchanalian Kuvera. Two other Bacchanalian groups, found among the sculptures in the Mathura Museum by Dr. Vogel and described by him, throw welcome light upon the date and meaning of the earlier discoveries described above. One of these groups,

A. Lotus forms, Amaravati

B. Lotus and *makara*, Amaravati.

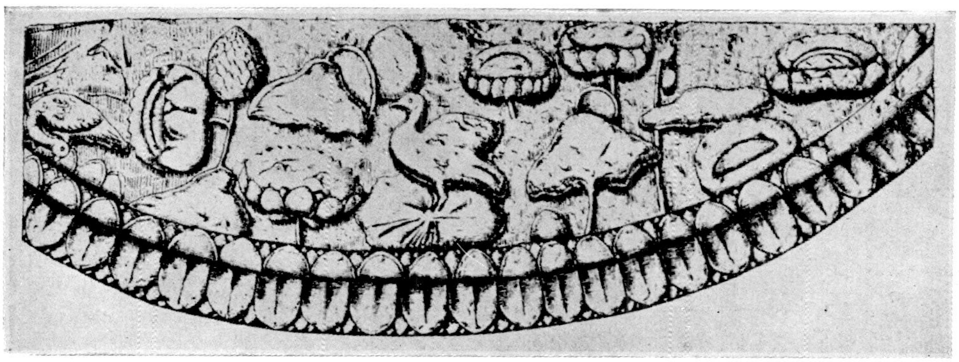

C. A pond, Amaravati.

(From Rea, *South Indian Buddhist Antiquities*)

PLATE 43

A. Court scene. Medallion, Amaravati. (2nd Cent. A.D. Satavahana period).

B. Enthronement of relics. Medallion, Amaravati. (2nd Cent. A.D. Satavahana period).

(*By Courtesy of the British Museum*)

1 foot 2 inches high (Plate 33B), represents a corpulent, coarse-looking man, apparently nude, squatted, and holding in his right hand a cup, which a female attendant is about to fill from a jar. His left hand grasps a long object, presumed to be a money-bag. This last attribute and the physique of the obese drinker permit of little doubt that the personage represented is Kuvera, the god of riches, whose podgy form has become familiar from the many images collected of late years in connexion with Buddhist monasteries from the Punjab to Ceylon. This sculpture, however, is medieval and closely corresponds to another of reddish sandstone, probably of Mathura workmanship, found at Osia, Rajputana.[1] Kuvera (also called *Vaisravana* and *Jambhala*) was king of the *Yaksha* demi-gods or sprites, and forms of his effigy are closely related to certain images from Gandhara. Dr. Vogel probably is right in associating all the Bacchanalian sculptures of Mathura with *Yaksha* worship[2] (A 9).

Naga sculptures.

Mr. Growse also published a mutilated statue, 3 feet 1 inch high, lying at Kukargrama in the Saadabad *pargana* of the Mathura District — a singularly graceful figure of a *Naga* youth with a canopy of seven cobra heads, holding his right hand above his head, while his left grasps a cup similar in shape to that seen on the Pali Khera block, but apparently without the curved handle. A garland of wild flowers is twined round his body, and he wears a high head-dress of a pattern commonly found in Kushan sculptures. The worship of the Nagas, the spirits of the waters, was much favoured by the ancient inhabitants of the Mathura region in Kushan times.[3] This drinking *Naga* is related to another fine life-size statue of a *Naga* water-sprite from Chhargaon, near Mathura, now in the Mathura Museum, the approximate date of which is fixed by an inscription on the back, recorded in the fortieth year during the reign of Huvishka. According to the chronology provisionally adopted in this work, the statue (Plate 32A), which is 5 feet high, may be ascribed to the year A.D. 117 or 118. The modelling is good. The arrangement of the waistcloth in a twisted roll is typically Kushan. The broken left hand probably held a cup.[4]

Subjects of Kushan sculptures.

Besides the Kushan Buddhas or Bodhisattvas and the *Nagas*, various canonical [and other] scenes are found in bas-relief (Plate 37). A common representation is the visit of Indra to Buddha in the *Indrasila* cave. The mountainous locality is conventionally indicated by 'rock-work' and its desolateness by birds and beasts looking out from their lairs. Plate 31A represents a three-tiered *stupa* with trees on either side of it and pairs of harpies (*Suparnas*) and centaurs (*Kinnaras*) bringing offerings and garlands. These 'offering-bearer' scenes are very common and, of course, are also to be found at Bharhut and Sanchi. At Mathura and in Gandhara they develop into processions and pageants as in the archway spandril

[1] 'Études de Sculpture bouddhique' (*Bull. de l'École francaise d'Extrême-Or.*, t. viii (1908), Nos. 3, 4, Fig. 2); *Ann. Rep. A. S., India*, 1906-7, 'The Mathura School of Sculpture', pp. 137-60. The second group in the Mathura Museum differs little from the one figured.

[2] See *A. S. Rep.*, 1906-7.

[3] loc. cit.

[4] Vogel in *Prog. Rep. A. S., N. Circle*, 1907-8, p. 38; *J. R. A. S.*, 1910, p. 1313 n. These so-called 'Bacchanalian' sculptures of Mathura cannot be at all understood if considered by themselves. They evidently belong to a large class of Buddhist works of art, represented by the 'scénes bacchiques' of Gandhara, which fill two plates of M. Foucher's book (Foucher, *L'Art gréco-bouddhique du Gandhara*, Figs. 127-33 *b*), several reliefs on railing pillars at Mathura, the 'Indian Bacchus' of the Tank silver dish, and the festive scenes depicted in the Aurangabad and Bagh Caves. All such works appear to be expressive, as Mr. Growse suggested, of a little understood sensual form of popular Buddhism, not indicated by literature until a time seemingly much later than the second century. But when the true history of Indian Buddhism comes to be written it must be based on the evidence of the sculptures and pictures as much as on the books. M. Roller's question, addressed to Christian ecclesiastical archaeologists with reference to the art of the Catacombs, may be repeated to Indianists: 'La pierre ne servirait-elle pas à contrôler le manuscrit?' (*Les Catacombes de Rome* (1881), Preface, p. ii.)

(Plate 37A). The figure-sculpture here is excellent, the garland-bearers of the middle band being portrayed with a fine rhythmic effect. The floral-bands are very simply treated and are typical of a common style of Kushan decoration.

It is to be noticed that just as there are fewer *Jataka* scenes at Sanchi than at Bharhut, there appear to be still fewer at Kushan Mathura. The canon is fast crystallizing into a literary form, to the exclusion of the ancient popular parables. The *Jatakas*, which are to be recognized at Ajanta, are on the whole of a different class, most of them being definitely literary.

Part II. AMARAVATI

Amaravat sculptures well known.

The sculptures from the *stupa* of Amaravati and its surrounding railing or screen of marble may claim the distinction of being the most accessible specimens of early Indian art. No visitor to the British Museum, however indifferent to Indian curiosities, can help seeing the spoils of the *stupa* and railing displayed on the walls of the grand staircase.

Destruction of the *stupa*.

The small town of Amaravati on the south bank of the Krishna (Kistna) river, in the Guntur District, Madras, represents a more important ancient city called Dharanikota, a place of considerable note from at least 200 B.C. A richly decorated *stupa*, known to have been in good repair and still venerated in the twelfth century, continued to exist to the south of the town up to the close of the eighteenth or the beginning of the nineteenth century, when it was utterly destroyed by a greedy local landholder, eager to obtain cheap building material and convinced that marble slabs, plain or carved, formed excellent food for a lime-kiln. About a century ago Colonel Mackenzie visited the place and had drawings made of numerous slabs, now no longer in existence. Various archaeological explorers have salved remnants of the sculptures, which are now mostly housed in either the British Museum or the Central Museum, Madras. Our knowledge of the extraordinary richness of the decoration of the *stupa* and its railing is derived from the poor remnants thus rescued and Colonel Mackenzie's drawings, which have been published fully by Mr. Fergusson and Dr. Burgess.

Date of the principal sculptures.

The *stupa* in its earliest form was of high antiquity, dating, as inscriptions prove, from about 200 B.C.[1] But the great mass of the sculpture is much later, and belongs to the Kushan period. The authority of the Kushan kings, however, did not extend as far south as Amaravati, which was then within the dominions of the powerful Andhra dynasty of the Deccan. By the help of two inscriptions mentioning Andhra kings, the construction of the great railing may be assigned to the half-century between 150 and 200 after Christ. The highly ornate slabs which cased the *stupa* itself may be a little later. We are almost certainly safe in saying that all the sculptures of the railing and casing fall within the hundred years between A.D. 150 and 250. Originally it was believed that there used to be two railings, and all the printed descriptions give details of an 'outer' and an 'inner' railing. But Dr. Burgess later stated that he and everybody else were mistaken, the fact being that no more than one railing, the so-called 'outer' one, ever existed. The slabs supposed to have belonged to an 'inner' railing really formed a casing applied to the body of the *stupa*.[2] However, two types of sculpture clearly

[1] These inscribed slabs are unsculptured. The characters are described as being of 'Mauryan type', a rather inexact phrase. Konow doubts whether any sculpture is pre-Christian. Buhler seems to regard the inscribed sculptures as being not earlier than second century A.D. and most of them later—on palaeographical evidence (A 11).

[2] Fergusson, *Hist. of Ind. and E. Archit.*, 2nd ed. (1910), vol. i, p. 119.

belonging to two different periods are distinguishable. In the first the Buddha figure is not found: in the second it is. The latter is stylistically also very much easier and richer. The bulk of the sculptures belong to this second period (A 10).

The railing, by far the most magnificent known example of such structures, was 192 feet in diameter, about 600 in circumference, and stood 13 or 14 feet high above the pavement. It was constructed of upright slabs connected by three cross-bars between each pair of uprights, which stood upon a plinth and supported a coping about 2 feet 9 inches in height. On the outer face each upright was adorned with a full disk in the centre and a half-disk at top and bottom, minor sculptures filling the interspaces. Similar but ever-varying disks decorated the cross-bars, and the coping was ornamented with a long wavy flower-roll carried by men, numerous figures being inserted in the open spaces. The plinth exhibited a frieze of animals and boys, often in comic or ludicrous attitudes. The decorations on the inner face were even more elaborate; the coping presenting a continued series of bas-reliefs, and the central disks being filled with delicate sculptures, treating every topic of Buddhist legend. Thus every part of the strucutre, with a surface of about 16,800 square feet, was covered with sculptured reliefs. The railing.

The slabs forming the casing of the lower part of the *stupa*, 162½ feet in diameter, were carved more richly even than the inner face of the railing, if that be possible. Apparently there were twelve in each quadrant, the principal object depicted on each slab being a highly decorated *stupa* with its railing, the rest of the surface being covered with an infinite variety of figures. Study of Plate 41A, reproducing the best preserved of such slabs, will dispense with the necessity for detailed description, and at the same time give a good notion of what the appearance of the Amaravati *stupa* must have been in the days of its glory. When fresh and perfect the structure must have produced an effect unrivalled in the world. However much severe taste may condemn the characteristic Indian lavishness of decoration which scorned to leave an inch of plain surface, the vast expanse of sculpture in white marble gleaming in the brilliant sunshine cannot have failed to exhibit a scene of unequalled splendour. The casing.

While abstaining from minute description of Plate 41A, which serves as a synopsis of the sculptures generally, I may invite the attention of the reader to a few points. In the relief picture the sculptured decoration is carried high up the dome, but the extant slabs seem to have been attached only to the lower part of the Amaravati *stupa*. It is possible that higher bands of decoration may have existed and been wholly destroyed. The railing in the relief has four cross-bars, and not only three as in the real monument. The 'moonstone' at the entrance agrees in form, though not in design, with the Ceylonese examples. The lions and some of the architectural forms are survivals of the Assyrio-Persian patterns of the Asokan age. The meaning of the five *stelae* or pilasters on the face of the *stupa* is not known (A 12). The worshippers in the central scene adoring the chair occupied only by an object which may be the sacred head-dress relic, might have appeared in a Sanchi or Bharhut relief, where images of Buddha are unknown; but here, at the top of the picture, we also find Buddha seated in the conventional *yogi* attitude. The frieze at the top of the slab contains nearly fifty figures, and the general effect, like that of nearly all the reliefs, is excessively elaborate. But the skill of the artist in design and drawing, and his technical powers of execution, are beyond dispute. Details.

Medallions

The infinite variety of the patterns used in the medallions and bars may be realized by study either of actual examples or of the relief pictures. Plate 42A is an excellent and well-preserved example of a charming decorative design based on the lotus-flower motive. The beauty and delicacy of the floral devices in the border and plinth deserve special notice and admiration. They will repay minute examination with a magnifying glass.

Decorative motives.

The treatment of floral and animal decorative motives has been illustrated above by photographs on a small scale. There specimens may be added from Mr. Rea's drawings on a larger scale, which have not been published except in his book (Plates 43A, B and C).

Buddhas.

A few separate images have been found at Amaravati. Two large marble statues, 6 feet 4 inches in height, are illustrated in Plate 42C. The opaque drapery is treated in a formalized style, quite different from the smooth transparent robes of the Gupta period, to be discussed in the next chapter, but to a certain extent resembling Gandhara work and the Mathura figures discussed above. These images may date from the third or fourth century, or even later; they closely correspond to the Buddhas painted on the columns in Cave X, Ajanta.

Criticism.

Fergusson's opinion that the sculptures of the Amaravati school mark 'the culmination of the art of sculpture in India', which was generally accepted until recently by English writers, including myself, does not now command such ready assent. I will not presume to say which work marks the 'culminating point', but it is certainly safe to affirm that the pre-eminence claimed for the Amaravati reliefs may be effectively challenged by compositions of later date, at least in some respects. All critics, however, can agree with Mr. Havell that the marbles of Amaravati offer 'delightful studies of animal life, combined with extremely beautiful conventionalized ornament', and that 'the most varied and difficult movements of the human figure are drawn and modelled with great freedom and skill' (Plates 41B, 42B, 44A and B, 45A). The obvious overcrowding of the compositions unfortunately is a defect common in Indian art. Historically, the sculptures are interesting as an academic development of the style of Sanchi and Bharhut. Mr. Havell may be right in believing that originally the effect of the Amaravati marbles was heightened by colour, and in holding that technically they should be regarded as 'painted relievos' rather than as true sculpture. But whether they were painted or not, they must have formed, when perfect, one of the most splendid exhibitions of artistic skill known in the history of the world.[1]

[1] Considering the geographical and political separation of the Kushan and Andhra empires, I think the presumption is that the sculptors of Amaravati had not direct knowledge of the Gandhara school, although it is possible that they may have had it. Hiuen Tsiang, the Chinese pilgrim, in the seventh century, did not really describe the *stupa* as being 'ornamented with all the magnificence of the palaces of Bactria (Tahia)', as Fergusson and Burgess suppose him to have done. A slight slip of the pen in the Chinese text used by Julien introduced the word mistranslated as 'Bactria'. The pilgrim really praised two monasteries in the Deccan as 'having all the artistic elegance of a great mansion and all the beauty of natural scenery'. The assumption made by Dr. Burgess and other authors that the account of *two monasteries* given by Hiuen Tsiang should be applied to the *stupa* of Amaravati is far from being established. Thus disappears the basis for Fergusson's argument that the school of Amaravati should be considered the offspring of the marriage of the art of the North—that is to say, Bactria as represented by Gandhara—with that of interior India as represented by Sanchi and Bharhut (Fergusson, *Hist. Ind. and. E. Arch.*, reprint of 1899, p. 103; new ed. by Burgess (1910), vol. i, p. 123). 'Instead of the *ta-hsia*, a "great mansion", here, the B text, used by Julien, has *ta hsia*, which is a Chinese name for the country called Bactria. But this is evidently a slip of the pen, and the proper reading is that of the other texts which means a "great mansion" ' (Watters, *On Yuan Chwang's Travels in India* (1905), vol. ii, p. 218). This material correction and Mr. Watters's comments on the current 'identification' of the pilgrim's *monasteries* with the Amaravati *stupa* have been overlooked in the revision of Fergusson's book. 'It is hard', Mr. Watters observes, 'to understand how any one could propose to identify a large monastery among hills and streams, and having spacious chambers and great corridors, with a building which is only a remarkable tope situated on a plain.' The error concurred in by Julien, Fergusson, and Dr. Burgess will not readily disappear from books on Indian art and antiquities.

A. Subjugation of the elephant Nalagiri by the Buddha. Medallion, Amaravati. 2nd Cent. A.D. Satavahana period. Madras Museum.

B. Scene from the life of the Buddha, Nagarjunakonda. 3rd Cent. A.D. Ikshavaku period.

Scenes from the life of the Buddha, from Nagarjunakonda. *Top*, Chanda giving out news of Siddhartha's departure. *Bottom*, Buddha and Nanda on a visit to heaven. 3rd Cent. A.D. Ikshavaku period.

PLATE 46

NOTES TO CHAPTER FOUR A 1

While dealing with early Indian art after the Mauryan period the most acceptable classification is one which recognizes the growth of an indigenous art in stone sculpture in Northern and Central India under the Sungas (*circa* 185 B.C. to 75 B.C.), to be followed by a Scythian period (Pl. 32B and D) under the Mathura Satraps such as Ranjula and Sodasa (1st century B.C.), merging into the splendid achievements of the Kushan period in the 1st and 2nd centuries A.D. at Mathura and elsewhere. As far as art in the Western and Eastern Deccan is concerned there is a great movement in the Krishna Valley. Its earliest manifestation is in the West at Bhaja (Pl. 25B and C) and in the East at Jagyyapetta, both about 100 B.C., if not earlier, and this is followed by the work of the other Western cave monasteries extending to the second half of the 2nd century A.D. as well as the work at famous sites such as Amaravati and Nagarjunakonda in the east right into the 3rd century A.D. All this early art of the Western Deccan and the Krishna Valley is designated as Andhra or Satavahana art. It was done under the Satavahanas and also under the Kshaharata Satraps who for some time ousted the Satavahanas in the Western Deccan. The reliefs of Nagarjunakonda belong to the rule of the A 2
Ikshavakus who were the successors of the Satavahanas in that area.

The year 78 A.D. for Kanishka is the theory generally accepted today though others have suggested 120 A.D. and 128 A.D. and recently 144 A.D. has been put forward though not on convincing grounds. Several magnificent portrait statues of the Kushan period have been found. That of the great Kanishka is reproduced as Plate 39A. It is inscribed with his name. The head is missing A 3
but we know his features from coins.

There is reason to believe that the Sarnath workshops of the Kushan period began to copy the Mathura style. A colossal Bodhisattva from Sarnath in the Sarnath Museum, in the characteristic A 4
buff stone, is obviously based on Mathura models.

The Kushan period haloes are almost invariably plain save for a scalloped edge. In the Kushan-Gupta transition period and in a few instances even during the Kushan period itself, decoration on A 5
the halo begins to appear. The Buddha head (Pl. 34D) belongs to the transition period.

These votive tablets pertaining to the Jain faith are known as *Ayyagapattas*, and are a characteristic A 6
of early Jain art at Mathura.

This image came from the Katra mound. There was a flourishing Bodhisattva cult at Mathura A 7
in the Kushan period. The whorl-like *ushnisha* is a characteristic of Kushan Buddha figures.

In fact, there is no foreign influence in these Kushan Bodhisattva figures (Pl. 33C and D). Plate 33D is from the Mahuli mound at Mathura. The great ancestor of the colossal standing A 8
Kushan Bodhisattva figures is the Parkham Yaksha (Pl. 11C).

The finest of all Bacchanalian groups was found at the Mahuli mound a few years ago (Pl. 38). It is sculptured on both sides and on the top is the Buddha's alms bowl. One side depicts the vice of drunkenness while the other depicts a courtesan enticing a young man. Such sculptures may have been intended to act as warnings against the pitfalls of life in the gay and opulent city of Mathura famed for its *ganikas* who were not common prostitutes but very superior courtesans. Another A 9
beautiful sculpture with a bowl is illustrated as Pl. 39B.

This does not appear to be so in all cases. Plate 38 has nothing to do with Yaksha worship. A 10

The generally accepted view is that there are four periods in the development of Amaravati extending from the early 1st century B.C. to the 2nd century A.D. Most of the sculptures of Amaravati A 11
are now in the Madras Museum and the British Museum.

This seems to be incorrect for the earliest sculptures must be well before the Christian era, though A 12
the majority belong to the 1st and 2nd centuries A.D.

These are what are known as *Ayaka* pillars. They are characteristic of the Krishna Valley Stupa architecture. A site of as great importance as Amaravati is that of Nagarjunakonda, also in the Krishna Valley, where there were extensive Buddhist monastic settlements. The sculpture of this site (Pls. 45B, 46) is a continuation of the Amaravati tradition and is equally fine. The work at Nagarjunakonda is associated with the Ikshvaku dynasty, the political successors of the Satavahanas in that area, in the 3rd century A.D. It is in the same greenish limestone and much that has come to light is well preserved. A stupa at Goli is also of the same period and has some interesting panels, now in the Madras Museum.

METAL SCULPTURE IN THE KUSHAN AND ANDHRA PERIODS

Till recently nothing was known of the art of metal sculpture in the 1st and 2nd centuries A.D. The metal sculpture of the Indus Valley civilization has already been referred to, but no examples of metal sculpture thereafter have come to light till we come to the rule of the Kushans in North India and of the Satavahanas in the Deccan. In 1945 the excavations at the Brahmapuri mound, Kolhapur in the Western Deccan, brought to light a miniature elephant with riders (Pl. 30C), closely resembling the elephant and rider capitals of the Western Indian cave temples such as those at Karle, Nasik and Kanheri. There is no doubt whatsoever that it belongs to the Satavahana period, probably mid-2nd century A.D. In the same hoard were found two circular metal rings surmounted with the heads of mythical creatures; a metal repoussé plaque of a mythical lion; and a small vessel engraved with an elephant on its lid, and wild animals, birds and aquatic creatures on the exterior of the vessel. Other objects in the hoard included a metal rod terminating in an elephant's head. The rod is part of a hanging lamp. A large plate engraved with typical Satavahana period figures of men and women has not yet been completely cleaned. Along with this hoard were found many other vessels for domestic and ritual use as also several objects of provincial Roman origin, further emphasizing the well known contacts between the West Coast of India and the Red Sea ports from where the ships engaged in the Roman trade set sail. The elephant with riders (Pl. 30C) is beautifully modelled and is a genuine example of metal sculpture in the round. It seems to have been an ornamental metal sculpture used as the finial of a lamp, incense burner or some other utilitarian or ritual object. The presence in this Satavahana period hoard of these miniature sculptured objects as well as articles with decorative figure engraving indicates that metal sculpture in miniature and engraving on metal must have had a considerable vogue as decorative features for articles of ritual and domestic use. The elephant with riders is skilfully fashioned indicating the existence of skilled craftsmen. Two well finished toy metal carts, such as are seen in a sculptured slab at Nagarjunakonda, were also found in the hoard which probably belonged to a trader in miscellaneous metal objects. A small plaque in the Baroda Museum depicting a man and woman seems to belong to the Satavahana period while a very unique miniature bronze was found at Nagarjunakonda.

With regard to metal sculpture in Kushan times a few images can with confidence be assigned to this period. One is of a female statuette corresponding to the Kushan railing figures of Mathura. It is now in an American Museum at Kansas City. The other, a male figure, was found in the excavations at Rupar (Pl. 40C). A hoard of Jain images from Chausa, Bihar, now in the Patna Museum, also offers most interesting material for a study of metal sculpture during the Kushan period. One example from this hoard is reproduced in Plate 40A while another, which probably belongs to the Kushan-Gupta transition period, is illustrated as Plate 40B. Though the metal sculpture of the Kushan and Andhra periods is very limited in quantity it is not lacking in that proficiency which is later on seen in the more refined Gupta period metal images.

A. Buddha, etc.; relief from Muhammad Nari.

B. Modified Corinthian capitals from Gandhara.

(By Courtesy of C. Whittingham and Griggs)

PLATE 47

A. Visit of Indra to Buddha, in Indrasaila Cave.
(Photo: Indian Museum, Calcutta)

B. Seated Buddha. Berlin Museum.
(*By Courtesy of C. Whittingham and Griggs*)

C. Gautama as emaciated ascetic.

PLATE 48

A. Hariti, from Sikri.

B. Kuvera and Hariti, from Sahri - Bahlol.

C. Bodhisattva. Lahore Museum.

E. Buddha seated under tree.

D. Buddha seated.

F. The first miracle at Sravasti.

G. The Great Miracle at Sravasti.

PLATE 49

A. Garuda and the Nagini, from Sanghao.

B. Kuvera. Lahore Museum.

C. Pallas Athene. Lahore Museum.

(By Courtesy of C. Whittingham and Griggs)

PLATE 50

Chapter Five

FOREIGN INFLUENCES ON INDIAN ART

Part I. THE HELLENISTIC SCULPTURE OF GANDHARA

Discovery of Indo-Hellenic art.

If Indian art as a whole may complain of undeserved depreciation and neglect, one branch of it, the Hellenistic sculpture of the regions on the north-western frontier, anciently known as Gandhara, has received its full share of attention in Europe and been the subject of voluminous discussion. The existence of an Indo-Hellenic school of sculpture was not recognized generally until 1870, when the late Dr. Leitner brought to England a considerable collection of specimens, to which he gave the name of Graeco-Buddhist. But so far back as 1833 Dr. Gerard had disinterred the first known example, a circular relief of Buddha, from the chamber of a ruined *stupa* near Kabul.[1] In 1836 James Prinsep published his account of the so-called 'Silenus' discovered by Colonel Stacy at Mathura, which has been already discussed; and in 1848 Cunningham examined the ruins of Jamalgarhi to the north-east of Peshawar. His observations, however, were not published until many years later. The first description of a selection of the Jamalgarhi sculptures was that printed by Sir E. C. Bayley in the *Journal of the Asiatic Society of Bengal* for 1852,[2] with illustrations so miserably rude that they gave little notion of the aesthetic value of the objects described. The sculptures thus imperfectly illustrated, having been subsequently brought to England, perished in the fire at the Crystal Palace which also destroyed Major Gill's copies of the Ajanta frescoes. Thus it happened that, as already observed, Dr. Leitner is entitled to the credit of having first convinced the learned world of the fact that during the early centuries of the Christian era North-Western India was the home of a school of Hellenistic sculpture of considerable artistic merit.

European interest in the subject.

The fact was so novel and surprising that one distinguished antiquary, Mr. W. Vaux, F.R.S., was bold enough to dispute it, and to declare his inability to perceive any manifest traces of Greek art on the sculptures procured by Dr. Leitner and other collectors in the neighbourhood of Peshawar. In a short time, however, evidence accumulated so rapidly that no possibility of doubt remained, and Professor Curtius was able to announce that the discoveries opened 'a new page in the history of Greek art'. That is the explanation of the keen interest taken in them by European scholars, who are eager to follow out in its most minute details the story of Greek art, on which that of modern Europe is based, while they usually remain indifferent, or even contemptuous, towards manifestations of artistic power in the nations of the East developed independently of the Hellenic tradition.

Abundance examples.

During the last forty years thousands of Indo-Hellenic sculptures have come to light, while considerable numbers, including most of the choicest specimens, have been catalogued, described, and photographed. The number, indeed, is so great that it is difficult to make a small selection thoroughly representative. Most of the examples chosen to illustrate this chapter have been selected in virtue of their conspicuous aesthetic merits, and may be regarded as evidence of the highest attainment of a school of artists working on Indian soil, and applying more or less modified Greek methods of composition and technique to Indian subjects.

[1] K. 1 of Indian Museum; Anderson, *Catal.*, Part I, p. 261.

[2] The approach to the subject by means of a postulated Hellenic artistic tradition progressively Indianized is by no means scientific. A period of initial Indianization, during which the whole body of the Indian canon was appropriated, must necessarily have preceded this so-called decline.

A few of the figures mark the gradual disappearance of the Hellenic tradition and the progressive Indianization of the treatment.[1]

The Gandhara territory.

The country from which comes this wonderful wealth of semi-foreign sculpture may be described in general terms as the North-Western Frontier. It includes the modern District of Peshawar, the valley of the Kabul river, Swat, Buner, and other tribal territories, as well as the western portion of the Punjab between the Indus and the Jhelum. The kingdom of which Peshawar (Purushapura) was the capital having been known in ancient times as Gandhara, the sculptures are usually described by that territorial name, although Graeco-Buddhist finds in Khotan and in the vicinity of Kabul render this title rather meaningless.

The richest sites as yet explored are those crowded together in the Yusufzai country to the north and north-east of Peshawar, comprising Jamalgarhi, Sahri-Bahlol, Takht-i-Bahi, and many more which it would be tedious to enumerate. Some of the best sculptures come from Swat, but the hostility of the tribes prevents systematic exploration of the antiquities beyond the British frontier.

Arrangement by subjects alone possible.

Even within the frontier most of the exploration done until recently has been the work of amateurs, conducted in a haphazard fashion, without the formation or preservation of adequate detailed record. Consequently, many buildings have been utterly destroyed, and the value of the large collections of sculptures found by many public institutions and private persons is seriously impaired by the lack of information concerning the provenance of the specimens. M. Foucher, the most learned and authoritative commentator on the sculptures, declares that it is impossible in the present state of knowledge to arrange them in chronological order. As a general rule, no doubt, the most Greek may be considered the oldest, and the most Indianized the latest, but the practical application of this principle presents many difficulties. Arrangement by localities is equally impracticable, because nobody knows where many of the best examples were found, and also because there is no distinct evidence of local variations in style. The general style over the whole region is fairly uniform. The result is that the only practicable arrangement is one by subjects. In this chapter it will not be possible to illustrate more than a few of the multifarious subjects treated by the artists, and students who wish to examine the whole field must be referred to special treatises. It is hoped, however, that the specimens reproduced will suffice to enable the reader to judge of the aesthetic qualities of the sculptures, and to place them in their due relation to Greek art on the one hand and to indigenous Indian art on the other, subject to a certain amount of vagueness in the chronology of the school.

Chronology.

Whenever the date of Kanishka, the celebrated king of Gandhara, shall be determined, that of the best period of the Hellenistic sculpture will also be known. Many of them undoubtedly are contemporary with him, though some are earlier and others later. Without going into complicated antiquarian discussions, it may suffice to say here that none of the sculptures are later than A.D. 600, few, if any, later than A.D. 400, and that in all probability extremely few are earlier

[1] Certain facts may be brought together which connect the sculptures at several localities with the Kushan kings: (1) coins of Kanishka in foundation deposit of Sanghao monastery (Cole, *Second Report*, p. cxx); (2) coin of Huviskha with a panel of best style at Takht-i-Bhai (*J. R. A. S.*, 1899, p. 422); (3) seven coins of Vasudeva with Jamalgarhi sculptures (Cunningham, *Reports*, v. 194); (4) coin of Huvishka in good condition at Ahinposh *stupa*, along with coins of Sabina, &c. (*Proc. A. S. B.*, 1879, p. 209); (5) some of the Mathura sculptures in Gandhara style bear Kushan inscriptions. For reasons stated already I now take the most probable date of the accession of Kanishka to be A.D. 78. With regard to these coin-finds and the chronology that has been built upon them, it must be realized that they actually only provide a *lower limit* for the dating of Gandharan art. The coins of several reigns and even dynasties are often together.

A. Boys armed as soldiers.

B. Hindu ascetic.

(*By Courtesy of C. Whittingham and Griggs*)

C. Man playing lyre (*vina*), from Yusufzai. (L. Dames, Berlin).

D. Buddha attended by Vajrapani, from Yusufzai. Dames Collection, Berlin.

E. Woman and tree, from Yusufzai. (L. Dames, Berlin).

PLATE 51

A. Procession of maskers and soldiers.
(By Courtesy of C. Whittingham and Griggs)

B. The Nativity of Buddha, from Yusufzai. (L. Dames, Berlin).

▼

PLATE 52

than the Christian era. The culmination of the art of the school may be dated from about A.D. 50 to A.D. 150 or 200. It is quite safe to affirm that the works of good quality belong to the first three centuries of the Christian era. Thus the best productions of the Gandhara Indo-Hellenistic school nearly synchronize with the art of the Flavian and Antonine periods in Western Asia and Europe, and in India with the reliefs on the great rail at Amaravati in the Deccan, as well as with many sculptures at Mathura on the Jumna, both of which will be discussed in the next chapter.

All the sculptures Buddhist.

Without exception, all the sculptures come from Buddhist sites and were executed in the service of the Buddhist religion, so far as is known. No trace of works of the pure Gandharan school dedicated to either Jainism or Brahmanical Hinduism has been discovered. Moreover, the subjects treated are not only Buddhist but purely Indian. Buddha may appear in the guise of Apollo, the god Brahma in that of St. Peter, or a door-keeper in that of Pallas Athene, but however Greek may be the form, the personages and incidents are all Indian, and centre round the person of Buddha, whose image dominates the compositions.

Dominance of the image of Buddha.

Herein lies the most obvious, and at the same time, perhaps, the most important difference between the ancient schools of interior India at Sanchi, Bharhut, or Bodh Gaya, and the school of Gandhara, and the contemporary art of Mathura and Amaravati. In Gandhara art, as M. Foucher observes, Buddha is everywhere; and whatever be the form which he assumes, as Prince Charming, emaciated ascetic, or ideal monk, or by whatever name he may be called, whether it be Siddhartha, Sramana Gautama, or Buddha Sakyamuni, he dominates almost every composition, so that the preparation of a full list of the sculptors' subjects is equivalent to writing an illustrated life of the Master. The early schools of Indian art, as we have seen, were content to indicate his supposed presence by mere symbols, and did not presume to imagine his bodily likeness.

Material.

The material of the sculptures is usually a blue clay-slate, described as 'hornblende-schist'. The stone was finished with fine plaster, like the rock sculptures of Ajanta and many other localities in India and Ceylon, and the effect was heightened by the free use of colour and gilding, traces of which are still nearly always discernible.

Plaster heads.

Great numbers of detached heads, made sometimes of stucco and sometimes of terra-cotta, have been found, varying in dimensions from tiny objects two or three inches high to life size. These heads, as various in character as in dimensions, are often of high artistic merit. One mode of their use is explained by an observation of Masson, who noted that at Hidda, near Jalalabad in the upper Kabul valley,

> 'idols in great numbers are found. They are small, of one and the same kind, about six or eight inches in height, and consist of a strong cast head fixed on a body of earth, whence the heads only can be brought away. They are seated and clothed in folds of drapery, and the hair is woven into rows of curls. The bodies are sometimes painted with red lead, and rarely covered with leaf-gold; they appear to have been interred in apartments, of which fragments are also found.'[1]

A period of work in stucco and clay seems to have succeeded the best period of work in schist. The latter work at Taxila is all stucco and clay.[2] Moulds were used for the wholesale reduplication of these heads. Buddhists consider the multiplication of sacred images an act of merit, and the practice of making

[1] *Ariana Antiqua*, p. 113. [2] Marshall, *Taxila Guide*, p. 108.

the bodies cheaply with clay enabled the pious donor to accumulate a credit balance of numerous good works without undue expense. Mr. J. P. Rawlins, who was stationed for a considerable time in the Hazara District, now in the North-Western Frontier Province, informs me that in that country he has seen numbers of perfect plaster casts, 'for the most part only of heads, of all sizes and descriptions, fastened to the walls in appropriate groupings or singly. Many of them seem to be portraits of living people at the time, full of expression, and with many and varied head-dresses.' My informant believed the practice to have 'come down from Greek times'. The age of the heads actually seen by Mr. Rawlins does not appear, but, whatever it may be, the practice referred to by him proves that the ancient stucco and terra-cotta heads might have been used to fix on walls as well as on clay images. When objects of this class were exhibited before the Asiatic Society of Bengal, Sir J. B. Phear remarked that similar heads from the neighbourhood of Peshawar preserved in the Indian Museum, Calcutta,

> 'obviously had been attached to masonry, and no doubt formed part of a subject worked out in high relief upon the frieze of some building. It was also remarkable that every one of them was unsymmetrical, i.e., compressed or flattened either on the right side or on the left side. The purpose of this must have been to adapt them to being seen with the greater artistic effect from a particular point of view; and it indicated considerable advance in knowledge of the peculiar conditions necessary for the success of sculptural ornament.'[1]

Examples.

The British Museum possesses about forty such detached heads, mostly from the Peshawar District, puchased in 1861, fifteen of which have been published by Dr. Burgess. Two of those are here reproduced (Plate 53A and B). Terra-cotta heads, somewhat similar in character, have been found in excavations at Sahet-Mahet in Oudh, supposed to be the site of Sravasti.[2]

No Greek architecture in India.

No trace of the existence of Greek architecture in either India proper or the borderland has ever been found, that is to say, no building yet examined was designed on a Greek plan, or with an elevation exhibiting one or other of the Greek orders, Doric, Ionic, or Corinthian. But the Indo-Hellenic architects freely used certain debased Greek architectural forms — columns, pilasters, and capitals — for decorative purposes, much in the same way as English architects of a century ago often applied a Greek pediment to the front of an English dwelling-house. The Ionic column has been found in two temples on the site of Taxila, associated in one case with coins of Azes I, who is supposed to have reigned between 90 and 40 B.C.[3] Growse noted the occurrence of a 'niche supported by columns with Ionic capitals' on a fragment of sculpture at Mathura,[4] and Simpson found the plaster fragment of a capital with corner volutes of the Romano-Ionic kind in the Ahinposh *stupa* near Jalalabad in the valley of the Kabul river.[5] More recently two more quasi-Ionic capitals have been discovered, one at Patna and the other at Sarnath, but they are really only variants of the Indian bracket-capital.[6] The Kashmir columns are often denominated 'Doric', but there is no real correspondence.

The abundance of modified Corinthian columns, pilasters, and capitals in the art of Gandhara contrasts strongly with the total lack of Doric and the extreme

[1] *Proc. A. S. B.*, 1870, p. 217.

[2] *J. A. S. B.*, Part I, vol. lxi (1892), extra No., Pl. XXVIII. For other Gandhara stucco heads from Sahri Bahlol see *Ann. Rep. A. S., India*, 1906-7, P. 107, Fig. 2 and Pl. XXXV.

[3] Cunningham, *A. S. Rep.*, vol. ii, p. 129; vol. v, pp. 69, 72, 190; vol. xiv, p. 9, Pl. VII: *Early Hist. of India*, 2nd ed., p. 227.

[4] *Mathura, A. District Memoir*, 3rd ed., p. 171.

[5] *Proc. A. S. B.*, 1879, p. 209, Pl. XI.

[6] *Hist. Ind. and E. Archit.*, 2nd ed. (1910), vol. i, p. 207, note and woodcut.

rarity of Ionic forms. Most of the Gandharan friezes exhibit representations of columns or pilasters with capitals more or less related to those of the Corinthian order, and which may be fairly called Indo-Corinthian. The shafts, whether round or square, are never fluted, and resemble those of the second or third century after Christ at Palmyra and Baalbec. The bases of structural pillars have been found at Jamalgarhi, and show that the shaft might be either cylindrical or square. The conviction of the architects that the form of column used concerned merely the decoration of a façade is well illustrated by the often-published slab from Muhammad Nari, on which Persepolitan columns are mixed up with Indo-Corinthian pilasters (Plate 47A).

Indo-Corinthian decorative forms.

The Indo-Corinthian capitals vary widely in detail, but all may be described as agreeing generally with the luxuriant cosmopolitan style in vogue throughout the Roman Empire during the early centuries of the Christian era. Six good specimens, believed to be from Jamalgarhi, are grouped together in Plate 47B. The introduction of figures of Buddha in two cases may be illustrated from Graeco-Roman art of the time of Augustus, and again, two centuries later, at the Baths of Caracalla. The shell canopy is found in the art of both Alexandria and Asia Minor. Even the modillions of cornices are sometimes made in the form of miniature Corinthian pilasters.[1] All capitals of the Indo-Corinthian class seem to be post-Christian, and their introduction appears to have been associated with the Kushan conquest of Kabul and the Punjab during the first century of the Christian era.

Two classes of figure sculpture.

The figure sculptures, as distinguished from detached heads and from merely decorative motives, may be grouped in two classes, as detached statues or small groups, often completely or nearly completely in the round, and relief pictures illustrating sacred stories in successive scenes. The reliefs, commonly spoken of as 'bas-reliefs', are, as a matter of fact, more often in high relief.

Infinite variety of subjects.

The statues and small groups represent Buddhas, Bodhisattvas, or saints on the way to become Buddhas, besides minor deities of the populous Buddhist pantheon. The stone pictures, like the later painted pictures at Ajanta, deal with the infinite variety of subjects presented by the scriptures, legends, and traditions of the developed system of Buddhism, known as the *Mahayana*, or 'Great Vehicle'. That system practically deified Gautama the Buddha, as well as other Buddhas, and surrounded them with a crowd of attendant deities, including Indra or Sakra, Brahma, and other members of the Brahmanical heavenly host, besides a multitude of attendant sprites, male and female, of diverse kinds and varying rank, in addition to human worshippers.

All the elements making up this motley retinue appear in the reliefs, and offer infinite opportunities for the exercise of fancy by the artists, who did not feel bound by strict rules, such as those of the *Silpa-sastras*. Although the accessible sculptures amount to only a small fraction of those which once existed, or even of those known to exist, they are thousands in number, and so varied in subject and treatment that several bulky volumes would be required for their adequate description and illustration. In this work it is not possible to give more than a small selection, representative so far as practicable.

The Gandhara sculptures suggest problems and speculations of many kinds. Regarded as an authentic expression of an obviously literary religious tradition,

[1] The purely Indian architecture of the earliest cave-temples makes great use of beam-ends, here decorated in the Corinthian manner.

Historical interest of the sculptures.

they control and illustrate the testimony of the Buddhist scriptures, throwing much fresh light upon the beliefs and practices of the early followers of the Great Vehicle. Viewed as a collection of sacred effigies they serve as a guide to the iconography of Buddhism, an aspect of the study specially attractive to Dr. Burgess and M. Foucher, which must be almost ignored in this volume.

Considered as pictures of human life, they present as in a mirror a vivid image of almost every phase of the life of Northern India, lay and clerical, during several centuries. The artists cause to pass before our eyes landscapes, towns, domestic interiors, streets, fields, trees, and animals, with unlimited realistic detail. All the material objects of the civilization of the times — furniture, vehicles, arms, tools, and the rest, are depicted as they were used by the ancients, and numberless illustrations of the manners and customs of the times bring clearly before our imagination the way in which those ancients passed their days. Every class of the population from prince to pariah is represented, and, in short, no subject of human interest was regarded as material unsuitable for the sculptor's chisel.[1]

Development of Buddha type.

Just as the sculptures and paintings of the Catacombs and the writings of the early Christian Fathers prove that no trustworthy tradition concerning the person of Jesus survived in the Church, and that artists for several centuries felt themselves at liberty to give free scope to their fancy in delineating His image, even so, during the first two or three centuries of the Christian era, Buddhist sculptors had not arrived at any settled convention as to the correct way of representing the effigy of Gautama the Buddha, whose real appearance in the flesh had been utterly forgotten. A long course of experiment was needed before Buddhist orthodoxy, guided by the later sculptors of the Gandhara school, settled down to the monotonous and insipid conventionality of the figures of Buddha now manufactured by the thousand, and adopted, with rare exceptions, in all Buddhist lands. Ultimately, the conception of the Indian *yogi* ascetic as worked out in Mathura, Amaravati, and Gandhara became dominant, and passed through Khotan to the Far East.

Buddha with moustaches.

A Buddha with long hair and moustaches, although not unknown even now in Japan, would seem strange and improper to most modern Buddhists. It is, indeed, essentially un-Indian. In Gandhara such a presentation of the Master long continued to be legitimate, and the legend of the cutting of his locks when he dismissed the charioteer, although known, was usually ignored in sculpture.

The Thunderbolt-Bearer.

The remarkable figure, which recurs frequently in variant forms at the Buddha's side, requires explanation. His characteristic attribute is the thunderbolt (Sanskrit *vajra*, Tibetan *dorje*) held in his left hand. The older writers on Buddhism wrongly identified the Thunderbolt-Bearer as Devadatta, the heresiarch enemy of Gautama Buddha; or as Mara, the Buddhist Satan; or as the god Sakra, the Indra of Brahmanical mythology. Dr. Vogel has developed a fourth theory, ingenious but not proved, that he should be regarded as a personification of Dharma, the Law. The best-supported hypothesis is that which treats him as a Yaksha, or attendant sprite, inseparable from the person of the Buddha. Probably the sculptors intended that he should be considered invisible to spectators, in accordance with a well-understood convention. The figure occurs on one relief of the Mathura

[1] This attitude may be criticized on two grounds: firstly, that Gandhara, the birth-place of this hybrid art, is not in India proper; the North-West has always been a land of mixed races and traditions: secondly, the Gandharan artists are inordinately clumsy in portraying many of the most ordinary eastern subjects—their lotuses are often almost unrecognizable, as also are their trees.

A. Head of Bodhisattva.

B. Head of old man.

C. Gautama riding away. Lahore Museum.

D. Worship of *trisula* symbol by monks.

E. Frieze of marine deities. B.M.

(A, B, E, from Burgess, *The Gandhara Sculptures*. D, *by Courtesy of C. Whittingham and Griggs*)

PLATE 53

A. "Bacchus", on left side of Aachen Pulpit.

(From a cast in the University Gallery, Oxford.)

B. "Woman and Tree", as carytid, from Upper Monastery, Nathu. Gandhara.

(*By Courtesy of C. Whittingham and Griggs*)

C. Part of a frieze from Mathura. Kushan Dynasty.

D. Atlantes from Jamalgarhi.

(Photos : Indian Museum, Calcutta)

school, a fragment of a stele found to the south of the city of Mathura (*Catal. Archaeol. Museum, Mathura,* No. H. 5, p. 127).

A seated Buddha in the Berlin Museum (Plate 48B) is one of the finest examples of the early Buddha type, with coiled hair, moustaches, and the robe falling over the feet.

The visit of Indra.

One of the most elaborate and beautiful products of Gandhara art is the relief panel from Loriyan Tangai in Swat (3 feet 10 inches × 2 feet 8 inches), representing the visit of the god Sakra (Indra) to Buddha while seated in a cave near Bodh Gaya (Plate 48A). Here the central figure has a sweet, calm dignity, while the numerous subordinate figures and the scenery are rendered with much grace and beauty. The device of exhibiting wild beasts looking out from their dens as a conventional indication that the scene is laid in a wild mountain country is common in early Indian art, and occurs more than once in sculptures of Gupta age.

The meaning of the composition is explained by Grunwedel:

> 'The Swat sculpture represents the visit of Sakra and his retinue, with the Gandharva harper Panchasika, to the Buddha while he was living in the *Indrasailaguha*, a cave near Bodh-Gaya. The entrance of the cave is surrounded by flames to represent the glory of the Teacher, "resplendent with a halo of many colours, extending to a fathom's length all round his person." Above and below, the birds, beasts, and trees indicate the isolation of the place. Indra appears as a royal personage on the right, doing reverence to the ascetic, with his parasol-bearer close behind, and the Devas [minor deities] of his train beyond on both sides. His peculiar crown or head-dress is very similar to what we find also in the Mathura sculpture. The figure of the Gandharva musician on the other side has been much damaged by the fracture of the stone, but his harp is still visible.'[1]

Sundry Buddhas.

Four various representations of Buddha are shown in Plate 49. In Fig. F the Master is depicted with flames issuing from his head and the water of life from his feet. This represents the fire and water miracle (*Yamaka-Pratiharva*) mentioned in Jataka, No. 483.[2] A remarkable parallel occurs in the Catacombs of Rome, where we find similar representations of the water of life streaming from the feet of Christ.[3] Fig. E shows Buddha seated under a tree. Fig. D is a good specimen of Buddha seated on the 'diamond throne', closely resembling the Berlin figure seated on a 'lion throne' (*ante*, Plate 48B). The remaining figure G is interesting as a distinctly more Indian Buddha type, on a 'lotus throne', and with the soles of the feet turned up in *yogi* fashion. The right shoulder is bared. This represents the latter part of the Great Miracle at Sravasti when the Buddha multiplied his person in the air and was heard preaching on all sides.'[4]

The Emaciated Buddha.

It is impossible to omit notice of the remarkable sculpture, 2 feet 8½ inches high, representing the Emaciated Buddha, or, more accurately, Bodhisattva, in the Lahore Museum, excavated from the ruins of a monastery at Sikri in 1889, which is the most notable known example of the treatment of a repulsive subject. It depicts the Master as he sat at Bodh-Gaya making the vain attempt to attain by the severest austerity that supreme knowledge which did not come to him, according to the story, until he abandoned the practice of self-torture (Plate 48C).[5] The subject is sometimes treated by Chinese and Japanese artists in another fashion,

[1] Grünwedel-Burgess, *Buddhist Art*, p. 142.
[2] Roller, *Les Catacombes de Rome* (1881), vol. ii, p. 291, Pl. LXXXVII, Figs. 2, 3, 4.
[3] See Rhys-Davids, *Buddhist Birth Stories*, p. 105; Spence Hardy, *Manual*, p. 331; Foucher, *Beginnings of Buddhist Art*, p. 153.
[4] The 'Indianized' style of a number of these Great Miracle reliefs and the fact that the subject does not appear in India proper until post-Gupta times, suggests a closer reliance of Gandhara upon India for inspiration than is usually acknowledged.
[5] *Lahore Museum Guide*, Pl. V; Senart, 'Notes d'Epigraphie Indienne,' iii, Pl. II (*Journal As.*, 1890).

as may be seen in the South Kensington Museum and the Musée Guimet. The Brahmanical parallel is Bhringi, an attendant of Siva, who 'was a model ascetic, and fasted so continuously that he became not only emaciated, but a living skeleton. He is so represented in the sculptures of the caves of Elephanta near Bombay.'[1]

Bodhisattvas. We cannot linger over the Buddha figures, or attempt to follow the personal history of Gautama from his conception and infancy to the funeral pyre and the distribution of his relics, as depicted in a long series of reliefs; but must pass on to another class of images, formerly described as 'kings' or 'royal personages', but now recognized as Bodhisattvas, or saints destined to become Buddhas. All considerable collections include specimens, and many have been published.

An image in the Lahore Museum (No. 0239), with finely sculptured drapery, is a beautiful work, and typical of its class (Plate 49C). The small relief on the pedestal follows the tradition of the Early School in the interior by abstaining from all attempt to image the dead Master, his presence being symbolized by the empty seat.

Kuvera. A larger statuette found near Peshawar, and generally regarded as the most striking piece in the large collection of sculptures in the Central Museum, Lahore, represents a royal personage seated in European fashion on a throne, with his left foot on a footstool and his left hand grasping a spear, his attitude being obviously reminiscent of that of the Zeus of Phidias (Plate 50B). This notable figure, at one time believed to be the portrait of an Indo-Scythian monarch, is now recognized as Kuvera or Vaisravana, god of riches and king of the Yakshas, who played a very important part in Indian Buddhism, and will be met with again in medieval times. The image is free from the tinge of effeminacy which mars some of the best finished works of the school, and must always command admiration for its virility and dignity.[2]

Kuvera and Hariti. Excavations at Sahri-Bahlol yielded another figure of the throned Kuvera with the goddess Hariti as his consort seated beside him (Plate 49B), which is one of the most delicately modelled works of the Gandhara school, and is presumably of early date. Hariti, in one of her aspects, was the protector of children from the dangers of epidemics. A standing figure from Sikri (Plate 49A) presents her in the same aspect of her character, but posed in quite another fashion. The clever and unusual treatment of the drapery may be noted.

Pallas Athene. One of the most interesting statuettes is the well-known image of Pallas Athene in the Lahore Museum (Plate 50C). The goddess is represented standing, facing front, wearing Greek costume, chiton and himation, and holding a spear across her body. Both hands have been lost. Probably the right hand grasping the spear was raised to her head, as was the right hand in the Pallas type of the coins of Azes I (? first century B.C.), while the left hand held the aegis. The late Dr. Bloch seems to have been right in interpreting the image as that of a foreign female guard set over the women's apartments of a palace, and forming part of a court scene.[3]

A panel from the Dames collection, now in Berlin (Plate 51E), is an uncommon

[1] Monier Williams, *Religious Thought and Life in India*, p. 441. 'A *muni* or sage—perhaps *Bringi* [sic]—very lean, with a long beard, and an offering in his left hand' (Burgess, *The Rock Temples of Elephanta or Gharapuri*, Bombay (1871), p. 23).

[2] Found at Tahkal on the old road from Peshawar to the Khyber Pass. A cast is in the Indian Section of the Victoria and Albert Museum, South Kensington. *J.A.S.B.*, Part I, vol. lviii (1889), p. 122, Pl. VIII; *Lahore Museum Guide*, Pl. III; Vogel, 'Note sur une Statue du Gandhara conservée au Musée de Lahore' (*B. E. F. E. O.*, Avril-Juin, 1903).

[3] A cast is in the Indian Section of the Victoria and Albert Museum, South Kensington. For the coin of Azes referred to see Gardner, *B. M. Catal.*, *Coins of Greek and Scythic Kings*, Pl. XVIII, 4. The statuette has been published in *J. A. S. B.*, Part I, vol. lviii (1889), p. 121, Pl. VII ; and *Lahore Museum Guide*, Pl. VI. For Bloch's remark see No. 1195 in *Indian Museum List of Negatives*.

A. Atlantes from Jamalgarhi.

B. From Lower Monastery, Nathu, Yusufzai.
(Photos : Indian Museum, Calcutta)

C. Frieze from Upper Monastery, Nathu, Yusufzai.
(By Courtesy of C. Whittingham and Griggs)

D. "Gigantomachia" from Jamalgarhi.

E. Garland from Sarnath.

PLATE 55

A. Door-jamb from Kankali Mound, Mathura.
(From *Jain Stupa of Mathura*)

B. Lotuses growing, Mathura.
(From *Jain Stupa of Mathura*)

C. Vase and plant, from Ghantasala.
(From Rea, *South Indian Buddhist Antiquities*)

PLATE 56

[Kanishka's casket. A.D. 100. Kushan period. (Front and side views).

(*Copyright by Department of Archaeology, Government of India*)

PLATE 57

A. The River-goddess Ganga, Udayagiri, Bhopal. (Early 5th Cent. A.D. Gupta period).
(Photo : Indian Museum, Calcutta)

B. The River-goddess Ganga, Besnagar. (5th Cent. A.D. Gupta period).

C. Varaha, from Udayagiri. Early 5th Cent. A.D. Gupta period.

D. Dwarapala, from Udayagiri. Early 5th Cent. A.D Gupta period.

PLATE 58

variant of the 'Woman and Tree' motive, which will be discussed later. The panel seems to be part of a larger composition, and is apparently of tolerably early date, although the figure is very Indian. Plate 51C, also from the Dames collection, is not equal in merit to the preceding, the drapery being treated in a more formal and commonplace manner. A man stands under a tree playing the *vina*, or lyre which, however, does not correspond to the Indian kind of to-day. These three figures apparently formed parts of a frieze or larger composition. The trees, necessarily treated conventionally in order to bring them within the limits of the panels, have a fine decorative effect.

Panels from Dames's Collection.

One Hellenistic group, known from at least five or six specimens, is of special interest as being demonstrably adapted from a masterpiece of Leochares, a famous Attic artist of the fourth century before Christ (372-330 B.C.). His bronze work, praised by Pliny (*d.* A.D. 79), but long since lost, inspired many later copyists, who translated the theme into marble, with variations. One of the marble copies, or imitations, is in the British Museum, another at Thessalonica, a third at Venice, and the fourth and finest is in the Museo Pio Clementino at the Vatican. The subject is the carrying off of the beautiful boy Ganymede by an eagle, represented sometimes as the messenger of Zeus, and sometimes as the god himself transformed. In the Vatican copy the eagle is shown as supported by the trunk of a tree in the background, with wings expanded and neck stretched upwards, grasping with tender firmness the nude youth, whose feet have just ceased to touch the receding earth. His robe, disclosing the nude figure, is so disposed as to protect his back from injury caused by the bird's talons. A dog, seated below, howls piteously for his vanishing master, as described by Virgil.[1] Nobody can look at Plate 50A, reproducing the best of the Buddhist adaptations, obtained from the monastery at Sanghao in the Yusufzai country, and compare it with the Vatican copy of the Attic artist's composition, without perceiving that the composition is essentially the same as that of Leochares, made familiar to the Hellenistic world in marble replicas. All the Buddhist adaptations omit the dog, and so agree with the groups preserved at Venice, Thessalonica, and in the British Museum, while in the pose of the eagle and the introduction of the trunk of the tree they resemble the Vatican example. The subject, although retaining the essentials of the Greek myth, has been thoroughly Indianized, both in general treatment and by the substitution of a heavily draped female for the nude boy. The notion once held that the woman should be regarded as Maya, the mother of Buddha, is erroneous. The better opinion is that the group was intended to represent to Indian minds the carrying off of a female *Naga*, or snake sprite, by a monstrous *Garuda*, the implacable enemy of the snake tribe. As in all the Gandhara sculptures, the subject is absolutely Indian, no matter how foreign the presentation of it may be in outward form.[2]

Adaptation of the Rape of Ganymede.

Plate 51A is a remarkable panel in the Lahore Museum (*Catal.*, Plate VII, 3), showing two boys of Greek appearance armed with the old Indian broad-sword, as described by Megasthenes and represented in the Bharhut and Sanchi sculptures.

[1] 'Puer . . . quem praepes ab Ida
Sublimem pedibus rapuit Iovis armiger uncis;
Longaevi palmas nequiquam ad sidera tendunt
Custodes, saevitque canum latratus in auras.'
(*Aen.* v. 252-7.)

[2] Full references to the marble groups will be found in *J. A. S. B.*, Part I, vol. lviii (1889), p. 134. The Vatican group is reproduced in Visconti, *Museo Pio-Clementino*, vol. iii, p. 149, in the histories of sculpture by Winckelmann, Lübke, and Perry, and *Encycl. Brit.*, 11th ed. 'Greek Art', Pl. I, Fig. 53.

The work is artistic and attractive, and, as Professor Gardner reminds me, recalls the Pergamene style.

The Nativity. I now proceed to illustrate a few representative relief scenic pictures of high quality, beginning with the Dames specimen of the Nativity, unpublished, and the finest example known to me of that favourite subject (Plate 52B). According to the legend, Gautama Buddha was born in a pure fashion by springing from his mother's side as she stood under a tree in the Lumbini Garden, the modern Rummindei, to the east of Kapilavastu. The composition is arranged in a perfectly symmetrical manner. On the left of the picture the god Indra, or Sakra, with his characteristic high head-dress, receives the child, behind him stands Brahma, and two other unnamed gods complete the divine party. The woman who supports the mother is her sister, and three attendants balance the gods on the other side. The figures are thoroughly naturalistic men and women, cleverly modelled, and ingeniously arranged so as not to interfere one with the other. The draperies are treated with freedom and variety. On the whole, I am disposed to regard this group as the finest of the more complex stone pictures produced by the school of Gandhara.

The 'Great Renunciation'. The story of the 'Great Renunciation' of domestic joys and the splendours of princely life by the young Gautama or Siddhartha when he went forth from his father's palace to take up the career of an ascetic, as told in both the books and the sculptures, comprises many incidents, which were treated in art with much freedom and variety of detail. Here I select for reproduction a rare representation of the groom Chandaka leading out the horse Kanthaka ready saddled for his master's use (Plate 53C). The modelling of the horse is better than that of the animal in Indian sculpture generally, which often fails with the horse, while almost always successful with the elephant. This minor accident is intended to serve as a symbol of the whole story.

Symbol worship. Plate 53D represents the worship, by shaven monks, of the *trisul* symbol, signifying Buddha, the Law, and the Church. It closely resembles the representation of the adoration of the *labarum* in the Catacombs.[1]

Demon hosts. The well-known unique relief representing a group of figures with demoniac faces attended by three soldiers (Plate 52A) has puzzled the interpreters, who usually assume the demons to be a part of the host by which Buddha was assailed in the Temptation. It was Dr. Leinter who remarked that the so-called demons are simply monks wearing masks for a 'devil dance', such as those now worn by Tibetan Lamas. The equipment of the soldiers has been described sometimes as Greek and sometimes as Roman. But it is neither. The men evidently belong to the Himalayan region, and wear the dress and armour used in that region about the time of Kanishka, say A.D. 100. The arrangement of the scales of the armour, probably made of leather, with the curved ends uppermost, is explained by Sir Aurel Stein's discoveries of similar scales at Dandan-Uiliq in Khotan, and by a suit of Tibetan mail preserved in the British Museum. The Khotan scales date from the seventh or eighth century, but there is no difficulty in believing that the fashion of armour may have remained unchanged for ages.[2]

Frieze of marine deities. An imperfect frieze in the British Museum, about 16 inches long by 6½ inches high (Plate 53E), which puzzled Dr. Burgess, has been convincingly interpreted

[1] Roller, *Les Catacombes de Rome*, Pl. LXXXVII.

[2] Stein, *Ancient Khotan*, pp. 252, 411, Pl. II, and Addenda, p. xvi. The stucco relief statue of a warrior in similar scale armour shown in Plate II may be as old as the second or third century, and approximately contemporary with the Gandhara relief.

A. The Mankuwar Buddha. (A.D. 448. Gupta period. Lucknow Museum).

B. Buddha from Mirpur Khas. Stucco. *c.* 500 A.D. Gupta period with some Gandhara influence. Prince of Wales Museum, Bombay.

C. Female head. 5th Cent. A.D. Gupta period.

D. Female head. 5th Cent. A.D. Gupta period. Mathura Museum.

A. Seated Buddha, Sarnath. (5th Cent. A.D. Gupta period. Sarnath Museum).

B. Buddha. Mathura Museum. (5th Cent. A.D. Gupta period).

(Copyright by Department of Archaeology, Government of India)

by M. Foucher as a representation of marine deities in a quasi-Greek fashion. The character of the personages as tritons or marine deities of some kind is established by the paddles which they carry and their kilts of fins cut in the shape of vine-leaves. The object borne in the right hand of the figure the second from the right end appears to be a dolphin, indicating that the holder was intended for Poseidon. The figure on the extreme left is in the familiar pose of Herakles. The Corinthian pillar on the right is in the style of Palmyrene work of the second or third century. The modelling of the forms would deserve praise but for the disfiguring exaggeration of the abdominal muscles. The bearded faces resemble that of an unmistakable triton, also in the British Museum, who has a fin and a curly tail (Foucher, Fig. 123).[1]

Apartness of Gandharan art.

The general impression produced by study of the Gandhara sculptures is that they form a class standing to a considerable extent apart from the main current of the evolution of art within the limits of India. M. Foucher has succeeded, I think, in demonstrating that the Gandhara school has no direct filial relations with the earlier art of Maurya and Sunga times, notwithstanding the appearance in both of certain elements common to the Hellenistic art of Western Asia. The artists of the north-west, who were masters of the technique of Asia Minor, had no need to copy tritons, centaurs, and so forth, from the works of their humbler predecessors in the interior. The true view seems to be that, whatever may be the sources and extent of foreign influence on the work of early Indian sculptors, the rapid development of the Gandhara school during the first century of the Christian era was the direct result of a fresh importation into the frontier regions, by accomplished artists introduced from outside, of Hellenistic ideas expressed in the forms then current throughout the Roman Empire.

Association with the Kushan dynasty.

According to Cunningham such importation of artists and ideas appears to have been closely associated with and dependent on the extension of the foreign Indo-Scythian and Kushan empires, as they gradually advanced their borders from the Oxus to the Ganges, and possibly as far as the Narbada. Unfortunately, as already observed, the chronology of those times is uncertain ; and until the chronological question, summed up as the problem of the date of Kanishka, shall be definitely solved, the exact relations of the art of Gandhara with that of the Graeco-Roman world and India proper cannot be elucidated with all the precision desirable.

It is, however, safe to affirm both that the Kushan kings had become lords of Kabul, with at all events part of the Punjab, before A.D. 100, and that sometime after that date the character of the Gandhara style was fixed. Much of the better sculpture of the Gandhara school undoubtedly was produced during the reigns of the later Kushans. The characteristic of this work is the modified Corinthian capital, similar in style to the capitals fashionable throughout the Roman empire in the early centuries of the Christian era.

Origin of the Gandhara school.

The appearance in sculpture of that specially Graeco-Roman form coincides with the introduction of the Kushan gold coinage, agreeing in weight with the Roman *aureus*, though somewhat debased in standard.[2] All the evidence leads to the inference that the rapid development and extension of the distinct Gandhara school, with its characteristic Indo-Corinthian capitals, were effected under the patronage of the great Kushan kings, who may even have imported foreign artists.

[1] Foucher, *L'Art gréco-bouddhique du Gandhara*, p. 244, Fig. 126.
[2] For details see Cunningham, *Coins of Mediaeval India*, p. 16.

Such foreign artists, accredited by royal authority and the fashion of the court, would have been readily accepted as teachers by the local Indian sculptors, who, after their accustomed manner, would have proceeded to adapt the new methods to their own purposes, sometimes, perhaps, bettering the instructions of their masters.[1]

Parallel case of Indo-Persian painting.

The popularization of the Persian style of painting in India under Akbar in the sixteenth century, and the immediate development of a prolific Indo-Persian school, surpassing its prototype in certain respects, while inferior in others, offer an almost exact parallel to the events which happened, as I believe, in the kingdom of Gandhara during the first century of the Christian era. The parallel fails in so far that the Persian style of painting, being congenial to Indian taste, readily admitted of certain modifications which may be reasonably regarded as improvements, whereas the ultimate models of the Gandhara sculptors having been the masterpieces of Attic and Ionic art, alien in spirit to the art of India, were usually susceptible of modification by Indian craftsmen only in the direction of degradation.

Indianization as a test of age.

It is obvious that the foreign elements in the art of Gandhara tended to diminish as time went on, and that, generally speaking, the sculptures with most clearly marked Greek character should be considered early, and those most Indianized as comparatively late. But, as already pointed out, this criterion affords no infallible test of age. Some of the best finished works in Hellenistic style may have been executed by clever Indian imitators long after the introduction of the style, just as among the Mughal paintings we find close imitations of Persian models side by side and contemporary with paintings profoundly Indianized.

Decadence or improvement?

Many European critics, convinced of the unapproachable excellence of the highest type of Greek art, the model of the less excellent Hellenistic art, see in the process of Indianization a decadence. But the critics of the 'nationalist' school are persuaded that this view is erroneous, and that the process of Indianization is in itself an artistic improvement. Mr. Havell, in general agreement with Dr. Coomaraswamy, teaches that the earliest Gandhara sculptors were no better than mechanical craftsmen, hirelings following more or less impure Hellenistic traditions, engaged by the frontier kings in the manufacture of inferior objects of handicraft, which are mere 'soulless puppets, debased types of the Greek and Roman pantheon posing uncomfortably in the attitudes of Indian asceticism', and tarred with the vices of commercialism, insincerity, and want of spirituality, most conspicuous in the earliest examples. The indictment continues:

'The insincerity and want of spirituality typical of nearly all the art of Gandhara are, as I have said, most conspicuous in the earliest examples, or those which are attributed to the first century of our era, when the Roman influence was strongest. Two centuries later, in the sculptures of the Loriyan Tangai Monastery, which Professor Grünwedel describes as belonging to the best period of Gandhara,[2] the art has become more Indian, more national, and more spiritual, but it has not yet achieved the true ideal of Indian art. Since, however, it is Indian influence, Indian thought, which has so far perfected the style, it is surely incorrect to say that the ideal of Indian Buddhist art has been created by foreigners. Foreign hands may have held the tools, but the influences which have dominated the art have been throughout Indian. . . .The perfected ideal of Indian art is as far in advance of the Gandharan type as the art of the Parthenon surpasses the art of Gandhara. Neither artistically nor technically is it possible to place the best Gandharan sculpture in the same plane with that of Borobodur, Elephanta, or Ellora, or even with the best modern Nepalese metal-work, such as the Buddha in Plate VI.'[3]

[1] This explanation of the rise of Gandhara art does not take into consideration the part played by Parthian and Sassanian Persia, intervening between East and West.

[2] Now in the Indian Museum, Calcutta. See Plate 48 A.

[3] *Indian Sculpture and Painting*, pp. 45-50.

The critic then proceeds to liken Gandharan art to 'cheap, modern Italian plaster work', and to extol the later medieval sculpture and bronzes as exhibiting 'quiet restrained dignity, calm conviction, and effacement of physical detail... the embodiment of a great national tradition, a synthesis of Eastern philosophy and religious art'. We are further told that the Brahmanical art of the eighth and ninth centuries expresses 'the true Indian conception of divinity in a superhuman, spiritualized body', or, as elsewhere phrased, 'the idea of a purified, transcendental body formed by the practice of *Dhyana* [meditation] and *Yoga* [ascetic restraint]'. So Dr. Coomaraswamy declares that

Alleged faults.

'just as through all Indian schools of thought there runs like a golden thread the fundamental idealism of the *Upanishads*—the *Vedanta*—so in all Indian art there is a unity that underlies all its bewildering variety. This unifying principle is here also Idealism, and this must of necessity have been so, for the synthesis of Indian thought is one, not many'.[1]

The spirit of early Buddhist art.

The substance of these criticisms seems to mean that all high-class Indian sculpture must be an expression of Brahmanical metaphysics, nothing else being truly Indian or national. But the Gandhara artists, who certainly did not worry about a 'superhuman, transcendental body', or take any interest in the Upanishads, agreed in those respects with the artists of all the early Buddhist schools, who were, nevertheless, just as Indian and national as any ninth-century Brahman could be. Although the technique of Gandhara differed widely from that of Bharhut, Sanchi, and the rest, all the early Buddhist schools alike, that of Gandhara included, were animated by the Buddhist kindly humanistic spirit, as different as possible from the *Tantric* notions dominating medieval art, both Brahmanical and Buddhist, but equally Indian. We are not entitled to denounce Gandharan art as 'lacking in spirituality', and so forth, merely because it does not express the ideas of Ellora and Elephanta. As a matter of fact, many of the good Gandhara sculptures may be fairly held to express with admirable feeling and sincerity the ideal of a saintly Indian man, and to be not lacking in 'restrained dignity'. For instance, the beautiful Bodhisattva (Plate 49C) is very far from being a 'soulless puppet'; the Lahore Museum Kuvera (Plate 50B) has a good share of 'restrained dignity'; and many of the Buddhas are quite equal to any of the Javanese or Ceylonese images. Much credit is given by the new school of critics to the achievements of medieval sculptors in the representation of gesture and strenuous action; but, without depreciating their work, it is permissible to insist on the similar merits of the Gandharan heads and Atlantes.

Restricted influence of Gandharan art in India.

Political conditions seem to have been responsible to a great extent for the failure of the art of the north-western frontier to penetrate deeply into the interior. The Kushan empire apparently broke up in the time of Vasudeva I, the successor of Huvishka, and was followed probably by a time of unrecorded anarchy. The next empire, that of the Guptas, who completed the conquest of the Gangetic valley about the middle of the fourth century, did not include the Punjab, and so was separated from Gandhara by foreign territory.

Gandhara the parent of Buddhist art in the Far East.

But outside India the Gandhara school achieved a grand success by becoming the parent of the Buddhist art of Eastern or Chinese Turkistan, Mongolia, China, Korea, and Japan. The stages of the transmission of the style to the Far East have been clearly disclosed by the abundant discoveries of sculptures and paintings in the manner of Gandhara throughout Chinese Turkistan, both to the north

[1] *The Aims of Indian Art* (Essex House Press), 1908.

and south of the Taklamakan (Gobi) Desert. Through China the imported forms of Buddhist art passed to Korea, and thence to Japan. Pious pilgrims, like Fa-hian and Hiuen Tsiang, played a large part in determining the course of Buddhist art in China by bringing back from the Indian Holy Land multitudes of images and pictures which became the authoritative models for Chinese monastic artists. The Indian influence, it must be clearly understood, affected the art of China and Japan only in its application to Buddhist uses. In other departments Chinese art, and its daughter in Japan, developed independently of Indian teaching.

The pursuit of the eastern ramifications of Indian Buddhist art lies beyond the scope of this work, but a slight sketch in outline of the process by which the Gandhara style became the basis of the art devoted to the service of Buddhism in the Far East is an almost indispensable supplement to an account of the Gandhara school, and may be presented in few words.

The progress of Indian Buddhist art eastwards.

Communications between China and the western countries were first opened up during the time of the Early Han Dynasty (226 B.C. to A.D. 25)[1] by means of the mission of Chang-Kien, who was sent as envoy to the Oxus region, and died about 114 B.C. That mission resulted in the establishment of regular intercourse between China and the Scythian powers, but did not involve contact with India. In the year A.D. 8 the official relations of the Chinese government with the western states came to an end, and when the first Han dynasty ceased to exist in A.D. 25 Chinese influence in those countries had vanished. But in A.D. 73 a great general named Pan-chao reduced the King of Khotan to subjection, and from that date continued his victorious career until his death in A.D. 102, when the power of China attained its greatest western extension. In the last decade of the first century Pan-chao inflicted a severe defeat on the Kushan king of Kabul somewhere beyond the Pamirs in the Yarkand or Kashgar country. Most probably that king was Kanishka. After Pan-chao's death the Kushan king retrieved his defeat and occupied Khotan, at some time between A.D. 102 and 123. To that Indo-Scythian conquest of Khotan I would attribute the rapid spread of Indian languages, scripts, religion, and art in Chinese Turkistan, as disclosed by the discoveries of recent years. Kanishka's defeat of the Chinese and conquest of Khotan afford an adequate explanation of the archaeological facts.[2] Probably the Indo-Scythian occupation of Khotan did not last very long, but no documentary evidence on the subject has yet been discovered. During the third century Buddhism effected considerable progress in China, and from the beginning of the fifth century to the eighth a constant stream of learned pilgrims devoted themselves to the task of saturating Chinese Buddhism with Indian ideas and Indian art. Early in the seventh century Bajna and his son, Wei-tschü I-song, distinguished painters from Khotan, visited the Chinese court, and founded an Indo-Chinese school of painting. China transmitted the Indian forms of Buddhist art to Korea, whence they passed to Japan. That is the outline of the facts.[3] During all the centuries mentioned there is no indication of a reflex action of Chinese on Indian art, the supposed Chinese influence on the Ajanta paintings a little before or after A.D. 600 being very doubtful.

[1] Chinese dynastic dates are given according to Tchang, le Père Mathias—*Synchronismes chinois* (Chang-hai, 1905).

[2] See *Ox. Hist. Ind.*, p. 128 for V. Smith's theory on this point.

[3] Hirth, F., *Ueber fremde Einflüsse in der chinesischen Kunst* (München und Leipzig, 1896), p. 83. For art of Gandhara style in Turkistan, see Stein's works, and the German publications giving the results of the first German expedition to Turfan, as enumerated by Dr. v. Le Coq in *J. R. A. S.*, 1909, p. 301.

A. Buddha from Sarnath. 5th Cent. A.D. Gupta period. National Museum, New Delhi.

B. Sultanganj Buddha, copper-casting now in the Birmingham Museum. (Colossal image. 6th Cent. A.D. Gupta period. The theory that this image is of the Pala period, 8th-9th Cent., is not acceptable).

PLATE 61

A, B. Sculptured door-jambs, Garwha. (5th Cent. A.D. Gupta period).

(Photos : Indian Museum, Calcutta)

E. Female head. 5th Cent. **A.D. Gupta** period. Mathura **Museum.**

C. Female image, stucco. Rajgir. (A nagini. 6th Cent. A.D. Gupta period. Now crumbled).

D. Female figure playing lyre. Terracotta from **Rupar.** 5th Cent. A.D. Gupta period.

The fact that the prevalent existing forms of Buddhist art in the Far East originated in Gandhara has been fully proved in detail by Professor Grünwedel and other authors, whose finding on that point is generally accepted.

Part II. THE EXTENT OF THE FOREIGN INFLUENCES

The isolation of India, so apparent on the map, has never been absolute. Her inhabitants from the most remote ages have always been exposed to the action of foreign ideas conveyed by one or all of three ways — by sea, through the passes of the north-eastern frontier, or through the more open passes of the north-west. The only foreign art which could influence India from the north-east being that of China, which certainly produced no considerable effect on Indian art prior to the Muhammadan conquest, the ingress of foreign artistic ideas through the north-eastern passes may be left out of account.

The channels of foreign influence.

Long before the dawn of history traders from distant lands had brought their wares to the ports of India, and in all probability introduced the alphabet and art of writing. But in those ancient days the sea, although open to the passage of adventurous merchants, was not the bond of union between distant lands which it has become in these latter times for a great naval power, and the influence exercised upon the art of the interior by small bodies of traders at the ports must have been comparatively trifling. The constant invasions and immigrations from the continent of Asia through the north-western passes had more effect;[1] and one prehistoric immigration, or series of immigrations, which brought the Vedic Aryans, ultimately settled the future of all India for all time by laying the foundations of the complex, exclusive, religious, and social system known as Hinduism. When history opens in the sixth century B.C., Northern India, at all events, was already largely Hinduized, and in the third century, when the earliest extant monuments came into existence, the Hindu system stood firmly established. In attempting to estimate the nature and extent of foreign influence on Indian art, as conveyed by sea and through the north-western passes, we must assume the existence of Hinduism as an accomplished fact, and acknowledge that nothing positive is known about Hindu art before the age of Asoka.

In his days the dominant foreign influence may be designated Persian, traceable clearly in his monolithic columns, in the pillars of structural buildings, and in architectural decoration. Capitals, crowned by *recumbent* bulls or other animals, are found at Bharhut, Sanchi and elsewhere, in the Gandhara reliefs, and at Eran in Central India, even as late as the fifth century of the Christian era, but these do not very exactly correspond with the true Achaemenian type. The capitals of the monolithic columns, likewise with their seated and standing animals, although distinctly reminiscent of Persia, differ widely from Persian models, and are artistically far superior to anything produced in Achaemenian times. Sir John Marshall, as already observed, can hardly be right in ascribing the beautiful design and execution of the Sarnath capital (*ante*, Plate 4) and its fellows to Asiatic Greeks in the service of Asoka.[2]

Early Persian influence.

We are thus led to consider the second foreign element in the most ancient

[1] Suggested indications of Babylonian influence include the earliest Indian astronomy, the knowledge of iron, urn-burial, and the marriage-mart at Taxila. See Kennedy, 'The Early Commerce of India with Babylon' (*J. R. A. S.*, 1898, pp. 241-88). This view does not accord with the ethnological facts. Any 'Babylonian' influence that left its mark on the land and its people must have been pre-Sumerian.

[2] See *J. R. A. S.*, 1907, p. 997, Pl. III ; ibid., 1908, p. 1092, Pl. IV, 6.

The Hellenistic element.

schools of Indian art, that is to say, the Greek element, expressed in Asiatic Hellenistic forms. In Asoka's age the chief schools of Greek sculpture were in Asia Minor at Pergamum, Ephesus, and other places, not in Greece, and the Hellenistic forms of Greek art had become largely modified by Asiatic and African traditions, reaching back to the ancient days of Assyria and Egypt. It is consequently difficult to disentangle the distinctively Greek element in early Indian art. The acanthus leaves, palmettos, centaurs, tritons, and the rest, all common factors in Hellenistic art, are as much Asiatic as Greek. The art of the Asokan monoliths is essentially foreign, with nothing Indian except details, and the fundamentally alien character of its style is proved by the feebleness of later attempts to copy it. I think that the brilliant work typified by the Sarnath capital may have been designed in its main lines by foreign artists acting under the orders of Asoka, while all the details were left to the taste of the Indian workmen, much in the same way as long afterwards the Kutb Minar was designed by a Muhammadan architect and built by Hindu masons, under the orders of the Sultan Altamsh.[1]

Post-Asokan art, essentially Indian.

Our knowledge of the fine art of Asoka's reign (273-232 B.C.) is restricted to the monolithic columns almost exclusively. The other sculptures of the Early Period probably are all, or nearly all, of later date. They present a great contrast, being essentially Indian, with nothing foreign except details, and they presuppose the existence of a long previous evolution of native art probably embodied in impermanent materials, and consequently not represented by actual remains.

Are we to regard these sculptures, and especially the reliefs of Bharhut, Sanchi, and Bodh Gaya, as purely Indian in origin and inspiration, or as clever adaptations of foreign models? The sudden apparition simultaneously of stone architecture, stone sculpture, and stone inscriptions during the reign of Asoka, when considered in connexion with the intimate relations known to have existed between the Maurya empire and the Hellenistic kingdoms of Asia, Africa, and Europe, raises a reasonable presumption that the novelties thus introduced into the ancient framework of Indian civilization must have been suggested from outside. That presumption is strengthened by the foreign style of the monolithic columns, which undoubtedly were a novelty brought into being by the command of an enlightened despot in close touch with the outer world. It must be remembered, however, that Early Indian architecture was essentially wooden. No sudden transition can be traced dating from Asoka's age. The small, square Gupta shrines are the earliest stone structures in India proper.

Probable Alexandrian suggestion of stone bas-reliefs.

Although I do not now feel justified in expressing as confidently as I once did my theory of the Alexandrian origin of Indian bas-relief sculpture *in stone*, I am still disposed to believe that such reliefs would never have been executed if works essentially similar had not previously existed in the Hellenistic countries, and especially at Alexandria.[2] The Indian reliefs certainly are not modelled on those of Persia, which are utterly distinct in character; and it seems unlikely that the Indians should have suddenly invented the full-blown art of stone bas-relief out of their own heads without any foreign suggestion. The Alexandrian reliefs were available as indications how stone reliefs should be executed, and the clever

[1] M. Foucher, writing of the Sanchi reliefs, observes that 'quantité de motifs decoratifs nous ont paru si directement empruntés à la Perse que leur importation ne s'explique guère autrement que par une immigration d'artisans iraniens'. (*La Porte Orientale du Stupa de Sânchi*, p. 34.)

[2] *Imp. Gaz.* (1908), vol. ii, p. 105; Hastings, *Encycl. of Religion and Ethics*, s.v. 'Amaravati'.

A. Temple at Sanchi. Early Gupta style. 5th Cent. A.D.

B. Temple at Deogarh. 6th Cent. A.D. Gupta period.

A. Siva as an ascetic (*mahayogi*), Deogarh. (Nar-Narayan. 6th Cent. A.D. Gupta period).

B. Vishnu on Ananta, Deogarh. (6th Cent. A.D. Gupta period).

PLATE 64

A. The Buddha with Bodhisattvas, Bagh Caves. *c.* 500 A.D. Gupta period.
(Copyright by Department of Archaeology, Government of India)

B. Ekmukha Linga, from Khoh. 6th Cent. A.D. Gupta period. Allahabad Museum

C. Female figure, from Bhumara. 6th Cent. A.D. Gupta period. Allahabad Museum.

A. Buddha from Kanheri Caves. 6th Cent. A.D. Deccan Gupta period. Influence possibly from Sarnath School.

B. Buddha from Ajanta Caves. 6th Cent. A.D. Deccan Gupta period. (Photo : A. L. Syed)

PLATE 66

Indian artists and craftsmen, once they had seized on the main idea, would have had no difficulty in transmuting it into purely Indian forms, just as the Hindu play-writer, mentioned by Weber, transformed the *Midsummer Night's Dream* into a piece thoroughly Indian in character, showing no trace of its English source.[1] Complicated relief pictures, like those of Bharhut and Sanchi, placed in exposed positions, could not have been satisfactorily executed in wood or ivory; but the trained wood and ivory carvers, who existed in India from time immemorial, could easily have applied their skill to making stone pictures as soon as the novel material had become the fashion. Carvers in wood and stone often are the same people and use tools substantially identical. The truth seems to be that the Indians illustrated the Jatakas with Indian scenes just as the Alexandrians illustrated pastoral poems with Greek scenes, and that the Indians got from abroad the idea of so doing. But the theory must be admitted to be incapable of decisive proof, although to my mind it appears to be highly probable. The subject-matter and treatment of the post-Asokan reliefs are certainly on the whole Indian, and such obviously foreign details as they exhibit are accessory rather than integral.

Indirect evidence of Greek influence.

M. Foucher, however, may be right when he discerns in the Sanchi sculptures more subtle indications of Hellenistic influence in certain examples of bold foreshortening, in clever presentations of the three-quarter face figure, and in the harmonious balancing of groups. It is, indeed, inconceivable that the Indian sculptors of Asoka's time should have failed to learn something from the Greek art if it was accessible to them. The exact channel of this foreign influence is not historically or geographically clear. And its extent is debatable if it existed at all. A great deal must be allowed for natural, purely native development, when discussing such improvement of skill as is visible in the East and West gates of Sanchi when compared with the North and South. But whatever was borrowed the Indian craftsmen made their own, so that their work as a whole is unmistakably Indian in character and original in substance.

I proceed to discuss in some detail certain motives of ancient Indian sculpture which seem to be of foreign origin, and in some cases lend support to the theory of specially Alexandrian influence.

The 'Woman and Tree' motive in sculpture.

The first to be considered is that which may be conveniently designated the 'Woman and Tree' (Plate 54B). The form which may be regarded as normal represents a woman standing under a vine or other tree, with her legs crossed, the left arm twined round a stem, and the right hand raised to her head. Many variations, however, occur. Occasionally, the left hand is raised above the head, as in an example from Mathura, in which also the right arm is not twined round a stem. Sometimes the legs are not crossed. The woman, in some cases, is more or less clothed, but frequently, and especially at Mathura, is unmistakably and aggressively naked. Very often, but not always, she stands on a dwarf, animal, or monster (Plate 32C).

The attitude is well calculated to display the charms of the female form, and, as M. Foucher observes, is frequently described in Sanskrit poetry, so that it may be regarded as 'la pose plastique par excellence' of India.[2] The dates of

[1] *Ind. Ant.*, vol. xxx (1901), p. 287, note 59, Weber relates a similar transformation in a Sanskrit adaptation of Euclid's *Elements*. 'All that remained of the original was the order of the contents and the substance of the examples. All the rest was Indian.' The Japanese treat European plays and tales in the same way.

[2] *L'Art gréco-bouddhique du Gandhara*, p. 229. A sculpture in the Mathura Museum exhibits a male figure in the same pose.

Sanskrit literature are so uncertain that it is quite possible that the descriptions may have been suggested by the statuary. It seems to me highly probable that the plastic rendering was a foreign introduction. Dates seem to forbid the suggestion that Western art might have borrowed it from India.

The motive in India.

The earliest Indian example known to me is the Bharhut draped figure of the Yakshi Chanda, who is represented in what I call the normal manner. That may be dated about 200 B.C.[1] The pose is in exact keeping with her character as a primitive godling. The lady also appears on the Sanchi gateways, and in Gandharan art over and over again with many variations. I cannot find her at Amaravati, but at Mathura she is specially characteristic of the local art, both Jain and Buddhist, and is often represented with lascivious suggestiveness in a manner to which the Mathura school was too much inclined. Slightly modified she becomes Maya, the mother of Buddha, in the Nativity scene (Plate 52B). The latest example that I can quote is a Brahmanical sculpture of the period at Vijayanagar Tadpatri (Plate 134B) in the Anantapur District, dating from the sixteenth century. Thus, it is established that in Indian sculpture the motive had an history of more than 1,700 years.

The motive in Greek art.

In Greek art it occurs in the fourth century B.C., a century or two before its first appearance in India at Bharhut. The Hellenistic artists transported the motive to Egypt, where, by reason of contact with native Egyptian sensual notions, its treatment acquired a lascivious tinge, agreeing strangely with the Mathura presentation, the nude figure, however, in Egypt being often male instead of female. M. Strzygowski gives the name of Copto-Alexandrian to the mixed or mongrel art produced by the intermingling of Hellenic and Coptic ideas. The art of Gandhara does not share with that of Mathura the reproach of lasciviousness. It deserves credit, as M. Foucher points out, for its 'irréprochable tenue' in dealing with the relations of the sexes.[2]

The Aachen 'Bacchus'.

The most striking illustration of the close resemblance between the Mathura presentation of the Woman and Tree motive and the Copto-Alexandrian form is found in an unexpected place, the cathedral of Aachen or Aix-la-Chapelle in Rhenish Prussia. Six remarkable ivory panels on the sides of the cathedral pulpit have been examined in a special disquisition by M. Strzygowski, who has proved to my satisfaction that the Aachen ivories are of Egyptian origin, and should be considered as examples of the Copto-Alexandrian school. They may have reached their resting-place by way of either Ravenna and Milan or Marseilles.[3]

Two figures, one on the right and one on the left of the pulpit, identical save in certain minor details, are known conventionally as 'Bacchus'. Each represents a nude young man facing, standing with the right leg straight and the left leg crossed over it. The body is supported by the left arm, which is twined round the stem of a vine overtopping and surrounding the youth with its foliage. His right hand is raised to the crown of his head (Plate 54A). The pose is precisely the same as that of the Woman and Tree motive in Indian art, and the resemblance between the Mathura and Aachen figures is so close that, in my judgement, it cannot be accidental. Both must have a common origin, which should be sought in Syria or Asia Minor, from which Egyptian Hellenistic art drew its inspiration.

[1] *Stupa of Bharhut*, Pl. XXII : Grünwedel-Burgess, *Buddhist Art*, Fig. 16.

[2] *L'Art gréco-bouddhique du Gandhara*, p. 248. The 'orgy' relief (ibid., Fig. 130 : *Gandhara Sculptures*, Pl. XXII. 7) is the only one open to a charge of impudicity.

[3] Strzygowski, J., 'Hellenistische und koptische Kunst in Alexandria' (*Bull. de la Soc. Archéol. d'Alexandrie* (Wien, Vienne), 1902).

A. Couple from Ajanta Caves. 6th. Cent. A.D. Deccan Gupta period.

(Photo : Vasudeo Muljimal)

B. Nagaraja and consort from Ajanta Caves. 6th cent. A.D. Deccan Gupta period.

(Photo : A. L. Syed)

PLATE 67

A. Flying couple, from Ajanta. 6th Cent. A.D. Deccan Gupta period.

B. Seated Buddha, from Ajanta. 6th Cent. A.D. Deccan Gupta period.

(Photos : **A. L. Syed**)

PLATE 68

The motive was variously treated in Egypt, and, at least in one case, a woman takes the place of the youth. There is no difficulty in believing in the transference of Alexandrian ideas to India either before or after the Christian era. From Asoka's time for several centuries intercourse between the ports of Egypt and India was continuous. The cupids, birds, and beasts interspersed in the foliage of the Aachen ivory are also often found in India. Compare, for instance, the Garhwa pillar (Plate 62A) and various Mathura sculptures.

The woman not a 'dancing-girl'.

The female figure in the Woman and Tree design used to be described as a 'dancing-girl'. But, whether nude or clothed, she is never represented as dancing, and Dr. Vogel certainly appears to be right in maintaining that she should be interpreted, not as a dancing-girl, but as a *Yakshi*, or female sprite.[1] The *Yakshas* and *Yakshis* played in ancient popular Indian Buddhism a prominent part comparable with that played by the *Nats* in modern Burmese Buddhism.

The Rider motive.

Other motives must be discussed more briefly. At Amaravati and in Gandhara a favourite subject is the departure of Gautama Buddha as Prince Siddhartha from Kapilavastu on horseback. Generally the horse is shown in profile, but occasionally is represented as emerging from a gateway, and facing the spectator, fore-shortened. This latter form of the design especially seems to be connected with the Rider motive as seen in the Barberini ivory diptych in the Louvre, of the fourth century, and in one of the Aachen panels, the origin of both being traced back by Strzygowski to the Egyptian representations of Horus triumphing over the powers of evil represented by a crocodile.

The earth-spirits.

The Indian sculptures usually show earth-spirits, or *Yakshas*, male or female, holding up the horse's hoofs. As Grünwedel and Strzygowski point out, the sculptures illustrate the Buddhist legend that the earth-goddess displayed half her form while she spoke to the departing hero, and also are a reminiscence or translation of the Greek motive of Gaia rising from the ground, familiar to Hellenic art from the fourth century B.C. Similar earth-spirits are seen in the Barberini diptych.[2] The Rider motive is used on the uprights of the Sanchi gateways, and there is a large Kushan Horse and Rider in the Mathura Museum.

Undulating garland or roll.

The use of a long undulating stem, band, garland, or roll to break up a long frieze into sections was familiar to Indian sculptors from early days. As seen on the Bharhut coping, the device used is a lotus stem with jack fruits attached. The stem is not carried by anybody. This design seems to be purely Indian.

But the later forms of the motive must be compared to the garland carried by *amorini*, *Erotes*, or cupids, which was constantly used in the later Hellenistic and Graeco-Roman art. In Gandhara an imbricated roll, quite in the Graeco-Roman fashion, carried by boys, equivalent to cupids or *Erotes* is substituted for the Indian lotus stem. At Mathura and Sarnath we find a smooth roll carried by men, not boys (Plate 54C), and at Amaravati a bulky tinsel roll with Indian decoration, also carried by men (Plate 41B).[3]

Pergamene influence.

The hippocamps, tritons, centaurs, and other weird creatures, which certainly were borrowed from Western art, occur, as we have seen in Chapter II, at Bodh Gaya and other places in the sculptures of the Early Period. It does not much matter whether we call them Hellenistic or Western Asiatic. Forms more or less

[1] *Ann. Rep. A. S. India*, 1906-7, p. 146.

[2] Grünwedel-Burgess, pp. 98-103, Figs. 50-4. See also *The Gandhara Sculptures*, Pl. XX, Fig. 1=*J. I. A. I.*, vol. viii (1898), Pl. XXII, Fig. 1, where the spirits are female.

[3] Anderson, *Catal. I. M.*, Part I, p. 241; Grünwedel-Burgess, p. 148, Figs. 99, 100; Foucher, *L'Art gréco-bouddhique du Gandhara*, p. 239, Figs. 116-18 ; *J. A. S. B.* Part I, vol. lviii (1889), p. 158, citing a Roman parallel.

similar recur at Mathura and Amaravati and in Gandhara. The strongly-marked muscles of some of the Gandhara figures and the snake-tailed monsters suggest the notion that the sculptors of the north-west felt the influence of the vigorous Pergamene school. The *Atlantes* of Jamalgarhi (Plates 54D and 55A) especially seem to be reminiscent of Pergamum; from the Buddhist point of view they may be regarded as *Yakshas.* A few of these Western Asiatic Hellenistic forms are shown together in Plate 55. *Atlantes* occur in later Hindu art in the form of dwarfs, usually four-armed.

Some architectural details.

Certain architectural details represented in ancient sculptures, in addition to the well-known Corinthian and Ionic capitals, may be mentioned as being common to Indian and Western Asiatic Hellenistic art. The fluted spiral column, frequently met with on the sarcophagi of Asia Minor and in later Roman work, does not seem to occur at Amaravati or in Gandhara, but is found at Mathura in sculptures which are difficult to date, but which seem to be post-Kushan.[1] Subsequently it was freely used in the cave-temples of Western India. The scallop shell of 'shell-niche' canopy, often seen on Asiatic sarcophagi and in Egyptian art, occurs in India, so far as I am aware, only in the details of the Corinthian capitals at Jamalgarhi. M. Strzygowski holds that the form probably originated in Mesopotamia, and that it was ultimately developed into the characteristic Muhammadan *mihrab.*[2] But that suggestion seems to be of doubtful validity. The rectangular incised panel frequently found on pilasters in Gandhara reliefs is specially characteristic of the Roman architecture of Palmyra (A.D. 105-273).[3] Much of the Gandhara art resembles that of Palmyra and Baalbec more closely than that of any other specific locality. The buildings at Baalbec date from the second century. It is, of course, unnecessary to point out in detail the numerous echoes of Greek art in the Gandhara sculptures. I have confined myself to noticing certain points of particular interest.

The vine

The introduction of the vine into Indian bas-reliefs used to be considered as in itself evidence of copying from Hellenistic models. But that view is not tenable. The vine is still largely grown in India proper, and until the recent Afghan conquest was freely cultivated in Kafiristan. Sir George Watt believes that the plant is indigenous on the lower Himalayan ranges, and is even inclined to think that its cultivation may have been diffused into Europe from that region. However that may be, it is certain that Indian artists had ample opportunities of studying the forms of vine-growth at first hand, and were under no necessity to seek foreign models.

Different style of treatment.

In certain cases, however, Indian sculptors chose to treat the vine motive after the European or West Asiatic manner.[4] The best example of such treatment is the well-known frieze from the Upper Monastery at Nathu, Yusufzai, which is almost a replica of a similar work at Palmyra, executed in the third century after Christ (Wood, *Palmyra*, Plate 41). The design (Plate 55C) consists of a vine stem knotted into five circles forming small panels, the first of which, to the left, contains leaves only; the second is occupied by a boy or 'genius' plucking grapes; the third exhibits a boy playing with a goat; the fourth displays a crudely executed goat nibbling the vine; and the fifth represents another boy plucking grapes. Plate 56A reproduces a Mathura sculpture treating the vine after the Indian manner, and admirably executed.

[1] *Jain Stupa of Mathura*, Pl. XLVIII, 3.
[2] *J. Hellenic Studies.* 1907, p. 114, Fig. 11.
[3] In Gandhara this 'panel' is a misunderstood conventional rendering of the octagonal railing-pillar. Codrington, *Ancient India*, Fig. 22.
[4] Letter dated 6 Nov. 1909.

The motive consisting of a vine or other conventionalized plant springing from a vase is common to Egyptian and ancient Indian art. M. Strzygowski gives three Egyptian examples in the essay cited above. The motive is found everywhere at Bharhut, Sanchi, and Amaravati, and is the basis of the later vase-and-foliage capital. Plant forms.

The Indian treatment of indigenous animals in both sculpture and painting is as original and artistic as that of plant motives. Animal motives.

'You have only', Sir George Watt writes, 'to look at the plants and animals employed in the most ancient designs to feel the strong Indian current of thought there conventionalized, which must have involved centuries of evolution. The treatment of the elephant, monkey, and serpent is Indian, and in no way Greek. No Greeks (as few Englishmen to-day) could give the life touches of those animals seen on all the oldest sculptures and frescoes.[1]

Those observations are perfectly true, and in all discussions of the foreign elements in Indian art we must remember that in certain respects Indian artists were not only free from obligation to the Greeks, but actually superior to them. The illustrations in this work bear abundant testimony to the Indian power of delineating indigenous living forms, both vegetable and animal. The Gandhara treatment of the elephants is inferior to that of the same subject by the artists of the interior, who were more familiar with that wonderful beast, which is not easy to model or draw well.

The general result of examination of the foreign influences upon Indian pre-Muhammadan art, whether sculpture, painting, or architecture, is to support the opinions of those who maintain the substantial originality of Indian art. It may be true that the general use of stone for architecture and sculpture was suggested by foreign example, and that the notion of making story-telling pictures in stone came from Alexandria; but, even if both those hypotheses be accepted, the substantial originality of the Indian works is not materially affected. The principal forms of Indian architecture, so far as appears, were developed in India, and it is impossible to connect them with Western forms. They have, as M. Le Bon observes, a character of 'frappante originalite'. The actually proved borrowings by India are confined to details, such as Persepolitan columns and capitals, and a multitude of decorative elements, some of which continued in use for many centuries. Substantial originality of Indian art.

M. Le Bon is well supported by facts in his opinion that India, Incompatibility of Indian and Greek ideals.

'malgre un contact assez prolongé avec la civilisation grecque, ne lui a emprunté, et ne pouvait lui emprunter aucun de ses arts. Les deux races étaient trop differéntes, leurs pensées trop dissemblables, leurs génies artistiques trop incompatibles pour qu'elles aient pu s'influencer. . . .Le génie hindou est tellement spécial que, quel que soit l'objet dont les nécessités lui imposent l'imitation, l'aspect de cet objet se transforme immédiatement pour devenir hindou.' The same author continues :—'Cette impuissance de l'art grec à influencer l'Inde a quelque chose de frappant, et il faut bien l'attribuer à cette incompatibilité que nous avons signalée entre le génie des deux races, et non à une sorte d'incapacité native de l'Inde à s'assimiler un art étranger.'[2]

The readiness of India to assimilate suitable foreign material is shown by her proved willingness to borrow freely from Persia in ancient times and again after the Muhammadan conquest.

Whatever influence Greece had exercised on Indian art was practically exhausted by A.D. 400. After that date the traces of Hellenistic ideas are too trifling to be worth mentioning. The medieval Brahmanical and Buddhist schools have nothing The end of Greek influence.

[1] *Les Monuments de l'Inde*, pp. 12-15.
[2] Bréhier, L., 'Les Origines de l'Art musulman' (*La Revue des Idées*, No. 75, Mars 1910, p. 190).

in common with Greek art, and the strange artistic forms introduced by the Muhammadan conquerors at the beginning of the thirteenth century were equally alien to Hellenic feeling. From the fifth century the art of India, whether Hindu or Muslim, must stand or fall on its own merits, without reference to Hellenic standards. The medieval Hindu revival and the advance of Islam, in large part synchronous, both involved a revolt against Hellenic ideas and a reversion to ancient Asiatic modes — a 'renaissance aux dépens des influences helléniques'.[1]

NOTE TO CHAPTER FIVE

The chronology of Gandharan sculpture is a very vexed problem and as such it has not been deemed necessary to deal with the pros and cons of conflicting theories. One thing seems fairly certain however and that is that many of the sculptures of the Gandharan school are later in point of time than they were originally thought to be. But much difficulty is experienced in coming to a definite conclusion by reason of the fact that the few dated examples we possess are not ascribable with confidence to any particular era. There is still a controversy as to which era a particular date should be ascribed and in fact some of the eras suggested are themselves matters of conjecture. Even stylistic analysis is not always helpful in this field of study. The famous Kanishka reliquary found at Peshawar (Pl. 57) itself raises problems for those who base chronology on style. The more so when Kanishka's date is so controversial. The art of Gandhara is generally referred to as Græco-Buddhist, but several writers have pointed out that the real and immediate influence is that of Roman sculpture and Roman art in general. This theory has in its turn been criticized and it has been maintained that the Western influence is really that of the Hellenistic period of Greek art. The truth may well be that more than one influence is to be discerned in Gandharan sculpture at all periods of its development. In its earlier stages the influence that dominated may well have been of the Hellenistic period, while in its later development a more dominating influence may have been that of Roman art. It must be remembered that a variety of craftsmen may have been employed in North-West India and that different groups of artisans may have been trained in different traditions.

The aesthetic merits of the art of Gandhara and the significance of the role it played in the history of Indian art have been widely debated. It has been dismissed as a debased art of little importance or as an isolated phenomenon of no real aesthetic or cultural value. On the other hand, it was regarded by the earliest writers on Indian art as the high water mark of Indian sculpture, no doubt, because it reflected the influence of Greek sculpture. The present editor at one time belonged to the former school of thought but has come to recognize that most of those who have debated this question have rather overstated their respective viewpoints. There is quite an appreciable body of Gandharan sculpture and stucco art from Afghanistan which merits serious consideration for a solution of certain problems of Indian sculpture and which at the same time can lay a claim to aesthetic merit. Broadly speaking, we have two fairly clear-cut groups of work in the plastic art of the North-West, loosely referred to as the school of Gandhara though it was produced over a much wider area than the ancient province of Gandhara. There are the stone narrative reliefs, stone Buddhas and stone Bodhisattvas in the gray schist of the region ; while from Afghanistan, as well as other sites, large quantities of terracotta figures, including the most fascinating individualistic portrait studies, have come to light. It has been suggested that most of the stone sculpture is anterior to most of the production in terracotta. This is again a problem of chronology and it has already been indicated that this problem still remains unsolved. Whoever seeks the feeling of Bharhut, Sanchi or Amaravati in the Gandharan reliefs is bound to be disappointed; but if one approaches this art and evaluates it within the ambits of its limitations, there is much, particularly in minor sculptural details, that will repay study and afford aesthetic pleasure. With regard to the stucco production there is a fair output of portrait studies which must surely be regarded as brilliant.

[1] Simpson (*J. Roy. Inst. Brit. Architects*, 1894, p. 100, Fig. 12) ; V. A. Smith (*J. A. S. B.*, Part I, vol. lviii, p. 160); Foucher, *L'Art gréco-bouddhique du Gandhara*, p, 240, Fig. 290).

A. Seated Buddha, from Ajanta. 6th Cent. A.D. Deccan Gupta period.

B. Temptation of the Buddha, from Ajanta. 6th Cent. A.D. Deccan Gupta period.

(Photos : M. V. Vijayakar)

PLATE 69

A. Facade of Chaitya Cave No. 19, Ajanta. 6th Cent. A.D. Deccan Gupta period.

(Photo : A. L. Syed)

B. Facade of Cave 1, Ajanta. 6th Cent. A.D. Deccan Gupta period.

PLATE 70

Chapter Six

THE GUPTA PERIOD

THE displacement of the Arsacid by the Sassanian dynasty of Persia in A.D. 226, the approximately simultaneous downfall of the Andhra kings who had ruled the Deccan for four-and-a-half centuries, and the disappearance of the Kushan or Indo-Scythian sovereigns of Northern India about the same time, unquestionably must have resulted in violent political and social disturbances on Indian soil during the third century. But hardly any record, archaeological or literary, has survived of that stormy interlude.

Revolutions in third century.

The rise in A.D. 320 of the Imperial Gupta dynasty, with its capital at Pataliputra (Patna), the ancient seat of empire, marks the beginning of a new epoch. Under a succession of able and long-lived monarchs the Gupta dominions rapidly increased, until in the first quarter of the fifth century they comprised in modern terms Central and Western Bengal, Bihar, the United Provinces of Agra and Oudh, part of the Central Provinces, and the whole of Malwa and Gujarat, with the peninsula of *Surashtra* or Kathiawar. We know from the contemporary testimony of the Chinese pilgrim Fa-hien that the compact empire thus formed was then well governed by Chandragupta II, surnamed Vikramaditya.

The Gupta empire.

During the last quarter of the fifth century the Gupta empire was shattered by the inrush of swarms of fierce Huns and allied nomad tribes from Central Asia. The short-lived Hun power was broken in India by a decisive victory gained by native princes about A.D. 528, but a long time elapsed before new political combinations of any stability could be formed. In the seventh century a great king named Harsha (606-47) reduced India north of the Narbada to obedience, while the Deccan submitted to his able contemporary Pulakesin II Chalukya, and the far south was governed by a powerful Pallava king. The Chalukya fell before the Pallava in 642, and five or six years later Harsha died childless, leaving the empire which he had won a prey to anarchy.

Hun invasions, Harsha, &c.

During the seventh and eighth centuries the foreign settlers had become Hinduized, tribes developing into castes. When the ninth century opens we find a new distribution of power among kingdoms mostly governed by so-called Rajputs, in many cases the descendants of chieftains belonging to the foreign tribes of Hunas, Gurjaras, and the like. The Huna or Hun invasions with the subsequent readjustments mark the division between the history of Ancient and that of Medieval India.

Limits of the Gupta period.

All students of Indian literature now recognize the fact that during the reigns of Chandragupta II and his next two successors, from about A.D. 375 to 490, every branch of Hindu literature, science, and art was vigorously cultivated under the stimulus of liberal royal patronage; and there is general agreement that Kalidasa, the greatest of Indian poets, graced the Gupta court and produced his masterpieces in the later years of the fifth century.[1] The plastic and pictorial arts shared in the good fortune of literature and science. In painting we have the frescoes of Ajanta and Bagh, and also those of Sigiriya in Ceylon. In coinage a marked improvement took place during the reigns of the earlier Gupta kings.[2]

Gupta literature, science, and art.

Until quite recently the merits of Gupta sculpture were not generally or freely

[1] For the history in detail see *Early Hist. India*, 2nd ed., chaps. xi-xiii.

[2] Marshall, *J. R. A. S.*, 1907, p. 1000. However, the supply of sculpture of the actual Gupta fifth century is small when compared with the bulk of medieval sculpture.

Gupta sculpture. recognized (A 1). Owing to the destruction wrought by iconoclast Muslim armies and kings who overran and held in strength almost every part of the Gupta empire, few remains of the period exist above ground, except in out-of-the-way localities, and our present knowledge of Gupta art is largely the result of excavation. Sarnath, especially, has proved to be a rich treasure-house of Gupta, as well as of Kushan and earlier art.[1] The ravages of the Huns did not wholly stop the practice of the arts of civilization, and one of the surprises of recent exploration has been the discovery of many large Buddhist monasteries at Sarnath and other places in Hindustan dating from the fifth and sixth centuries. The sculpture of the period is mainly Buddhist and Brahmanical, the Jain works being few and of little artistic interest (A 2).

Earliest Gupa works. Except certain coins of high artistic quality, as judged by an Indian standard, no work of art yet discovered can be referred to the reign of Samudragupta (A.D.*c.* 335-75), the victorious general, and accomplished poet and musician, who has recorded his achievements on Asoka's pillar at Allahabad. The earliest known Gupta remains date from the beginning of the fifth century (A 3).

Gupta architecture. In the fifth century were built the earliest stone buildings that have survived. They are chiefly tiny shrines (Plate 63A) situated in out-of-the-way places. Cunningham treated those little edifices as examples of the 'Gupta style', and enumerated seven characteristics of that style, namely,

(1) flat roofs, without steeples of any kind;
(2) prolongation of the head of the doorway beyond the jambs;
(3) statues of the personified Ganges and Jumna guarding the entrance;
(4) pillars with a massive square capital, surmounted by two lions back to back, often with a tree between them;
(5) bosses over the capitals, and peculiar friezes;
(6) continuation of the architrave of the portico as a moulding round the building; and
(7) deviation of the plan from the cardinal points.

A characteristic example exists at Tigowa in the Jabalpur District, Central Provinces[2] (A 4).

These small shrines are really the prototypes of much of the architecture of the great cave temples at Ajanta and Ellora. All the known examples are Brahmanical. At Udayagiri caves are to be found cut in the rock on exactly the above plan. At Ajanta the Buddhist rock-cut *Vihara*, which was originally nothing but a large pillared hall with cells for dwelling purposes leading into it on the three inner sides, was converted to ritual purposes by cutting a shrine exactly corresponding to the Gupta structural shrines in the back wall. The doorways, with their pilasters and river-goddesses are reproduced in detail, proving the near relation of Ajanta architecture to the Gupta. Some of these shrines actually stand free, having a circumambulation passage cut around them. In the *Saiva* caves at Ellora and Elephanta the shrine is pushed forward into the body of the hall directly in front of the main entrance. These *Linga* shrines have doorways and door guardians on all four sides. The river-goddesses of the true [early] Gupta shrines are placed on the level of the lintel on either side of the door [as at Udayagiri caves excavated in A.D. 401-402, Plate 58A]. *Ganga* stands on her *Makara* (Plate 58B) and

[1] Greek influence has been suggested in the drama of Kalidasa. Vincent Smith finds European influence in the Gupta coins, but owns to a lack of proof. The Gupta coinage may best be taken as an orderly development of the numismatic art of the Kushans.

[2] [Now Madhya Pradesh].

A. Bracket figure from Badami.

B. Verandah pillar, Cave III, Badami.

Early western Chalukyan school with some Gupta influence. Last quarter of the 6th Century A.D.

PLATE 71

A. Love scene. Medallion from **Badami** Caves.

Early western Chalukyan school with some Gupta influence. Last quarter of the 6th Cent. A.D.

B. Bas-relief from **Badami Caves.**

PLATE 72

A. Nataraja from Badami Caves.

B. Figures from Badami Caves.

Early western Chalukyan school with some Gupta influence. Last quarter of the 6th Cent. A.D.

(Photos : A. L. Syed)

PLATE 73

A. Flying figures from Aihole.

B. A couple from Aihole.

Early western Chalukyan school with some Gupta influence. *c.* 600 A. D.

PLATE 74

Yamuna on her tortoise. At Udayagiri, on the doorway of the Chandragupta Cave excavated in A.D. 401-2, the goddesses are represented without their vehicles. Here and elsewhere they stand beneath trees usually in the Woman and Tree posture. It seems that originally they were tree-spirits, like the *Yakshis* at Bharhut, and only became river-deities later.[1] [Other sculptures from Udayagiri of the early 5th century, A.D. are illustrated as Plate 58C and D].

In the Ajanta frescoes it is evident that the palace and town architecture was entirely of wood, beautifully carved and painted.

Siva and Parvati.

Although in the matter of style no distinctions based on the religious destination of particular images can be drawn, it will be convenient to finish the description of selected Brahmanical stone sculptures before proceeding to the discussion of the Jain and Buddhist works and the metal castings.

The Indian Museum, Calcutta, possesses a remarkable group of Siva and Parvati (Km. 40) from Kosam in the Allahabad District, bearing an inscription dated A.D. 458-9. The consorts stand side by side, each with the right hand raised and the open palm turned to the front. The head-dress of the goddess is described as a most elaborate construction, which recalls that 'of some Dutch women, and consists of a huge, transverse, comb-like ornament projecting beyond the side of the head, and terminating on both sides in large wheel-like ornaments, from the centre of which depends a large tassel. There are huge ear-ornaments and very massive bangles.'[2]

Siva as *mahayogi*.

A temple at Deogarh (Plate 63B), in the Lalitpur subdivision of the Jhansi District, U. P., is adorned with sculptures of exceptionally good quality in panels inserted in the plinth and walls, which may date from the first half of the sixth century. That region probably escaped the Hun troubles owing to its remote situation. A panel on the eastern facade, representing Siva in the garb of an ascetic (*mahayogi*), attended by another *yogi* and various heavenly beings hovering in the air (Plate 64A), may claim a place among the best efforts of Indian sculpture. The principal image is so beautifully modelled and so tastefully posed that we almost forget the inartistic excrescence of the extra pair of arms. The flying figures are admirably designed so as to give the appearance of aerial flight. The modelling of the feet and hands deserves particular notice, and the decorative carvings are in good taste. The close-fitting garments of all the figures and the wigs of some of the attendants are characteristic of the period.

Vishnu on Ananta.

Another panel from the south facade of the same temple is equally good (Plate 64B). The subject is Vishnu as the Eternal, reclining on the serpent Ananta, the symbol of eternity, with the other gods watching from above. The principal image is beautifully posed, and the extra arms most dexterously arranged. The wig-like dressing of the hair is very prominent in this fine group.[3]

A Rajgir sculpture.

The little-known ruins at Rajgir, the ancient capital of Magadha, include a relief of a female, facing front, which is of the Gupta age (Plate 62C)[4] (A 5). The sculptures at Nachna-Kuthara in Ajaigarh State are very fine, especially the doorways of the two shrines. Cunningham describes them as 'being much superior to all medieval sculptures, both in ease and gracefulness of their attitudes, as well as in real beauty of the forms'.

[1] Cunningham, *A. S. Rep.*, vol. x, pp. 48-56; Ibid., vol. ix, pp. 42-6 ; Bloch, *Progr. Rep. A. S., East. Circle*, 1907-8 ; Cousens, *Progr. Rep. A. S , West. Ind.*, 1903-4.

[2] Anderson, *Catal.*, Part II, p. 286 ; Cunningham, *A. S. Rep.*, vol. x, p. 3 ; photo. 669 in I. M. *List*.

[3] For Deogarh antiquities see Cunningham, *A. S. Rep.*, vol. x, pp. 100-4, Pl. XXXIII-VI. The groups of sculpture have not been published previously.

[4] Cunningham, *Rep.* vol. xxi, p. 96.

Fifth-century Garhwa sculptures.

Several ancient sites in the south-western part of the Allahabad District have yielded to slight excavation many remarkable Buddhist sculptures in stone, proved by dated inscriptions to be assignable to the reigns of Chandragupta II, his son Kumaragupta I, and his grandson Skandagupta in the fifth century.

The vigorous, and at the same time refined, sculpture adorning the ruins of a Gupta temple at Garhwa, twenty-five miles south-west of Allahabad, is illustrated on Plate 62A and B, giving back and side views of one pillar. The panels on the front are arranged according to the ancient Indian fashion, and the style is related to the art of Sanchi and Bharhut much more closely than to medieval art. There is no trace whatever of Gandharan influence. The figures are well drawn, and modelled on purely naturalistic principles.

The beautiful ornament on the side is described by Cunningham as consisting of—

> 'the undulating stem of a creeper, with large curling and intertwining leaves, and small human figures, both male and female, climbing up the stem, or sitting on the leaves in various attitudes. The whole scroll is deeply sunk and very clearly and carefully carved; and . . . is one of the most pleasing and graceful specimens of Indian architectural ornament.'[1]

The commendation is fully justified; nothing better can be found in the earlier work at Mathura, and the Garhwa design would do credit to an Italian fifteenth-century artist.

Seated Buddha from Sarnath.

Among the numerous excellent sculptures of Gupta age, disclosed by recent excavations at Sarnath (Plates 60A, 61A), the most pleasing, perhaps, is the seated Buddha in white sandstone, 5¼ feet in height (Plate 60A).

The deer-park at Sarnath having been the place where the Wheel of the Law was first turned, or, in other words, the doctrine of the Buddhist way of salvation was first publicly preached by Gautama Buddha, his effigy is naturally represented with the fingers in the position (*mudra*) associated by canonical rule with the act commemorated. The wheel symbolizing the Law and the five adoring disciples to whom it was first preached are depicted on the pedestal. The woman with a child on the left probably is intended for the pious donor of the image. The beautifully decorated halo characteristic of the period is in marked contrast with the severely plain halos of the Kushan age. The style, marked by refined restraint, is absolutely free from all extravagance or monstrosity. Allowance being made for the Hindu canon prohibiting the display of muscular detail, the modelling must be allowed to display high artistic skill. The angels hovering above may be compared with the similar figures at Deogarh. The close-fitting smooth robe is one of the most distinctive marks of the style, which is singularly original and absolutely independent of the Gandhara school.[2] The composition is so pictorial that it might have been designed after the model of a painted fresco.

Standing Buddha at Mathura.

An excellently inscribed standing Buddha of the fifth century in the Mathura Museum (Plate 60B), height 7 feet 2½ inches, while clearly related to the Sarnath seated image in several respects, differs widely in the treatment of the drapery, which at Mathura shows a reminiscence of Hellenistic forms. The skill with

[1] The Garhwa remains are fully described and illustrated by Cunningham, *A. S. Rep.*, vol. iii, pp. 53-61 ; vol. x, pp. 9-15, with plates.

[2] Foreign influence has been discerned in the Gupta coins. The conquest of Western India undoubtedly opened the western ports to Northern India, which suggests a channel of influence via the Red Sea. 'The period when mathematics flourished in India commenced about A.D. 400 and ended about A.D. 650, after which deterioration set in. This period is characterized by quite an extraordinary amount of intercourse between India and foreign countries' (Kaye, *J. R. A. S.*, 1910, p. 759). Many Indian 'embassies' to China and the Roman empire are recorded during this period. All that is of value in the Hindu mathematics of the time, according to Mr. Kaye, is Greek.

A. Durga, Mahisha-mardini, Mahisa Mandapa, Mamallapuram. (Durga slaying the demon Mahisa, Mahabalipuram. 7th Cent. A.D. Post-Gupta Pallava period).

(Photo: Indian Office

C. Kartikeya riding his peacock vehicle. *c.* 600 A.D. Immediate post-Gupta period, Northern India. Mathura Museum.

B. Siva from Shamlaji. Early 7th Cent. A.D. Immediate post-Gupta period, Southern Rajasthan and Northern Gujarat. Baroda Museum.

(By Courtesy of Wales Museum, Bombay)

PLATE 75

.A

B.

C.

A. Elephants from the rock-sculpture of Arjuna's Penance, Mahabalipuram. B, C. Sculptures from the raths at Mahabalipuram. 7th Cent. A.D. Post-Gupta Pallava period. The former identification of the rock-sculpture as the Descent of the Ganges is no longer acceptable.

PLATE 76

which the body is shown through the transparent garments is characteristic of the best Gupta sculpture.[1](A 6).

Colossal copper Buddha.

The unique copper colossus of Buddha, about 7½ feet high, now in the Museum and Art Gallery, Birmingham (Plate 61B), is, perhaps, more closely akin to the Sarnath than to the Mathura image, the robes being almost smooth, with the folds marked very faintly. The transparency of the garments is clearly marked. The statue was excavated by certain railway engineers in 1862 from the hall of a ruined monastery situated between the modern mart and the railway station at Sultanganj, on the Ganges, in the Bhagalpur District, Bengal. One of the discoverers brought it home, and some years later presented it to the Birmingham Museum. The image was found lying on the ground, having been wrenched from its massive granite pedestal; but was practically perfect, except that the left foot was broken off above the ankle. The earliest possible date is indicated by the discovery in an adjoining *stupa* of a coin of the last Western Satrap of Surashtra, accompanied by one of his conquerors, Chandragupta II, Vikramaditya, who annexed his dominions about A.D. 390. The statue, therefore, may be dated early fifth century (A 7).

Technique of the colossus.

According to Rajendralala Mitra, the material is 'very pure copper', cast in two distinct layers, the inner of which was moulded on an earthy, cinderlike core, composed of a mixture of sand, clay, charcoal, and paddy (rice) husks. The segments of this inner layer were held together by much corroded iron bands, originally three-quarters of an inch thick. The outer layer of copper seems to have been cast over the inner one, presumably by the *cire perdue* process. It was made in several sections, one of which consisted of the face and connected parts down to the breast.

Lumps of copper ore found close by indicate that the smelting and casting were done on the spot. The hand of another large copper statue was picked up, and three small Buddhas of the same metal were discovered. One, nearly destroyed by rust, was seated, the three others were standing, with halos broken and detached. A large Bihar image of carboniferous shale was found nearby: this image is also in the Birmingham Museum.[2]

The Mankuwar Buddha.

At the adjoining village of Mankuwar a very perfect seated Buddha of unusual type was found (Plate 59A), bearing a dedicatory inscription dated in the year 129 G.E. = A.D. 448-9. The peculiar head-dress, if it be a head-dress, is, as Cunningham remarked, like that now worn by the Abbots of Bhutan, and the image may be the work of a northern artist.[3] The webbed hand was one of the traditional marks of a Buddha, according to some schools. The wheel below symbolizes the turning of the Wheel of the Law, that is to say, the preaching of the doctrine destined to traverse the world like the chariot wheels of a conquering monarch. The expression of the face differs from that of most images, and the work undoubtedly is a notable example of fifth-century sculpture. The clothing

[1] Careful study of an adequate number of examples might disclose the existence of several well-marked local schools of sculpture during the Gupta period; but it would be premature at present to attempt such refinement in the treatment of a subject which needs to be first sketched on broader lines. Vincent Smith accentuates the division into local schools of Indian art too much. The development of Indian art is a matter of periods rather than geography, as the affinities between Mathura and Amaravati show.

[2] The Sultanganj discoveries are described in *J. A. S. B.*, vol. xxxiii (1864), pp. 361 seqq. with lithograph: Cunningham, *A. S. Rep.*, vol. x, p. 127; xv, p. 126: Anderson, *Catalogue, I. M.*, Part II, p. 481. The modern *cire perdue* process of casting bronze over a core made of modelling clay mixed with pounded brick and plaster of Paris is described, ibid., p. 85. The Sultanganj process seems to have been essentially the same, with the addition of a second layer of copper.

[3] According to Dr. Bloch (*J. A. S. B.*, vol. lxvi, Part I, p. 283), what looks like a close-fitting cap really is a conventional arrangement of the hair.

is merely the Indian waist-cloth, quite different from the robe of the ordinary Buddha.

The Iron Pillar of Delhi.

The existence of the Sultanganj Buddha, weighing nearly a ton, is good evidence of Indian proficiency in metallurgy at the beginning of the fifth century. Still stronger testimony to that skill is borne by the celebrated Iron Pillar of Delhi, set up about A.D. 415 by Kumaragupta I in honour of his father, Chandragupta II, Vikramaditya. The total length of the pillar from the top of the bell capital to the bottom of the base is 23 feet 8 inches, and the diameter diminishes from 16.4 inches below to 12.05 inches above. The material is pure malleable iron of 7.66 specific gravity welded together, and the weight is estimated to exceed six tons. 'It is not many years since the production of such a pillar would have been an impossibility in the largest foundries of the world, and even now there are comparatively few where a similar mass of metal could be turned out.' The statue originally surmounting the pillar having disappeared, this marvellous metallurgical triumph does not further concern a history of fine art.[1]

Gupta monolithic columns.

The old Asokan practice of erecting isolated monumental columns, usually monolithic, was revived in Gupta times. Samudragupta, perhaps the most brilliant of an able dynasty, does not seem to have erected pillars of his own, and was content to record the history of his reign on a pillar of Asoka, now at Allahabad (*Prayaga*), which, apparently, has been removed from Kausambi. The earliest extant stone pillar of Gupta age is that erected at Bhitari in the Ghazipur District, U.P., by Skandagupta about A.D. 456 to commemorate his wars with the Huns and Pushyamitras. The next, set up at Kahaon in the Gorakhpur District, U.P., in A.D. 460-1, early in the reign of the same king, by a private member of the Jain community, is adorned with the images of five Jain saints, one in a niche at the base, and four on the summit. The statues, as usual with the Jains, are conventional and of little artistic interest.

The third in date is the fine monolithic pillar, 43 feet high, set up at Eran in the Sagar District, C.P., as 'the flag-staff of *four-armed* Vishnu', in A.D. 484-5. The statue now on the top is a *two-armed* male figure with two faces and a radiated halo — a form not easy of interpretation.

Two great monolithic columns, the better preserved of which is 39 feet 5 inches long, excluding the detached abacus, lie at Sondani or Songni, near Mandasor in Sindhia's Dominions, and bear inscriptions recording the decisive defeat of the Huns by King Yasodharman about A.D. 528. Several specimens of good contemporary sculpture adjoin.

Another great monolithic column, with a worn inscription of late Gupta age, and 47 feet high, stands at Pathari, about thirteen miles to the south-west of Eran.

Furthermore, Cunningham's illustration of the Sanchi torso, now in the Victoria and Albert Museum, South Kensington, proves it to have stood at the base of a column. It is to be dated *c.* A.D. 500[2] (A 8).

Gupta forms of capital.

The Gupta form of capital is generally characterized by a large square abacus of twice the breadth of the shaft, surmounted by two lions sitting back to back, sometimes with a tree or human figure between them. The Budhagupta column has four lions, one at each corner. The process by which the medieval capital was evolved from the Persepolitan through the Gupta forms is explained by Cunningham as follows:

[1] V. A. Smith, 'The Iron Pillar of Delhi (Mihrauli)' (*J. R. A. S.*, 1907, pp. 1-18). The passage quoted is from V. Ball, *Economic Geology of India*, p. 338, 1st ed., 1881.

[2] *A. S. I.*, vol. x.

'The old bell-capital of the Asoka period has now been considerably altered by bands of ornament and the addition of foliated turn-overs. In later times these turnovers were greatly increased in size, while the body of the bell was lessened until it resembled a water-vessel or *kumbha*, which eventually became its well-known designation. This curious change from the old bell-capital of Asoka to the water-vessel of the medieval temples is very clearly traceable in the different examples of the Gupta period.'[1]

The foregoing select illustrations (A 9) will, it is hoped, be considered sufficient to establish the claims of the Gupta sculpture of Northern India (A 10) to favourable consideration on its merits as art. It is, as Sir John Marshall observes, endowed with 'freshness and vitality', while the designs are singularly refined and the technical execution of the best pieces is exquisite. Students who desire to pursue the subject further will find more material in the publications noted below.[2]

A transition sculpture.

NOTES TO CHAPTER SIX

Gupta art covers the period 320 A.D. to *circa* 600 A.D. even though the Imperial Guptas ceased to reign in the first half of the 6th century. The Gupta idiom continued to influence Indian art both in the north and the south even after 600 A.D. and that is why it is essential to recognize a post-Gupta period from about 600 A.D. to 800 A.D. It is an error to characterize the art of this post-Gupta period as medieval. It is not merely a matter of nomenclature. Post-Gupta sculpture is different in concept and treatment from the marked architectonic sculpture of the medieval period namely, *circa* 800 A.D. to 1300 A.D. A 1

Some of the Jain Tirthankaras of Mathura, belonging to the 5th century A.D., are indeed very fine. They can be seen in the Mathura and Lucknow Museums. A 2

It would be more correct to say that the earliest dated Gupta sculpture belongs to the last quarter of the 4th century A.D., judging by an example dated 383 A.D. in the reign of a ruler named Trikamala, probably a feudatory of the Guptas. It is a Buddha in Mathura red-stone and was found at Gaya. It is now in the Indian Museum, Calcutta. Its stylistic characteristics indicate that the Gupta idiom was already being formulated in the reign of Samudragupta. A 3

See Plate 63A where the lovely Gupta shrine at Sanchi is illustrated. It belongs to the 5th century A.D. and is characteristic of the early Gupta temple without *shikara* (spire). It has the classic simplicity of early Gupta art. A 4

These stucco sculptures have now crumbled. A 5

Diaphanous drapery is a characteristic of the Sarnath school, but that is not the case with the Mathura school where the folds of Buddha's garments are emphasized by delicately carved lines. A 6

This magnificent image is ascribed by some writers to the 7th and 8th century. They do not regard it as an example of Gupta art. This viewpoint is difficult to comprehend in view of its marked Gupta characteristics. A 7

It appears to be considerably later and is not a Gupta period sculpture. A 8

Gupta sculpture is famed for many exquisite female heads and two fine specimens are illustrated on Plate 59C and D and Plate 62E. A female nymph from Bhumara (Pl. 65C) is characteristic of this period. Terracotta art was also at its height during the Gupta age and its variety and excellence deserve a separate volume with varied illustrations. The excavations at several sites such as Rajghat near Banaras, Kausambi, Ahicchatra, etc., have brought to light many thousands of terracottas of the Gupta and pre-Gupta periods. A Gupta terracotta of a female lyrist from Rupar is reproduced as Plate 62D. Amongst the several *ekamukha* Gupta lingas known, that from Khoh (Pl. 65B) is perhaps the finest. It is marked by great dignity and feeling. A 9

It is essential to recognize that the Gupta idiom is not confined to Northern India. It spread into Central India (Pl. 65A) which was under the direct sway of the Guptas and it also influenced the contemporary art of the Deccan and nearby in no small measure when the powerful Vakatakas, A 10

[1] *A. S. Rep.*, x. 88. References for the pillars are :— *Bhitari*—Cunningham, *A. S. Rep.*, vol. i, p. 38, Pls. XXIX, XXX : Fleet, *Gupta Inscr.*, No. 13. *Kahaon*—Cunningham, *Rep.*, vol. i, p. 92, Pl. XXX : Fleet, *op. cit.*, No. 15. *Eran*—Cunningham, *Rep.*, vol. vii, p. 88 ; x, p. 81, Pl. XXVI : Fleet, *op. cit.*, No. 19. *Sondani*—*Ind. Ant.*, 1908, p. 107, with plates : Fleet, *op. cit.*, Nos. 33-5. *Pathari*—Cunningham, *Rep.*, vol. vii, p. 67; x, p. 70 : not in Fleet. Smaller pillars or *stelae* of Gupta age exist at several places.

[2] *J. R. A. S.*, 1907, pp. 996-1000 : *Ann. Rep. A. S., India*, 1903-4, pp. 213-26 ; 1904-5, pp. 43-58 and 59-104 ; 1905-6, pp. 61-85 and 135-40 ; 1906-7, pp. 44-67 and 68-101.

and thereafter the Chalukyas of Badami, were the leading dynasties in that area. Thus the nomenclature "Deccan Gupta School" has now come to be well recognized. This Deccan Gupta art varies from site to site. A strong influence, probably emanating from Sarnath, is to be seen in some of the figures at Kanheri near Bombay, such as Plate 66A. On the other hand characteristically heavier types resulting from the fusion of Gupta and Vakataka idioms are seen at Ajanta (Plates 66B, 67A and B, 68A and B, 69A and B, 70A and B). In the Chalukyan districts of Badami and Aihole during the 6th century the Gupta influence though present is considerably transformed by marked local preferences both in the handling of form and the portrayal of facial types. It is generally referred to as the early Chalukyan school and its output is often of a very high order indeed (Plates 71A and B, 72A and B, 73A and B, 74A and B).

Even in Sind at Mirpur Khas, a strong Gupta influence is to be seen in the beautiful stucco sculptures of a Buddhist Stupa (Pl. 59B). They belong probably to the late 4th or early 5th century A.D. and reveal the presence of art currents from the North-West intermingling with the Gupta idiom.

A.

B.

C.

D.

A. Sculpture from a rath at Mahabalipuram. B, C. Details from the rock-sculpture of Arjuna's Penance, Mahabalipuram. D. The monkey family, from Mahabalipuram. 7th Cent. A.D. Post-Gupta Pallava period.

PLATE 77

A.

B.

A. Marriage of Siva and Parvati, Elephanta. B. Descent of the river Ganga. (First half of the 7th Cent. A.D. Post-Gupta period. The theory that the Elephanta sculptures belong to the 8th Cent. is no longer acceptable).

(*Copyright by Department of Archaeology, Government of India*) (Photo : E. S. Mahalingam)

PLATE 78

Chapter Seven

THE MEDIEVAL CAVE-TEMPLES

Ajanta sculptures.

WHILE the most characteristic and distinctive sculptures of Gupta age occur in Northern India, the rock-cut shrines and monasteries of the Deccan are adorned with numerous sculptures more or less closely related to those of the north. These as a whole are later and must be considered as intermediate between the Gupta work and the later medieval. At Ajanta, interest having been concentrated chiefly on the paintings, the accounts of the sculptures are meagre and detailed photographs are scarce (A 1).

The Temptation.

The numerous sculptures in Cave XXVI include a gigantic recumbent Dying Buddha, 23¼ feet in length, bearing a general resemblance to the fifth-century image at Kasia in the Gorakhpur District, U.P. The most notable sculpture on the walls is the large and crowded composition representing the Temptation of Buddha, which Dr. Burgess describes as 'beautiful', adding that 'several of the faces are beautifully cut'. The subject is also treated at Ajanta in fresco and at Borobudur, Java, in sculpture. The fantastically dressed hair, characteristic of the period, worn by several of the figures in the Ajanta sculpture should be noted. The elephants are well drawn, as usual.

Chase of wild bull.

In Cave I, supposed to be the latest of the completed excavations, a great quantity of rich sculpture exists, dealing chiefly with incidents in the lives of Buddha. A scene depicting the chase of the wild bull is praised as being 'spiritedly carved'.

Sculptures of the Bagh caves.

The sculptures in the Bagh caves, Gwalior State, until recently known only through drawings prepared for Dr. Burgess, have since been officially photographed. The best images, representing Buddha, or possibly a Bodhisattva, with two attendants, are the south-western group in the Gosain's Cave, No. II. The style connects them with the Gupta rather than the medieval period, and especially with the sculptures in Cave IX, Ajanta. They may have been executed in the latter half of the sixth century (A 2). The pose is easy and the modelling good.[1]

Aurangabad caves.

The late Buddhist caves at Aurangabad in the Nizam's dominions, not far from Ellora, are supposed to date from the 'seventh century of our era, and perhaps towards the end of it'.[2] Whatever their exact date may be, the sculptures (Plate 86A) are related more closely to those of the Gupta age than to the Tantric works of the medieval period.

The 'Drunkard's Progress'.

The principal cave, No. III, contains many columns most elaborately decorated with figure sculpture as well as complex patterns. On certain of these columns a sixteen-sided portion is

> 'carved with sixteen scenes which may be an anticipation of Cruikshank or John Adam, for they seem intended to picture the "Drunkard's Progress". The number of figures varies from two to four in each. Two persons are represented sitting together, apparently drinking in the most friendly way, then staggering along, then dancing with their backs to each other, then quarrelling; one is being dragged along helpless between two men, and so on in successive panels'.[3]

It is a pity that no reproductions of these lively stone pictures have been published. The subjects recall the much earlier 'Bacchanalian' sculptures of Mathura, and suggest speculations concerning certain varieties of Buddhism in practice.

A frieze.

In the same cave an architrave bears on the front a long frieze of fourteen scenes

[1] The Bagh caves (India Society, London).
[2] Burgess, in *Hist. Ind. and E. Archit.*, 2nd ed. (1910), vol. i, p. 205. The Aurangabad work seems more nearly related to Ajanta than to Ellora or Badami. It is probably mid-sixth century.
[3] Burgess, *A.S.W.I.*, vol. iii, p. 67.

of the *Jataka* kind in relief, including an impalement, a battle in a forest, and other incidents, the meaning of which is not known. The drawing in Dr. Burgess's volume is on such a small scale that it is impossible to judge fairly the quality of the art, but, so far as can be seen, the action is vigorously depicted.

Egyptian-like heads.

Certain groups of kneeling worshippers in the same excavation are extremely curious. The mode of hair-dressing has quite an Egyptian appearance.

The later cave temples.

At Ajanta much of the sculpture is reminiscent of the Gupta fifth-century style. In the later caves the work is definitely medieval, being based on the iconography of the time. It is almost entirely hieratic. It is distinguished from the earlier work, also, by its richly crowded design. The bands of masks ('face of fame', *kirtti-mukha*), the grotesque animals with foliated tails, and many motives based on jewellery designs, distinguish it from the Gupta. For the purpose of illustration it will suffice to reproduce a few select specimens from the shrines at Badami, Ellora, and Elephanta, with two sculptures from temples of later date. The cave sculptures of interest range in date from the sixth to the eighth century.

The Brahmanical the most important.

The works of art are shared by all the three indigenous Indian religions — Brahmanical Hinduism, Buddhism, and Jainism. The Buddhist and Brahmanical works are both numerous and very much alike in spirit and style. The spirit of the new art will be most easily understood from study of the Brahmanical sculptures, to which the few illustrations for which there is space will be restricted. In those days Buddhism was a dying faith, slowly perishing by absorption into the enveloping mass of Hinduism. The Brahmanical works of art exceed the Buddhist, not only in number but in merit. To Mr. Havell and Dr. Coomaraswamy the compositions in the cave temples are 'examples of the finest period of Hindu sculpture, from about the sixth to the eighth century, when orthodox Hinduism had triumphed over Buddhism'; but most European observers experience difficulty in appreciating the artistic qualities of those compositions. Mr. Fry, commenting on Mr. Havell's book, is more appreciative than many writers: 'The free and picturesque composition from Ellora', he says, 'representing *Ravana under the mountain of Kailasa*, complicated though it is, is held together by the dramatic beauty of movement of the figures of Siva and Parvati. The same dramatic vitality is apparent in the struggle between *Narasinha* and *Hiranya-Kasipu*, also from Ellora. Indeed, all the Ellora sculptures here reproduced appeal to the European eye by a relatively greater observance of the laws of co-ordination, and by evidence of dramatic force which indicates that Indian art did not always convey its meaning in a strange tongue.'[1] To be judged fairly the sculptures should be seen in the mass and among their solemn surroundings. They undoubtedly suffer grievously by being excerpted in bits and reproduced in illustrations a few inches square. While fully conscious of the difficulties inherent in the attempt to illustrate the colossal and fantastic creations of the cave sculptors within the limits of an ordinary page, I have tried to select fairly a small number of examples generally recognized as among the best.

Sculptures at Badami.

The cave temples at Badami in the Bijapur District, Bombay, exhibit among other decorations long sculptured story-telling friezes (Plate 72A and B), extremely curious, but so clumsily executed as hardly to deserve the name of works of art (A 3). They date from the closing years of the sixth century.[2] From an artistic

[1] *Imp. Gaz.*, s.v. Abu. *Quart. Rev.*, 1910, p. 235.

[2] Described, and illustrated with other sculptures, by seven plates in *Ind. Ant.*, vi. pp. 354-66. Also Burgess, *Arch. Rep., Belgam and Kaladgi*; Rea, *Chalukian Architecture*, and the monograph, Arch. Sur. Memoirs.

Colossal image of Mahesvarimurti, Elephanta. First half of the 7th Cent. A.D. Post-Gupta period. This famous image is commonly but erroneously referred to as the Trimurti.

(Copyright by Department of Archaeology, Government of India)

PLATE 79

A. Siva as the Great Ascetic, Elephanta. (First half of the 7th Cent. A.D. Post-Gupta period).
(Copyright by Prince of Wales Museum, Bombay)

B. Krishna, Kailasa, Ellora. (Second half of the 8th Cent. A.D. Post-Gupta Rashtrakuta period).
(By Courtesy of A. A. Macdonell)

C, D. Sculptures from Ellora. Second half of the 8th Cent. A.D. Post-Gupta Rashtrakuta period.
(Photos : A. L. Syed)

PLATE 80

A. Vishnu as the Man-lion Narasimha slaying the impious Hiryankasipu. Dasavatara Cave, Ellora. 7th Cent. A.D. Post-Gupta, early Rashtrakuta period.

B. The Goddess Yamuna. Lankesvara Shrine, Ellora. (The river goddess on her vehicle the tortoise, 2nd half of the 8th Cent. A.D. Post-Gupta Rashtrakuta period).

PLATE 81

A. Siva and Parvati, Ellora. 2nd half of the 8th Cent. A.D. Post-Gupta Rashtrakuta period.

B. Ravana shaking Kailasa, Ellora. 2nd half of the 8th Cent. A.D. Post-Gupta Rashtrakuta period.

PLATE 82

point of view the bracket figures of a god and goddess on the top of a pilaster, as shown in Plate 71A and B and Plate 73B, are by far the best things at Badami.

There are four cave-temples, all *linga-shrines*, at Badami, all cut on the same plan and at more or less the same time. As has been said, at Ajanta many of the shrines inset in the back wall of the so-called *Viharas* are simply reproductions of the flat-roofed, structural Gupta shrines of the fifth century, with doorway and four-pillared verandah accurately reproduced. At Badami the shrine is cut in the same position but is simplified into a plain cell without verandah. At Ellora this cell was cut away from the rock by means of a circumambulation passage. The stylobate of Cave I is carved with a distinctive frieze of dancing dwarfs, which also appears at the base of sculptured panels and in the other caves. The sculpture of Caves 2 and 3 is Vaishnava, and contains magnificent sculptures of the Man-Lion and Boar incarnations, and a fine *Bhogasanamurti*. Cave 3 contains an inscription of the Chalukyan king, Mangalesvara, dated in A.D. 578. Cave No. 4 is Jain. [Plate 73A is a dancing Shiva from Badami, being one of the earliest representations of the theme].

Bhairava and *Kali*, Ellora.

The iconographical nature of the subjects chosen by the cave sculptors is well exemplified by the *Bhairava* and *Kali* group in the *Das Avatara*, or 'Ten Incarnations' temple at Ellora, dating from about A.D. 700 (Plate 85A), described by Dr. Burgess as follows:

> 'Beginning on the north side with the Saiva sculptures — the first from the door is Bhairava or Mahadeva in his terrible form; and a more vivid picture of the terrific a very diseased imagination only could embody. The gigantic figure lounges forward holding up his elephant-hide, with necklace of skulls (*mundmala*) depending below his loins; round him a cobra is knotted, his open mouth showing large teeth, while with his *trisula* [trident] he has transfixed one victim, who, writhing on its prongs, seems to supplicate pity from the pitiless; while he holds another by the heels with one of his left hands, raising the *damru* [small drum] as if to rattle it in joy, while he catches the blood with which to quench his demon thirst. To add to the elements of horror, *Kali*, gaunt and grim, stretches her skeleton length below, with huge mouth, bushy hair, and sunken eyeballs, having a crooked knife in her right hand, and reaching out the other with a bowl, as if eager to share in the gore of its [*sic*] victim; behind her head is the owl [one species is called *Bhairava*], the symbol of destruction, or a vampire, as fit witness of the scene. On the right, in front of the skeleton, is *Parvati;* and higher up, near the feet of the victim *Ratnasura*, is a grinning face drawing out its tongue. Altogether the group is a picture of the devilish; the very armlets Bhairava wears are ogre faces'.[1]

Rescue of *Markandeya.*

A subject rarely represented in sculpture, the rescue by the god *Siva* of his worshipper *Markandeya* from the clutches of the messenger of *Yama*, god of death,[2] appears twice at Ellora, and is treated with less grimness than the Bhairava group. The earlier composition in the *Das Avatara* Cave is more vigorous than that at the Kailasa, half a century or more later in date.

Siva dancing.

The sculptures in the *Lankesvara* section of the *Kailasa* temple are commended as having been 'executed with great care and minute detail'. The best known,

[1] Fergusson and Burgess, *The Cave Temples of India*, p. 346 (1880).

Vincent Smith's attitude to Brahmanical Indian art was not sympathetic: 'The religion which finds expression in imagery so truly devilish is not a pleasant subject of contemplation, and no amount of executive skill or cleverness in the production of scenic effect can justify, on aesthetic grounds, such a composition, which is frankly hideous. Its claim to be considered a work of art rests solely upon its display of power in a semi-barbaric fashion. The horror of the subject and its treatment is not redeemed by any apparent ethical lesson. Indeed Puranic and Tantric Hinduism (including late Buddhism) concerns itself little with ethics. The earlier Buddhism, as a religion, busied itself mainly with morals, and consciously aimed at "the welfare and happiness of all creatures", a noble ideal which found its utterance in art. In Brahmanical Hinduism of all varieties each man seeks at the most his own personal salvation, and so Brahmanical art seldom exhibits a trace of human sympathy, a defect dearly purchased by its much praised idealism.'

[2] This is a common subject in the later sculpture of the south.

and perhaps the most meritorious, is that exhibiting Siva performing the *Tandava* dance (see below), a work remarkable for the good modelling of the principal image, and the scrupulous exactitude of the carving. The river-goddess from this cave is especially fine (Plate 81B).

Siva dancing ; in Lankesvara temple.

A good Vishnu at Ellora is shown in Plate 80B. The god is imagined as striding through the seven regions of the universe in three steps, and is here shown as taking the third step.[1] [Other masterpieces from Ellora are reproduced as Plates 80C and D, 81A, 82A and B, 83A and B, 84A and C. All depict Brahmanical themes. Some imposing Jain sculptures of the 9th century are also seen at Ellora in Plates 85B and C].

[1] The sculpture is unfinished. It is more probably a rendering of Krishna lifting up *Govardhan* and sheltering the flocks.

A. Ravana shaking Kailasa, Ellora.

B. Dance of Siva, Ellora.

8th Cent. A.D. Post-Gupta Rashtrakuta period.

PLATE 83

A. Siva and Parvati, Ellora. 8th Cent. A.D. Post-Gupta Rashtrakuta period.

B. Buddha, Ellora. 7th Cent. A.D. Post-Gupta period.

C. Sculpture from Ellora, 8th Cent. A.D. Post-Gupta Rashtrakuta period.

PLATE 84

The famous caves on the island of Elephanta in Bombay Harbour are usually supposed to date from the eighth century (A 4). The colossal sculptures are most imposing and effective (Plates 78A and B, 79, 80A) when viewed in the recesses of the caverns. The first of the two specimens selected is the favourite subject of the marriage of Siva with Parvati; and the second is the representation of Siva as the Great Ascetic (Plates 78A, 80A), which may be compared with Siva at Elephanta.

Das Avatára Cave, Ellora.

the far finer Gupta treatment of the same subject. The most imposing of the Elephanta sculptures is the gigantic *Trimurti* (Plate 79) or Trinity (A 5), which is the first thing discerned as the eyes become accustomed to the gloom, on approaching the cave through the present main entrance. The original main entrance is to one side and leads direct to the square *Linga* shrine.[1]

[1] For the survival of Buddhist traits in the Saiva cults see *Or. Qu. Mag.*, vii. 218 *seqq ; Languages, &c. of Nepal*, 133 *seqq.*, as quoted by Sir R. Temple in *Ind. Ant.*, xxii, 363.

Chronology of medieval caves.

The chronology of these caves must be deduced from the following facts:

I. The likeness of the Ajanta shrines to the Gupta fifth century shrines, taking into consideration their plan, the sculptured doorways, and the Vakataka epigraphy.

II. The *Visvakarma* Cave at Ellora is linked with Ajanta by the style of its sculptured *stupa*. The seated Buddha on it is in the style of certain later sculptural additions at Ajanta such as the bas-relief Temptation of the Buddha in Cave XXVI. It is also linked with Badami by the little frieze of dancing dwarfs in the bas-relief pavilions on either side of the *chaitya*-window. It may be dated in the second half of the sixth century. The sculpture of the Buddhist caves at Ellora (Plate 84B) corresponds most exactly with the Ajanta frescoes in style, especially the doorway of Cave VI.[1]

III. At Ellora two other styles of sculpture exist, which may be respectively typified by the dynamic Brahmanical sculptures of the *Das Avatara* Cave and the later *Kailasa* sculptures. The *Kailasa* is accepted as having been excavated in the second half of the eighth century. The Brahamanical caves at Ellora would seem to belong to the earlier half of the same century (A 6).

NOTES TO CHAPTER SEVEN

A 1 The sculpture at Ajanta which is characterstic of Deccan Gupta art is very fine indeed. See Notes to Chapter Six.

A 2 Bagh can be dated to the 5th century A.D., being approximately contemporary with caves 16 and 17 of Ajanta. See Notes to Chapter Six.

A 3 This approach to the Badami friezes is not likely to be accepted today. Badami belongs to the early Chalukyan school, which was influenced to a considerable extent by the idiom of Deccan Gupta art. See Notes to Chapter Six.

A 4 Elephanta can confidently be assigned to a period not later than 650 A.D. It represents the high-water mark of post-Gupta art, along with Ellora and Mahabhalipuram. The sculptures of Mahabhalipuram near Madras are illustrated as Plates 75A, 76A, B and C, 77A, B, C and D. They belong to the mid-seventh century and represent the finest achievement of art under the Pallavas. Plate 76A and Plate 77B and C are from the great rock relief depicting Arjuna's Penance and formerly identified as the Gangavatarana myth. The slender elongated figures are characterstic of this post-Gupta development in the south where the other dominating influence was that of Amaravati. In the immediate post-Gupta period, *circa* 600 A.D., fine sculptures also were produced in other parts of the country. The Shiva from Shamlaji, Gujarat State (Pl. 75B), is one such example and another from Mathura is Kartikeyya (Plate 75C).

A 5 The famous so called Trimurti is really a Maheshwari Murti. It depicts the great god Shiva and not the three gods of the Trinity — Shiva, Vishnu and Brahma.

A 6 Some of the caves are likely to be even earlier.

[1] Fergusson and Burgess, *Cave Temples*, Pl. LXI.

Chapter Eight

THE EARLY SCHOOLS OF INDIAN PAINTING

Part I. AJANTA AND BAGH (A1)

Long history of painting in India and Ceylon.

FEW, very few, people realize that the art of painting in India and Ceylon has a long history, illustrated by extant examples ranging over a period exceeding two thousand years, and that during the so-called Dark Ages the Indian and Ceylonese painters attained a degree of proficiency not matched in Europe before the fourteenth or fifteen century. Nevertheless, such are the facts. In this chapter and the next following the history of the art in India and Ceylon, so far as its practice was dominated by Hindu ideas, will be traced from the earliest times of which there is record until the present day; but, unfortunately, the incompleteness of the record compels the historian to leave many gaps in his narrative. The widest of those gaps lies between the close of the Ajanta series in the seventh and the introduction of the Indo-Persian style by Akbar in the sixteenth century. During that long period of more than nine hundred years hardly anything definite is known concerning the productions of Indian and Ceylonese painters.

Literary evidence.

The ancient literature of India and Ceylon contains many references to pictorial art, the earliest, perhaps, being those in books of the Pali Buddhist canon dating from some three or four centuries before the Christian era. Several passages in those books tell of pleasure-houses belonging to the kings of Magadha and Kosala in Northern India as being adorned with painted figures and decorative patterns, presumably similar to the earliest known frescoes in Orissa and at Ajanta.[1] Painted halls are also mentioned in the *Ramayana;* and allusions to portraits are frequent in the dramas of Kalidasa and his successors from the fifth to the eighth century after Christ. The Ceylonese chronicle, the *Mahavamsa*, composed probably in the fifth century, tells of the mural paintings decorating the relic-chamber of the Ruwanweli *dagaba* constructed by King Dutthagamini about 150 B.C. The testimony of native writers is confirmed by that of the Chinese pilgrims in the fifth, sixth, and seventh centuries, who notice several examples of celebrated Buddhist pictures; and by Taranath, the Tibetan historian of Buddhism, who, when writing at the beginning of the seventeenth century, ascribes the most ancient pictures to the gods, and declares that they were so marvellous as to bewilder beholders by their realism.[2]

Range in time of extant remains.

The literary evidence thus summarily indicated would alone amply prove the early and continuous practice of the painter's art in both India and Ceylon; but it is unnecessary to labour the proof from books, because evidence of a more satisfactory kind is furnished by the considerable surviving remains of ancient painting from the second century before Christ; which, even in their present fragmentary and mutilated state, enable the modern critic to appraise the style of the early Indian artists, and to recognize the just claim of the art of India and Ceylon to take high rank among the ancient schools of painting. We will now proceed to give in this chapter an account of the extant remains of Indian and Ceylonese painting from the second century before Christ to the middle of the seventh century of the Christian era.

[1] Rhys-Davids, *Buddhist India*, p. 96 ; citing *Vin.*, ii. 151 ; iv. 47, 61, 298 ; *Sam.*, 42, 84.

[2] *Geschichte des Buddhismus*, ch. xxiv, transl. Schiefner, p. 278. His testimony will be discussed in the next chapter.

The oldest paintings.

The oldest Indian pictures are found in the Jogimara Cave of the Ramgarh Hill to the south of the Mirzapur District now attached to the Central Provinces.

These pictures, apparently executed in the customary Indian method of fresco, which will be explained presently, are divided into concentric circles by bands of red and yellow, sometimes enriched with a geometrical design, these circles seemingly being again subdivided into panels. The general nature of the subjects of the four best preserved panels can be understood from the following brief description:

Description.

A. In the centre a male figure is seated under a tree, with dancing girls and musicians to the left, and a procession, including an elephant, to the right.

B. This panel exhibits several male figures, a wheel, and sundry geometrical ornaments.

C. One half of this panel merely shows indistinct traces of flowers, horses, and clothed human figures.

In the other half is seen a tree having a bird and apparently a nude child in its branches, while round the tree are grouped other nude human figures, wearing their hair tied in a knot on the left side of the head.

D. The upper part of one half of this panel contains a nude male figure seated and attended by three clothed men standing, with two similar seated figures and three more attendants on one side. In the lower part are depicted a house with the horseshoe or so-called *chaitya* window, an elephant, and three clothed men standing in front. Near this group are shown a chariot drawn by three horses and surmounted by an umbrella, and a second elephant with an attendant. In the second half of the panel the figures are generally similar in character.

Date and style.

The early date of the paintings, which are fairly well preserved, is attested by inscriptions, evidently contemporary, and by the style, which recalls that of the sculptures at Sanchi and Bharhut. They probably date from the second century, and cannot well be later than the first century before Christ. The subjects cannot be interpreted at present, but the nudity of the principal figures suggests a connexion with the Jain rather than the Buddhist religion, if the cave and paintings had any religious significance, which is doubtful. As regards technique, the designs are painted usually in red, but occasionally in black, on a white ground. The outlines of the human and animal figures are drawn in black. Clothing is white with red outlines, hair is black, and eyes are white. Yellow appears in the dividing bands only, and blue does not seem to occur.[1]

Topography.

The story of the art of painting in India is continued by the celebrated frescoes of the Ajanta caves in the west, ranging in date from about A.D. 50 or earlier, to about the sixth century, a period of some six or seven centuries, and constituting the most important mass of ancient painting extant in the world, Pompeii only excepted. The caves, twenty-nine in number, are 'excavated in the face of an almost perpendicular scarp of rock about 250 feet high, sweeping round in a curve of fully a semicircle, and forming the north or outer side of a wild and lonely glen, down which comes a small stream'. This glen or ravine, a scene of great natural beauty and perfect seclusion, admirably adapted for a monastic retreat, is situated about three and a half miles south-west from Phardapur, a small town in the Nizam's Dominions, standing at the foot of a pass across the Indhyadri Hills, which divide the tableland of the Deccan from the Khandesh District in

[1] The only information on the subject is recorded by the late Dr. Bloch in *Ann. Rep. A. S., Bengal Circle*, 1903-4, pp. 12-14 ; and *Ann. Rep. A. S., India*, 1903-4, p. 130.

A. Bhairava. Dasavatara Cave, Ellora. (7th Cent. A.D. Post-Gupta. early Rashtrakuta period).
(Copyright by Department of Archaeology, Government of India)

B, C. Indra (*left*) and Ambika (*right*). Jain deities from the Jain rock-temple, Ellora. 9th Cent. A.D. End of the post-Gupta period.

PLATE 85

A. Dance scene from Aurangabad Caves. 7th Cent. A.D. Immediate post-Gupta period in the Deccan.

(*Copyright by Department of Archaeology, Government of India*)

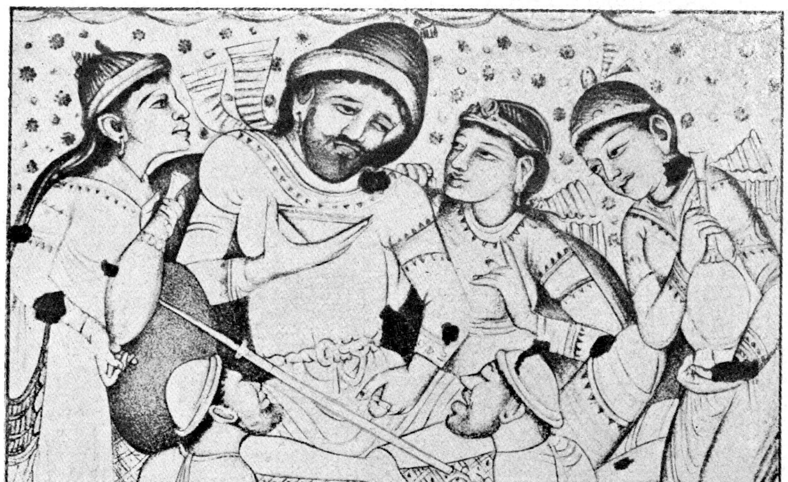

B. Group of foreigners, from Ceiling of Cave I, Ajanta. (Bacchanalian scene. Probably Panchisika and Hariti. This panel appears to be the work of artists from North-West India or beyond. 6th Century, A.D.).

(From Griffiths, *The Paintings of the Cave Temples of Ajanta*)

PLATE 86

the Tapti valley, and four miles WNW. from the town of Ajanta, not far from the battle-field of Assaye.

The caves.

'The caves extend for a distance of about 600 yards from east to west round the concave wall of amygdaloid trap which hems in the stream on its north or left side, and vary in elevation from about 35 to 100 feet above the level of the torrent.' The numbers by which authors have agreed to designate them begin at the east end. Four of the excavations, Nos. IX, X, XIX, and XXVI, are churches (the so-called *chaityas*), the rest being monastic residences, the *viharas* of English writers. Some have never been completed. The principal works are elaborate architectural compositions, executed in the solid rock, the nature of which is very inadequately expressed by the term 'caves'.

Extent and date of paintings.

In 1879 paintings to a greater or lesser extent remained in sixteen caves, Nos. I, II, IV, VI, VII, IX, X, XI, XV, XVI, XVII, XIX, XX, XXI, XXII, and XXVI. The most important fragments were then to be seen in nine caves, Nos. I, II, IX, X, XI, XVI, XVII, XIX, and XXI, those in Cave XVII being the most extensive.[1] The most ancient excavations, Nos. VIII, XII, and XIII, have no paintings. No. XIII, perhaps the earliest of all, has polished walls, and may date from 200 B.C. Six of the caves, Nos. VIII, IX, X, XI (with some sculpture possibly later), XII, and XIII are concerned with the early *Hinayana* form of Buddhism, and may be considered to cover a period of about three and a half centuries from 200 B.C. to A.D. 150. All the others were dedicated to the *Mahayana* forms of worship. Nos. VI and VII may be assigned to the century between A.D. 450 and 550. The rest, namely Nos. XIV to XX, XXI-XXIX, and I-V seem to have been excavated between *c.* A.D. 500, several having been left incomplete. No. I was held by Fergusson to be the latest of the completed works.

The paintings are not necessarily of exactly the same age as the caves which they adorn. The most ancient unquestionably are certain works in Caves IX and X, partially overlaid by later pictures. These earliest paintings are so closely related to the Sanchi sculptures that they may be referred to approximately the same age, about the beginning of the Christian era, or earlier. They may, perhaps, be credited to the patronage of the powerful Andhra kings of the Deccan, who, even if not themselves Buddhists, certainly put no obstacle in the way of Buddhist worship. So far as appears, no paintings were executed for centuries afterwards.[2]

The bulk of the paintings unquestionably must be assigned to the time of the great Chalukya kings (A.D. 550-642) and of the earlier Vakataka kings of Berar. A Vakataka inscription exists in Cave XVI. It is unlikely that any can have been executed later than the second date named, when Pulakesin II was dethroned and presumably killed by the Pallava king of the South. The resulting political conditions must have been unfavourable for the execution of costly works of art dedicated to the service of Buddhism, the Pallava kings having been, as a rule, ardent worshippers of Siva. The related paintings at Bagh in Malwa may be dated at some time in the sixth century, or the first half of the seventh. A close relation exists between the frescoes and certain sculptural additions at Ajanta such

[1] The amount remaining is now much reduced. In 1909-10 Mrs. Herringham found considerable remains only in Caves I, II, IX, X, XVI, and XVII (*Burlington Magazine*, vol. xvii, June 1910, pp. 136-8, with two Plates). See also her remarks in *Catalogue and Guide to the Indian Court, Festival of Empire*, published in July 1911.

[2] The Buddhas on the pillars of Cave X have been considered to antedate the bulk of the paintings, but they show signs of poor craftsmanship rather than of antiquity. According to Mrs. Herringham, these are the only paintings now left in Cave X. The wall-paintings described by Burgess in 1879 have disappeared.

as the Temptation scene in Cave 26 as well as with the earliest work at Ellora which is also Buddhist.

Recent history of the paintings.

The Ajanta paintings first became known to Europeans in 1819, but failed to attract much attention until 1843, when Mr. James Fergusson, the historian of architecture, published a description of them and persuaded the Directors of the East India Company to sanction the preparation of copies at the public expense. In pursuance of the orders of the Court, Major Gill, a competent and conscientious artist, was deputed some years later, and continued at work until the outbreak of the Mutiny in 1857.[1] The copies then executed, thirty or more in number, were sent home from time to time, and with the exception of five, the last executed, perished in 1866 in a fire at the Crystal Palace, where they were exhibited. Nothing remains of the lost copies except a few small-scale outline engravings in Mrs. Speir's *Ancient India* (1856), and reproductions of them in *Ancient and Medieval India* (1869) by the same lady under the name of Manning, and also in the *Notes on the Bauddha Rock-Temples of Ajanta* (1879) by Dr. Burgess.

Since then fresh copies have been prepared between 1872 and 1885 by Mr. Griffiths of the Bombay School of Art, and his pupils, which have been published in two magnificent atlas folio volumes entitled *The Paintings of the Buddhist Cave Temples of Ajanta, Khandesh, India* (1896). The India Office also possesses a fine volume of photographs arranged by Dr. Burgess (A 2).

The Crystal Palace fire did not exhaust the ill-luck of these famous paintings. A subsequent fire at the South Kensington Museum destroyed or damaged many of Mr. Griffiths's copies, as shown in detail in the Appendix to volume ii of his work. The copies, more than a hundred in number, which escaped the fires are exhibited in the Indian Section of the Victoria and Albert Museum at South Kensington, but many of them have been damaged.

Injuries suffered by the paintings.

Publicity has been fatal to the originals, and the Government of H.H. the Nizam, in whose territories the caves are situated, for some time showed little concern for their preservation. Indeed, thirty years ago one of his subordinate officials wrought much damage by cutting out heads to present to visitors; and, shameful to say, Dr. Bird, a Bombay archaeologist, was guilty of the same crime with the intention of benefiting the Museum at Bombay. Of course, all the fragments of plaster thus abstracted crumbled to dust and were lost irretrievably. Much injury also has been done by smoke from the fires of Hindu ascetics camping in the caves, by the folly of irresponsible scribblers of various nationalities, and by the unchecked action of bats, birds, and nest-building insects. In 1903-4 wire screens were fixed up in all the more important caves, and a good deal of cleaning was done. In 1908 the Department submitted a scheme for further conservation to the Government of the Nizam. Since then the caves have been amply protected and a curator appointed. Exact copies have also been made of the frescoes by means of tracing and photography and the frescoes themselves have been finely preserved.

The long-continued neglect of these precious remains offers a painful contrast to the vigorous and effective action taken by the Government of Ceylon to preserve the fifth-century paintings at Sigiriya which will be described in due course. At Ajanta the result of neglect and wilful injury is that the existing paintings are

[1] His portrait appears in Plate 34 of Fergusson's scarce octavo work entitled *The Rock-cut Temples of India, illustrated by 74 photographs taken on the spot by Major Gill* (Murray, 1864); photograph No. 616 in *India office List of Negatives.*

A

B

C

D

E

A, B, C, D, E. Small panels from ceiling of Cave 1, Ajanta.
(6th Century A. D. Deccan Gupta period).

F. Figures in spandril of central ceiling panel, Cave 1, Ajanta.
(6th Century A.D. Deccan Gupta period).

(From Griffiths, *The Paintings of the Buddhist Cave Temples of Ajanta*)

A. Female figure, Cave II, Ajanta. (6th Cent. A.D. Deccan Gupta period).

B. Seated woman, Cave IX, Ajanta. (1st Cent. A.D. Satavahana period).

C. Woman carrying child, Cave XVII, Ajanta. (Late 5th Cent. A.D. Deccan Gupta period under the Vakatakas).

D. Buddha, Cave X, Ajanta. (5th Cent. A.D. Deccan Gupta period under the Vakatakas).

(From Griffiths, *The Paintings of the Buddhist Cave Temples of Ajanta*)

A. Wall painting from Vaishnavite Cave, Badami. Last quarter of the 6th Cent. A.D. Early western Chalukyan school with some Gupta influence.

B. Wall painting from Jain Caves, Sittanavasal, from Pudukottai State. 7th Cent. A.D. Pallava idiom. Post-Gupta period.

PLATE 89

A. Sigiriya frescoes; 'Pocket B', Figs. 3, 4.

B. Sigiriya frescoes; 'Pocket B', Figs. 7, 8.
(*Copyright by Archaeology Department, Ceylon*)

PLATE 90

only a small fraction of those visible in 1819, when the caves were first brought to notice. Nevertheless, in spite of all mischances, enough either remains or has been recorded to indicate the course of Indian pictorial art for some six centuries or more.

Many of the paintings referred to in this chapter, which existed in 1879, when Dr. Burgess wrote, have since disappeared.

The paintings are frescoes of the Indian kind.

The Ajanta pictures may be correctly termed frescoes, although the process used is not exactly the same as any practised in Europe.

'The Indian practice of wall-painting at Ajanta, as elsewhere', Mr. Griffiths observes, 'is in fact a combination of tempera with fresco. The hydraulic nature of Indian lime, or *chunam*, makes it possible to keep a surface moist for a longer time than in Europe, and the Indian practice of trowelling the work—unknown in Europe—produced a closer and more intimate *liaison* between the colour and the lime, and a more durable and damp-resisting face than the open texture of European fresco. The art has been practised all over India since the time of the Ajanta frescoes, and to this day houses, mosques, and temples are thus decorated. The modern method is first to spread a ground of coarse mortar (*chunam*) of the thickness of from half to one inch on the wall. This is allowed to stand for a day. If on the next day the ground is too dry, it is moistened, and then tapped all over with the edge of a small piece of wood of triangular section, to roughen it and give it a tooth. Then, with a coarse brush, a thin coating of fine white plaster (*chunam*) is applied, and the work is allowed to stand till the next day, being moistened all the time. If the painting is to be highly finished, the ground is carefully smoothed with a small flat iron trowel about the size of a dessert spoon, which produces a surface on which the design is first sketched, or transferred by pouncing from a perforated drawing on paper, and then painted.

The outline is usually put in first in brown or black; local colour is filled in with flat washes, on which the details are painted.

The colours are ground with rice or linseed-water with a little coarse molasses (*gur*), and water only is used in painting. Then, when the painting is completed, it is again rubbed over with the same small trowel. . . . It is considered absolutely necessary that the work should be kept damp from beginning to finish, so that the plaster is not allowed to set until the completion of the picture. When once the smoothly trowelled surface is dry, it bears a distinct sheen or gloss and the colours withstand washing.

The process used at Ajanta.

Between the methods of modern India and that employed at Ajanta, the only difference is that instead of a first coat of mortar, a mixture of clay, cow-dung, and pulverized trap rock was first applied to the walls and thoroughly pressed into its [*sic*] surface, when the small cavities and air-holes peculiar to volcanic rock and the rough chisel marks left by the excavators served as keys. In some instances, especially in the ceilings, rice husks were used.

This first layer—which, according to our modern notions, promises no great permanence—was laid to a thickness varying from one-eighth to three-quarters of an inch, and on it an egg-shell coat of fine white plaster was spread. This skin of plaster, in fact, overlaid everything—mouldings, columns, carven ornaments, and figure sculptures, but, in the case of carved details, without the intervention of the coat of earthen rough-cast; and, from what remains, it is clear that the whole of each cave was thus plaster-coated and painted. The texture of the volcanic rock, which is at once hard, open, impervious to damp, and yet full of air-holes, is especially suitable for this treatment. Great pains were taken with the statues of Buddha; one in the small chamber to the right of the first floor of Cave VI is covered with a layer of the finest plaster one-eighth of an inch thick, so painted and polished that the face has the smoothness and sheen of porcelain.[1]

It will be seen that a parallel to the technique of the Ajanta paintings is scarcely to be found in the Italian frescoes. But it is evident from specimens of the Egyptian work in the British Museum that loam or clay mixed with chopped straw formed the substratum over which, as at Ajanta, a layer of fine plaster was laid to receive the final painting.

It may not be impertinent again to point out the exceeding simplicity of the Indian and Egyptian methods, which have ensured a durability denied to more recent attempts executed with all the aids of modern chemical science.'[2]

[1] In Cave IX the early picture H which Mr. Griffiths exposed and copied, after removing a later damaged painting, was executed on a coat of finest plaster, 1/32 inch thick, applied directly to the rock, and polished like porcelain.

[2] Griffiths, op. cit., p. 18.

The foregoing description of the technique of the Ajanta paintings, based upon Mr. Griffiths's patient study for thirteen years on the spot, may be accepted with confidence as authoritative, although Mr. Havell may be right in adding that the pictures were sometimes touched up in tempera after the surface had dried. Italian workers in true fresco (*fresco buono*) often permit themselves the same liberty.[1]

Observations of Mrs. Herringham.

But it will be well to supplement Mr. Griffiths's account by the recent observations of Mrs. Herringham, also an expert artist, who writes:

'The technique adopted, with perhaps some few exceptions, is a bold red line-drawing on the white plaster. Sometimes nothing else is left. This drawing gives all the essentials with force or delicacy as may be required, and with knowledge and intention. Next comes a thinnish terra-verde monochrome showing some of the red through it; then the local colour; then a strengthening of the outlines with blacks and browns giving great decision, but also a certain flatness; last, a little shading if necessary. There is not much definite light and shade modelling, but there is great definition given by the use of contrasting local colour and of emphatic blacks and whites.'

Mr. Griffiths, it will be observed, does not mention the first outline in red.

Pigments.

The nature of fresco-painting in any of its forms implies the use of a limited range of pigments capable of resisting the decomposing action of lime, and consequently composed of natural earths. At Ajanta and Bagh the colours most freely used are white, red, and brown in various shades, a dull green, and blue. The white is opaque, mainly composed of sulphate of lime; the reds and browns derive their tints solely from compounds of iron; the green is a silicate, similar to the mineral now known as *terre verte;* and the blue is ultramarine, which was obtained in ancient times by grinding calcined lapis lazuli, a costly semi-precious mineral usually imported from either Persia or Badakshan. All the other pigments are to be found locally. The long panels of the ceilings in Cave II, dating from about A.D. 600, offer well-preserved examples of charming floral decorations in blue (Griffiths, Plates 123-5). In the early paintings of the Ramgarh Hill, Orissa (*ante*, p. 273), and the fifth-century works at Sigiriya in Ceylon (*post*, Sec. 5 of this chapter), blue never occurs. At Ajanta, yellow, so largely used at Anuradhapura in Ceylon, apparently is very rare. The yellow of ancient painters is believed to have been always orpiment, a natural arsenic sulphide.

Subjects of pictures.

The subjects of the pictures, as distinguished from the purely decorative devices, are almost exclusively Buddhist. They include, of course, numerous figures of Buddha and representations of sacred objects and symbols. The more complex compositions for the most part deal with either the incidents of the life of Gautama Buddha or those related in the Jataka stories, which narrate the events of his former births. In at least two cases the Jataka story is indicated beyond dispute by a painted label, but the fragmentary condition of the pictures renders difficult the identification of most of the scenes.[2] There is, however, no difficulty in recognizing in Cave X the tale of the six-tusked elephant, and a few other legends may be identified with more or less certainty.[3] Miscellaneous edifying Buddhist

[1] For a good summary account of the European processes see the article 'Fresco' in Chambers's *Encyclopaedia* (1905). Mr. J. L. Kipling, a competent authority, states that the fresco-painting on the walls of the mosque of Wazir Khan at Lahore, 'which is very freely painted and in good style, is true fresco-painting, the *buono fresco* of the Italians, and, like the inlaid ceramic work, is now no longer practised, modern native decoration being usually *fresco secco*, or mere distemper painting' (*Lahore Guide*, 1876; quoted in Birdwood, *Industrial Arts of India* (1880), p. 228).

[2] Close upon twenty Jatakas may be identified. *Guide Ajanta Frescoes*. Arch. Dep. Hyderabad State.

[3] In Cave XVII the story of Sibi Raja, who gave his eyes to the beggar (No. 499; Cowell and Rouse, *transl.*, vol. iv, p. 250) is labelled. In Cave II the Kshantivadin and Maitribala *jataka* pictures are accompanied by quotations from the *Jataka Mala* of Arya Sura inscribed in characters of about the sixth century, the former being also labelled by name (Heinrich Lüders, 'Arya Sura's Jatakamala und die Fresken von Ajanta', *Nachr. d königl. Gesellschaft d. Wissenschaften zu Gottingen, Phil.-Hist. Klasse*, 1902, p. 758). The story of the six-tusked elephant is No. 514 (Cowell and Francis, vol. v, p. 20).

A. Sigiriya frescoes; 'Pocket B', Figs. 11, 12.
(*Copyright by Archaeology Department, Ceylon*)

B. *Kinnara* and lotuses. Ruwanweli, Anuradhapura.

C. Dwarf. Ruwanweli, Anuradhapura.

(From Smither, *Architecture Remains, Anuradhapura, Ceylon*)

A. General view of Muktesvara Temple, Bhuvanesvar, Orissa. *Cir.* 900 A.D.

B. Rajarani Temple, Bhuvanesvar, Orissa. *Cir.* 10th Cent. A.D.

subjects, not taken from the Jataka collection, include the *Litany of Avalokitesvara* and consecutive scenes from the life of the Buddha; the Wheel of Life, formerly miscalled the Zodiac.[1]

Decorative designs.

The high achievement of the Ajanta artists in decorative design executed with masterly skill is most freely exhibited in the ceiling panels of Cave I, painted in the first half of the seventh century (Plate 87A to F). Mr. Griffiths, who took so much pleasure in copying the designs, describes their variety as infinite, carried into the smallest details, so that repetition is very rare; fancy is given full play, and the simplest objects of nature, being pressed into the artist's service, are converted into pleasing and effective ornament.

'The smaller panels', he observes, 'are ornamented with designs as varied and graceful as they are fanciful. Some with grotesque little figures, rich in humour and quaintly dressed in Persian turbans, coats, and striped stockings; gambolling amid fruits and flowers; dancing, drinking, or playing upon instruments; or chattering together; some with animals combined with the lotus, drawn with remarkable fidelity and action: as the elephant, humped bull, and the monkey; parrots, geese, and conventional birds singly and in pairs, with foliated crests, and tails convoluted like heraldic lambrequins, showing the upper and under surface of the ornament. Some contain the large pink lotus, full-bloom, half-bloom, and in bud, as well as the smaller red and white; some with the mango (*Mangifera indica*), custard apple (*Anona squamosa*); a round fruit which may be the *bel* (*Aegle marmelos*) or the lime (*limbu*); another that looks like the brinjal or aubergine (*Solanum melongena*), and many others.

The ornament in these panels is painted alternately on a black and red ground. The ground colour was first laid over the panel, and then the ornament painted solidly upon this in white. It was further developed by thin transparent colours over the white.'[2]

Examples of small panels.

The reader who desires to realize fully the justice of Mr. Griffiths's panegyric must study his numerous plates, or the full-sized copies in the Indian Section of the Victoria and Albert Museum at South Kensington; or, best of all, Mrs. Herringham's recent copies. Here it is not possible to give more than a few specimens.

Panels in Cave II

Cave II presents some very good work. The circular panels (Griffiths, Plates 115, 117-19 coloured and 120, 121 uncoloured) are very fine, the figures in the spandrils being particularly good and full of movement. These circular panels have a distant resemblance to the carved moonstones of Ceylon. The long ceiling panels (Griffiths, Plates 122-31 coloured and 132 uncoloured) are admirable.

Picture of fighting bulls.

The decorative designs in Cave I include a minor picture of considerable interest painted on a bracket capital (Griffiths, Plate 114). The subject is that of two bulls fighting, and its treatment proves the artist's knowledge of animal form and his power of expressing vigorous action. The same subject, with variations of detail, is treated in a sculpture at the ancient cave of Bhaja, dating from about the beginning of the Christian era or earlier, and again in a sixteenth-century painting at Akbar's capital, Fatehpur Sikri. It occurs also in a well-known sculpture in the Louvre, brought from the Doric temple at Assos in the Troad, and dating from about 500 B.C.[3]

Cave XVII.

In the sixth-century Cave XVII, the charming floral designs combined with human figures on the panels of the pillars (Griffiths, Plates 144-9) are closely related to the slightly earlier sculptured work on the Garhwa pillars in Northern India

[1] Fergusson identified one of the scenes in Cave I portraying foreigners in pointed caps as the reception of an embassy from Khushru Parviz, King of Persia, to Pulakesin II, *c.* A.D. 626: the representation of such a secular scene is contrary to the general trend of Ajanta painting and Indian art as a whole.

[2] Griffiths, op. cit., pp. 41, 42.

[3] For Bhaja see Fergusson and Burgess, *The Cave Temples of India* (1880), p. 536; for Assos, Texier and Pullan, *Principal Buildings in Asia Minor*, Pl. I; or Texier, *Asie Mineure*, vol. ii, pp. 112-14. The Fathpur Sikri frescoes are reproduced by E. W. Smith, *Fathpur-Sikri*, vol. i, Pl. XI-XIII, XV, *a*, *b*, *c*; CIX-CXX, and also partly in the *J. I. A. I.* (July 1894), and Griffiths, op. cit.

(*ante*, p. 166). The *kirttimukha* grinning faces in Plate 146 are common throughout medieval Indian art. As chaste decoration it would be difficult to surpass the frets in Griffiths, Plates 143 and 149.

Spandril picture in Cave I. The pair of lovers in a spandril of the central panel of the ceiling of Cave I is admirably drawn, and although forming only a subordinate member of a decorative design, is worthy of reproduction as a cabinet picture (Plate 87F).

Wall-pictures. We now proceed to describe, so far as space permits, characteristic examples of the larger pictures on the walls of the caves in chronological order. But the pictures being too large to admit of intelligible reproduction as complete compositions, except on a scale far beyond the dimensions of this book, the illustrations will be confined to extracts from the paintings, which are generally overcrowded and lacking in the unity derived from skilled composition.

Early pictures in Cave IX. The earliest works, as already stated, are certain paintings in Caves IX and X, closely related to the Sanchi sculptures. The seated woman is a pleasing example from the painting H in Cave IX (Plate 88B), which Mr. Griffiths exposed by

Outline of elephant in Cave X, Ajanta.

removing a later and damaged picture. The old composition was painted on a thin porcelain-like skin of fine plaster applied direct to the rock.

Early pictures in Cave X; elephants. In cave X the remains of early paintings are, or were thirty years ago, more extensive. The fragments on the right-hand wall then consisted chiefly of elephants drawn in outline 'in a strikingly bold and true style'.

On the left 'was a procession of men, some on foot, some on horseback, variously armed, some with halberts, and differently dressed; and behind were groups of women; but all have been defaced by native visitors within the last twenty years or less', that is to say, prior to 1879. Numerous heads and figures in these scenes, admirably drawn and full of spirit and character, are reproduced in Plates VIII-X of Dr. Burgess's *Notes*, from drawings preserved at the India Office, made by a Hindu student of the School of Art, Jayrao Raghoba. The group shown in his Plate X, a Raja in the midst of eight female attendants (see illustration on p. 94), is unusually well composed. The perspective of the numerous figures is satisfactory, and the drawing of the hands and arms is particularly good.

Figures of Buddha.

I am disposed to think that the figures of Buddha painted on the pillars of Cave X (Griffiths, Plates 42, 43, and cover) are the next in date, and should be assigned to the fifth century, but they might be later. The nimbus and draperies recall early Christian art and the sculptures of Gandhara. The best is shown in Plate 88D. These are now (1910) the only paintings left in Cave X.

Cave XVI.

The whole interior of Cave XVI was once covered with paintings of high merit, but even thirty years ago many of them had been destroyed. The plates in Mr. Griffiths's work include little from this cave, although his copies, execpt three burnt, are preserved at South Kensington.

The 'Dying Princess'.

The scene known as the 'Dying Princess', reproduced by Mr. Griffiths in 1874, was deservedly praised by him in glowing language, endorsed by Dr. Burgess and Mr. Fergusson, which merits quotation:

> 'A lady of rank sits on a couch leaning her left arm on the pillow, and an attendant behind holds her up. A girl in the background places her hand on her breast and looks towards the lady. Another with a sash across her breast wields the *pankha* [fan], and an old man in a white cap looks in at the door, while another sits beside a pillar. In the foreground sit two women. In another apartment are two figures; one with a Persian cap has a water-vessel (*kalasa*) and a cup in the mouth of it; the other, with negro-like hair, wants something from him. To the right two *kanchukinis* [female servants] sit in a separate compartment. . . . For pathos and sentiment and the unmistakable way of telling its story this picture, I consider, cannot be surpassed in the history of art. The Florentine could have put better drawing, and the Venetian better colour, but neither could have thrown greater expression into it. The dying woman, with drooping head, half-closed eyes, and languid limbs, reclines on a bed, the like of which may be found in any native house of the present day. She is tenderly supported by a female attendant; whilst another with eager gaze is looking into her face, and holding the sick woman's arm as if in the act of feeling her pulse. The expression on her face is one of deep anxiety as she seems to realize how soon life will be extinct in the one she loves. Another female behind is in attendance with a *pankha*, whilst two men on the left are looking on with the expression of profound grief depicted in their faces. Below are seated on the floor other relations, who appear to have given up all hope and to have begun their days of mourning, for one woman has buried her face in her hand and apparently is weeping bitterly.'[1]

Persian figures.

Other figures wearing the Persian cap appear in a second painting (No. 6 of Burgess) in the same cave, and may be compared with the representation of the so-called Persian embassy and connected minor pictures in Cave I.

Cave XVII.

Cave XVII, which is little later in date than Cave XVI, and thirty years ago, whatever may be the case now, could show more painting than any of the others, may fairly be considered the most interesting of the series.[2] No less than sixty-one distinct scenes are described in Dr. Burgess's *Notes.* The two large pictures, reproduced in outline in his Plates XVIII and XIX, are so excessively crowded with figures and so deficient in unity of composition that they cannot be presented satisfactorily except on an enormous scale.

The 'Wheel of Life', &c.

The representation in the left end of the verandah of the Buddhist Wheel of Life, commonly miscalled the Zodiac, is interesting rather as an illustration of popular Buddhist teaching in the sixth century than as a work of art. Similar pictures are still frequently exhibited in Tibetan monasteries and used by the Lamas for purposes of instruction. The dimensions of the Ajanta painting, now

[1] *Ind. Ant.*, vol. iii, pp. 25 *seqq.*, with uncoloured plate. The text is quoted in Burgess, *Notes*, p. 58. He numbers the painting as 5. The picture is not included in Mr. Griffith's special work.

[2] Mrs. Herringham notes that 'in Cave XVI, slightly the earlier, nearly everything is obscured, but in Cave XVII many interesting subjects still remain intelligible'.

Raja and women, Early painting, Cave X, Ajanta.

A. Parasuramesvara Temple, Bhuvanesvar, Orissa. 9th Cent. A.D

B. Temple of the Sun, Konarak, Orissa. 13th Century.

PLATE 93

A. Temple of Vishvanath, Khajuraho. *Cir.* 1000 A.D.
(*Copyright by Department of Archaeology, Government of India*)

B. The Council Hall, Vijayanagar. 16th Century.
(Photo: Klein and Peyerl)

PLATE 94

a mere fragment, are 8 feet 7 inches by 5 feet 1 inch.[1] The huge painting indicated in Burgess's Plate XIX was supposed to represent the legend of the landing of King Vijaya in Ceylon and his coronation as described in the Pali chronicles, but is actually a faithful rendering of the *Simhala Avadana*. Painting No. LIV (Griffiths, Plate 82) gives the story of Sibi Raja, already mentioned.

Cave XIX. Among the later caves the *Chaitya* or church, Cave XIX, which is elaborately carved throughout and has its porch and whole front covered with beautiful sculpture, was considered by Mr. Fergusson to be 'one of the most perfect specimens of Buddhist art in India'. The paintings include many effigies of Buddha (Griffiths, Plate 89), and some exquisite panels on the roof of the front aisle, as well as rich floriated patterns on the roofs of the side aisles.

Cave II. We now pass to Caves I and II, No. I being probably the latest of the completed works.

Mr. Griffiths has devoted a large number of plates (Nos. 20-35 and 115-32) to Cave II, besides nine text illustrations. The individual figures are remarkable for clever drawing, the artist having apparently gone out of his way to invent specially difficult poses. Mr. Griffiths's figure 8, a woman prostrating herself, and figure 16, snake-hooded *Nagas*, or water-sprites, are good examples of such *tours de force*. The woman standing, with her left leg bent up (Plate 88A), is capital, the feet being as well drawn as the hands; and the woman in the swing (Fig. 66) is pleasing and life-like. Fig. 5 of Griffiths is reproduced (Plate 88C).

Cave I. The elegant decorative designs of Cave I have already been described. The numerous large wall-pictures include the Temptation of Buddha, a subject also effectively treated in sculpture in Cave XXVI, not far removed in date. In this cave is also the so-called Persian embassy scene. The identification is based (*a*) upon the pointed caps which are considered to be Persian; (*b*) upon the statement of an Arab historian that an embassy was sent by Pulakesin II to the Persian court in A.D. 626 (A 3).

Khusru Parviz. Four smaller pictures placed symmetrically at the corners of the central square of the principal design of the roof, and all replicas of one subject, with variations, evidently have some connexion with the other 'Persian' pictures, which measures 15 by 6½ feet. The best of these small compositions has been illustrated by Mr. Griffiths both from a photograph (Plate 95, Fig. 4) and from a water-colour drawing (Plate 94, Fig. 4). The colours of the latter seem to be too brilliant, and a more faithful reproduction by Mr. Griggs was published by Fergusson, which is here reproduced uncoloured by permission of the Council of the Royal Asiatic Society (Plate 86B). Fergusson, developing the Persian myth, assumed that the principal personages depicted must be King Khusru and his famous consort, Shirin, but this attractive hypothesis cannot be said to be proved.[2] (A 4).

Aesthetic value. The foregoing descriptions and illustrations will enable the reader to form a judgement concerning the aesthetic value of the Ajanta paintings, and I trust that nobody will be found to agree with the opinion expressed in Sir George Watt's

[1] The picture and its Tibetan counterparts are discussed fully by Col. Waddell in 'The Budhist Pictorial Wheel of Life (Zodiac)' in *J. A. S. B.*, vol. lxi (1892), Part I, pp. 133-55, with plates. His Pl. VII corresponds with Griffiths, Pl. 56.

[2] J. Fergusson, 'On the Identification of the portrait of Chosroes II among the Paintings in the Caves at Ajanta' (*J. R. A. S.*, April, 1879); Rajendralala Mitra, 'On Representations of Foreigners in the Ajanta Frescos' (*J. A. S. B.*, vol. xlvii (1878), Part I, pp. 66-72, and four uncoloured plates). His Pl. IV corresponds with Fergusson's plate and the small outline copy in Burgess, *Notes*, Pl. IV, Fig. 2.

book that they 'can hardly be classed among the fine arts'.[1] The pictures and decorative designs in the caves, when compared with Egyptian, Chinese, or other ancient paintings, which did not profess to show the relief effect of modern pictures, are fairly entitled to high rank as works of fine art. In judging them the critic should remember that the wall-paintings were executed on an enormous scale, some being more than 20 feet in diameter, and that they were intended to be looked at in the mass from a distance, and not in minute detail. Small reproductions on a page a few inches long cannot possibly give a just idea of the effects aimed at by the artists. Moreover, those artists were much concerned to tell sacred stories, and make their pictures serve for the edification of devout worshippers as instructive illustrations of the Buddhist Bible; whereas all the religious sentiment in the spectator on which they relied for sympathetic understanding is wanting in the modern European critic. Yet, in spite of the disadvantages inherent in small-scale reproductions and criticism by judges out of touch with the spirit of the artists, the paintings stand the unfair test wonderfully well, and excite respectful admiration as the production of painters capable of deep emotion, full of sympathy with the nature of men, women, children, animals, and plants, and endowed with masterly powers of execution.

Mr. Griffiths's verdict.

The considered verdict of Mr. Griffiths, the artist who spent thirteen years in the close, loving study of the paintings, may be accepted as a sound general criticism, not attempting to distinguish periods and styles :—

> 'In spite', he writes, 'of its obvious limitations, I find the work so accomplished in execution, so consistent in convention, so vivacious and varied in design, and full of such evident delight in beautiful form and colour, that I cannot help ranking it with some of the early art which the world has agreed to praise in Italy. . . . The Ajanta workmanship is admirable; long subtle curves are drawn with great precision in a line of unvarying thickness with one sweep of the brush; the touch is often bold and vigorous, the handling broad, and in some cases the *impasto* is as solid as in the best Pompeian work. . . . The draperies, too, are thoroughly understood, and though the folds may be somewhat conventionally drawn, they express most thoroughly the peculiarities of the Oriental treatment of unsewn cloth. . . . For the purposes of art-education no better examples could be placed before an Indian art-student than those to be found in the caves of Ajanta. Here we have art with life in it, human faces full of expression, limbs drawn with grace and action, flowers which bloom, birds which soar, and beasts that spring, or fight, or patiently carry burdens; all are taken from Nature's book—growing after her pattern, and in this respect differing entirely from Muhammadan art, which is unreal, unnatural, and therefore incapable of development.'[2]

Comparison with early Italian art.

Whatever be the value of the incidental criticism on Muhammadan art—a subject to be discussed in due course—Mr. Griffiths's hearty appreciation of the Ajanta frescoes is, in my judgement, just and well deserved.

In support of his comparison with the performance of the early Italians, he aptly cites the fragment of a fresco with heads of nuns by Ambrogio Lorenzetti, executed in the fourteenth century, and now in the Sienese Room of the National Gallery, as being 'singularly like the Ajanta work in colour, execution, and treatment; the forms being drawn with a delicate brown outline, and the flesh-tints

[1] It is only fair to quote this dictum in full :—'*Painting.*—This may be said to be divided into three distinct styles. The Buddhist, exemplified by the frescos on the walls of the caves of Ajanta. . . . The first mentioned is more decorative than pictorial, so that it can hardly be classed among the Fine Arts, and is therefore omitted from a description of what is intended to be an account of painting in the pictorial sense only. The earliest true pictures, therefore, of which we have any record are the productions of the old Moghul painters' (Sir George Watt, *Indian Art at Delhi* (1904), p. 454). The opinions recorded in the book are partly those of Mr. Percy Brown.

[2] Griffiths, *The Paintings of the Buddhist Caves of Ajanta*, pp. 7, 9; *Ind. Ant.*, iii. 28. The work done by the Bombay students shows that they were capable of appreciating the ancient models set before them. Many of the designs have been used for the decoration of pottery made at the Bombay School of Art. Examples are shown in the Indian Section of the Victoria and Albert Museum.

A. Ceiling of Tejpal Temple, Mt. Abu. A.D. 1230. Late Solanki style.
(Photo : A. L. Syed)

B. Sculpture from Dilwara Temple, Mt. Abu. 13th Cent. A.D.
Late Solanki style. (Photo : Damoder Hansraj)

PLATE 95

A. Pillars of upper hall of Tejpal's Temple, Mt. Abu. A.D. 1230.

B. Temple of the Sun at Osia, Jodhpur State, Rajputana (Rajasthan). Late 9th Century.

A. Details of temple of Martand, Kashmir. 8th Century.
(From a drawing by W. Simpson)
(By Courtesy of Royal Institute of British Architects)

C. Buddha from Kurkihar. Lucknow Museum.
(10th-11th Cent. A.D. Pala school).
(Copyright by Department of Archaeology, Government of India)

B. Indrani, Jajpur, Bengal. 10th Century.

D. Buddha from near Rajgir. (10th-11th Cent. A.D. Pala school).
(By Courtesy of Royal Asiatic Society of Bengal)

A. Marichi, Goddess of Dawn, from Kurkihar. Lucknow Museum. (11th Cent. A.D. Pala school).

(Copyright by Department of Archaeology, Government of India)

B. Surya, excavated in the Rajmahai Hills, Santal Parganas, Bengal. Ind. Sec., V & A. Museum. (11th-12th Cent. A.D. Pala-Sena school).

C. Ardhanarisvara. 11th-12th Cent. A.D. Pala-Sena school. Rajshahi Museum.

(Copyright by Department of Archaeology, Government of India)

PLATE 98

and drapery flatly put in with very little modelling'. The obvious comparison with ancient Italian art was also made by Mr. Fergusson, who considered the Ajanta paintings to be better than anything in Europe before the time of Orcagna in the fourteenth, or even Fiesole (Fra Angelico) in the fifteenth century. Similarly, Mr. Havell, another trained artist, who selects the charming Mother and Child in Cave XVII (Griffiths, Fig. 76) as the most attractive specimen of Ajanta art, finds in the frescoes 'the same intense love of nature and spiritual devotion as are evident in the sculptures of Borobodur', and compares the 'exquisite sentiment' of the picture selected with the wonderful Madonnas of Giovanni Bellini'.[1]

Comparison with Chinese art.

Mr. Fergusson was of opinion that while the art of Ajanta resembled that of China in flatness and want of shadow,[2] he had never seen 'anything in China approaching its perfection'. Forty years ago so little was known in England about Chinese art that this sentiment might pass muster, but Fergusson's dictum could not now be accepted in the light of fuller knowledge. It is interesting to set against it the deliberate judgement of Mr. Laurence Binyon, a learned connoisseur in the art of the Far East.

'The art of Ajanta', he observes, 'is characterized by the strong outline which marks the early Asiatic style; the colouring appears to have been heavy and hot; the figures and faces are animated—there is force and individuality in them, a strong sense of life. We feel that the painters were possessed by their subject; they worked with fervour and devotion. . . . This, and the scale of the frescoes, make a forcible and imposing impression. Yet the art of Ajanta has not passed the primitive stage. With all the feeling for life in individual figures that the painters show, they betray as yet little of that instinct by which an art develops—the instinct towards unity, towards the conception of a subject as a synthetic whole. Their compositions are crowded and incoherent. In details and in single groups and forms, on the other hand, there is grace, dignity and character.. . . . What is lacking in the Ajanta paintings, what is so signally manifest in Chinese painting throughout its history, is that powerful creative instinct and aesthetic perception which make for synthetic unity in art, that sense of controlling rhythm and balance which inspires all fine design.'[3]

Various periods and styles.

The expert criticisms above quoted all agree in being general in their terms. Lady Herringham, in the too brief article already cited more than once, carries the aesthetic valuation of the paintings farther by distinguishing various periods and styles. She holds that the frescoes 'fall into about six distinct groups, representing various schools and periods rather than the steady development of one school'. Going a little into detail, the critic proceeds:

'I have already alluded to several styles and classes of painting in Caves 1 and 9, 16 and 17. There are besides, later developments of the narrative style of Cave 17, which we find in Caves 1 and 2. These are (1) a more emphatic and stylistic manner, with more formalism in the drawing, more action and less tenderness; (2) a more popular, lively, and forcible dramatic narrative, with more incidents and less idealism.

In Cave 2 are three more distinct styles: on both the side walls of a secondary shrine we find four or five elaborately posed, nearly nude life-size figures. These are sinuous in outline, quite Cimabuesque in proportion, attitude and general feeling; the arrangement suggests bas-relief. The late date of this cave indicates the period of the painting. In a similar shrine on the opposite side are corresponding decorations, and the figures on the main west wall might, but for the type, be an assemblage of Chinese sages; they are drawn with a magnificent bravura. There is not much colour left, but the somewhat caligraphic drawing in forcible blacks and reddish browns is so freely executed that

[1] *Indian Sculpture and Painting* (1908), p. 164.

[2] Actually the painting at Ajanta is not at all flat but renders the contours delicately and faithfully.

[3] Laurence Binyon, *Painting in the Far East* (1908), pp. 35, 50. See also the same author's article, 'A Chinese Painting of the Fourth Century' in *Burlington Magazine*, Jan. 1904, p. 44. One Japanese work, the fresco in the temple of Horiuji, which was repaired or built between A.D. 708 and 715, is quite Indian in character, and 'there seems no doubt that it is modelled upon the Ajanta frescoes' (*Painting in the Far East*, p. 87). Anderson gives the date as 607, but other critics date it a century later.

one scarcely regrets the destruction which has laid bare such vital work. On a separate part of this west wall there is a subject of men and white geese in a water-lily pool, which, though closely linked to the earlier definitely Indian types of painting, suggests the freedom and at the same time the perfect balance of the very best Chinese period. The colour scheme is very beautiful—brilliant white, deep purple-brown, a vivid but rich malachite-green, with touches of a clear red.

Three notable paintings.

Further, in Cave 17 there are three paintings by one hand very different from all the rest. They are (1) a hunt of lions and black buck;[1] (2) a hunt of elephants;[2] and (3) an elephant salaaming in a king's court—the companion picture to No. 2. These pictures are composed in a light and shade scheme which can scarcely be paralleled in Italy before the seventeenth century. They are nearly monochrome (warm and cool greys understood), except that the foliage and grass are dull green. The whole posing and grouping is curiously natural and modern, the drawing easy, light and sketchy, and the painting suggestively laid in with solid brush strokes—in the flesh not unlike some examples of modern French painting. The animals—horses, elephants, dogs and black buck—are extremely well drawn.'

Paintings in caves at Bagh.

The development of criticism on the lines indicated by Lady Herringham would require a bulky monograph based on detailed notes taken on the spot by a competent expert. It is impossible to work out the differences of the supposed schools merely from the fragmentary published reproductions.[3]

The vigorous school of art which produced the Ajanta frescoes did not confine its operations to the caves at that place (A 5). Several similar excavations near Bagh, a village or decayed small town in the Gwalior State, situated on an ancient road connecting Gujarat with Malwa, exhibit traces of a set of works resembling in general style the Ajanta paintings, and at one time of almost equal importance. Unfortunately, the crumbling of the rock, and absolute neglect, combined with the effects of the smoke from vagrants' fires, have left hardly anything of compositions which once covered thousands of square feet.

The principal group of caves contains eight excavations, the largest being 94 feet square. The whole of the roof, walls, and columns of this great chamber was coated with fine stucco and decorated with paintings of high merit and infinite variety. Smaller remnants of painting may be still discerned in two other caves, and there is reason to believe that the work is not all of one period.[4]

Subjects of the paintings.

The paintings appear to have rivalled those of Ajanta in variety of design, vigorous execution, and decorative quality, life being treated in both places with equal gaiety and hardly a trace of asceticism. Two of the Bagh groups illustrate the performance of the *hallisaka*, a kind of operetta or musical play, acted by a troupe of women led by a man. According to the books the female performers should number seven, eight, or ten. At Bagh they are six in one case and seven in the other. They are represented as elaborately dressed, singing, and performing with much enjoyment on drums, cymbals, and other instruments. Our surprise at finding such gay scenes depicted on the walls of a Buddhist monastery may be lessened when we consider the nature of many of the sculptures at Mathura

[1] Burgess, *Notes*, Cave XVII, No. 28.

[2] Ibid., Nos. 36, 37. I cannot trace the 'companion picture'. Burgess does not notice the distinctions of style.

[3] Lady Herringham has generously presented her copies of the frescoes to the India Society. They were exhibited in the Indian Section of the Festival of Empire (1911). In the *Catalogue and Guide to the Indian Court, Festival of Empire*, p. 92, Lady Herringham states that 'there are at least twenty different kinds of painting. Some pictures recall Greek and Roman composition and proportions, a few late ones resemble the Chinese manner to a certain extent, but the majority belong to a phase of art which one can call nothing except Indian, for it is found nowhere else.'

[4] The existing paintings have since been copied. References are :—Dangerfield, Capt., 'Some Account of the Caves near Baug, called the Panch Pandoo, with three drawings' (*Trans. Lit. Soc., Bombay*, vol. ii (1820), pp. 194-204). Impey, Dr., 'Description of the Caves of Bagh, in Rath' (*J. Bo. Br. R. A. S.*, vol. v, pp. 543-73). Burgess, J., *Notes on the Bauddha Rock-Temples of Ajanta* (1879), pp. 94, 95. Luard, Major C. E., 'The Buddhist Caves of Central India' (*Ind, Ant.*, vol. xxxix, August 1910, pp. 225-35, with plans and plates). The Bagh Caves (*Ind. Soc., London*).

A. Scroll on Parasuramesvara Temple, Bhuvanesvar.

B. Scroll with birds, etc., Rajarani Temple, Bhuvanesvar.

C. Antelope frieze, Muktesvara Temple, Bhuvanesvar.
(From *Antiquities of Orissa*)

PLATE 99

A. A colossal horse, Konarak. (Orissa, 13th Cent. A.D.).

B. A wheel, Konarak. (Orissa, 13th Cent. A.D.).
(Photos : Raj Bedi)

PLATE 100

and in the Aurangabad caves; but we do not know quite enough about the real nature of the later popular Buddhism in India to understand fully the significance of such frivolous sculptures and paintings.[1]

The Bagh caves do not contain an inscription of any kind (A 6), and their date can be determined only by considerations of style. The hair-dressing of many of the male figures and the transparent close-fitting robes connect the sculptures with the later Gupta rather than with the medieval period. The general character of the paintings is sufficiently known to make it certain that they are not earlier than the late works at Ajanta. Probably the paintings may have been executed between the middle of the sixth and that of the seventh century. The paintings include patterns executed in black and white with touches of Indian red, as well as works executed in 'excessively vivid' colours, with 'marked contrasts in blue, red, and yellow'. The two styles may belong to different ages. Chronology.

Part II. CEYLON.

Having been constrained to comment upon the long-continued neglect of the Ajanta and Bagh paintings, and the failure of the authorities to take the simple measures needed to save priceless works from destruction, it is a pleasure to turn to Ceylon and recognize the well-considered and successful policy of the island government with regard to the closely related frescoes at Sigiriya.[2] Sigiriya.

The marvellous citadel at that place, perched upon the summit of an isolated, tower-shaped hill, 600 feet high, and rising abruptly from the plain, was constructed as an impregnable refuge by the parricide king, Kasyapa I, who reigned from A.D. 479 to 497. The rock-cut galleries leading to the tyrant's aerie having crumbled away in the course of ages, the summit had become inaccessible save to occasional adventurous cragsmen. The work of excavation, repair, and restoration undertaken in 1895 by the Government of Ceylon was carried on systematically under the capable guidance of Mr. H. C. P. Bell, Archaeological Commissioner, until its completion some ten years later, as recorded in Sessional Paper XX of 1909. The paintings, with which alone we are now concerned, have been secured by wire nettings and other devices in such a way that 'they can be examined closely, without difficulty, and in perfect safety; from one end of the caves to the other they are for ever secure from further damage'. The story of the operations, as related in Mr. Bell's *Reports*, terminating with the document cited above, is a most interesting record of successful wrestling with formidable engineering difficulties, and of the completion of a well-devised plan, without parsimony and without extravagance.

The paintings are found in two irregular rock-chambers, usually described as 'pockets', situated on the western cliff, about fifteen yards above the floor of the southern end of the gallery. Six such 'pockets' exist, but the remains of painting are confined to four, and those of any importance exist only in 'pockets A and B'—two rough, natural chambers forming a cave 67½ feet in length, divided into two sections by a cramped ledge. 'Pocket B', 41¼ feet long, is comparatively roomy, whereas 'Pocket A', 26¼ feet in length, is cramped. Position of the paintings.

The paintings comprise twenty-one half or three-quarter-length female portraits,

[1] For the definition of *hallisaka* see Sylvain, Lévi, *Théâtre Indien*, App. p. 30.

[2] The name, in all its forms, means 'Lion-hill', with reference to the passage connecting the galleries, which was wrought in the shape of a gigantic lion. The hill stands in the Inamaluwa Korale of the Matale District, Central Province, about twenty miles almost due west from the medieval capital, Polonnaruwa.

besides the hand of another figure. Seventeen of these are in 'Pocket B' and only five in 'Pocket A'. The figures in the more spacious chamber B are mostly above life-size, while those in chamber A, where space was limited, are below life-size.

Copies. In 1889 Mr. A. Murray succeeded with great difficulty in obtaining copies of thirteen figures in either pastel or coloured photographs, now preserved in the Colombo Museum. His meritorious work, performed when the 'pockets' were all but inaccessible, has been superseded by a magnificent series of facsimile copies made in oils on canvas by Mr. Perera, which also are exhibited at Colombo. These copies, which are described as reproducing with minute accuracy every detail of the originals in size, colour, and all other respects, have been carefully photographed. Some of the photographs have been reproduced in Mr. Bell's *Reports* and Mr. Havell's book, and a selection is now given from copies liberally supplied by the Government of Ceylon.

Technique. The paintings were executed on a carefully prepared surface formed by the application of fine lime-plaster from a quarter to half an inch thick laid on a bed about half an inch in thickness, composed of tempered clay mixed with kaolin, and strengthened by the admixture of rice-husks, with, perhaps, some coco-nut fibre. Mr. Bell believes that the pictures were wrought in tempera on a dry surface. The process, possibly, did not differ much from that used at Ajanta. Except that Fig. 14 in 'pocket B' has a black background, the range of colours is confined to three—red, yellow, and green. The blues, so conspicuous at Ajanta and Bagh, are absent.

Subject. The subject is a procession of noble ladies carrying flowers, and attended by female servants, all moving in the direction of the Pidurangala Buddhist temple to the north of the hill, as if about to make offerings at that shrine. All the figures are fully clothed from the waist downwards in coloured *kambaiyas*, and above the waist in short-sleeved jackets made of the finest material, and in some cases barely indicated by a line of deeper colour.

The noble ladies are painted in pale yellow or orange, their attendants being distinguished by a greenish complexion. All the women are decked with a profusion of ornaments. Each ends below in a cloud-like mass, a peculiarity best explained by Mr. Bell's suggestion that it is due to the irregular form of the cramped rock space available, on which the artist could not have drawn the legs without unsightly distortion. The suggestion made by another author that the clouds are intended to indicate the divine character of the personages appears to be incorrect. In accordance with the usual Indian practice, the figures were first outlined in red and black, and then painted in, not necessarily by the same hand. In one instance it is apparent that the outline was not exactly followed.

Chronology and criticism. The date of the frescoes in the closing years of the fifth century is fixed with sufficient accuracy by the known limits of the reign of Kasyapa I, A.D. 479 and 497. They are, therefore, practically contemporary with the paintings at Ajanta; all critics recognize the fact that the art of Sigiriya is closely related to that of Ajanta. For instance, the lady carrying a lotus in Plate 90B may be compared with the similar figure in Cave II at Ajanta, as reproduced in Griffiths, Plate 31. But the limitation of the colours and the total absence of blue in the Ceylonese paintings are important differences, and I do not think that the Sigiriya work equals the best at Ajanta. Mr. Havell is bold enough to credit the ladies of Sigiriya with 'Botticellian grace', a criticism which may not meet with universal acceptance. But, whatever may be the final verdict of experts as to the intrinsic merits of the

Ceylonese paintings, there can be no doubt that they are extremely remarkable productions of their age, and well deserving of careful study and serious criticism. There is nothing to indicate who the Ceylonese artists were, whence they came, or how they learned their skill.

The Sigiriya figures (Plates 90A and B, 91A), although by far the most important and interesting, are by no means the only remains of ancient painting in the island. Numerous traces of early wall-paintings have been detected at Anuradhapura, of which the best preserved are those on the walls of the detached building ('frontispiece' of Smither) on the eastern side of the Ruwanweli *dagaba*. Besides white, three primary colours, yellow, red, and blue, are used, the yellow and blue being sometimes combined to produce green. Yellow in various shades is the favourite, and was obtained from the natural arsenic sulphide called orpiment. The blue is indigo, not lapis lazuli.

Paintings at Anuradhapura.

The style of the specimens reproduced in colour by Mr. Smither is distinctly antique and closely allied to that of the later Ajanta paintings, being characterized, as they are, by bold free-hand execution of curves, with a truthful and at the same time decorative treatment of plant motives. Two examples are offered (Plate 91B and C), which may be dated at any time from the sixth to the eighth century. The date of the building of the *dagaba*, of course, gives no clue to the date of mural decorations, which, in all probability, were retouched from time to time on the old lines. The colours are white and tints of brownish yellow.

Ancient paintings are necessarily so rare that a work hitherto unpublished cannot be passed over, although it is of but slight intrinsic importance. Mr. Bell discovered two caves at a place called Tamankaduwa (Pulligoda galkanda), in a southerly direction from Kuda Ulpota and Dimbulagala, North Central Province, one of which contains a painting of five men, with halos and conical head-dresses, seated in an attitude of adoration. The colours are said to be 'well preserved', but no further details are recorded, and the 'short inscription' in the adjoining cave does not appear to have been deciphered. The age of the painting, therefore, is doubtful, but, so far as can be judged from a photograph, it must be of early date, possibly of the seventh century. It may, however, be later.

Cave painting at Tamankaduwa.

NOTES TO CHAPTER EIGHT

See Note to Chapter 15, on painting. A 1

Four magnficient volumes in colour photography by G. Yazdani have been brought out by the Archaeological Department of the former Hyderabad State. They are the finest reproductions yet made of Ajanta. A 2

This identification is no longer accepted by scholars. A 3

Plate 86B shows a well-known type of Bacchanalian scene and the principal figures are perhaps meant to be Panchisika and Hariti with attendants. But there can be no doubt that here we have the work of some foreign artist from the North-West or further afield. The Sassanian type of flying ribbons should be noted. A 4

There are Brahmanical paintings of the 6th century at Badami in the Bijapur district (Plate 89A). So also the Jain frescoes at Sittanavasal in South India (Plate 89B) evidence the Pallava idiom of the 7th century though some critics opine that they are Pandyan work of the 9th century which does not appear improbable. Nevertheless the Pallava idiom is certainly present. A 5

But the discovery of a copper plate there indicates the 5th century A.D. The style supports that view. A 6

Chapter Nine

ARCHITECTURE AND SCULPTURE OF THE MEDIEVAL PERIOD

Part I. MEDIEVAL ARCHITECTURE

Jain and Hindu temples.

THROUGHOUT India, except Buddhist remains, there is hardly anything standing which can be dated earlier than A.D. 450. No early examples of civil architecture exist. After the date named Buddhist structures become scarce. The styles of Indian architecture in the medieval period, therefore, must be deduced from Brahmanical and Jain temples, or from the buildings represented in the Ajanta frescoes (A 1).

It is now admitted that the variety of styles which may be distinguished depends not on differences of creed, but on date and, to a certain degree, on locality. At Khajuraho, for instance, Jain and Brahmanical temples are built in the same style.

Early stages of Indian styles lost.

All authors who treat of Indian architecture notice, and are embarrassed by the fact, that each style when it first comes to our knowledge is full-grown and complete. The earliest specimens betray no signs of tentative effort, and in no case is it possible to trace the progressive evolution of a given style from rude beginnings. The extensive destruction of ancient monuments, especially those built of brick, no doubt supplies a partial, though not adequate, explanation.[1] I am convinced that the more fundamental explanation is to be found in the assumption that all the Indian styles are derived from prototypes constructed in timber, bamboos, and other perishable materials.[2] We have seen how easily the *stupa* railings can be accounted for in this way, and by the extension of the theory an adequate reason for the non-existence of the missing links in the chain of architectural evolution is supplied. In the essay previously cited, Mr. Simpson has quoted from the *Satapatha Brahmana* (*S.B.E.*, vols. xii, xxvi) a long description of an early Brahmanical temple as constructed some five or six or seven hundred years before the Christian era. That temple consisted simply of two sheds, which were 'merely formed of posts and beams, covered with reeds and mats, and could only be described as belonging to the "thatch period" in architecture'. From such an edifice to the temples of Mount Abu and Tanjore the distance is great, but there seems to be little reason to doubt that the intervening stages were worked out for the most part by experiments with evanescent materials. Brick, the intermediate stage between the 'thatch period' and the 'stone period', offers such a ready prey to the spoiler that it may be reckoned as only 'semi-permanent' material.[3] Whatever be the validity of this theory, we must take the styles ready-made as we find them, and briefly consider their several peculiarities, so far as may be necessary for the intelligent appreciation of the ancillary fine arts, which form the main subject of this work.

[1] Cunningham, *A. S. Rep.*, vol. xi, pp. 40-6, pls. XIV-XVII; Vogel, *Ann. Rep. A. S. Northern Circle*, 1907-8, p. 31.

[2] The Ajanta frescoes make it plain.

[3] 'The earlier temples, I believe, were built wholly in brick. At Aunda we find a small one built almost entirely of that material, while the star-shaped plan and sharp crisp mouldings are maintained as well almost as if built in stone. Remains of some of these early brick temples are found in North Gujarat and the foundations and platforms on which the older stone ones are erected are frequently constructed with a brick core. Brick was, without doubt, the prevalent building material before stone came into general use, and probably immediately succeeded the more primitive wooden structures whose [*sic*] forms are reproduced in many of the earliest caves' (Cousens, *Progr. Rep. A. S. W. I.*, 1894-5, p. 6). In some regions where stone was abundant the brick stage may not have intervened. For N. Gujarat see Burgess, vol. ix, *A. S. W. I.*, vol. xxxii of New Imperial Series.

A. Colossal elephant, Konarak. (Orissa, 13th Cent. A.D.).
(Photo : Raj Bedi)

B. Bala-Krishna, Konarak. (The identification is incorrect. The seated figure is King Narasimha himself, the builder of the Sun Temple, Orissa. 13th Cent. A.D.).

C. Vishnu, Konarak.
(Orissa, 13th Cent. A.D.).

(By Courtesy of the Council of the Royal Asiatic Society)

PLATE 101

A, B. Details of sculptures from the Sun Temple, Konarak, Orissa. 13th Cent. A.D.
(Copyright by Department of Archaeology, Government of India)

PLATE 102

In an ordinary Hindu temple the essential part is the rectangular cell or shrine containing the image or symbol of the god, and such a plain cell constitutes the simplest form of temple. The small shrines of the Gupta period have already been described. In the medieval period dignity was gained by the addition of a high roof or steeple, and by prefixing a porch, or nave with or without side-aisles, transepts, and subsidiary steeples, until an architectural composition of extreme complexity was evolved. Another type, built frequently by Jains and occasionally by Brahmanists, is a modification of the monastery, the monks' cells round the quadrangle being replaced by niches enshrining images. The modifications of both ground-plan and superstructure are, indeed, endless.[1] All forms offer abundant opportunity for artistic decoration.

Essentials of a temple.

In the crowd of varieties two leading styles of temple architecture—the Northern or Indo-Aryan of Fergusson, and the Southern or Dravidian—may be readily distinguished (A 2).[2] If it be possible to amend the nomenclature so long established by Fergusson's authority, it would be preferable to give territorial names to all styles, calling the Indo-Aryan style that of *Aryavarta* or Hindustan, the great plain between the Himalayas and the Narbada.[3] The term Dravidian is free from objection, *Dravida* being the ancient name of peninsular India. The two styles may more simply be denominated Northern and Southern.

Two leading styles.

The *Aryavarta*, or Northern style, examples of which to the south of the Narbada are rare, is characterized by the bulging steeple with curvilinear vertical ribs, placed over the sanctuary, and frequently reproduced on other parts of the building. Miniature repetitions of the form are often used with good effect as decorations of the steeples themselves. In spite of theories as to the bamboo origins of the curvilinear spire, its form is obviously inherent in the Indian corbelling methods of building. It appears to have been evolved first of all in brick as in the Great Temple at Bodh-Gaya.

Aryavarta or Indo-Aryan style.

The best early examples are found at Bhuvanesvar (Plates 92A and B, 93A), in the Puri District, Orissa, where the temples, numbering several hundreds, illustrate the history of the style from the ninth or tenth to the thirteenth century. The earliest specimens have steeples comparatively low and squat (Plate 93A), but pleasing to an eye which has become accustomed to the design. The porch is a walled chamber with a low, massive roof, and internal pillars are wholly wanting. The combination of vertical and horizontal lines is skilfully arranged so as to give dignity to buildings of moderate height. This early astylar form of temple is best illustrated by the *Muktesvara* shrine, which Fergusson called 'the gem of Orissan art' (Plate 92A).[4]

Temples at Bhuvanesvar.

A second, and later, variety of the style is adequately represented by the Great Temple, which has a high steeple tower, with sides vertical for the most part, and curving only near the top. The roof of the porch has considerable elevation, and in many details the design differs from that of the earlier variety. Sculptures of remarkable merit are introduced in panels on the basement and elsewhere.

The Great Temple.

The third, or 'decorated', variety of the Bhuvanesvar style, in which columns become prominent, dates from the twelfth or thirteenth century. The most

the *Rajarani* temple.

[1] At Aihole, Bijapur District, Bombay, 'we have an unbroken sequence in the styles from the fifth to the fourteenth century—from the early cave to the latest mediaeval temple' (Cousens, *Progr. Rep. A. S. W. I.*, 1908-9, p. 35).

[2] This classification does not apply to Ceylon.

[3] The term Indo-Aryan implies a disputable theory. The two styles of architecture, although rising from different origins, are related chronologically, for the Southern style reached its highest development after decadence had set in in the North.

[4] See *Ann. Rep. A. S., India*, 1902-3, pp. 46-50; ibid., 1903-4, pp. 46-8; *Progr. Rep. E. Circle* 1908-9, p. 18.

charming example is the *Rajarani* temple (Plate 92B). Some exquisite details of this building are illustrated in Plate 62B[1].

Temple of the Sun at Konarak.

The most renowned achievement of the vigorous Orissan school of architects is the temple of the Sun at Konarak (*vulgo* 'Kanaruc') on the coast, known to sailors as the Black Pagoda, in order to distinguish it from the White Pagoda, or temple of *Jagannath* at Puri. The remains of the main steeple, never completed, which had been overwhelmed long ago by the drifting sand, have been lately exposed by excavation. The porch, which stands practically perfect, is covered by a beautifully designed pyramidal roof, justly praised by Fergusson, and described by the Workmans as the most perfectly proportioned structure which they had seen in the course of years of study devoted to Indian temples. The temple, when in better condition than it now is, was admired enthusiastically by Abul Fazl, the minister and historian of Akbar in the sixteenth century. It is said to have been built by King Narasimha, who reigned between A.D. 1240 and 1280, a time when high-class work was not often produced. Considering its exceptional excellence, it is strangely late in date. A large book might be devoted to the description and illustration of this building and its sculptures. Plate 93B, from a photograph kindly supplied by the Director-General of the Archaeological Survey, shows the recently excavated remains of the steeple, as well as the porch seen from the north-west[2].

Temples at Khajuraho.

The Bhuvanesvar group of temples stands first in importance among the examples of the *Aryavarta* style by reason of the immense number of buildings, usually in fairly good condition, and their variety, which marks the stages in the history of the style for at least three centuries. The group next in importance, situated at Khajuraho in the Chhatarpur State, Bundelkhand, although far inferior in both numbers and variety, includes some admirable buildings designed on a grand scale and richly adorned with sculpture (A 3). The temples, in more or less satisfactory preservation, numbering between twenty and thirty, were all erected by order of the Chandel kings *c.* A.D. 1000. They are executed in a fine sandstone, which offers great facilities to the sculptor. Several of the domes, constructed in the Indian manner with horizontal overlapping courses of stone, are remarkable achievements, the largest being 22 feet in diameter. The cusps hanging from the centre of some of the domes are beautiful, although, of course, not so elaborately carved as the similar works executed slightly later and in more manageable marble at Mount Abu. Plate 94A gives a good notion of one of the best of the Khajuraho temples. The steeple is nearly 100 feet high.

The Gujarati, or so-called Jain style.

A beautiful variation of the *Aryavarta* or Indo-Aryan style, found in Rajputana and Gujarat, is characterized by a free use of columns carved with all imaginable richness, strut brackets, and exquisite marble ceilings with cusped pendants, at least equal to the best Tudor work of the kind. By an unfortunate error Fergusson described this Western or Gujarati style as the 'Jain style' (A 4). In reality it has no concern with any special kind of religion, and is Jain merely because Jains were numerous and wealthy in Western India in the late medieval period as they are still. When power passed into Muslim hands the so-called Jain style, that is to say the local style, was applied with the necessary modifications to the needs of Muhammadan worship.

[1] [This plate reference is to the previous edition. It has been omitted from the Third Edition and so this sentence is inapplicable].

[2] [This photograph has been replaced in the Third Edition with a later one and not from the same angle, but also supplied by the Department of Archaeology, Government of India].

A, B. Details of sculptures from the Sun Temple, Konarak, Orissa. 13th Cent. A.D. (Photos : P. Braham)

C. Mother and Child, Temple of Jagannath, Puri. (Orissa, 12th Cent. A.D.).

PLATE 103

A. Detail of sculpture from Mokalji's Temple, Chitor. 11th Cent. A.D.

B. Sculptures on a wall of Mokalji's Temple, Chitor.

C. Face in wall of Temple, Vasantgarh.

(*Copyright by Department of Archaelogy, Government of India*)

PLATE 104

A. Kuvera, Temple No. 9, Osia. (Rajasthan. 9th Cent. A.D.).

B. Statuette of Vishnu. Mathura Museum. (11th Cent. A.D.).

PLATE 105

A. Ardhanarisvara, from Ambaneri, near Bharatpur.

B. A musical scene, from Ambaneri, near Bharatpur.

8th Cent. A.D. Post-Gupta period.

Two temples at Mount Abu, built wholly of white marble, are famous as unsurpassed models of this wonderful style. The earlier, dedicated to *Adinath*, was built by a minister or governor named Vimala in A.D. 1031; the later was consecrated by Tejpal two centuries afterwards, in A.D. 1230. Notwithstanding the considerable difference in age both temples are very similar in style. Illustrations are given showing half of the ceiling (Plate 95A) and some of the columns in the upper hall of Tejpal's temple (Plate 96A). It is needless to comment on the beauty and delicacy of the carving and the richness of the design in both cases (Plate 95B).

Temples on Mount Abu.

It would be easy to fill many pages with more or less similar specimens of work in the medieval style. I am tempted, however, to add a photograph (Plate 96B) of a charming temple of the Sun at Osia in the Jodhpur State, Rajputana, brought to notice by Mr. D. R. Bhandarkar, and treated in a much simpler fashion—an example of the originals of the huge piles at Khajuraho and Mount Abu, probably dating from the ninth century. Osia possesses no less than twelve large ancient temples, some Jain and some Brahmanical, and all, apparently, dating from the eighth and ninth centuries. The residents of the town show their appreciation of these works of art by using them as public latrines.[1]

Temples at Osia.

Northern India is full of examples of the style, ancient, medieval, and modern, mostly in stone, but occasionally in brick. The oldest brick specimen in preservation sufficiently good to allow of the recognition of the style is that at Bhitargaon in the Cawnpore District, which is probably of the fifth century. With it must be classed the great temple at Bodh-Gaya. Another well-preserved ancient brick temple, referred doubtfully to the eighth century, stands at Konch in South Bihar.[2] There are many fine brick-temples in the Central Provinces, the finest of which is at Sirpur. These temples have massively carved stone door-posts, lintels, and pillars. The beautifully decorated burnt-brick *Stupa* at Mirpur Khas must also be mentioned as belonging to the first half of the medieval period. The art of these sites is the forerunner of the art of Khajuraho and Bhuvanesvar. There is reason to believe (as already observed) that the transition from wooden to stone architecture was made through brick, and that the scarcity of old brick buildings is due to the facility with which the material could be utilized for other constructions. The decorations of brick buildings were carried out in terra-cotta, and carved as well as moulded bricks were used. Such bricks of good design are often seen built into later structures. The art of carving brick appears to be extinct.

Brick temples.

The late medieval Bengal variety, showing signs of Muhammadan influence is characterized by the use of the bent cornice, obviously copied from the bamboo eaves of an ordinary Bengal hut, and by a peculiar arrangement of the curvilinear steeples; one lofty steeple placed over the centre being surrounded by four, eight, or sixteen smaller towers of the same form. Fergusson has described the temple at Kantonagar in Dinajpur District, finished in 1722, and decorated with applied terra-cottas of slight artistic merit. This variety of the *Aryavarta* style is peculiar to Bengal.[3] The only example recorded outside that province is one at Bilhari, Central Provinces, built to the order of a Bengali immigrant.

Bengal variety of the *Aryavarta* style.

[1] *Progr. Rep. A. S. W. I.*, 1906-7, p. 36.

[2] Cunningham described and illustrated both temples: Bhitargaon, *A. S. Rep.*, vol. xi, pp. 40-4, Pls. XIV-XVII; and Konch, ibid., vol. viii, p. 54, Pl. VI; vol. xvi, pp. 50-8, Pls. XVI-XVIII.

[3] Manmohan Chakravarti, 'Bengali Temples and their General Characteristics' (*J. A. S. B.*, vol. v, New Ser. (1909)).

Modern temples.

In the modern temples of Northern India the tendency is to reduce the curvature of the steeple, and to make the form approximate to that of an English slender spire. The effect is sometimes pleasing, but lacking in the massive dignity of the best designs at Bhuvanesvar and Khajuraho. The contemptible sculptured and painted decorations of the modern buildings testify plainly to the general lack of artistic feeling.

Numerous recent buildings, sacred and secular, combine the Muhammadan dome with the Bengali cornice, omitting the steeple. Such buildings are erected freely by Hindus for purely Hindu purposes, as, for instance, the elegant mausoleum built at Benares to the memory of the lately deceased saint, Swami Bhaskaranand, which looks like a Muslim building.

The Kashmir style.

The peculiar styles of architecture prevalent in the Himalayan kingdoms of Kashmir and Nepal demand brief notice.

The Kashmir style proper is restricted to the Valley, although a modification of it is found in the Salt Range region of the Panjab. The temples in this style, varying in date from about A.D. 750 to 1200, are all of small size, but in some cases the dignity of magnitude is attained by the addition of a walled quadrangle of imposing dimensions.

The best-known example is the temple of Martanda or Martand—a local name of Vishnu as the Sun-god—which was erected about the middle of the eighth century by Lalitaditya (A.D. 724-60), the most powerful sovereign of Kashmir. This building, although the largest of its kind, is of modest dimensions, being a rectangle measuring 60 feet long by 38 feet wide. The width of the facade, however, is increased to 60 feet by the addition of wings, and the walled enclosure measures internally 220 by 142 feet. The colonnade lining the wall is composed of eighty-four pillars, with intervening niches surmounted by the trefoil arches and triangular pediments or gables characteristic of the style. The cell, or chapel, which occupied the centre of each face of the enclosure, originally reached a height of about 30 feet. All the roofs have disappeared completely, so that it is uncertain whether they were of wood or stone.

Peculiarities of the style.

Plate 97A clearly illustrates most of the peculiarities of the architecture, which may be summed up as consisting of pyramidal roofs, gables, trefoil arches, quasi-Doric columns, and dentil ornaments.

Various examples.

The temple at Buniar (*Bhaniyar*), of uncertain date, which resembles that of Martand in being surrounded by a colonnade, differs by being of smaller dimensions and in almost perfect preservation. The central shrine is now covered with wooden shingles, which may or may not have been the original form of roof.

The more ornate temples at Vantpar (*Avantipura*) were erected during the reign of Avantivarman (A.D. 855-83). The well-known little shrine at Payer, which Fergusson assigned to the thirteenth century, is older than he supposed, and probably dates from the tenth century.[1] The notion, started by Cunningham and accepted by certain other authors, that the quadrangles of the more important temples were designed to be filled with water, so that the shrines might be placed more immediately under the protection of the *Nagas*, or water-sprites, is absolutely baseless.[2]

Two peculiarities of Kashmir architecture—the trefoil arch and the quasi-Doric columns—have given rise to much discussion. The trefoil arch recurs in certain

[1] Miscalled Payech by Vigne and many subsequent authors (Stein, transl. *Rajatarangini*, vol. ii, p. 473).

[2] Ibid., Bk. iv, v. 192 note.

A. Sculpture from Udayeswara Temple, Udaipur, former Gwalior State. 11th Cent. A.D.

B. Sculpture from Rudra Mahal, Siddhpur, North Gujarat. 11th Cent. A.D.

Sculpture from the Sun Temple, Modhera, North Gujarat. *c.* 1025 A.D.

PLATE 107

A, B. Sculptures from Khajuraho. *c.* 1000 A.D.

Trefoil arches and Indo-Doric columns.

temples at Malot, Katas, and other places in the Salt Range, which was subject to the crown of Kashmir in the seventh century;[1] and when employed structurally, appears to be derived from the similar form frequently used as a canopy to a statue.[2]

The columns of the Kashmir temples are usually described as Indo-Doric on the assumption that their design is derived ultimately from Greek models. Mr. Tavenor Perry has thrown doubt upon this assumption because the Kashmir columns have sixteen flutes and are associated with very unclassical gables and trefoil arches.[3] As usual in India, the stages of the evolution of the Kashmir style cannot be traced in detail. It is possible that the Salt Range temples alluded to, and others at Gop, Sutrapada, and Kadwar in Kathiawar, which resemble the Kashmir buildings in certain respects, may be older than those in the Valley, but no clear evidence on the subject is available.[4]

Nepalese style.

The small valley of Nepal proper, measuring about 20 miles by 15, is said to contain more than two thousand temples.[5] Most of them are designed in a style differing but slightly from the familiar Chinese pattern, in which the roof is the main element, the walls being mere screens set between pillars. An excellent illustration of this style is afforded by a temple built at Bhatgaon in 1703.

Temples and tombs, S. Kanara.

Certain temples and tombs of Jain priests in the South Kanara District on the western coast of the Madras Presidency, built in a style obviously derived from wooden originals, possess a surprising and unexplained resemblance to the buildings in distant Nepal.[6]

Part II. MEDIEVAL AND MODERN SCULPTURE

Constrast between early and medieval sculpture.

The Gupta period may be regarded as one of transition between ancient and medieval art, as it was between the polities of ancient and medieval India. From the sixth century we find in sculpture few traces of the kindly, human spirit and naturalistic treatment which distinguished the ancient schools, mainly devoted to the service of Buddhism; and we pass into a world of art which scorns to represent the daily life of men and women, concerning itself almost exclusively with either asceticism of the self-contained *yogi* type or the weird imaginings of the later Hindu mythology, including that of the Mahayanist Buddhists, almost indistinguishable from that of the Brahmans. The beautiful story-telling reliefs of Borobudur in Java form a delightful exception to this generalization, and carry on the spirit of the old Bharhut and Sanchi artists with a delicacy and refinement of style peculiar to themselves. The Jain sculpture is so strictly conventional that it may be almost left out of consideration. The spirit of medieval sculpture is chiefly expressed in Brahmanical and Buddhist works, which alike exalt the ascetic ideal and reflect the teachings of *Puranic* and *Tantric* literature.

The ascetic ideal.

Buddha no longer appears as the sympathetic human teacher moving about among his disciples and instructing them in the Good Law. His image is now generally made to conform to the ideal of the passionless *yogi*, as described in the *Bhagavad-Gita*:—

[1] Fergusson, *Hist. Ind. and E. Architecture*, 2nd ed., i. 270; Cunningham, *A. S. Rep.*, vol. v, pp. 85-92, Pls. XXV-XXVII; vol. xiv, p. 35, Pl. XV; Beal, *Buddhist Records*, i. 143; Watters, *On Yuan Chwang's Travels*, i. 249.

[2] It is so used at Konarak in Orissa (*Ann. Rep. A. S., India*, 1903-4, Pl. XXII *a*).

[3] *Trans. Roy. Inst. British Architects*, 3rd Ser., vol. i, p. 158.

[4] For the Kathiawar temples see *A. S. W. India*, vol. ii, p. 187, Pls. LI-LIII; Cousens, *Progr. Rep. A. S. W. I.*, 1898-9, pp. 14-18.

[5] Illustrations of styles used in Nepal will be found in Le Bon, *Les Monuments de l'Inde*.

[6] Fergusson, *Hist. Ind. and E. Archit.*, 2nd ed., Figs. 303, 304, 307.

'Who fixed in faith on Me,
Dotes upon none, scorns none; rejoices not,
And grieves not, letting good or evil hap
Light when it will, and when it will depart,
That man I love ! Who, unto friend and foe
Keeping an equal heart, with equal mind
Bears shame and glory; with an equal peace
Takes heat and cold, pleasure and pain; abides
Quit of desires, hears praise or calumny
In passionless restraint, unmoved by each;
Linked by no ties to earth, steadfast in Me,
That man I love!'[1]

The representation of 'passionless restraint', however true to Hindu nature, affords a strictly limited field for the exercise of the sculptor's powers, and there is necessarily much monotony in the images, whether of Buddha or other personages, which are devoted to the expression of the ascetic ideal.

Expression of passion.

Another dominant note in medieval sculpture is struck by the endeavour of the artists to express violent superhuman emotion or demoniac passion, as represented by the whirling dances of *Siva*, the strivings of *Marichi*, the struggling of *Ravana* beneath his mountain load, and many other iconographical compositions. Multitudes of sculptures are simply the formal images of innumerable gods and goddesses, adorned with all the attributes and accessories prescribed by various scriptures.

Medieval sculpture peculiarly Hindu.

The sculpture of the early Indian schools makes an appeal far more universal than that of medieval times, which demands from the spectator a certain amount of recondite knowledge of the ideas underlying the later mythology. Its enthusiastic admirers never weary of extolling its 'idealism', and of glorying in the fact that it is so peculiarly and exclusively Hindu as to be often unintelligible to the ordinary well-educated critic. The feelings which prompt such eulogies appear to be largely influenced by the modern nationalist movement.

Modern art continuous with medieval.

The Brahmanical (including later Buddhist) art, as evolved during the seventh, eighth, and subsequent centuries, continues to this day. No clear line of demarcation can be drawn between medieval and modern sculpture, although, unfortunately, modern work of any considerable degree of excellence is very rare. This chapter, therefore, deals with both medieval and modern art as being essentially one, the outcome of the Brahmanical reaction by which Buddhism was slowly strangled.

The selection of medieval sculptures reproduced in this chapter will, it is hoped, be adequate to enable every reader to form his own judgement concerning the merits of the compositions as works of art. The first part of the medieval period is illustrated by the great cave-temples of Ajanta, Badami, and Ellora.

Two art provinces, Bihar, &c., and Orissa.

Apart from the great shrines of Rajputana, Khajuraho, and Mount Abu, late medieval sculpture falls into two main territorial divisions, namely, (1) Bihar, both North and South, with certain adjoining districts of Bengal and the Agra Provinces, which collectively formed the dominions of the *Pala* dynasty for more than four centuries from about A.D. 775 to 1193, the date of the Muhammadan conquest; and (2) Orissa, on the coast of the Bay of Bengal, which never was included in the *Pala* realm (A 5).

The *Pala* kings having been devout Buddhists to the last, Buddhism continued

[1] *Bhagavad-Gita*, Bk. XII, transl. Edwin Arnold.

to be the dominant religion in their territories long after it had become either extinct or moribund in most parts of India; and the Buddhist monasteries of Bihar, especially the wealthy foundation at Nalanda (modern Bargaon), were crowded with thousands of monks, who cultivated with success the arts required for the decoration of the sacred buildings. In consequence, a large proportion of the sculpture in Bihar and the neighbouring regions is Buddhist. The later Buddhism, as we have occasion to remark more than once, was of the *Mahayana* or '*Great Vehicle*' kind, delighting in the use of images, and closely related to Hinduism. The Brahmanical faiths, of course, never died out, and their votaries contributed their share to the art production. Late survival of Buddhism in Bihar.

During the first half of the seventh century, when the Chinese pilgrim Hiuen Tsang recorded his invaluable notes, the Buddhists of Orissa outnumbered the Brahmanical Hindus, but notwithstanding that fact, Buddhist sculpture is rare in the province, and the extant specimens, often of a high class, are mainly Brahmanical. From the point of view of the historian of art, as already observed, religious distinctions in the medieval period are unimportant, sculptors making use of the style of their own age and country, irrespective of the creed to the service of which their works were dedicated. Brahmanical sculpture of Orissa.

In Bihar the Muslim onslaught at the close of the twelfth century overthrew Buddhism suddenly, and scattered all over India those few monks who survived the indiscriminate massacres committed by the iconoclast armies of Islam. The rich monasteries of Sarnath near Benares soon shared the fate of the communities in Bihar, and layers of ashes in the ruins testify to this day the violence of the conquerors. Hindu art of all kinds, Buddhist included, was practically stamped out in the north-eastern provinces by the Muhammadan conquest. It lingered, however, in Orissa longer than in Bihar, and some of the best Orissan work dates from the thirteenth century. The conquest of Orissa was not completed until Akbar's time in the sixteenth century, but it may be said that from the fourteenth century the history of art in all the north-eastern provinces is concerned only with Muslim forms. Hindu art destroyed by Muslim conquest.

In quite recent days a slight revival of Hindu art may be discerned. Practically the history of Hindu sculpture in Bengal, Bihar, and Orissa closes with the thirteenth century.

The innumerable ancient sites in Magadha or South Bihar and the neighbouring districts are full of well-executed images, mostly dating from the times of *Pala* rule, between the eighth and twelfth centuries (Plates 97B, C and D, 98A, B and C). The destruction due to Muhammadan hatred of images has been less complete than in the upper provinces. Medieval Buddhism in its *Tantric* forms approximated so closely to the Brahmanical Hinduism that even a skilled observer may sometimes hesitate to decide as to the religion for the service of which the image was destined—the Buddhist *Tara*, for instance, is not easily distinguishable from the Hindu *Lakshmi*. Although the style of the sculptures is always dominated by the formalism of ritual prescription, artists of exceptional ability and skill could make their powers more or less clearly apparent, and so raise compositions mainly conventional to the rank of works of art. A few specimens which possess merit greater than ordinary have been selected from the mass. Abundance of sculpture.

An elaborately decorated seated Buddha, in basalt, from Kurkihar in the same region, similarly proved by its inscription to date from the ninth century, carries on the history. The folds of the drapery are marked by formal lines, and the A ninth-century Buddha.

resemblance to work of the Gupta period has disappeared (Plate 97C). The details are wrought with the highest possible finish, but the type was too rigidly determined by rule to allow the sculptor much scope for the exercise of his taste.

Marichi. The *Tantric* image of *Marichi*, goddess of dawn, a weird form with three heads and six arms (Plate 98A), offers greater opportunities to an artist in the delineation of active exertion. The goddess is supposed to be standing in a chariot drawn by seven boars, but the chariot and team are treated merely as formal accessories, the spectator's attention being invited solely to the sculptor's attempt to express the idea of radiant energy in the person of the goddess. The pose is that technically called the 'archer' attitude.

The Rajmahal Sun-god. One of the best and most characteristic examples of Bihar sculpture is the large group of the Sun-god and his attendants now in the Indian Section of the Victoria and Albert Museum, which stands 5½ feet high, and is in nearly perfect preservation (Plate 98B). The god is represented standing in a lotus-shaped chariot drawn by seven horses, and driven by the legless *Aruna*, the Dawn. The artist, like the sculptor of *Marichi*, has concentrated his attention on the effigy of the god, reducing the chariot, horses, and charioteer to the position of minor accessories, in such a way that a casual spectator might fail to perceive their significance. The body of the principal figure is carefully modelled with considerable regard to realism, and the same commendation may be bestowed on the two female attendants with fly-whisks. The decorative framework is skilfully treated, and the whole composition produces an imposing and very pleasing effect. The mechanical execution of the carving is perfect, and the design is more restrained than that of much Hindu sculpture of the same period. The material is a black carboniferous shale, or clay slate, well adapted to the sculptor's purpose, and the twelfth century may be assigned as an approximate date. The Rajmahal Hills, where this remarkable work was excavated, lie to the south of Monghyr, and, although outside the limits of Bihar, were doubtless subject to the *Pala* rulers of that province.

A Rajgir Buddha. One more illustration of the medieval art of Bihar may suffice—a beautifully modelled and exquisitely finished seated Buddha in black Monghyr stone found by Mr. Grierson near Rajgir (Plate 97D). The standing figures are the *Bodhisattvas Avalokitesvara* and *Vajrapani*. The seated goddesses are the two forms of *Tara*, the Green and the White. The composition as a whole is a compendium of the symbolism of *Mahayanist* Buddhism. As a work of art its interest lies chiefly in the careful modelling of the principal figure. The script of the inscription, the usual 'Buddhist creed', indicates that the work is approximately contemporary with the Rajmahal Sun-god.

Other good images. It may be well to mention the existence of other excellent specimens of the medieval Bihar style, without detailed description or illustration. (1) Sir John Marshall notes as the most beautiful of the later finds at Sarnath, dating from the eleventh or twelfth century, a tiny figure of *Avalokitesvara*, 3½ inches high, the carving of which, though somewhat stereotyped in character, is said to be executed with a delicacy and refinement which would do credit to a Chinese artist;[1] (2) the large Buddha called *Mata Kunwar* at the famous site near Kasia, Gorakhpur District;[2] (3) a fine Vishnu at Devathala, Dinajpur District, Bengal;[3] and (4) sundry Buddhist sculptures from Kurkihar and Bishanpur, especially a remarkable relief

[1] *J. R. A. S.*, 1908, p. 1093, not reproduced.

[2] Martin (Buchanan-Hamilton), *Eastern India*, ii, 357, with sketch.

[3] Cunningham, *A. S. Rep.*, vol. xv, Pl. XXVII.

(Photo : P. C. Patel)

A, B. Sculptures from Khajuraho. *c.* 1000 A.D.

PLATE 109

(Photo : E. S. Mahalingam)

(Photo : P. Braham)

A, B. Sculptures from Khajuraho. *c.* 1000 A.D.

PLATE 110

of a *Bodhisattva* teaching, as described and illustrated by Stein.[1] The list might be largely extended from the collections in the Indian Museum, Calcutta, the Provincial Museum, Lucknow, and at other places.

The medieval sculptures of Orissa are chiefly associated with the Brahmanical temples of three localities—Bhuvanesvar, Konarak, and Puri—all in the Puri District, and ranging in date from perhaps the ninth century to the thirteenth. The peculiarities of the architecture have already been noticed. The oldest sculptures, usually in sandstone, are at Bhuvanesvar; the best statues, mostly in chlorite, are at Konarak. Localities of Orissan sculptures.

The temples and shrines at Bhuvanesvar, said to be five or six hundred in number, are usually richly decorated, and so offer a wide field for selection, limited to some extent by the fact that many of the sculptures are grossly obscene, constituting, it is said, a complete set of illustrations of the Sanskrit *Kamasastra*, or erotic treatises. Sculptures at Bhuvanesvar.

The sculptures, both decorative and statuary, are well represented in the Indian Museum, Calcutta, by a series of 128 casts taken in 1869, under the supervision of the Principal of the Calcutta School of Art at the time. 'The Orissa carver of those days', Dr. Anderson observes, 'went direct to nature for his designs, and the results of his labours in combining groups of animals with foliage show that he must have been a keen observer. They are extremely pleasing pieces of art, not only on account of the beauty of their execution, but by reason of their truthfulness to nature.'[2]

In justification of this criticism a few examples from Rajendralala Mitra's work may be given, beginning with a scroll on the Parasuramesvara temple, one of the oldest, possibly dating from the eighth or ninth century (Plate 99A). Another scroll, including birds, &c., is from the small *Rajarani* temple of later date (Plate 99B). A frieze of antelopes from the *Muktesvara* temple (Plate 99C), perhaps of the ninth century, illustrates the successful realistic treatment of animal forms. Examples of decorative work.

The Great Temple is supposed to date from the tenth century. Some of the minor accessory figures on it are pleasing, the sculptor having more liberty for the exercise of his fancy and taste in treating them than he had when modelling the canonical images of the gods. Plate 74A is from the *Baital Dewal*, a barrel-roofed shrine, like a Southern *Gopuram*, of about the same period.[3] Minor figures.

The chlorite *Bhagavati*, 7 feet high, on the tower of the Great Temple is an excellent example of the numerous elaborate and carefully carved statues of deities modelled according to strict rule. Such images are exhibitions of the skill of the stone-cutter rather than of creative sculpture. A goddess.

At the famous temple of Jagannath, Puri, built about A.D. 1100, a well-executed group representing a Hindu mother with her baby (Plate 103C) offers a welcome change on gods and goddesses. Human sentiment is painfully rare in Indian medieval sculpture. This group seems to me to be of great merit. Mother and child.

The unfinished temple at Konarak, dedicated to the Sun, and erected between A.D. 1240 and 1280, was designed to simulate a gigantic solar car drawn by horses. Eight great wheels, each 9 feet 8 inches in diameter, accordingly are carved above the plinth, and remarkable statues of seven horses stand outside. The wheels, the most perfect of which is shown in Plate 100B, are carved with wonderful patience and admirable skill. Wheel at Konarak.

[1] *Ind. Ant.*, xxx (1901), pp. 85, 90, 91, with photographic plates.

[2] *Catal. Archaeol.*, Coll. *I. M.*, Part II, p. 221.

[3] [This plate has been omitted from the Third Edition].

Colossal horses.

One of the detached colossal horses is shown in Plate 100A. It is the best preserved. Another, placed outside the southern facade, is described by Mr. Havell as 'one of the grandest examples of Indian sculpture extant'. Mr. Havell's judgement of these works is as follows :—

'here Indian sculptors have shown that they can express with as much fire and passion as the greatest European art the pride of victory and the glory of triumphant warfare; for not even the Homeric grandeur of the Elgin marbles surpasses the magnificent movement and modelling of this Indian Achilles, and the superbly monumental horse in its massive strength and vigour is not unworthy of comparison with Verrocchio's famous masterpiece at Venice'.[1]

Elephant colossus.

The elephant colossi are also finely executed. One, shown in Plate 101A renders with mastery the character of the creature.

Chloriti statues.

The recent explorations carried out under Sir John Marshall's direction have revealed many finely executed chlorite statues in addition to those previously known. Two of the most noticeable of these discoveries are here reproduced. The image of Vishnu standing, equipped with all his canonical attributes, and attended by earthly and heavenly worshippers (Plate 101C), may be fairly credited with no small degree of beauty, notwithstanding the hieratic style and the four arms. The flying figures are good and the carving is perfect. [Some of the sculptures, including erotic themes, is of a high order. See plates 102A and B, 103A and B].

The effigy of *Bala-Krishna* (A 6), the god as a boy in a swing, on the contrary, is ugly (Plate 101B), and chiefly of interest as a *tour de force* in stone-cutting. Nobody but a Hindu would think of making such claims in stone. The trefoil arch may be noted.

Modern Orissan art.

Orissan art practically ceases with Konarak. A small tract by Mr. Havell proves that the artist families have never died out altogether, nor have they wholly lost their ancient skill. The author holds, and gives reasons for holding, that 'there are carvers still to be found, whose work, in spite of all the discouraging conditions which surround them, is hardly inferior in artistic perception and technical skill to that of their predecessors'. He considers the men of Orissa to be superior to the north-western workers in sandstone, because they have 'not hampered themselves by the limitations of a wood-carver's technique, but have fully realized the technical possibilities of their material for producing bold effects of light and shade suitable for architectural work'. I have no doubt that some of the living Orissan stone-carvers possess artistic feeling and could produce sculpture of considerable merit, if they received adequate patronage. At present their abilities are usually frittered away on pretty trifles in soapstone.[2]

Iconoclasm.

In the Punjab and the United Provinces of Agra and Oudh thousands of Hindu temples and other edifices must have been destroyed by the Muslim conquerors during the seven centuries intervening between the raids of Mahmud of Ghazni and the death of Aurangzeb in 1707. The detailed records of the devastation wrought at Kanauj, Mathura, Benares, and many other notable cities fully justify the assertion that the buildings and monuments destroyed must have been numbered by thousands. Medieval sculpture, consequently, is scarce in the

[1] Mr. Havell freely admits the defects of the statues in 'equine anatomy'. Verrocchio died in A.D. 1488. His masterpiece is the equestrian statue of Bartolomeo Colleoni. Mr. Fry so far agrees with Mr. Havell as to describe the horse published by that author as 'a superb colossa figure', possessing 'in the highest degree the qualities of great monumental design' (*Quart. Rev.*, 1910, p. 236).

[2] E. B. Havell, *Stone Carving in Bengal*, thin quarto, 16 pp., 5 plates (Bengal Secretariat Dépôt, Calcutta, 1906).

A. Metal image of Jivantaswami, from Akota, near Baroda. *c.* 600 A.D. Late Gupta or early post-Gupta period in North Gujarat, Southern Rajasthan. Baroda Museum.

B. Metal image of Bodhisattva, from Sirpur, Central India. 9th Century A.D.

C. Metal image, from Khinkhini, Central India. 9th Century A.D.

(*Copyright by Prince of Wales Museum, Bombay*)

PLATE 111

A. Metal image of the Buddha with attendants, from Sirpur, Central India. 9th Century A.D.

B. Metal head of Tara, from Nalanda. 9th Century A.D. Pala school.

PLATE 112

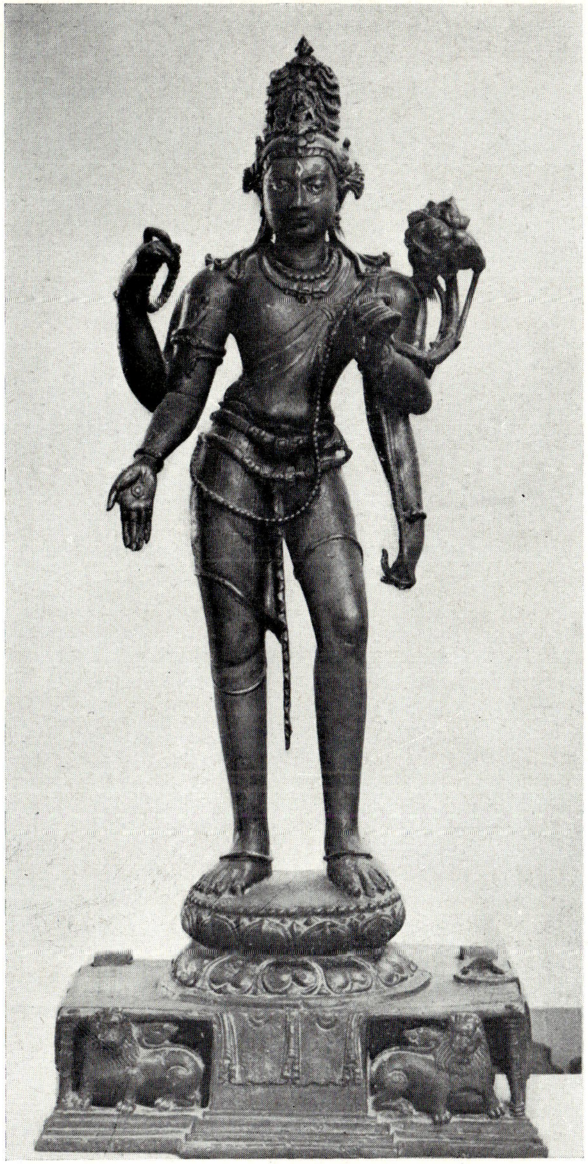

A. Metal image of Bodhisattva Avalokitesvara, from Kurkihar. 9th Century A.D. Pala school. Patna Museum.

B. Gilt-metal image of Bodhisattva Avalokitesvara, from Kurkihar. 12th Century A.D. Patna Museum.

PLATE 113

A. Metal image from Kurkihar. 9th Century A.D. Pala school. Patna Museum.

B. Metal image of the Buddha, from Kurkihar. 10th Century A.D. Pala school. Patna Museum.

PLATE 114

territories strongly held by the Musalman powers.[1] (A 7). The more considerable remains are to be found only in regions lying remote from the track of the Muslim armies, such as Khajuraho in the Chhatarpur State of the Central India Agency, and the more inaccessible parts of Rajputana and the Central Provinces.

Sculpture at Khajuraho.

Plates 108A and B, 109A and B, 110A and B, give some slight indication of the sculptured wealth of the greater temples at Khajuraho erected during the tenth and eleventh centuries by the kings of the Chandel dynasty. I visited the temples many years ago and can testify that the crowd of figures is far more numerous than would appear from the photograph (Plate 110B). But this 'peuple de pierre', as M. Le Bon calls it, was designed for the purpose of architectural decoration in the mass, not as an assemblage of individual works of fine art. The group of medieval temples at Khajuraho is the largest and most important in Upper India. At minor sites we find the same lack of individual works of artistic distinction and, as a rule, the same absence of detailed record. The temples of Mount Abu in Rajputana undoubtedly exhibit masses of sculptured decoration of the most marvellous richness and delicacy, but there does not seem to be anything deserving of isolation from the mass for study as a separate work of art.

Tower of Victory at Chitor.

The Tower of Victory, over 120 feet in height, at Chitor in Rajputana, built in the fifteenth century to commemorate the military successes of a local chieftain, is covered from top to bottom, inside and out, with an infinite multitude of images, representing, so far as may be, all the denizens of the Hindu pantheon, with their names attached, and constituting an 'illustrated dictionary of Hindu mythology'. Besides the effigies of the more ordinary deities, there are images representing the seasons, rivers, weapons, and other things as yet unpublished. Whenever this series of sculptures shall be reproduced it will be invaluable as a key to Brahmanical iconography, but is not likely to contribute much to the history of art.[2] The better class of art in Rajputana dates from an earlier period, ending with the twelfth century.

Relief-sculptures at Chitor.

If the description recorded by Mr. Garrick, Sir A. Cunningham's assistant, can be depended on, certain relief sculptures at the Mokalji temple on the famous rock of Chitor possess high merit as works of art (Plate 104A and B). The darkness of the chamber in which they are placed unfortunately frustrated attempts to photograph them. The temple, originally erected in the eleventh century, was reconstructed in the fifteenth century during the reign of Mokalji (A.D. 1428-38). The pillars bearing the reliefs evidently belong to the earlier building.[3] The bas-reliefs, sixteen in number, are carved on octagonal bands of the eastern pair of pillars supporting the principal chamber of the temple, eight scenes on each pillar. The first scene on the southern column of the pair, according to Mr. Garrick,

'depicts five human figures, of which two are large and three small; one of the former represents a woman carrying a water-jar on her head, and a man standing before her with hands joined in an attitude of adoration. The minor figures are much broken. This sculpture, along with the others of this set, is remarkable for the elaborate detail and technical excellence of its workmanship, the woman's hair being most minutely delineated.... The third carving is very well modelled and proportioned, and depicts two standing figures, male and female.... The fifth scene is filled with

[1] The case of the Bulandshahr District, U.P., illustrates what happened. 'As might have been expected from its nearness to Delhi, the Muhammadans have made a clean sweep of the district, and razed to the ground every building, secular or religious, that had been erected by its former Hindu rulers' (Growse, *J. A. S. B.*, Pt. I, vol. lii (1883), p. 280).

[2] Cousens, *Progr. Rep. A. S. W. I.*, 1900-1, p 9.

[3] Ibid., 1903-4, p. 38.

vigorous action, and consists of a musical festival; six male figures play six musical instruments . . the sixth and last figure of this interesting group is seen full to the front, blowing a flute (*murali or bansi*) in a very animated position as if he were dancing. . . .'

On the northern column of the pair—

'the seventh scene is in all probability the most interesting of the whole series, and in its half a dozen figures gives us both a duel and an execution. The upper pair of men fight with shields and sabres, and their armour, accoutrements, &c., even to the knobs and bosses on their shields, are most carefully delineated, and show that the manufacture of these articles has altered as little during the last eight centuries as that of the musical instruments figured elsewhere. The lower portion of this comprehensive and instructive scene shows a pair of kneeling figures bound hand and foot, while an executioner holds his knife to the neck of the male figure to our left; but the female with him may possibly be a mere witness, though it is pretty clear from the general distribution of action in this trio that she awaits her turn for immolation.'[1]

Mokalji's temple, as a whole, is decorated with an extraordinary wealth of sculpture, very effective in the mass, but not of quality sufficiently high to permit of small excerpts appearing to advantage. In order to give some notion of the powers of Rajputana sculptors in the first half of the fifteenth century, a specimen from the later sculptures of the temple, in high relief, with the images almost detached (Plate 104B), is presented.

Face in a window. The most artistic object discovered by Mr. D. R. Bhandarkar during his rambles in Rajputana—so fruitful in additions to historical knowledge—is the face looking out from a stone window in a wall of an old temple of the Sun at Vasantgarh in the Sirohi State (Plate 104C). Mr. Bhandarkar supposes it to date from the seventh century,[2] but, whatever its exact age, it is a beautiful work, and unique, to the best of my knowledge. The surrounding ornament is in an excellent style.

Image of Kuvera. The ancient town of Osia in the Jodhpur or Marwar State possesses no less than twelve old temples. In one of these, No. 9, known as the shrine of *Devi*, is the image of *Kuvera*, the god of riches, which may be compared with the effigies of the same deity in Gandhara and elsewhere (Plate 105A).[3]

Vishnu at Mathura. A beautifully wrought figure of Vishnu in the Mathura Museum, about 26 inches in height, and presumably produced in the local workshops (Plate 105B), may be compared with the Konarak Vishnu (Plate 101C). The two images, while largely in agreement, differ in a multitude of details.[4] The Mathura figure is not likely to be later than the tenth century, the temples of the city having been burnt by Mahmud of Ghazni at the close of A.D. 1018.

NOTES TO CHAPTER NINE

A 1 The term medieval should in general be restricted to work after 800 A.D. The period 600 — 800 A.D. is best designated as post-Gupta. There is a fundamental difference in the approach to sculpture during the two periods. In the post-Gupta period, as at Elephanta, Ellora and Mahabalipuram, sculpture retains its importance and fulfils a role which is not mainly architectonic as during the medieval period.

[1] Garrick, in Cunningham's *Archaeol. Survey Reports*, vol. xxiii, pp. 120-3. Mr. Garrick's tour took place in 1883-4.

[2] *Progr. Rep. A. S. W. I.*, 1905-6, pp. 51, 52. It is, however, typically medieval, *c.* A.D. tenth century.

[3] Ibid., 1906-7, p. 36. Bhandarkar dates most of the Osia shrines in the eighth century, but they can best be compared to Khajuraho and cannot be much earlier than A.D. 900.

[4] At Panthia near Mandhata, the ancient Mahishmati, on the Narbada, there are twenty-four different forms of Vishnu duly labelled and distinguished by variations in the attributes and position of the hands.

A

B

C

A. Rock-sculpture of Arjuna's Penance, Mahabalipuram. 7th Century A.D. Pallava period.

B. Rath at Mahabalipuram. 7th Century A.D. Pallava period. (Photo : A. L. Syed)

C. Muktesvara Temple, Kanchi, from the south-west. 8th Century A.D. Pallava period. (From Rea, *Pallava Architecture*)

PLATE 115

A, B, C. Shaivite sculptures from Kailasanatha Temple, Kanchipuram. 8th Century A.D. Pallava period.
(Photos : E. S. Mahalingam)

PLATE 116

The question of the nomenclature to be adopted in classifying Indian temples is somewhat intricate. The texts on temple architecture indicate three main styles, namely Nagara (Northern or the Indo-Aryan of Fergusson), the Dravida (Southern or the Dravidian style) and Vesara (probably the Orissan Style). But an even more elaborate classification is necessary to distinguish the very early flat-roofed Gupta shrine from the subsequent development of the shrine with shikara (spire). So also the Kashmir, Chalukyan and Orissa styles must be differentiated from the Northern style as seen at Khajuraho. A 2

The Khajuraho temples are famed for their wealth of erotic sculpture which is a mixture of obscenity, crudely pictured, and sexual passion rendered without reticence but with undeniable beauty from the sculptural point of view. A 3

This style is best known as Solanki style of Gujarat. It is to be seen in Hindu and Jain temples. It grew up under the Solanki kings and continued with their successors, the Vaghelas. It is also found in Rajputana (Rajasthan). A 4

There is a wealth of medieval period sculpture all over India as can be seen from the examples reproduced from Abaneri near Bharatpur (Pl. 106A and B), Udaipur in Madhya Pradesh (Pl. 107A) and Gujarat (Pl. 107B and C). A 5

The figure is not Bala Krishna but King Narasimha, the builder of the temple. A 6

This is not quite accurate. For instance, despite the rule of the Muslim Sultans at Gujarat, there is no dearth of Hindu and Jain temples there. A 7

METAL IMAGES FROM CENTRAL AND EASTERN INDIA

During the medieval period there was an outburst of activity with regard to the production of metal images. This is a feature common to many parts of the country. A fine group, some as early as *circa* 600 A.D. (Pl. 111A), was discovered at Ākota near Baroda and other interesting groups come from Sirpur and Khinkhini in Central India (Plates 111B and C and 112A). In Eastern India during Pala rule, the output was prolific extending from the 8th century or even earlier to the 13th century. These Pala bronzes vary greatly in quality and the later products are often apt to be mechanical. Characteristic styles are reproduced as Plates 112B, 113A and B and 114A and B. All these images are meant for worship in shrines and some could have been for household worship. In fact, we know that the Pala production of Buddha metal images was part of a movement of Buddhist monasteries to revitalize and popularise Buddhism.

Chapter Ten

SOUTHERN INDIA

Part I. ARCHITECTURE

THE Dravidian or Southern style of architecture is sharply distinguished from the Northern by the fact that its tower or spire is straight-lined and pyramidal in form, divided into stories by horizontal bands, and surmounted by either a barrel-roof or a dome derived directly from the ancient wooden architecture. The central shrine originally stood alone, but in later times it was enclosed in an immense walled court, usually including numerous subsidiary temples, tanks, and sculptured halls or cloisters. The quadrangle is entered by lofty gateways (*gopuram*), which in later temples overtop the central shrine, and so spoil the effect of the architectural composition. But the great temple of Tanjore, its smaller replica at Gangaikondapuram, and some of the earlier temples at Conjeeveram (*Kanchi*) are designed on correct principles, with the central mass dominating the composition. Sometimes there are several quadrangles, one within the other.

Rathas of Mamallapuram.

The history of the style begins in the seventh century with the *Dharmaraja Ratha*, the earliest of the rock-cut *rathas* at Mamallapuram, thirty-five miles south of Madras, commonly known as the Seven Pagodas, which were excavated in the reigns of the Pallava kings of the South during the seventh century (A 1). I give an illustration of the *Ganesa Ratha* (*c.* A.D. 680), with a ridge roof[1]. Some of the others are crowned by domes.

Structural temples at Kanchi.

The next stage in the development of the style is marked by the structural temples at Conjeeveram (*Kanchi*), the Pallava capital, which became known only a few years ago, and have been described in detail by Mr. A. Rea. Six temples of the Pallava period exist in or close to the town[2] (A 2). Inscriptions prove that the two principal edifices, the *Kailasanatha* and the *Vaikuntha-Perumal*, were erected by the sons of King Rajasimha, great-grandson of Narasimha-varman (A 3). The *Muktesvara* temple of about the same date, say A.D. 700 to A.D. 750, with a domical roof, is a typical example (Plate 115C)[3].

Further development was effected under the patronage of the powerful Chola kings, Rajaraja and his son Rajendra (985 to 1035), the builders respectively of the Great Temple at Tanjore and its fellow at Gangaikondapuram in the Trichinopoly District (A 4). At this period the shrine was designed on huge proportions, towering above the subsidiary gateways and pavilions.

Later temples.

The gigantic South-Indian temples, with vast quadrangular enclosures and lofty *gopurams* (Plates 133B, 134 A) overtopping the central shrine, extend in date from the sixteenth century to the present day. Fergusson speaks of 'upwards of thirty great Dravidian temples, or groups of temples, any one of which must have cost as much to build as an English cathedral — some a great deal more'. Several such edifices, at Ramesvaram, Tinnevelly, Madura, and other

[1] [In this Edition, the illustration of the Ganesa Ratha has been replaced by Plate 115B which is of a Ratha with a barrel roof].

[2] Rea, *Pallava Architecture*, 4to, Madras, 1909, being vol. xxxiv of *Archaeol. S. Rep., India*, New Imp. Series, and vol. xi of the Southern India Series. The standard work is Jouveau-Dubreuil, *Architecture du Sud de l'Inde*. See also his *Pallavas*.

[3] For relation of Pallava caves and temples see Venkayya, 'The Pallavas' (*Ann. Rep. A. S., India*, 1906-7, pp. 226-35), and Dr. Hultzsch (*Ep. Ind.*, vol. x, pp. 1-14).

places, are described in his book. The buildings at Madura are of special interest because they can be dated closely, having been erected by Tirumal Naik, a local chieftain, who reigned from 1623 to 1659. Plate 133B gives a general view of the Madura temple, a typical example. The corridors or cloisters connected with such temples are of wonderfully large dimensions — those of Ramesvaram, for instance, aggregating nearly 4,000 feet in length — and are filled with weird, fantastic sculpture. Perhaps the most marvellous of all Dravidian temples is the well-known rock-cut *Kailasa* temple at Ellora, excavated from a hill-side by a *Rashtrakuta* king in the eighth century. In style the *Kailasa* is a development of the Pallava shrines, but its sculpture is finer than anything produced in the South. At Badami and Pattadkal in the Bijapur District are other shrines of the same type; these are all structural.

The Vijayanagar style.

The immense ruins of the city of Vijayanagar (Plate 132A and B), dating from the fifteenth and sixteenth centuries, surrounding Hampi village in the Bellary District, Madras, present numerous examples of a special local variety of Dravidian architecture. The royal palaces and apartments here show signs of Islamic influence (Plate 94B). The temples are purely southern Indian in style with high gateways and many-pillared pavilions.

The Deccan or Chalukyan style.

The style intermediate in both locality and character between the Northern and Southern styles is that which received from Fergusson the inappropriate name of *Chalukyan*. It is true that the *Chalukya* clan supplied one of the leading royal families of the Deccan from the middle of the sixth to the middle of the eighth century, and again from A.D. 973 to the Muhammadan conquest, but the typical examples of the style are the work of *Hoysala*, not *Chalukya* kings; and, if a dynastic designation be given, the style should be named *Hoysala* rather than *Chalukya*. Territorial designations are, however, preferable to dynastic, and if it be practicable to modify Fergusson's established nomenclature, the style may be better described either as that of the Deccan, or that of Mysore, in which province the finest specimens occur, at Halebid, the ancient capital, Belur, and many other localities less known to fame.

The Belur and other temples.

This style, whatever name be bestowed upon it, is characterized by a richly carved base or plinth, supporting the temple, which is polygonal, star-shaped in plan, and roofed by a low pyramidal tower, surmounted by a vase-like ornament. The temple of Vishnu in the village of Nuggehalli, in the Tiplur Taluk, Mysore, as shown in Plate 119A, from an unpublished photograph, gives a good notion of this extraordinarily ornate style. The stellate plan appears clearly in the view of the Somnathpur temple (Plate 120A). The Belur temple is known to have been erected in A.D. 1117 by a *Hoysala* king named *Bettiga*, converted from Jainism to faith in Vishnu. The more magnificent temples at Halebid, the *Hoysalesvara* and *Kedaresvara*, are somewhat later in date, and necessarily must have been under construction for many years. Not long ago the disintegrating action of the roots of a banyan tree unfortunately reduced the *Kedaresvara* to a heap of ruins.[1]

Sculptures at Halebid.

Plate 122, showing a small portion of the sculptures on the *Hoysalesvara* temple, will give the reader a faint notion of 'one of the most marvellous exhibitions of human labour to be found even in the patient East'. The architectural frame-

[1] The principal temples in this style range in date between A.D. 1117 and 1268 (Rice, *Mysore and Coorg from the Inscriptions*, Constable, 1909, p. 194). See Workman, *Through Town and Jungle* (1904), ch. v, with many excellent illustrations.

work, it will be observed, is used mainly as a background for the display of an infinity of superb decoration, which leaves no space uncovered and gives the eye no rest.

'The building', Fergusson writes, 'stands on a terrace ranging from 5 to 6 feet in height, and paved with large slabs. On this stands a frieze of elephants, following all the sinuosities of the plan and extending to some 710 feet in length, and containing not less than two thousand elephants, most of them with riders and trappings, sculptured as only an Oriental can represent the wisest of brutes. Above these is a frieze of *sardulas*, or conventional lions—the emblems of the Hoysala Ballalas who built the temple.[1] Then comes a scroll of infinite beauty and variety of design ; over this a frieze of horsemen and another scroll ; over which is a bas-relief of scenes from the *Ramayana*, representing, the conquest of Ceylon and all the varied incidents of that epic. This, like the other, is about 700 feet long. (The frieze of the Parthenon is less than 550 feet.) Then some celestial beasts and celestial birds, and all along the east front a frieze of groups from human life, and then a cornice, with a rail, divided into panels, each containing two figures. Over this are windows of pierced slabs, like those of Belur, though not so rich or varied.'

The *Hoysalesvara* and several other buildings of its class are twin temples consisting of two distinct shrines set side by side and joined together. The beautiful building at Somnathpur (Plate 120A) is a triple temple. A special feature of interest in these Mysore temples is the record of the names of the Kanarese artists, who executed individual statues. At Belur there are twelve such signatures, and at the *Hoysalesvara* fourteen, all different. Eight signatures on the Somnathpur temple have been noted, among them that of *Mallitamma*, who executed forty images.[2]

The Ballari temples.

Certain temples near the Tungabhadra river situated in the western part of the Bellary District, Madras, wedged in between Mysore territory on the south and the Nizam's Dominions on the north, form the subject of an excellent monograph by Mr. Rea, entitled *Chalukyan Architecture*. The title is so far justified that the buildings were erected to the order of *Chalukya* kings in the twelfth century. But the style is a modification of the Dravidian or Southern, not of the Deccan or Mysore style called *Chalukyan* by Mr. Fergusson. The plans are rectangular, not star-shaped, and the towers are distinctly Dravidian in design. The buildings, as Mr. Rea correctly observes, 'exhibit a preponderance of Dravidian forms. They might best be described as an embodiment of *Chalukyan* details engrafted on a Dravidian building.' Although the statues, individually regarded, are not of high merit, and present much of the grotesqueness of commonplace Hindu sculpture, the ornament, considered as a whole, is superb. It is impossible, we are assured, to describe the exquisite finish of the greenstone or hornblende pillars, or to exaggerate the marvellous intricacy and artistic finish of the decoration in even the minutest details. The ornament is generally completely undercut, and is sometimes attached to the solid masonry by the most slender of stalks, producing the effect of an incrustation of foliage on the wall. Both the intricate geometrical patterns of the ceilings and the foliated work covering every other part of the building exhibit the greatest possible exuberance of varied forms boldly designed and executed with consummate mastery of technical details. No chased work in gold or silver could possibly be finer, and the patterns to this day are copied by goldsmiths, who take casts and moulds from them, although unable to reproduce the sharpness and finish of the originals.

[1] The lions are there, not as the emblem of the Hoysala kings, but as part of the canonical scheme of decoration — elephants, lions, horses, men.

[2] In *Epigraphia Carnatica*, vol. v, Part I, pp. xxxvi, xxxviii, Mr. Rice describes and illustrates several temples. See also *Ann. Rep. Archaeol. S., Mysore*, 1909-10, para. 25.

A. Brahma.

B. Siva.

10th Century A.D. Early Chola school, South India.

(*By Courtesy of Museum of Fine Arts, Boston*)

PLATE 117

A. Siva and Parvati, on north wall of great (Chola) temple Gangaikonda-Cholapuram, Trichinopoly. 11th Century.
(*Copyright by Department of Archaeology, Government of India*)

B. Ardhanarisvara, from Kondiyur, Tanjore district. 10th Century A.D. Early Chola period.
(*Copyright by Government Museum, Madras*)

C, D. Siva as Bhikshatana (*left*) and dancing Siva (*right*), from the Great Temple, Tanjore. Early 11th Century A.D. Chola period.

E. Siva and Parvati, on north wall of Great (Chola) Temple Gangaikonda-Cholapuram, Trichinopoly. 11th Century.
(*Copyright by Department of Archaeology, Government of India*)

PLATE 118

Opinions may differ as to the propriety of employing such jewellers' work as architectural decoration, but concerning the beauty of the result and the high standard of executive skill no two opinions are possible. The annexed plan of a ceiling in the *Suryanarayanaswami* temple at Magala (Plate 120B) may suffice to give some notion of the exquisite carving characteristic of the Bellary variety of the Dravidian style, as favoured by *Chalukya* Kings. A ceiling.

Part II. SCULPTURE AND BRONZES

The arts of sculpture and decorative carving in stone continued to be practised in India to the south of the Narbada under the patronage of many dynasties throughout the medieval period, and even to this day are cultivated with considerable success whenever encouragement on an adequate scale is offered. But, excepting certain Chola statuary of the eleventh century, which is pre-eminently excellent, the Southern figure sculpture does not often attain high quality. In quantity it is enormous, the gigantic temples and halls characteristic of the Dravidian kingdoms being commonly overloaded with sculptured ornament on every member. Mythological subjects from the *Puranas* and *Tantras* are the favourites, and the tendency is to treat the conceptions of a luxuriant mythology with exuberant fancy. The result too often is merely grotesque, and very few of the individual images can claim to be beautiful. The sculpture of the South is really the successor of the medieval art of the North. The figure-sculpture is purely iconographical, and executed exactly according to the literary canon. Character of Southern sculpture.

The purely decorative designs carved on the twelfth-century *Chalukya* and *Hoysala* temples and elsewhere are unsurpassed, but the statuary of the same buildings is too often conventional and rarely of much merit.

During the seventh century the kings of the Pallava dynasty of *Kanchi* (Conjeeveram) succeeded in making themselves the dominant power in Southern India, overshadowing the ancient *Chola*, *Chera*, and *Pandya* dynasties of the Tamil region, and, for a time, obscuring the glory of the powerful *Chalukya* sovereigns of the Deccan. The Pallava king named Mahendra-varman I (*c.* A.D. 600-25), a great builder, is responsible for many rock-cut temples in the North Arcot, South Arcot, Chingleput, and Trichinopoly Districts. The earliest *rathas*, or monolithic shrines, at Mamallapuram, or the Seven Pagodas, also probably should be ascribed to his reign. His son, Narasimha-varman I, surnamed Mahamalla, the most mighty prince of his line, gave his name to Mamallapuram, and constructed or rather caused to be excavated, some of the *rathas* at that place. The family taste for architecture survived in the descendants of Narasimha-varman, the so-called 'Shore Temple' at Mamallapuram and the early structural temples at Kanchi being ascribed partly to his great-grandson, Rajasimha, and partly to Rajasimha's sons. The Pallava dynasty.

The most notable remains of Pallava art are those dating from the seventh and eighth centuries at Mamallapuram, which include, besides the well-known *rathas*, numerous less familar monuments, comprising temples, statues in the round, and gigantic sculptures in relief carved on the face of the rocks (Plate 115A). Among the sculptures in the round mention may be made of a lion, seven feet in length, which is said to be well-proportioned and of a noble appearance. Remains at Mamallapuram.

Several authors concur in the opinion that the most artistic of the reliefs is the great composition depicting the victory of the Good, represented by the goddess *Durga* mounted on a lion, over evil personified in the buffalo-headed demon, Durga and Mahishasura.

Mahishasura (Plate 75A). The scene undoubtedly is full of life and movement, and the goddess is a dignified figure.

The Great Bas-Relief.

The great bas-relief at Mamallapuram (Plate 115A), covers a sheet of rock 96 feet in length and 43 feet in breadth. Around a central figure, now missing, all creation, heavenly and earthly are gathered in worship. Before the great deity even the animals do penance, while seers and lesser gods and the spirits of the air unite in adoration. This gigantic sculpture was erroneously identified as representing Arjuna's Penance, after the story in the *Mahabharata* (A 5).

Relief at Trichinopoly.

Another and smaller relief of Pallava age at Trichinopoly seems to be of earlier date and is in a better style of art. This group, consisting of five large figures, in addition to the crouching dwarf on whose hand the central deity, apparently a form of Siva, rests his right foot, is symmetrically composed, due prominence being given to the god, who stands in a natural and easy attitude. He has four arms, but only two are prominent, and all the other figures are quite free from monstrosity. The kneeling worshippers are excellently modelled and pleasing in appearance. The style, in fact, is much more akin to that of Northern India, and especially to the work at Badami, than to the sculpture commonly seen in the South.

The Begur and Atakur reliefs.

Two spirited bas-relief sculptures from Mysore territory, now in the Bangalore Museum, although too crude to rank as fine art, perhaps deserve passing mention. The first, on the Bagur stone, dating from about A.D. 934-8, gives a vivid picture of a battle between the force commanded by a chief mounted on an elephant and another led by a rival on horseback. The second, on the Atakur stone dated A.D. 949-50, commemorating a set fight between a mighty hound and a great boar in which both combatants were killed, represents an incident in the struggle, the hound having his teeth fixed in the boar's snout.[1] The design is better than the execution.

The Chola dynasty.

The *Cholas*, who succeeded the *Pallavas* as the paramount power in the South, may be said to have filled the principal places in the Tamil countries with their edifices, religious and secular, all richly sculptured (Plate 117A and B). Rajaraja the Great (985-1018), the most famous king of a capable dynasty, extended his power over nearly the whole of the Madras Presidency, Ceylon, and a large part of Mysore, while his navy ranged as far as the Laccadive and Maldive islands. A king so powerful and wealthy naturally spent freely on building, and the world owes to him the temple at Tanjore, his capital, the best designed of all the great South Indian temples.

Gangaikonda-Cholapuram.

His son and successor, Rajendra-Choladeva I, surnamed Gangaikonda (1018-35), continued and extended Rajaraja's victories by sea and land. In memory of the subjugation of the Ganga territory in Mysore, or, as others say, to commemorate his march northwards as far as the Ganges, Rajendra built a new capital, Gangaikonda-Cholapuram, in the Trichinopoly District, and constructed there an enormous artificial lake with an embankment sixteen miles long. The principal temple, designed on the noble model of the Tanjore temple, enshrined a huge monolithic lingam, thirty feet high, and the precincts of the city included a palace and many other notable buildings, now either vanished or in complete ruin. The sculptures in panels on the walls of the great temple are remarkable

[1] Fleet, 'Three Western Ganga Records in the Mysore Government Museum at Bangalore' (*Ep. Ind.*, vi, p. 40, with plates). A larger photograph of the Begur stone in *Ep. Carnatica*, vol. xi, frontispiece.

A. Temple at Nuggehalli, Mysore. A.D. 1249
(*Copyright by Department of Archaeology, Government of India*)

B. Stone Bull from Hanamkonda. 11th Century A.D. Chalukyan school.
(Photo : E. S. Mahalingam)

PLATE 119

A. Somnathpur Temple, Mysore. A.D. 1268. (Hoysala school).
(Copyright by Department of Archaeology, Government of India)

B. Plan of Ceiling in Suryanarayanaswami Temple at Magala. (11th Century A.D. Chalukyan school).
(From Rea, *Chalukyan Architecture*)

C. Bracket statuette; Karvati Temple. (Correctly, Kuruvati Temple. 11th Century A.D. Chalukyan school).

Jain sculpture and ornament on north face of Jinanathpur Basti, near Sravana Belgola. 12th Century A.D.
(*Copyright by Department of Archaeology, Government of India*)

Sculptures from Hoysalesvara Temple, Halebid. 12th Century A.D. Hoysala school.

PLATE 122

for their elegance and beauty (Plate 118A, C, D and E). [Late Chola sculpture is seen in Plates 127A and B and 128A].

Twelfth-century sculpture of Mysore temples.

The excessively exuberant, and yet fascinating, massed architectural sculpture of the Mysore temples built by the *Hoysala* kings in the twelfth century has been already illustrated sufficiently (Plates 121, 122, 123A and B, 124A and B, 125A and B, 126A and B). The artists who designed such enormous sheets of rich sculpture aimed at producing an imposing effect by the splendour of a mass of carvings of the highest complexity, rather than by inviting attention to individual figures. Nevertheless, the individual figures will bear examination in detail, the elephants especially being exquisitely true to nature. As already observed many of the larger statues of the Mysore temples are signed by the artists.

Chalukyan sculpture in Bellary District.

The approximately contemporary temples erected in the Bellary District, Madras, under the patronage of the *Chalukyan* kings are remarkable for the unequalled richness and delicacy of their deeply undercut decorative carving (Plate 120B). The figure sculpture (Plate 120C), notwithstanding the perfection of its mechanical execution, is generally conventional in design and semi-barbarous in style. [A Chalukyan bull from Hanamkonda is illustrated as Plate 119B].

The kingdom at Vijayanagar.

In the year 1336 two Hindu brothers established a principality with its capital at Vijayanagar on the Tungabhadra river, which rapidly developed into an empire comprising all Southern India beyond the Kistna. The state attained the height of its prosperity early in the sixteenth century during the reign of Krishna Deva Raya, the contemporary of Henry VIII of England, who stoutly maintained the Hindu cause against the Muslim Sultans of the Deccan until 1565, when he was utterly defeated by the combined forces of the Muhammadan princes, and his capital taken. The victors devoted their energies for five months to the deliberate destruction of the city, heaping up bonfires round the principal monuments, and hacking and mutilating the graven images. They succeeded in converting one of the richest and most splendid capitals of Asia into the abode of wild beasts, which has remained desolate to this day, save for the huts of a tiny hamlet nestling amidst the ruins.

Site of the city.

The actual site of the city covers an area of nine square miles, but the fortifications and outposts include a space far larger. In the days of its greatness the capital was filled with magnificent granite edifices erected by forced labour, and adorned in the most lavish manner with every form of decoration agreeable to the taste of a semi-barbaric court. The extant detailed accounts of the glories of Vijayanagar in the sixteenth century recall the familar stories of the Aztec capital as it was seen by its Spanish conquerors, the administration of both courts combining unbridled luxury with ferocious cruelty.

Style of art.

The semi-barbarism of the court is reflected in the forms of art. The giant monolithic Man-lion (*Narasimha*) statue, 22 feet high, and the huge Monkey-god *Hanuman*, although wrought with exquisite finish, are hideous inartistic monsters; and the sculpture generally, however perfect in mechanical execution, is lacking in beauty and refinement.

Bas-reliefs of *Hazara Ramaswami.*

In the palace enclosure the most striking building is the temple known as *Hazara Ramaswami*, 'the Thousand Lord Ramas', used by the old kings as their Chapel Royal. The walls of the courtyard of this edifice are covered with bas-reliefs depicting scenes from the *Ramayana*, described by Mr. Rea as being 'beautifully executed and carved with great life and spirit'. The specimens illustrated in

Scroll, Harihareswara temple, Bellary District.

Makara torana (arch), Malikarjuna temple, Kuruvatti.

Plate 132A and B will show how far such praise is justified.[1]

Sculptures on Vitthala-swami temple and throne.

One of the most notable of the ruins is the temple of Vishnu under the name of *Vitthalaswami*, begun early in the sixteenth century, and still unfinished when the city fell in 1565, never to rise again. The great hall in front of the shrine

'rests on a richly sculptured basement, and its roof is supported by huge masses of granite, 15 feet high, each consisting of a central pillar surrounded by detached shafts, figures mounted on demons, and other ornament, all cut from a single block of stone. These are surmounted by an elaborate and equally massive cornice ; and the whole is carved with a boldness and expression of power nowhere surpassed in the buildings of its class, showing the extreme limit in florid magnificence to which the style advanced. This beautiful building has been grievously injured by the destroyers of the city. Several of the carved pillars have been attacked with such fury that they are hardly more than shapeless blocks of stone, and a large portion of the centre has been destroyed utterly. (*Imp. Gaz.*)

[1] For the history see Sewell, *A Forgotten Empire* (*Vijayanagar*), *a Contribution to the History of India* (1900), a valuable and deeply interesting book. A photograph of the Man-lion faces p. 163. The Monkey-god forms the frontispiece to Meadows Taylor and Fergusson, *Architecture in Dharwar and Mysore* (atlas fol., 1866). The whole of the *Ramayana* reliefs is given in Pls. LXVIII, LXIX of that work. [This plate does not appear in the Third Edition but has been substituted].

A, B. Sculptures from Hoysalesvara Temple, Halebid. 12th Century A.D. Hoysala school.
(Photos : D. Hansraj)

PLATE 123

(Photo : A. K. Banerji)

A, B. Madanikas from the temple at Belur, Mysore. 12th Cent. A.D. Hoysala school.

Yali, or rampant lion, in Vijayanagar style, at Virinchipuram.

Female figure at Jinji (Gingee).

The sculptures on the walls of the throne are also commended, but no illustrations of the works referred to have been published. [This is no longer true. Plate 132A and B].

Sculptures of Tarpatri temple.

The best examples of the Vijayanagar style are to be found, perhaps, not at the capital, but at Tadpatri (Tarpatri), Anantapur District, Madras, in gateways (Plate 134B) erected during the sixteenth century by a prince subordinate to the kings of Vijayanagar. Fergusson, who devoted two full-page plates to the illustration of the Tadpatri greenstone sculptures, judged them to be 'on the whole, perhaps, in better taste than anything else in this style'.[1] [The style prevails all over Southern India. Plates 128B and C, 129A and B, 130A, B and C, 131A, B and C].

Yali, or rampant lion, at Virinchipuram.

The *Margasahayar* temple at Virinchipuram in the North Arcot District, 7½ miles to the west of Vellore, is believed to have been erected late in the fifteenth century, while the district was included in the dominions of Vijayanagar. One of the columns offers a good example of the *yali*, or conventional rampant lion, an effective, bold form of decoration very fashionable and characteristic of the country in both South India and Ceylon during medieval times. The lion, about 5½ feet in height, is designed and executed with spirit.

Ancient motive of figure at Gingee.

The statue of a goddess on the entrance of the temple of *Venkata-ramanasvami* at the famous fortress of Gingee in the South Arcot District, probably built during the time of the Vijayanagar rule a little before or after A.D. 1500, is of special interest as proving, like the Tadpatri figures, the persistence of a very ancient motive, common in Gandhara and Mathura art (see illustration above). This late southern example preserves all the essentials of the design — the female figure, the crossed legs, the raised right arm, and the left arm twined round the stem.

Sculptures at Udaiyarpalaiyam.

The palace of the Udaiyarpalaiyam zamindar in the Trichinopoly District contains some good figure and decorative sculpture associated with Indo-Muhammadan architecture, and evidently not older than the seventeenth century. It is executed in a rather soft stone. My attention was drawn to the sculptures by the remarks of Mr. J. P. Bedford, I.C.S., who made a communication to the Archaeological Survey and wrote:

'One of the big halls is in general design something after the fashion of Tirumal Naik's famous hall in Madura ; but the spandrels of the arches are one mass of carving of birds, flowers, &c., showing extraordinary fancy and spirit, while the arches themselves are worked out in the most

[1] A new temple at Tadpatri is adorned with elaboration equal to that of the old one; but, although the decorative carving is good, the figure sculpture is grotesque and contemptible. The work has been fully illustrated by Mr. Rea in his book, *Stone Carving and Inlaying in Southern India*.

exquisite tracery, with a niche above each column containing some god or saint. Above the level of the spandrels is a deep colonnade running round the whole hall, corresponding to the clerestory of an English cathedral—also a mass of spirited carving in relief. The effect of the whole is, so far as the writer's experience goes, absolutely unique so far as an Indian building is concerned; but it is very suggestive of Northern European Gothic, say the porches of Chartres Cathedral.'[1]

Seventeenth-century sculpture.

The numerous [usually] gigantic temples (Plates 133A and B, 134A) of Southern India in the Dravidian style, erected from the sixteenth century to the present day, with their appurtenant corridors and 'halls of 1000 columns', are covered with sculpture, mostly of a fantastic and *outre* character. The most famous princely builder was Tirumal (Trimul) Naik, who ruled at Madura from 1621 to 1657. His celebrated pillared hall, or *choultry*, at that city is 333 feet long and 105 feet wide, with four ranges of columns, all different, and all most elaborately sculptured.

Fergusson's criticism.

'The facade of this hall,' Fergusson observes, 'like that of almost all the great halls in the south of India, is adorned either with *yalis*—monsters of the lion type trampling on an elephant—or, even more generally, by a group consisting of a warrior sitting on a rearing horse, whose feet are supported on the shields of foot-soldiers, sometimes slaying men, sometimes tigers. These groups are found literally in hundreds in Southern India, and, as works exhibiting difficulties overcome by patient labour, they are unrivalled, so far as I know, by anything found elsewhere.

'As works of art they are the most barbarous, it may be said the most vulgar, to be found in India, and do more to shake one's faith in the civilization of the people who produced them than anything they did in any other department of art. Where these monstrosities are not introduced, the pillars of entrances are only enriched a little more than those of the interior, where the ornamentation is in better taste, and generally quite sufficiently rich for its purpose.'[2]

Fergusson's criticism fails to give the Southern sculptors due credit for their power of expressing vigorous movement, and, in my judgement, is too harsh. Such figures appear to be unknown elsewhere, and it is not apparent how they became so much favoured in the Tamil country. Fergusson probably was right in his suggestion that the rampant horses, *yalis*, and heavy cornices with double curvature, characteristic of the Dravidian temples in the South, were derived from primitive terra-cotta forms.[3]

Character of late Southern sculpture.

The Southern sculpture, remarkable, as already observed, for its enormous quantity, fantastic character, often degenerating into the grotesque, and marvellous elaboration, rarely, if ever, exhibits the higher qualities of art. The sculptures being designed to be viewed in the mass, not as individual works, reproductions of a few separate figures cannot do full justice either to the sculptors' intention or to the general effect. But, subject to that caution, a few specimens may be cited to give some idea of the style. The best of this class of work dates from the seventeenth century, while the most recent is the worst; indeed, modern figure sculpture, as a rule, hardly deserves to be called the work of artists.

Examples.

Examples of seventeenth- and eighteenth-century sculpture might be multiplied indefinitely. Selected specimens from buildings in the Madura District will suffice as typical illustrations (Plate 134C and D). One of the best images among the crowd at Tirumal Naik's *choultry* (1623-65) is that of Siva in an unusual attitude as a supplicant to some other deity. The effigy of the woman holding a doll-like baby, from the Great Temple at Madura (Plate 134C), is welcome as introducing a rare touch of human sentiment, but is far inferior to the treatment of a similar

[1] *Ann. Progr. Rep. A. S. Madras and Coorg*, 1604-5, p. 44.
[2] *Hist. of Ind. and E. Archit.* (1899), p. 363; ed. 1910, vol. i, p. 389.
[3] However, the use of large terra-cotta figures to decorate gateways, &c., is comparatively modern.

subject at Puri (*ante*, Plate 103C). The blotchy appearance of the photograph is due to the whitewash or paint with which the statue has been smeared. The sculptures from the Ramesvaram temple are somewhat later, dating from the close of the seventeenth or the beginning of the eighteenth century. The image of the female carrying a male deity on her back (Plate 134E) is characteristically grotesque. It too has been smudged with paint or whitewash. The modelling of the woman is not destitute of merit.

Modern sculpture.

The capabilities of modern sculptors in the South are best proved by the decorations of the new palace in the town of Mysore, executed to the order of H.H. the Maharaja and described and illustrated by Mr. A. Rea. Skill is not confined to the members of any one caste, and the Maharaja has been willing to employ capable men from any district. The material used is sometimes soapstone and sometimes stone of considerable hardness. The soapstone is employed in fairly large masses, a clever figure of Vishnu, for instance, being two feet in height. The drapery of that figure looks as if it had been imitated from photographs of Gandhara work. The style throughout is frankly eclectic and imitative, and it is obvious that the artists have studied models of various periods and schools. One decorative motive is admittedly borrowed from a picture by Ravi Varma, and the more direct influence of modern European art can be clearly traced. A relief representing the marriage of *Rukmini* looks as if it had been suggested by study of photographs of the Borobudur bas-reliefs. Some of the female figures are very pretty. Artistically, the best things are certain decorative soapstone panels wrought with floral and other designs, thoroughly Indian in character and of first-rate quality.[1]

South Indian brass and copper castings

Many images cast in copper by the *cire perdue* process exist and also a few castings in brass. In modern times casting in brass has been carried on mainly in Mysore and Western India, and not in the South. The better specimens of these castings seem to range in date from the twelfth to the eighteenth century. [The best from the 8th to the 13th century. Plates 135A and B, 136A and B, 137A and B, 138A and B, 139A and B, 140A. They come from various localities and provincial styles can often be located]. The modern work is usually on a small scale and of very poor craftsmanship.

Vijayanagar brass portrait statues.

Exceptional interest attaches to the brass images reproduced in Plate 140B, which are certified by inscriptions on the shoulders to be portraits, apparently contemporary, of Krishna Raya, the famous king of Vijayanagar in the early years of the sixteenth century, and two of his queens. They stand inside a temple on the sacred hill of Tirumalai or Upper Tirupati, and were photographed by a high-caste Hindu, no European or Musalman being permitted to enter any temple on the hill. The town of Tirupati is famous for the skill of its workers in brass.[2] The images, although formal in design, are defective in expression.

Siva Nataraja.

Numerous figures of *Siva Nataraja* exist, some of which have been illustrated in the works of Dr. Coomaraswamy and Mr. Havell. The figure lent by Lord Ampthill to the Indian Museum, South Kensington, which was shown at the India Section of the Festival of Empire in 1911, is perhaps the finest of all (A 6). The

[1] A. Rea, *Monograph on Stone Carving and Inlaying in Southern India*, with thirty-one plates; Madras Government Press, 1906; quarto in paper covers. The half-tone blocks cannot be reproduced. Some of the best objects are shown in Pls. XXIV-XXVI.

[2] *Imp. Gaz.*, s.v. Tirumala; *Annual Report, A. S., India*, 1902-3, p. 227; citing Hultzsch (*Progr. Report*, 1903, in *Madras G. O. Public*, Nos. 655, 656, dated 24 July 1903). Dr. Hultzsch's recommendation to have the images photographed by a high-caste Hindu was carried out by the Survey in the following year, but no description of the statues was recorded.

explanation of the symbolism of these representations of the dancing god will be reserved until the Ceylonese examples are discussed.

The date of Southern Indian castings.

The best of these images, such as the *Nataraja*, described above, are directly comparable with Pallava and Chola sculpture, and are probably pre-eleventh century. It is very difficult to date the later works. As a whole, the scale of the castings is very much reduced. The jewellery and costume is also over-emphasized, the waist-cloths of the goddesses being shown round the legs and not merely indicated by tooling on the legs. Many of the large, early figures are fitted with rings at the base for transport in processions. The later figures, for the most part on a small scale and much tooled, are probably to be associated with Tanjore.

The image of *Parvati*, now in the Boston Museum (Plate 138A), is not very dissimilar in style from the Polonnaruwa bronzes, and may, perhaps, date from about the same period, the twelfth century. It is well modelled; the hands are specially good.

NOTES TO CHAPTER TEN

A 1 In fact the heyday of the style begins with the rock-cut shrines excavated by the great Pallava ruler Mahendravarman I, at Trichinopoly and other places. The raths of Mahabalipuram and the great rock carving of Arjuna's Penance (Pl. 115A) represents the second stage in the development of the style.

A 2 The structural temples of Conjeeveram mark the third stage in the development of Pallava architecture. Much of their fine sculpture was covered with plaster in later times making it difficult to appreciate their beauty (Plates 116A, B and C).

A 3 The Kailasnatha was erected by Rajasimha, but the Vaikuntha Perumal was erected by his successor, Nandivarman Pallavamalla.

A 4 Prior to the period of Rajaraja and Rajendra, the early Chola shrine developed in the late 9th and the 10th century A.D. These shrines are only now becoming well known. The sculpture of the early Chola (Plates 117A and B, 118B) and Pallava-Chola transition shrines is of very high merit.

A 5 In fact it is now recognized that this identification is correct.

A 6 It has already been pointed out in the Notes to Chapter I, that many superior examples exist, as for instance, Plate 137A.

SOUTH INDIAN METAL IMAGES

At one time it was thought that the beginnings of South Indian metal sculpture do not antedate the rule of the Cholas. But this view has been proved to be incorrect. Metal images of high quality were also made during Pallava rule. It is true that the Pallava images which have come to light are a mere score or two at the most as compared to the thousands of Chola and post-Chola images still to be seen.

In 600 A.D., the South was ready for a religious upheaval such as was seldom witnessed in any age. Buddhism had failed to maintain its original outlook and had lost all its early vigour by schisms that seem utterly puerile to us today, as also by a mode of life that did little credit to the monastic orders. To what extent morals in these monastic orders had deteriorated can be gauged by the fact that when Buddhism became an almost forgotten religion in the greater part of the South, the mounds covering the old Buddhist stupas and monasteries were widely referred to as the courtesan mounds.

Methaphysical speculations were all very well for learned men, but the masses were groping for a creed which would not entail intricate mental processes and which would provide an anchorage for storm-tossed spirits. It was not a new creed that suddenly revitalized the whole South. It was the doctrine of Bhakti, but it was presented in a manner, and with a vigour so new, that it assumed almost the aspect of a new religion. This revival was brought about by a band of hymnists whose songs reveal such frenzied devotion to the Lord Shiva that one is not surprised at the manner which

(Photo : D. Hansraj)

(Photo : A. K. Banerji)

A, B. Sculptures from the Hoysalesvara Temple, Halebid, Mysore. 12th Century A.D. Hoysala school.

PLATE 125

A, B. Madanikas from the temple at Belur, Mysore. 12th Century A.D. Hoysala school.

(Photos : A. K. Banerji)

their emotional outbursts invigorated simple minds. With two such hymnists as Appar and Sambandar living in the same century, little wonder that the dominant ruling house of the Pallavas in South India during 600-700 A.D. became ardent patrons of the great Shiva legend.

The Satavahana Empire had crumbled in the first half of the 3rd century A.D., due in all probability to weakness at the centre and the consequent revolt of provincial governors, who carved out small kingdoms for themselves and threw off the last vestiges of the rule that was once the Imperial Andhras. We know of a Vishnugopa at Kanchi who is mentioned by Samudragupta in his list of feudatories on the Allahabad Pillar inscription. This Vishnugopa was doubtless a Pallava chief for the Pallavas themselves were once the viceroys of the Satavahanas. Therefore the family, whatever its origin, had inevitably imbibed the artistic legacy of Andhra art. We are not concerned with the early Pallavas though we may be justified in assuming that the artistic greatness which this family was later to achieve, was due in considerable measure to the cultural background which the Andhras had created and which was too deep rooted to disappear with that dynasty. In the reconsideration of the chronology of South Indian bronzes it is to the Pallavas of Kanchi that we must look for the beginnings.

The South India bronzes though mostly Brahmanical also pertain to the Jain (Pl. 135A) and Buddhist (Pl. 135B) faiths. It seems that the greatest production was in the Tanjore district, but the art of metal images for worship was nevertheless widespread. Chalukyan (Plates 135A, 136B, 139A) and Kakatiya (Pl. 136A) bronzes are known and a systematic study enables us to classify those of other districts also. The best South India bronzes are amongst the finest achievement of metal sculpture in the world.

Chapter Eleven

CEYLON AND JAVA

Part I. SINGHALESE ARCHITECTURE AND SCULPTURE

The two capitals. THE principal architectural remains in Ceylon are found at the two most notable of the ancient capitals, namely, Anuradhapura and Polonnaruwa, both situated in the North Central Province. The former city, a royal residence for more than a thousand years, was superseded in the eighth century by Polonnaruwa, the glory of which lasted, with interruptions, until the early years of the thirteenth century. The antiquities, therefore, belong to two widely separated series. Those at Anuradhapura go back to the time of Asoka, but mostly date from the earliest centuries of the Christian era; whereas the most important buildings at Polonnaruwa were constructed during the second half of the twelfth century (A.D. 1153-97) in the reigns of Parakrama Bahu the Great and Kirti Nissanka Malla.[1]

Anuradhapura. Anuradhapura, when in its prime, was a city of colossal proportions, 'une véritable Rome bouddhique', at least 8 miles in diameter, and crowded with magnificent buildings. After the removal of the court everything went to ruin, but many edifices were repaired and restored by Parakrama Bahu, to whose energy the splendours of Polonnaruwa also are largely due. After his death the ancient capital again became desolate, and remained buried in dense forest until recent times. During the last forty years the ruins have been systematically and efficiently explored, with the result that the principal remains have been exposed, mapped, and more or less completely described.

Dagabas. The most conspicuous structures are the great Buddhist *dagabas* (*stupas*), far exceeding in dimensions anything of the kind now standing in India. That commonly called the Jetawanarama, still 251 feet high, stands on a stone platform nearly 8 acres in extent, while the space included within the walled enclosure measures nearly 14 acres. The Abhayagiri *dagabas*, almost equal in mass, is said to have been originally erected in the first century B.C. The earliest, the Thuparama, built in the days of Asoka, has been covered up in recent times, like most of the others, by later additions.[2]

Other sacred buildings. The *dagabas*, huge masses of masonry, wonderful as stupendous monuments of laborious engineering, are not in themselves interesting as examples of architectural art. The work of the artist must be sought in the numerous and splendid associated buildings. The stone railing never attained in Ceylon the development which in India made it the vehicle for much of the highest art of the country. The only considerable example in the island, situated at Anuradhapura, and discovered and rebuilt by Mr. Bell, was a well-designed structure of uncertain date, perfectly plain, as at Sanchi, except for sculptured guard-posts at the entrance.

[1] Polonnaruwa, alias Kalingapura, or Pulastipura, the modern Topavewa or Topawa, represents a much more ancient city, Wijitapura, of which some remains seem to be traceable (Parker, *Ancient Ceylon*, pp. 239-41). For the dates of the medieval kings see *Epigraphia Zeylanica*, vol. i, p. 156. The traditional date for the foundation of Anuradhapura is 457 B.C. Polonnaruwa was abandoned finally in A.D. 1240.

[2] See *Architectural Remains, Anuradhapura, Ceylon: comprising the Dagabas and certain other Ruined Structures*. Measured, drawn, and described by James G. Smither, F.R.I.B.A., late Architect to the Government of Ceylon. Sixty-seven Plates. Published by order of the Ceylon Government (Atlas folio, N. D.). The drawings, finished in 1877, were not published until 1894. Mr. Parker (*Ancient Ceylon*, p. 300) gives good reasons for believing that the real Abhayagiri is now miscalled the Jetavana. The true Jetavana, according to him, stands to the east of the Sela Chaitya.

Musicians and dancers, from Chindabaram. Probably early Vijayanagar period.
(Photos : A. L. Syed)

PLATE 127

A. Dancers and musicians, from Chidambaram. Probably early Vijayanagar period.
(Photo : A. L. Syed)

B. Sculpture from Temple at Vellore. 16th Century A.D. Vijayanagar period.
(Photo : E. S. Mahalingam)

C. Figure of musician from Nataraja Temple, Chidambaram. 16th Century A.D. Vijayanagar period.

(Photo : S. R. Rajagopal)

A, B. Sculptures from the temple at Vellore. 16th Century A.D. Vijayanagar period.
(Photos : E. S. Mahalingam)

A, B, C. Sculptures from the temple at Vellore. 16th Century A.D. Vijayanagar period.
(Photos : E. S. Mahalingam)

It surrounded a rectangular pillared hall, not a *dagaba* (Plate 141A)[1]. The monasteries and temples connected with the *dagabas* included every variety of edifice needful for the accommodation of thousands of monks and for the ritual of a highly ceremonial religion.

Mr. Bell's description of the Vijayarama at Anuradhapura, erected in or about the eighth century for the use of a community of Tantric Mahayanist Buddhists, will serve to give a notion of the form and extent of an early monastic establishment of the more important kind in Ceylon. **A typical monastery.**

'Here existed', he writes, 'a typical *sangharama*, or Buddhist establishment, perfect in itself, with its shrines and meeting-hall, its priestly residences, bath-house, store-rooms, ponds, &c.

Broadly, the monastery consisted of a raised quadrangle, 288 feet north and south by 268 feet east and west, walled, with entrances at the cardinal points, enclosing a *dagaba* and three *vihares* [temples], and having an open hall attached to the north. Outside this *temenos* was first a walk, then twelve annexes, evenly grouped, surrounded by a moat, with the chief *pansala* [monks' residences], a bathing-house, and a few other buildings on the south and west; the whole covering an area of 12½ acres, bounded by a quadrangular wall of stone, 200 yards by 300 yards, traces of which may still be seen. From the lodge (*mura-ge*) a broad street led straight to the inner quadrangle.'[2]

It would be difficult to point out the ruins of an Indian monastery equally extensive. The unlimited field for the exercise of the painter's and sculptor's arts presented by such a mass of buildings was sedulously cultivated.

The Buddhist temples in Ceylon, differing widely from Indian models, ordinarily were rectangular buildings of either brick or stone, approached through a vestibule, and sometimes with only a single entrance, but often with four entrances facing the cardinal points. They were frequently arranged *quincunx* fashion in groups of five, four small shrines being placed symmetrically round a larger central one. **Temples.**

Shrines of the Hindu gods find honoured places among the Buddhist buildings, Vishnu, for instance, being regarded as the protector of Ceylon, and worshipped in subordination to Buddha. Hindu temples intended for Brahmanical worship, as practised by the Tamil invaders, also exist. One illustration of such a temple at Polonnaruwa, dedicated to Siva, and dating probably from the eleventh or twelfth century, may be given to show how far the Ceylonese Hindu buildings resemble the South Indian Chola types.[3] The Tivanka Vihare at Polonnaruwa, built by Parakrama Bahu, and generally miscalled the Thuparama, has a high pyramidal roof in Dravidian style, and, generally speaking, the Polonnaruwa buildings have a distinctly Dravidian character, but the huge Dravidian gateways (*gopuram*) are unknown in Ceylon.

The basements are sometimes adorned with relief figures in stucco of some merit (Plate 141C). **Stucco reliefs.**

Circular temples or shrines, of which three notable examples are known, are the most original and peculiar of Ceylonese buildings. That at Polonnaruwa, erected by King Nissanka Malla at the close of the twelfth century, is considered by Mr. Bell to be 'the most beautiful specimen of Buddhistic stone architecture existing in Ceylon'. He declares that 'no photographs or drawings can adequately reproduce, nor can words but faintly outline, the inexpressible charm' of the inner **Circular shrines.**

[1] Full details in *Ann. Rep. A. S., Ceylon*, for 1892 (xxxvii, 1904), p. 1. As a decorative pattern the railing was familiar in the island (see *Anc. Ceylon*, p. 278).

[2] *Ann. Rep. A. S., Ceylon*, for 1891 (xxxvi, 1904), p. 4. The existence of Tantric Mahayanist Buddhism in Ceylon deserves special notice.

[3] Fully described and illustrated in *Ann. Rep. A. S., Ceylon*, 1907, pp. 17-24, 36, Pls. XVI-XIX, and plan. This purely Brahmanical building is locally miscalled the *Dalada Maligawa*, or 'Shrine of the Tooth Relic'. The fine Hindu bronzes described *post*, chap. vii, sec. 7 *b*, were found by digging a trench outside a southern extension of the eastern wall of the enclosure of this temple, to which they evidently belonged.

platform. The structure, about 80 feet in diameter, is circular, standing on a terrace, also circular, and 125 yards in diameter. It was intended for the reception of the tooth-relic. The centre was occupied by a small *dagaba* surrounded by sixteen statues, and two concentric circles of granite columns, twenty and sixteen in number respectively. The entrance was through a portico on the north-east. The elaborate decoration was lavished chiefly on the stylobate of the inner platform and on the staircase. A portion of the exterior is shown in Plate 144C, and the western stairs in Plate 143C.[1]

The Medirigiriya example.

A second and earlier building of the same class has been discovered at a place called Medirigiriya in the Tamankaduwa District, North Central Province, hidden in the heart of the forest, six miles from the nearest village. It stands on the highest point of a mass of rock, and like its fellow at Polonnaruwa is surrounded by a slab wall, carved with surface ornament. There are

'three concentric rows of graceful columns (sixty-eight in all) of the type seen at Thuparama and Lankarama, Anuradhapura. The inner and second row[s] of pillars bear single lions and pilasters on their capitals, the outermost [bears] posturing *ganas* (dwarfs). In height this row of columns is but 9 ft. 9 in., while the two inner rows reach 16 ft. All are octagonal, and all are unbroken, save four; but several have lost their spreading capitals. Within the circle of pillars, seated on an *asanaya*, is a Buddha in stone; probably one of four cardinally placed, with their backs to a small central *dagaba*. The design on the stone slab wall encircling the *dagaba* and columns is the "Buddhist railing" pattern, in this differing from the flowered ornamentation of the Polonnaruwa "*Wala-da-ge*".'

An inscribed pillar close by was erected in the third year of King Kasyapa V (929-39), which may be taken as the date of the building.[2] Plate 144D shows the best-preserved part of the enclosure.

The Toluvila example.

The third example, discovered in 1894, to the north of the great Toluvila monastery at Anuradhapura, is of small size, with an enclosure 37 feet in diameter, surrounding a miniature *dagaba* with a diameter of only 8 feet, and two concentric rings of slender columns.[3]

Circles of columns.

Such concentric circles of detached, slender, monolithic columns are a characteristic feature of Ceylonese architecture. They occur, in addition to the examples already cited, at the Thuparama and Lankarama *dagabas* of Anuradhapura, as well as at the Ambusthala *dagaba* of Mihintale, distant eight miles from the early capital. Their purpose has been much discussed. Mr. Smither has demonstrated that those at the Thuparama could not have carried a roof of any kind.[4] It is possible that in some cases they may have been used to support sacred Buddhist symbols, but ordinarily, as Mr. Parker argues, those round the large buildings appear to have been intended primarily as a barrier against evil spirits, and secondarily to support festoons of lamps suspended on great occasions. At the *wata-da-ge* shrines, according to Mr. Bell, the pillars were intended to 'hold up a roof to shelter the small *stupa* and worshippers at the shrine'.[5]

Shafts and capitals of columns.

The forms of shaft and capital, differing widely from Indian types, are illustrated on a larger scale on Plate 142. But it is impossible to go into detail here, or to discuss

[1] The building is fully described and illustrated by half-tone blocks in Mr. Bell's *Ann. Rep.* for 1903, 1904, and 1907 (Sess. Papers LXV, LXVI of 1908, and V of 1911). It has been extensively restored by the replacing of fallen members.

[2] Bell, *Ann. Rep.* for 1897, p. 7; for 1907, Pls. XXVIII, XXIX (Sess. Papers XLII, 1904; V, 1911).

[3] *Ann. Rep. A. S., Ceylon*, 1904, P. 2 (Sess. Paper LXVI of 1908). In *Ann. Rep. A. S., Ceylon*, 1907, p. 3, Mr. Bell notes the existence of six small circular brick shrines (*wata-geval*) at the Vessagiriya Monastery, Anuradhapura, besides one at the Abhayagiriya and one at the Toluvila. These seem to be different from the *wata-da-ge* type described in the text.

[4] General de Beylié maintains that the Thuparama columns supported 'un toit à l'indienne, à étages superposés' (*L'Architecture hindoue en Extrême-Orient*, Paris, 1907, p. 361).

[5] *Ancient Ceylon*, p. 289; *Ann. Rep. A. S., Ceylon*, 1904, p. 2.

A, B. Sculptures from Venugopala Temple, Srirangam. 16th Century A.D. Vijayanagar period.
(Photos : K. Arunachalam)

C. Sculpture from Varadaraja Temple, Kanchipuram, 16th Century A.D. Vijayanagar period.
(Photo : E. S. Mahalingam)

PLATE 131

Sculptured reliefs from Vijayanagar. 16th Century A D. Vijayanagar period.
(Photos : A. L. Syed)

PLATE 132

the age and evolution of the various types. Mr. Parker supposes the Thuparama columns to date from the period between 100 B.C. and A.D. 100.[1]

Sat Mahal Prasadaya.

This necessarily slight notice of architecture in Ceylon may be concluded by mention of a unique building at Polonnaruwa known as the *Sat Mahal Prasadaya*, a seven-storied square brick tower, built in diminishing stages, and rising from a low basement, which measures 39 feet 2 inches each way at ground level. The brickwork was covered with fine lime plaster, probably once coloured, and twenty niches contained as many stucco statues, eleven of which still exist. The edifice was erected by order of King Nissanka Malla a little before A.D. 1200, in imitation of Cambodian models, and probably for the use of the Cambodian mercenaries then in the service of the Ceylonese monarch.[2]

Ceylonese sculpture abundant.

Ceylon is rich in sculpture of many kinds, beginning probably from the early centuries of the era. Fergusson's belief that the 'almost total absence of sculpture' was one of the most striking peculiarities of Ceylonese art has been disproved abundantly by the fruitful researches of the Archaeological Department. But it is extremely difficult to affix dates, even approximate, to the numerous specimens of the Ceylonese sculptors' skill. Dated dedicatory inscriptions, so common in India, are rare in the island, and the principal monuments have been subject to such extensive alterations at various times that it is almost impossible to distinguish the sculptures of different periods. It is possible that when systematic study shall be applied to the local styles of art closer discrimination will be feasible, but in the present state of knowledge anything like accurate chronological classification of the sculptures of Ceylon is unattainable. The brief discussion of the subject which limits of space permit will be arranged under two headings, Early and Medieval; the former comprising everything up to about A.D. 700, and the latter everything later. Ceylon has not produced any noticeable modern sculpture. Mr. Hocart, the present Commissioner, is engaged upon an analysis of the sculptures which bids fair to solve these problems. An epigraphist has also recently been appointed.

Inferior in quality to Indian.

The general impression on my mind is that, with the exception of some of the colossal statues, the bronzes, which are very good, but may have been cast in India, and a few other works, the production of the island sculptors is by no means equal to that of the best artists on the mainland. The style is Indian, with a difference. We must remember that many of the Ceylonese images were originally plastered and coloured, and that the rough, weatherworn blocks now visible do not produce the effect designed by the artists.

Stelae.

The highly decorated stelae at the entrances to chapels connected with the great *dagabas* are characteristic of Ceylonese art. The examples chosen from the Abhayagiri *dagaba* at Anuradhapura may be assigned with considerable probability to the time of King Gajabahu I, in the second century of the Christian era, but it is possible that they may be later, or even earlier. The floral patterns differ widely from those used in the medieval stelae of Polonnaruwa. The devices springing from vases (Plate 143D) recall many examples of the same motive in Alexandrian and Indian art.

The human figures in panels have a general resemblance to those at Sanchi, but are more advanced in style.[3] The dwarf in the *Atlas* pose may be noticed

[1] *Ancient Ceylon*, p. 268.

[2] *Ann. Rep. A. S., Ceylon*, 1903, pp. 14-16, Pls. XIII-XV (Sess. Paper LXV of 1908). See also *Ann. Rep.* 1906, p. 17.

[3] Third century(?). In India these figures can only be compared to Kushan art.

in Plate 143A. The seven-headed *Naga* or cobra shown in Fig. B is a good example of an art form extremely common in Ceylon, and usually well sculptured; the number of heads varies, nine being the maximum. Doorkeepers intended to ward off the attacks of evil spirits were deemed essential for most Ceylonese buildings. This *Naga* at Ruwanveli (Plate 143B) is a good example.[1] Ugly dwarfs were regarded as very effective janitors. The specimens from the Ruwanveli and Jetawanarama *dagabas* (Plate 144A and B) are typical. They may be compared with the somewhat similar figures on the capitals of the western gateway at Sanchi, but are much later.[2] Plate 142F is a characteristic example of the small grotesque figures used decoratively in Ceylonese art. Like Gothic gargoyles, they are cleverly done, though ugly, and very like the Badami dwarf-friezes.

Reputed statues of kings.

Portrait statues supposed to be those of ancient kings are said to be a speciality of Ceylonese art. Mr. Smither has described two battered examples which seem to be of high antiquity. One of these, traditionally believed to represent King Devanampiya Tissa, the contemporary and friend of Asoka, which was found near the Ambusthala *dagaba* at Mihintale, eight miles from Anuradhapura, may be correctly attributed by the popular voice. It is described as follows:

'The stone was in four pieces, but these have been put together and the statue placed erect on its circular base. The figure, which is 6 feet 5 inches in height, originally stood facing the *dagaba*, and doubtless in a devotional attitude; the arms, however, are broken off close to the shoulders and cannot be found. The king is clothed in the "dhoti", or waist-cloth wrapped round the loins and falling to the ankles, the upper part of the body being uncovered. The head-dress consists of a plain and slightly elevated pear-shaped cap, encircled by a jewelled band, or diadem; the ears are adorned with pendant ear-rings, and the neck with a jewelled neck-piece. The base is carved to represent an expanded lotus-flower, and is precisely similar in design to that found at the Thuparama *dagaba*. Both statue and base are much weather-worn, although originally sheltered beneath a covered structure of which three stone octagonal pillars, formerly surmounted by capitals, are the only remains.'[3]

The second example is the reputed portrait of King Bhatika Abhaya (*Batiya Tissa*), who reigned during the first century of the Christian era. It was found near the Ruwanveli *dagaba*, and has been set up, after undergoing repair. The material is hard dolomite, much weather-worn, and the height is about 8 feet. The dress of the figure resembles that of another statue commonly believed to represent King Dutthagamini, which stands on the terrace of the Ruwanveli *dagaba*, and has been published by Mr. Havell. It seems probable that these works represent saints or religious teachers rather than kings.[4]

A curious collection of eight life-size images on the embankment of a tank at Minneriya, N. C. P., is popularly believed to represent King Mahasena (*c.* A.D. 300) with his wives and courtiers. The images obviously are ancient, but too much injured for appraisement as works of art.[5]

Buddhas.

Large and often colossal images of Buddha, seated, standing, or recumbent, are numerous in the island, some of which undoubtedly must be very ancient. One of the oldest, probably, is a battered seated figure at Tantrimalai, which wears a conical cap, and is believed by Mr. Parker to date from about the beginning of the Christian era.[6]

[1] Seventh century (?). The costume is medieval and also the pose.
[2] Seventh century (?).
[3] Smither, *Anuradhapura*, p. 11.
[4] Smither, *op. cit.*, p. 11; Havell, *Indian Sculpture and Painting*, Pl. XII; Parker, *Ancient Ceylon*, Fig. 72. The dates of early kings of Ceylon are uncertain; Bhatika Abhaya is assigned to A.D. 42-70, and Dutthagamini to 106-84 B.C.
[5] *Ann. Rep. A. S., Ceylon*, 1893, p. 10; photographs A. 344-7, C. 806.
[6] Parker, *Ancient Ceylon*, pp. 219, 244; Bell, *A. S. Rep.*, 1896, p. 8.

One of the best Buddhas of early age is the now well-known image from the Toluvila ruins, Anuradhapura, represented *in situ* in Plate 145B, with a native seated beside it in exactly the same attitude. The photograph helps the European reader to realize the facts on which the forms of the canonical images are based.

The Kapila relief.

I think that I am right in including among the early works a fine sculpture of uncertain date, proved by Dr. Coomaraswamy to represent Kapila, a legendary sage (Plate 145A). It is cut in rather high relief on the face of the rock on the right-hand side of the Isurumuniya Vihara at Anuradhapura, where many other notable works of sculpture exist. They appear to be of various ages and to deserve more attention than they have received.

The subject is a man curled up in the attitude technically described as 'kingly ease' (*maharaja lila*), with his left hand resting on the seat, and his right hand extended over the raised knee, holding the halter of a horse, the head of which appears on the rock, but is not included in the photograph. The man's head, covered with thick hair, is partly turned towards the proper left and averted from the horse, which he seems to ignore. The expression is that of calm and abstracted but not unconscious dignity, while the difficult pose is modelled with consummate skill and yet with perfect simplicity.[1]

The legend, as told in the *Ramayana*, may be briefly summarized as follows: Sagara, King of Ajodhya, had by his queen Sumati 60,000 sons, whose impiety was such that the gods complained to Vishnu and the sage Kapila. King Sagara, having undertaken to perform the rite of the horse sacrifice (*asvamedha*) in token of his universal sovereignty, deputed the duty of guarding the intended victim to his 60,000 sons, who failed in the trust committed to their charge, and allowed the animal to be carried off to the nether regions (*Patala*). Their father having directed them to recover the horse, they dug down and down until they found him grazing in Hades, with the sage Kapila seated close by, and engaged in deep meditation. The princes menaced him with their weapons, but were reduced to ashes by the flames which darted from his person, when he turned his glance upon them.

This relief seems to me to be one of the most remarkable productions of Indian art, whether on the mainland or in the island of Ceylon.[2]

'Moonstones.'

The 'moonstone', a semicircular slab placed at the foot of a staircase and carved elaborately in low relief, is specially characteristic of, although not absolutely peculiar to, Ceylonese art. The design is always based on the open lotus flower, the pattern being arranged in concentric circles. At Anuradhapura, where some specimens may be very ancient, the standard arrangement is that of an outermost circle with the 'cobra pattern', resembling acanthus leaves in effect; then a procession of quadrupeds in a fixed order moving from left to right—horse, elephant, humped bull, and lion; next, a belt of graceful foliage, which is followed by a row of sacred geese, while the central circles represent the lotus in bud, leaf, and flower. The animal symbolism is perhaps the same as that of the Asoka pillars.[3]

The notable statue of an aged bearded man cut in the face of a boulder to

[1] Bell, *A. S. Rep.*, 1906, p. 8. Neither Mr. Bell nor Mr. Cave mentions the Kapila relief, the merit of which was first recognized by Dr. Coomaraswamy. The critical opinion expressed in the text is confirmed by Mr. Lawrence Binyon, who holds that 'the rock-carved "Kapila" in Ceylon is a tremendous work, impossible to forget when once seen' (*Sat. Rev.* 18 Feb. 1911).

[2] For the identification see Coomaraswamy in *Spolia Zeylanica*, vol. vi (1909), p. 132. The legend is given in Dowson, *Classical Dict. of Hindu Mythology*, s.v. Sagara. Some description of the shrines of Isurumuniya is given in Cave, *The Ruined Cities of Ceylon*, pp. 47-9.

[3] A good early example from the Dalada Maligawa in Smither, Pl. LVII. See also Tennent, *Ceylon*, 2nd ed., p. 619.

The so-called Parakrama Bahu statue.

the east of the Topaveva embankment at Polonnaruwa, popularly known as the image of King Parakrama Bahu the Great, who reigned from A.D. 1153 to 1186, certainly is not what it is supposed to be. The figure, cut in gneiss (granite), and 11½ feet high, stands full face, fronting nearly south, in an easy attitude, with the right leg slightly bent. The costume is confined to a tall cap and simple loin-cloth held up by a band knotted in front. The hands support a model of a palm-leaf book (*ola*) held across the body. The expression of the face is grave, and the half-closed eyes look down upon the manuscript. A long rounded beard and drooping moustache add to the gravity of the countenance. These details are inconsistent with the popular attribution. Mr. Bell is of opinion that the book and the whole appearance and pose of the figure stamp it unmistakably as the portrait of a reverend religious teacher from the Indian continent. He suggests that the statue may represent an ascetic named Kapila, for whom Parakrama Bahu built a richly adorned dwelling.[1]

Seated Buddhas.

Two seated Buddhas strike me as being excellent works and out of the common — namely, the colossal image at the Pankuliya Vihare, Anuradhapura, and the smaller image from Vihare, No. 2, Polonnaruwa (Plate 146A and B). The characteristic points of each appear sufficiently from the photographs without detailed comment. Mr. Bell conjectures that the Pankuliya statue may date from the tenth century; the Polonnaruwa image may be two centuries later.

Standing Buddhas.

The largest statue in the island, and perhaps the most impressive, is the colossal standing image of Buddha at Awkana, N. C. P., 46 feet in height, including the pedestal. It is cut from the face of an enormous boulder, practically in the round, being joined to the rock only by slight support. Local tradition attributes the work to the reign of Parakrama Bahu. The expression of calm majesty is given successfully (Plate 146 D). A similar, and nearly as large, but less effective colossus, carved merely in high relief, and inferior in execution, stands at Saseruwa, N. W. P., and may be assigned to the same period.[2]

'Ananda.'

The stately colossal standing image at the Gal-vihare, Polonnaruwa, popularly known, and apparently rightly, as that of Ananda, the disciple of Buddha, is one of the most imposing and interesting statues in Ceylon (Plate 146 C). The faithful attendant stands watching a colossal recumbent figure of his dying Master.

The 'stone book'.

No monument in the island is more extraordinary than the gigantic 'stone book' (*gal-pota*) at Polonnaruwa, a monolith brought from Mihintale, eighty miles distant, at the close of the twelfth century by Nissanka's 'mighty men', as recorded in a long inscription on its surface. It is nearly 27 feet long, 4 feet 7 inches broad, and varies in depth from 1 foot 4 inches, to 2 feet 2 inches. The relief sculpture treats of the common Indian subject, elephants pouring water over Sri or Lakshmi — the goddess of good fortune.

Bas-relief scenes.

More artistic bas-reliefs of uncertain date occur elsewhere. Perhaps the most remarkable is that at Pokuna (masonry tank) A, Anuradhapura, which vividly depicts elephants bathing, and then charging away when scared. The relief is so low that the photographs are not sufficiently distinct for successful reproduction. Mr. Bell describes this work, which is in two sections, as an absolutely unique piece of carving, and without exception the most spirited and life-like to be seen

[1] *A. S. Rep.*, 1906, p. 11, Pl. XI; *Guide to Colombo Museum* (1905), p. 21; *Ruined Cities of Ceylon* (1897), p. 119.

[2] Bell, *A. S. Rep.*, 1895, pp. 6, 12; Tennent, *Ceylon*, 2nd ed., vol. ii, p. 604, with woodcut.

A. Temple of Subrahmanya, Tanjore. (17th Century A.D. Post-Vijayanagar period).

B. Golden lily pond and gopurams, Madurai Temple. 17th Century A.D. Nayak period.

A. Gopuram, Madurai Temple. 17th Cent. A.D. Nayak period.

B. Part of jamp of N. gopura, Tadpatri, Anantapur District. (16th Cent. A.D. Vijayanagar period).

C. Woman and baby, Great Temple, Madura.

D. Siva, Tirumal Naik's choultry, Madura.

E. Female carrying male deity, Ramesvaram Temple.

(17th Cent. A.D. Nayak period)

PLATE 134

anywhere among the ruins of Anuradhapura.[1] It is supposed to date from the time of Parakrama Bahu.

Part II. SINGHALESE METAL CASTINGS

The remarkable richness of Ceylon in art-works of metal, chiefly copper, was not realized until recent discoveries compelled attention to the fact. Before 1905 a few objects of interest had been collected by the casual exertions of individuals, but since that date the numerous additions to the public collections have been acquired by the systematic operations of the Archaeological Survey. Few, if any, of the castings are earlier than the tenth century, and most of them are a great deal later. As a whole there is little that is distinctive about them and it is better to consider them as one with the Southern Indian castings. Ceylonese copper castings.

Perhaps the most notable of the Ceylon bronzes is an image of the goddess *Pattini Devi*, found near the north-eastern coast somewhere between Trincomalee and Batticalwa, and presented to the British Museum in 1830. It stands 4 feet 9½ inches in height and is composed of a metal which looks like brass, but may be a pale bronze (Plate 147A). It seems to have been originally gilt. The age of the work is doubtful. The cleverness with which the transparency of the skirt is shown recalls similar skill exhibited in the Gupta sculpture of the fifth century in Northern India, but it would be rash to attribute such an early date to the Ceylonese image for that reason only, and it is difficult to find any other test of its age. *Pattini Devi.*

The nudity above the waist, which may offend the European eye, is in accordance with the ancient custom of Southern India and Ceylon, not wholly disused even in these days. The waist is rather too much attenuated, in conformity with common Indian practice, examples of which may be found even in the Bharhut sculptures; but, except for that defect, the modelling is good, and the hands especially are admirable.

Pattini is one of the most popular deities in Ceylon, and her worship is still kept up on the mainland also, whence it was introduced into the island, most probably in the reign of Gajabahu I at some time in the second century of the Christian era. The cult seems to have originated in the *Chera* territory (Coimbatore and Salem), but some of the legends connect its beginnings with a *Pandya* King of Madura. The goddess is considered to be the guardian of female chastity, and is also credited with power over epidemics, whether of man or beast. Two wooden images of her and her husband found in a cave at the Nikawaewa monastery are supposed to date from the eleventh century. The British Museum casting may be quite as early[2] (A 1).

Some good castings, believed to date from about the tenth century, have been obtained from various localities within the area of the ancient capital, Anuradhapura. They include a pair of miniature feet apparently belonging to a lost statuette, and only three inches in length, which are described as 'excellently modelled'.[3] Like the great Buddha in the Birmingham Museum, they were cast on a core, in this case of iron. The best piece, from the aesthetic point of view, is a statuette supposed to be that of a *Bodhisattva* (Plate 148B). The statuette, 20¼ inches high, was found to the south of the Thuparama. The person represented stands Bronzes from Anuradhapura.

[1] *Ann. Rep. Arch. S.*, 1901, p. 6; photographs A. 405, 406, C. 1304.

[2] The legend of the goddess is too long to quote. See *The Tamilian Antiquary*, No. 3 (1909), p. vii note; ibid., No. 5, p. 47: and Dr. Coomaraswamy in *J. R. A. S.*, 1909, P. 293, with references. The wooden images are figured in Parker, *Ancient Ceylon*, Fig. 272.

[3] Bell, *Anuradhapura and the North-Central Province, 7th Progress Report* (xiii, 1896), Pl. XVII.

in the pose with a double bend, known technically as *tivanka.* The drapery is gracefully treated, the modelling, especially of the hands, is truthful, and the serene expression of the face is pleasing.[1] The style closely resembles that of some of the Polonnaruwa castings, which are ascribed to the twelfth century, and the Anuradhapura statuette may be as late (A 2).

Bronzes from Polonnaruwa.

The few figures collected at Polonnaruwa in 1906, forming the first series in the Colombo Museum (Nos. 40-52), are not of much importance; but the second and third series, excavated in 1907 and 1908 from the Siva Dewale and neighbouring sites, may be fairly said to add a new chapter to the history of art in Ceylon. Nothing like them was known before, except the Anuradhapura *Bodhisattva*, if that be the correct designation for it. A few of the best have been selected from a set of good photographs taken by Dr. Andreas Nell and kindly supplied by the Government of Ceylon. The identification of the images has been effected by the Honourable Mr. P. Arunachalam. These figures, all massive and very heavy, are ascribed to the twelfth and thirteenth centuries. Their large size proves that the artists of those days knew how to overcome the difficulties of casting copper on a considerable scale, and gives the images an importance and dignity which cannot be claimed by miniature works a few inches high. In the opinion of Dr. A. Willey, F.R.S., late Director of the Colombo Museum, they 'are Polonnaruwa *bronzes* for better or for worse', and certainly were not imported from the mainland.[2] But I am disposed to agree with Mr. Bell that they were executed in India.

Siva *Nataraja.*

The place of honour may be given to the spirited images of Siva as *Nataraja*, 'Lord of the Dance', the first of their kind to be found in Ceylon (Plates 147B, 148C); which compare favourably with the best examples of similar compositions in Southern India (A 3). A specimen in the Madras Museum arouses enthusiasm, which few can share fully, in the breast of Dr. A. K. Coomaraswamy, who first published photographs of the work. In order to make the Ceylonese bronzes intelligible, the explanation of the legend of Siva's manifestation as 'Lord of the Dance', given in the *Koyil Puranam,* and said to be familiar to all southern worshippers of the god, is quoted from the eloquent pages of the author referred to:

The legend.

'Siva appeared in disguise amongst a congregation of the thousand sages, and in the course of disputation, confuted them and so angered them thereby, that they endeavoured by incantations to destroy Him. A fierce tiger was created in sacrificial flames, and rushed upon Him, but smiling gently, He seized it with His sacred hands, and with the nail of His little finger stripped off its skin, which He wrapped about Himself as if it had been a silken cloth. Undiscouraged by failure, the sages renewed their offerings, and there was produced a monstrous serpent, which He seized and wreathed about His neck. Then He began to dance; but there rushed upon Him a last monster in the shape of a hideous malignant dwarf. Upon him the God pressed the tip of His foot, and broke the creature's back, so that it writhed upon the ground; and so, His last foe prostrate, Siva resumed the dance of which the gods were witnesses.

One interpretation of this legend explains that He wraps about Him as a garment, the tiger fury of human passion; the guile and malice of mankind He wears as a necklace, and beneath His feet is for ever crushed the embodiment of evil. More characteristic of Indian thought is the symbolism, in terms of the marvellous grace and rhythm of Indian dancing, the effortless ease with which the God in his grace supports the cosmos; it is his sport. The five acts of creation, preservation, destruction, embodiment and gracious release are his ceaseless mystic dance. In sacred Tillai, the "New Jerusalem", the dance shall be revealed; and Tillai is the very centre of the Universe, that is, His dance is within the cosmos and the soul.'[3]

[1] See *Burlington Magazine*, 1910, p. 87, Pl. I, 3.
[2] *Spolia Zeylanica*, Sept. 1909, p. 67 note.
[3] *The Aims of Indian Art* (pamphlet, Essex House Press, 1908).

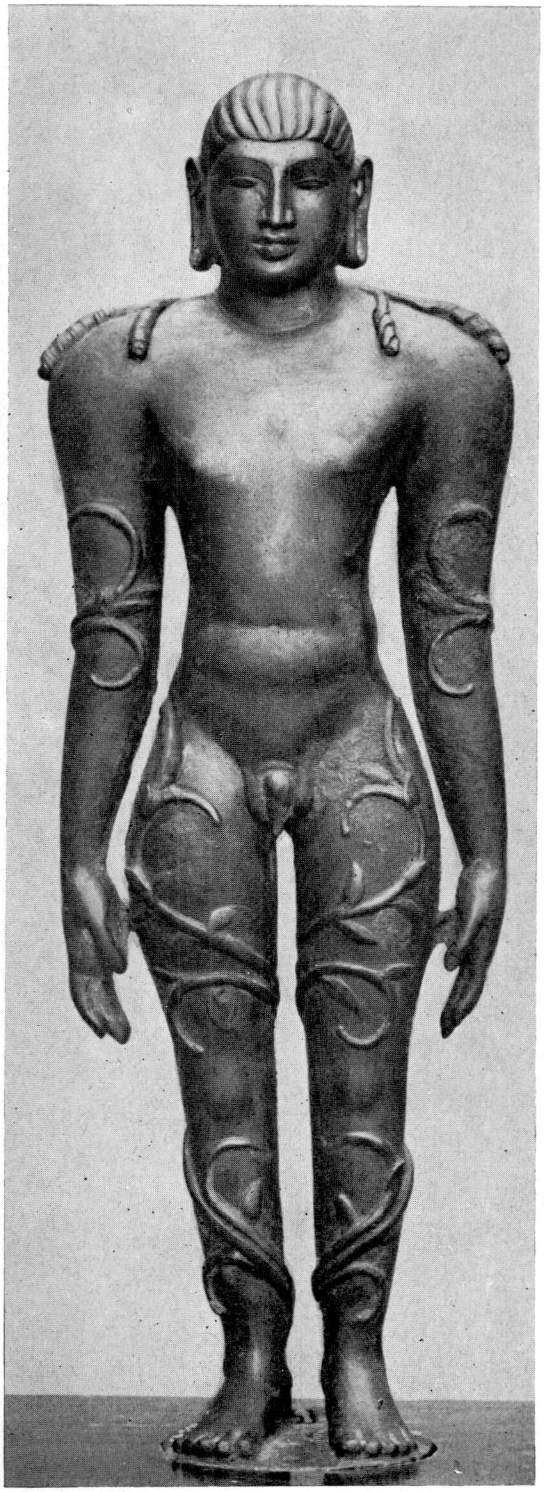

A. Metal image of Bahubali. 9th Cent. A.D. Chalukyan school. Prince of Wales Museum, Bombay.

B. Metal image of the Buddha from Nagapatnam. 10th Cent. A.D. Chola period.

PLATE 135

A. Female lamp bearer. Bronze. Warangal. Probably 11th. Cent. Hyderabad Museum.

(Copyright by Department of Archaeology, Government of India)

B. Chandrasekhara. Bronze. 13th Cent. A.D. Chalukyan period. Probably from Mysore or Bellary District. National Museum, New Delhi.

A. Nataraja from Tiruvarangulam, Pudukottai District. Bronze. 10th Cent A.D. Early Chola period. National Museum, New Delhi.

B. Balakrishna. Bronze. 12th Cent. A.D. Chola period. Prince of Wales Museum, Bombay.

PLATE 137

A. Parvati. Probably from a Somaskanda group. Bronze. 11th Cent. A.D. Chola period.

B. Nataraja. Bronze. 13th Cent. A.D. Late Chola period.

(*By Courtesy of Museum of Fine Arts, Boston*)

The more prosaic description of the group by Mr. Arunachalam, slightly condensed, will enable the student to appreciate the intention of the formal symbolism. The god's hair is braided, forming a crown at the top and a circular coil at the back, the lower braids whirling in the dance, which is named *Tandava*. The mermaid on the right braid (indistinct in the photograph) symbolizes the Ganges; a crescent moon and serpent decorate the left braid. Other serpents coiled round his body are regarded as symbols of Siva's energy. His three eyes, one in the forehead, represent the sun, moon, and fire; the skull at the base of the crown is a symbol of destruction, and the necklace, composed of skulls of Brahmas, Vishnus, and Rudras, symbolizes the evolution and involution of the universe throughout the aeons. The bisexual nature of the diety is indicated by the long man's ear-ring in the right, and the woman's circular ear-ring in the left ear. Fire, a symbol of both destruction and divine purifying grace, is held in the left upper hand, and also surrounds the group. The small drum in the right upper hand is supposed to suggest vibration, the first stage in evolution. The right lower hand is raised in assurance of protection to the worshipper, while the left lower hand points to the uplifted foot, the refuge of the suppliant. The monster trampled on personifies the powers of evil and illusion from which the deity delivers the soul. The composition as a whole is understood to represent the control of the operations of the universe by Siva.

The symbolism.

The greater part of the foregoing commentaries has nothing to do with the merits of the compositions as works of art. Any competent coppersmith can make to order rings symbolizing fire and other formal attributes in accordance with written rules, and such accessories, whether well or ill made, will be equally significant to the devout Hindu versed in the legends and metaphysics of his faith. The general lines of the principal image, too, are determined by pattern sketches, of which Dr. Coomaraswamy has published a specimen. Consequently, a perfectly correct group, with all the needful apparatus for edification, can be made passably well by any skilled bronze founder, whose work need not be anything higher than mere manufacture. The scope for the display of aesthetic feeling and creative skill, which distinguish an artist from a skilful mechanic, is restricted almost exclusively to the manner of rendering the action of dancing with passion, including, of course, the modelling of the principal figure. When various examples of the treatment of the prescribed theme are examined and compared they will be found to differ widely according to the degree of artistic power possessed by the maker of each. Among good examples may be classed Dr. Coomaraswamy's favourite in the Madras Museum, the Tanjore specimen, and No. 1 from Polonnaruwa (Plate 147B). The No. 15 Polonnaruwa image (Plate 148C), without the ring of fire, is the most artistic of all. It is described as being 'the best finished of all the *bronzes*', and is deserving of the care spent on its production. A third Polonnaruwa specimen (No. 24) is coarsely executed and of inferior quality. The same criticism applies to a second example in the Madras Museum, to another in the British Museum, and to the South Kensington image from Malabar. The 'belle statue de bronze ancien' in the Musée Guimet may be placed in the higher class.[1]

Limits of artist's scope.

[1] The S. Kensington bronze, two feet in height, found long ago at Chaoghat in Malabar, was presented by Jonathan Duncan, Governor of Bombay, to the Indian Office Museum, and thence has passed into the India Section of the Victoria and Albert Museum. It is engraved as Pl. XIV of Moor's *Hindu Pantheon* (1810; =frontispiece of Higginbotham's edition, Madras, 1864), but the engraving is not faithful, having been 'improved' by the artist. For the 'belle statue' see figure on p. 94 of the *Petit Guide Illustré du Musée Guimet*. The subject is often treated in stone sculpture.

The standing image of Siva (No. 12), striking an attitude in another of his dances (*sandhyanirtta*), is gracefully posed, and well modelled, save for the excessive thickness of the arms (Plate 148D). The figure of the Sun-god (No. 18), with a halo, holding a lotus bud in each hand, is dignified, and the type is unusual (Plate 149A). One ideal of the goddess *Parvati*, consort of Siva, is expressed in No. 7, with the characteristic Indian bend (Plate 149B). The image closely resembles that labelled as *Lakshmi* in the Musée Guimet (*Petit Guide Ill*, Plate p. 62). Another conception of Parvati (No. 20) is shown in Plate 149C. The figure and pose are natural and pleasing.

Images of Tamil saints. An interesting group of images deals with popular Tamil saints, whose effigies have been identified by Mr. Arunachalam. Probably the best of this group is No. 16, representing *Sundara-murti Swami*, an apostle and psalmist of Siva about A.D. 700. He was a native of Tiruvarur, near Negapatam in the Madras Presidency; called to be an apostle on his wedding-day, hence dressed in the clothes and ornaments of a bridegroom. The clothes are somewhat scanty. The artist has rendered with remarkable success the attitude and facial expression of religious ecstasy powerful enough to tear away a bridegroom from the side of his bride (Plate 148A). The image has strong claims to be considered the finest of the Polonnaruwa bronzes, or, at least, to be placed second only to the *Nataraja*, No. 15.

Statuette of Avalokitesvara. Certain small miscellaneous bronze images from Ceylon, of which the exact find-spots are not recorded, are of sufficient interest to deserve special notice. A little figure, presumably that of the *Mahayanist* deity (if the expression be allowed) named *Avalokitesvara* or *Padmapani*, only $3\frac{5}{8}$ inches in height, in Dr. Coomaraswamy's collection now at Boston, and ascribed to the sixth or seventh century, is regarded by him, and not without reason, as the best of all the Ceylonese images (Plate 150A). He praises the 'perfection and abstraction of the style', claiming that 'the divine ideal is fully realized both in expression and in physical form'.

Jambhala, or Kuvera. Another excellent little image, $3\frac{1}{8}$ inches high, from the same collection, represents the minor deity *Jambhala*, or *Kuvera*, the well-contented god of riches (Plate 150B), whose effigy in various forms is frequently found in the ruins of Buddhist monasteries in India and Java. His right hand grasps a fruit; the left rests upon the mongoose, or ichneumon, sacred to him. Dr. Coomaraswamy's criticism is as follows:

> 'The artistic interest of this figure lies in its frank realism, contrasting with the idealistic treatment of the figures so far referred to. The God of Wealth, far less remote and hard to reach than so exalted a being as a Bodhisattva, is worshipped for material rather than spiritual benefits; he is represented as the very image of a fat trader seated in his booth awaiting customers. The patron saint of prosperity and trade is a comfortable, worldly person! The realistic treatment of the firm flesh is as masterly in its own way as the generalization of the more ideal types, such as the Avalokitesvara.'[1]

The Badulla Buddha. The Colombo Museum possesses many other bronze objects, including several Buddhas. One of these (Plate 150C), a Buddha 'of unique design' and uncertain

[1] Coomaraswamy, 'Mahayana Buddhist Images from Ceylon and Java', *J. R. A. S.*, 1909, p. 288. That valuable article, and another entitled 'Indian Bronzes' in *Burlington Magazine*, May 1910, discuss in detail many images which cannot be noticed here. Kuvera (= Jambhala= Vaisravana) was chief of the Yakshas. He was specially honoured in Khotan and Chinese Turkestan generally. A manuscript from Turfan calls him 'the highest of the gods' (von Holstein, 'Tisastvustik,' pp. 97, 122 note, *Bibl. Buddhica*, No. xii, St. Pétersbourg, 1910). 'Jambhala of Ceylon' was known even in distant Nepal (Foucher, *Iconographie bouddhique*, Pl. IX, 2).

A. Jain Tirthankara. Bronze. 9th-10th Cent. A.D. Chalukyan period. Pudukottai Museum.

B. Somaskanda group. Bronze. 14th-15th Cent. A.D. Early Vijayanagar period. Indian Museum, Calcutta.

PLATE 139

A. Umasahiti. Bronze. 12th Cent. A.D. Chola period. Indian Museum, Calcutta.

B. Cast metal portrait images of Krishna Raya of Vijayanagar (A.D. 1510-29) and his Queens; in the Sri Nivasa Perumal temple on the hill of Tirumalai near Tirupati, N. Arcot District. (Vijayanagar period).

(Copyright by Department of Archaeology, Government of India)

PLATE 140

date, found below Badulla, possesses considerable merit.[1] It belongs to the same early period as the two Boston figures described above.

Part III. JAVA

Indian colonies in the Far East.

The extensive and long-continued emigration from India to the Far East — including Pegu, Siam, and Cambodia on the mainland, and Java, Sumatra, Bali and Borneo among the islands of the Malay Archipelago — and the consequent establishment of Indian institutions and art in the countries named, constitute one of the darkest mysteries of history.[2] The reality of the debt due to India by those distant lands is attested abundantly by material remains, by the existence to this day of both the Buddhist and Brahmanical religions in the island of Bali to the east of Java, by Chinese history, and by numerous traditions preserved in India, Pegu, Siam, and the Archipelago. But when the attempt is made to transmute vague, conflicting traditions and imperfectly known archaeological facts into orderly history the difficulties in the way of success appear to be largely insurmountable. But, in order to render at all intelligible the fact of the existence of magnificent achievements of Indian art in Java, to which island the summary observations in this work will be confined, some attempt, however imperfect, at historical explanation is indispensable. In Java the forms of art are thoroughly Indian in subject and style, of high aesthetic quality, and sufficiently dated to permit of their correlation with the art of India. The less purely Indian and less meritorious ramifications of Hindu art in the other countries of the Far East must be left unnoticed.

Some traditional dates.

It is certain that during the early centuries of the Christian era India possessed an active and enterprising seafaring population on both coasts — that of the Bay of Bengal on the east, and that of the Arabian Sea on the west; and it is highly probable that from the first to the eighth century emigration to the Malay Archipelago continued to proceed from both sides of India. If Javanese tradition may be believed, a large body of Indian emigrants, led by Aji Saka, landed in the island from the east of India in the year 1 of the local era, equivalent to A.D. 75 or A.D. 78 according to various computations, but the details of the story are obviously open to sceptical criticism.

The observation of Fa-hien, the Chinese Buddhist pilgrim who visited Java in A.D. 414, and found 'plenty of heretics and Brahmans, but not enough Buddhism to be worth mentioning',[3] is excellent evidence that a strong Indian colony professing the Brahmanical religion must have been then already settled in the island for a long time. The statement made in a late Chinese work that an Indian colony arrived in Java during the reign of the Han emperor, Kwang Wu-ti (A.D. 25-57), is credible, although the authority on which it is based has not been found.[4] From the testimony of Fa-hien and other indications there is no doubt that Brahmanical Hinduism reached Java long before Buddhism. According to the Chinese *History of the Sung Dynasty*, the conversion of the island to Buddhism

[1] A rough list of bronzes and other objects is printed in the *Catalogue of Finds, Archaeological Survey of Ceylon; deposited in the Colombo Museum*, 1906-7, p. 27, supplied by the Government of Ceylon. The *Guide* to the Museum (1905) is published in *Spolia Zeylanica*, Part IX. Badulla is in the hill country; the image was found in the plain below.

[2] The Hinduized Javanese founded considerable colonies in Madagascar during the early centuries of the Christian era (*Journal Asiatique*, 1910, p. 330).

[3] *Travels*, chap. xl, in Giles's version. The other versions (Laidlay, Beal, Legge) agree subtantially with Giles. Fa-hien's statement is corroborated by certain nearly contemporary inscriptions in Java and at Koetei in Borneo (Kern, 'Gedenkteekenen der oude indische beschaving in Kambodja,' *Onze Eeuw*, 4 Jan. 1904, p. 46).

[4] *The Pilgrimage of Fa Hian* (Calcutta, 1848), p. 363, Laidlay's translation of Klaproth's note.

was effected by Gunavarman, Crown Prince of Kashmir, who had renounced his rank in order to become a monk. He then joined a monastery in China and died at Nanking in A.D. 431. This statement dates the conversion immediately after Fa-hien's visit.[1]

Javanese writers, supported to some extent by local traditions of Gujarat and Southern Marwar in Rajputana, affirm that in the year A.D. 603 a numerous body of colonists sailed from Western India to Java.[2] The Siamese annals record that in the year A.D. 685 (*Saka* 607)

'great political disturbances occurred all over India, and the inhabitants, finding it impossible to make a living, were forced in large numbers to leave their home and country and settle among other nations.... At that time four tribes of Brahmans, consisting of a considerable number of persons, made their way eastward from "Wanilara" to Burma, Pegu, then independent, the Laos States, Siam, and Cambodia.'[3]

Traditional dates like those cited notoriously require to be treated with caution, but in this case both the dates in the seventh century happen to be credible, as marking times of ascertained political disturbance in India. The earlier date, A.D. 603, which falls within the period of anarchy and strife due to the Hun invasions, precedes by a few years the consolidation of the empires founded by Harsha in the north and by Pulakesin II Chalukya in the Deccan. The later date, A.D. 685, approximately coincides with the fall of Valabhi, which is believed to have been destroyed about that time by the Arabs then settled in Sind.[4] The Chinese statement in the *History of the Sung Dynasty* dating the conversion of the island between A.D. 414 and 431 is the most trustworthy of all, though of course the assertion that the whole population was converted cannot be accepted. As in India, Brahmanical Hinduism continued to exist side by side with Buddhism. The earliest known dated Indo-Javanese inscription is said to be one of the year A.D. 732.[5] We are, therefore, justified in believing that the ancient Indian Brahmanical colonies in Java received strong reinforcements from the mother-country during the fifth, seventh, and eighth centuries. Considering that all, or nearly all, the Buddhist remains in the island are later than the middle of the eighth century, we may further infer that the new-comers were largely Buddhist in religion, and included many skilled craftsmen. The most ancient objects in the island possessing value as works of art are Buddhist. The late Dr. Brandes, who had a good right to express an authoritative opinion, held that the buildings at Borobudur, with their incomparable sculptures, should be dated between A.D. 778 and 928 (=700-850 Saka). According to M. Tissandier the Kali Bening and Sari temples at Prambanam (Brambanam) were begun in A.D. 779.[6] Other Indo-Javanese works, however, are much later, the Chandi Sewa temple, for example, being assigned to A.D. 1098. The Hindu kingdom of Majapahit in Eastern Java was overthrown by the Muhammadans in A.D. 1478, when the persecuted Hindus fled to Bali, where their descendants still practise Brahmanical rites, including *sati* (suttee) in its most appalling form, while another section of the population is Buddhist.

[1] de Beylié, *L'Architecture hindoue en Extrême-Orient*, p. 335; Pelliot, *Bull. E. F. E. O.*, iv. 274.

[2] A. M. Jackson in *Bombay Gazetteer* (1896), vol. i, Part I, App.

[3] A. Steffen, art. No. 125, *Man*, 1902. 'Wanilara' has not been identified. *Quaere* does *lara*=Lata=Gujarat?

[4] *A. S. W. I.*, vi. 3; ix. 4.

[5] According to the late Dr. Brandes quoted by Mr. Sewell (*J. R. A. S.*, 1906, p. 421). Earlier Indian inscriptions not bearing precise dates exist from the fifth century. In Cambodia the earliest recorded Indian ruler, Srutavarman or Kaundinya, lived in the middle of the fifth century. In the following age Bhavavarman founded many temples in honour of Indian deities, especially Siva, at which daily readings of the epics and *Puranas* were held. Indian influence was at its height in Cambodia in the sixth century (Kern, *op. cit.*, p. 47).

[6] *Cambodge et Java*, Paris, 1896, p. 126.

From these facts it follows that the whole history of Indo-Javanese Buddhist art must lie between A.D. 420 and 1478, a period of more than a thousand years. The finest works may be assigned to the ninth century.

Hinduized Buddhism.

In Java, as elsewhere, the late *Mahayanist* Buddhism so closely approximated to Hinduism that sculptures which at first sight appear to be purely Brahmanical may be really Buddhist. 'Brambanam and Chandi Sewa', Mr. Sewell observes, 'are to all external appearances purely Brahmanical, though we learn on examination that Brahma, Vishnu, and Siva were there held to be Bodhisattvas and not gods. And this is the case everywhere in Eastern Java, the temples being mostly Hindu in type (though always with a difference), and having statues adapted generally from Brahmanical originals.'

Borobudur.

The best known monument in the island is the vast pyramidal pile of Borobudur, 'a hill in nine stages', combining the character of a *stupa* or *dagaba* with that of a temple. As an architectural composition the building, more than 400 feet square at the base, is of small account. Its importance in the history of art depends upon the immense series of about 2,000 bas-reliefs adorning the galleries, which, if laid end to end, would extend more than two miles. The best reliefs are the panels of the so-called 'second gallery', exceeding two hundred in number, which are arranged in two series. The upper series presents in easily recognizable stone pictures the life of Buddha, as told in the ancient Sanskrit work the *Lalita Vistara*. The scenes of the lower series, artistically of equal merit, resisted interpretation until lately, but have now been proved to be illustrations of the *Divyavadana* and other Buddhist romances, including some of the *Jatakas*, or stories of the former lives of Buddha. About two-thirds of the 120 panels in that series have now been identified, and in time the balance probably will yield their secrets. The intention of the designer of the monument was that the worshipper, while making his ritual perambulation (*pradakshina*) of the building, should be instructed ocularly in the whole doctrine of Buddhism, according to the system of the *Mahayana*, or 'Great Vehicle'.[1]

Example of bas-reliefs.

It is difficult to choose among the numerous beautiful reliefs of the 'second gallery' of Borobudur. Several of the best have been reproduced by Mr. Havell and in the new edition of the *History of Indian and Eastern Architecture*. I select one from the lower series (Plate 151A).

Criticism.

All critics can go so far as to concur in M. Tissandier's rather faint praise that the bas-reliefs are 'motifs ciselés dans la pierre avec une puissance rare'; or M. Foucher's more liberal criticism that they are justly celebrated for their good proportions, naturalness of gesture, and the variety of attitude in the figures. But not everybody can agree with Mr. Havell that the reliefs exhibit 'supremely devout and spontaneous art', far excelling by their simplicity, unaffected *naiveté*, artistic feeling, imagination, and magnificent conventionalism of the accessories the work of Ghiberti on the bronze doors of the Baptistery at Florence, which Michael Angelo declared 'to be worthy to be the gates of Paradise'. The same critic holds that the simple life led by the artists of Borobudur left them in peace

[1] The name Boro-Budur means 'the many Buddhas' (cf. Sanskrit, *Brihad-devata*). The older books give erroneous interpretations. The building, although apparently a staged pyramid, is really constructed on the plan of a circular *stupa*, all the angles being inscribed in circles. The so-called 'second gallery', designed to be the first, became the second when the original plinth was encased in a structure of late masonry. The literary works illustrated by the reliefs all belong to the *Mula-Sarvastivadin* school of Buddhism, to which the seventh-century pilgrim, I-tsing, adhered (Foucher, 'Notes, d'archéologie bouddhique', *B. E. F. E. O.*, Janv-Mars, 1909 pp. 1-50).

to concentrate their whole soul on this work, and kept their minds free and able to listen to the voices of Nature and of their own inspiration —'the soul of Nature speaking to the soul of man'. In reality, as M. Foucher truly observes, the immense processions of scenes at Borobudur have a 'caractère livresque' in virtue of their being illustrations of sacred story-books, which deprives them of the spontaneity and emotional (*vibrant*) expression that can spring only from contact with living oral tradition. The compositions were prompted, not by the 'voices of Nature', but by a business-like, systematic endeavour to give visual expression to set passages in favourite authors; and we have not the slightest reason for believing that the artists led particularly simple lives. We know, in fact, nothing whatever about them or their lives. A certain uniformity of effeminacy (*mollesse*) characterizes the forms, as it does some of the much earlier compositions of Gandhara. But, although it is true that the reliefs are carefully planned and must be criticized as selected book illustrations rather than as the spontaneous utterance of simple souls in direct contact with nature, they are extremely good and charming. Fergusson thought that the art of the later cave-temples was 'nearly identical' with Borobudur.[1] As a whole the Pallava and Chola sculpture of the South is nearer to the Javanese work. They deserve the most careful critical study by professional sculptors, who alone would be in a position to realize how much praise is due to artists capable of executing more than two miles of stone pictures, almost uniform in beauty and the display of technical skill of a high order.

Numerous ancient cities.

Notable sites, crowded with ancient buildings, are far too numerous in Java to be even named. The most important, perhaps, after Borobudur is Prambanam (*Brambanam*), an early capital, where the temples are said to include six large and 150 small ones, supposed to date from about the tenth century.

Detached images and bronzes.

The Javanese sculptures, in addition to reliefs, comprise multitudes of large detached stone images and small bronzes, of which only a small number of specimens can be illustrated here. From van Kinsbergen's plates I select a very pleasing image of Sarasvati, consort of Brahma and goddess of speech and learning, who is represented enthroned. The mongoose or ichneumon is her special attribute (Plate 151B).

The other illustrations are from photographs kindly supplied by Dr. Coomaraswamy and already published by him, and also, in part, by Mr. Havell.

The stone Buddha (Plate 152A) is one of several similar images, nearly equal in quality, which exhibit the Indian *yogi* ideal in an exceptionally dignified and agreeable manner. The expressive modelling of the right hand deserves special commendation.

Plate 151C gives a side view of the beautiful image of *Prajna-Paramita* now at Leyden, of which Mr. Havell has published a front view. The name is that of the most sacred book of the *Mahayanist* scriptures, ascribed to Nagarjuna, and thence transferred to a personification of Supreme Wisdom in female form. Mr. Havell, who regards the image as being 'one of the most spiritual creations of any art, Eastern or Western', compares it with the Madonnas of Giovanni Bellini.

The little bronze (Plate 152B), supposed to represent *Manjusri*, is one of the most attractive of the Raffles collection in the British Museum.

[1] *Hist. Ind. and E. Arch.* (1910), ii. p. 426.

A. Stone railing at Anuradhapura, as restored.

B. Siva Temple No. 1, at Polonnaruwa, west wall.

C. Stucco reliefs on porch of the Hetadage, Polonnaruwa.

A. Capital at Abhayagiri vihare, Anuradhapura.

D. Column in Ruwanveli area, Anuradhapura; 9 ft. 4 in. high.

B. Capital at Abhayagiri vihare, Anuradhapura.

C. Sculptured stele at Abhayagiri *dagaba*, Anuradhapura.

E. Sculptured stele at Abhayagiri *dagaba*, Anuradhapura.

F. Part of dado, Ruwanveli *dagaba*, vihare.

NOTES TO CHAPTER ELEVEN

Pattini Devi is probably the work of South Indian metal sculptors settled in Ceylon during the 11th century. It has the characteristics of Chola art of that period. A 1

The Boddhisattva from Anuradhapura is earlier than the 12th century. Its most likely date would be the 9th century when the Pallava metal casters were producing masterpieces in South India. It may be the work of a South Indian *stapathi*. A 2

In fact, they are much inferior to the best Natarajas of the South Indian temples. A 3

Chapter Twelve

CENTRAL ASIA, TIBET, AND NEPAL

Part I. CHINESE TURKISTAN

Recent discoveries.

THE explorations carried on since 1896 by Sir Aurel Stein, Professor Grünwedel, Dr. v. Le Coq, and other savants, in the vast regions of Chinese Turkistan, lying north of Tibet, to the west of China, and both north and south of the Taklamakan Desert ('Gobi' of the older maps), have revealed 'sand-buried' and other ruins full of the remains of ancient civilizations.[1] Those remains, which include thousands of manuscripts written in many scripts and languages, known and unknown, also comprise multitudes of works of art, pictorial and plastic, which, by their characteristics, mark Chinese Turkistan as the meeting-ground of Hellenistic, Indian, Persian, and Chinese forms of civilization.

Immense amount of material.

The wide extension of Indian languages, literature, and art from the second century of the Christian era thus demonstrated has been a surprise to the learned world, but the huge mass of material collected is so unmanageable that many years must elapse before 'the most interesting subject', as Dr. v. Le Coq calls it, of the relations between the early civilizations of India, Persia, China, and the Far East can be worked out so as to admit of firmly established conclusions. At present it is not possible to present in a few pages a satisfactory abstract of the new knowledge concerning the diffusion of Indian art and learning in the Chinese Turkistan countries. The paintings seem to be assignable mostly to the seventh or eighth centuries, and so help to fill up the gap in the story of Indian painting between Ajanta and Akbar. In this section no more can be attempted than a slight indication of the extent to which Indian schools of painting, modified by external influences, penetrated Turkistan, and, through it, the Far East.

Remains of eighth century at Dandan-Uiliq.

The discoveries made by Sir Aurel Stein during his various expeditions into the Desert having been published in considerable detail, a fair idea can be formed of the achievements of painters following Indian models more or less closely during the seventh and eighth centuries in Turkistan. Numerous fresco or distemper paintings on wood and plaster were found at a place called Dandan-Uiliq, which was abandoned soon after A.D. 791. All these works may be referred with confidence to the eighth century, and thus afford evidence of a sufficiently dated stage in the evolution of Indian painting when exposed to the influence of the Persian and Chinese schools. A few of the more striking examples are reproduced by permission.

Mounted personages on panel.

One of the best preserved paintings is that on a panel (D. vii, 5), 15 inches high and nearly 7 inches broad, which represents two sacred or princely personages, mounted, one on a piebald Yarkandi pony and the other on a camel (Plate 153B). The nimbus behind the head of each rider indicates either his high rank or his sacred character. The artists of the Mughal court in India were accustomed to give this emblem of sanctity to the emperors and even to members of their families, and in Khotan during the eighth century the same practice seems to have prevailed. The picture speaks for itself so clearly that detailed description is unnecessary, but the blending of Indian and Chinese features in the face of the horseman may be noted, and the free drawing of the camel

[1] The word 'Gobi' simply means 'desert' (Stein).

A. North stele, east chapel. Abhayagiri.

B. Naga door-keeper, Ruwanveli *vihare*.

C. Western stairs of circular shrine (*wata-da-ge*) at Polonnaruwa.

D. Sculptured stele at Abhayagiri *dagaba*. Anuradhapura.

PLATE 143

A. Dwarf right-handed door-keeper of south porch of west chapel of Jetawanarama.

B. Dwarf door-keeper, Ruwanveli *dagaba*.

C. Circular shrine (*wata-da-ge*) at Polonnaruwa; part of north-east quadrant.

D. Circular shrine (*wata-da-ge*) at Medirigiriya, N.C.P.

PLATE 144

A. Kapila relief, Isurumuniya, Anuradhapura.
(By Courtesy of Dr. A. K. Coomaraswamy)

B. Seated Buddha (5 ft. 9 in.) *in situ* at Toluvila, Anuradhapura; now in Colombo Museum.
(Copyright by Department of Archaeology, Government of India)

PLATE 145

A. Seated Buddha (6 ft. 9 in.); Pankuliya Vihare, Anuradhapura.

B. Seated Buddha, from Vihare No. 2, Polonnaruwa; now in Colombo Museum.

C. Colossal statue of "Ananda", Polonnaruwa.

D. Colossal Buddha at Awkana, N.C.P.

(Copyright by Department af Archaeology, Government of India)

deserves commendation. The horseman is repeated on D. x, 5 (Stein, Plate LXII), but the identity of either figure has not yet been determined.

Painting in Tibetan manner.

The ugly picture on the obverse of panel D. vii, 6, measuring $12\frac{3}{4} \times 8$ inches, representing a three-faced, four-armed deity, supposed to be a Tantric form of *Avalokitesvara*, squatting on a chequered cushion supported by two white bulls, is purely Indian, and is so closely related to the modern *Lamaist* compositions that it might be described as the oldest extant Tibetan painting. The body and front face of the deity are dark blue, the face on the proper right, with a feminine expression, is white, and the demoniac face on the proper left is yellow. The outline is drawn in thick black lines, and the work has little aesthetic merit (Stein, Plate LX).

A Persian Bodhisattva.

The reverse of the same panel offers a surprise by presenting a picture of a four-armed Buddhist saint or *Bodhisattva* in the guise of a Persian with black beard and whiskers, holding a thunderbolt (*vajra*) in his left hand. The combination on one panel of this almost purely Persian figure with the Indian image on the other side suggests questions, at present insoluble, concerning the forms which Buddhism may have assumed in Iranian lands. The art, seemingly of higher quality than that of the obverse picture, is certainly more pleasing. The four arms are a distinctly Indian feature (Plate 153A). The existence of this queer figure may help us in some measure to understand the introduction of Persian figures into the Buddhist pictures of Ajanta, which may yet be proved to be an Indian development of Central Asiatic Buddhist art. But that hypothesis at present lacks historical support.

The water-sprite fresco.

The most interesting of the Dandan-Uiliq paintings is the fresco depicting some legend connected with a female water-sprite, probably the tale told by Hiuen Tsiang of the minister who married the widow of the *Naga* king in order to secure the flow of water over the lands of Khotan. However that may be, the design and execution of the composition are of considerable merit, and well illustrate the variety of elements combined in the medieval art of Khotan. The pose of the lady, whose figure in the original projects about 18 inches above the water, is plainly a reminiscence of some Hellenistic Venus, such as the de' Medici or the Capitoline, and the vine-leaf guarding her modesty equally recalls the conventional fig-leaf. Her ornaments are Indian, her face Chinese. Thus in this one figure we can trace the meeting of the three civilizations, Greek, Indian, and Chinese. The seated figures are more Chinese in type than anything else. I do not perceive any Persian factors in this work (Plate 154A).

Chinese princess fresco.

Another painting (D. x, 4), more primitive in style, illustrates the story of the Queen of Khotan, a Chinese princess, who secretly introduced silk cocoons into her adopted country by concealing them in the folds of her head-dress. The central effigy of the princess, boldly sketched with a few etching-like strokes, will suffice as an example of the style (Fig. 154B). It will be observed that the head of the princess, like the heads of the three other persons in the picture, is surrounded by a nimbus or halo, apparently affording clear evidence that in Khotan art of the eighth century, as in Mughal art of the seventeenth, the nimbus was given to persons of royal birth as well as to divinities and saints. The lady's features are Indian rather than Chinese.

Sketch of camel and calf.

Further east, at Endere, between Niya and Cherchen, in ruins of somewhat earlier date than those at Dandan-Uiliq, Sir Aurel Stein found a scrap of faded fresco on stucco with 'delicate and harmonious colouring', and an Indian-ink sketch on paper depicting a Bactrian she-camel suckling her calf, drawn in the fewest possible bold strokes with considerable spirit and vigour. A slight attempt to indicate the solidity or roundness of the body has been made by adding a wash of faint colour round the contours (Plate 154C). The drawing seems to have been executed with a brush, not a pen, and is free from conventionality.

Art to the north of the desert.

The countries to the north of the great desert have proved to be equally fertile in finds of astonishing richness. At the ruined city of Idiqut-i-Shahri the German explorers found the remains of Buddhist, Manichean, and Nestorian buildings and art associated in such a way as to show that for centuries the adherents of the rival creeds managed to live together. Ultimately, in or about the ninth century, the Buddhists were massacred by the Chinese, a fact of which Dr. v. Le Coq discovered terrible proof when he opened a chamber filled with the skeletons of monks and other signs of ruthless slaughter. At this site curious votive flags, both Manichean and Buddhist, were found with designs painted on plaster applied to long strips of cotton, in the manner still practised by Tibetan Lamas.

At Yar-Khoto, to the west of Turfan, paintings on silk, described as being exquisitely wrought and harmoniously coloured, were obtained. Stein also brought home from his second expedition a large quantity of similar silk designs obtained in a walled-up temple near the Kan-su border, many of which are in the finest condition.[1] The Yar-Khoto pictures are both Manichean and Buddhist, the latter never failing to retain a distinctly Indian character. At the Basaklik monastery Dr. v. Le Coq discovered wall-paintings executed on a surface of plaster composed of loam and chopped straw.

The pictures at Chiqqan Kol and Toyoq are in the archaic Indian style, whereas in other places the Indian features have been much modified by Chinese and Persian influence. It is evident that the Turkistan paintings range over a long time, and that, when their sequence shall have been worked out, much light will be thrown upon the development of the pictorial art of Asia, including India.

Indian origin of Buddhist art of the Far East.

Students of Chinese and Japanese painting have been aware for some years past that the specially Buddhist forms of art in China were derived from India through Khotan, and passed on through Korea to Japan, the principal agent in the transmission to Korea, and so to Japan, having been Wei-chi I-song, son of Bajna of Khotan. Bajna was one of the numerous foreign artists in the service of the Chinese Emperor, Yang-ti (A.D. 605-17), and had been preceded at the imperial court by two Indian monks, with names something like Kabodha and Dharmakuksha. Both Bajna and his son, according to Chinese critics, worked in a foreign, that is to say, Indian manner, and enjoyed high repute as Buddhist artists. The marked Indian element in early Japanese art is thus amply accounted for.[2]

Indian influence confined to Buddhist art.

Although the descent of the specially Buddhist varieties of the art of the Far East from India, and more particularly from Indo-Greek prototypes in Gandhara on the north-western frontier, is abundantly proved, the evidence does not warrant the larger inference drawn by Mr. Anderson that 'a previously undeveloped art' in China was dependent upon importations from India for its growth and development.[3] The earliest extant Chinese painting, the fourth-century picture by Ku K'ai-chih in the British Museum, does not show the slightest trace of either Indian

[1] A series was exhibited in the Indian Court of the Festival of Empire, 1911, and described by Stein in the *Catalogue* of the Court, pp. 14-26.

[2] Hirth, *Ueber fremde Einflüsse in der chines. Kunst*, pp. 34, 38, 39, 43-60.

[3] Anderson, *Descriptive and Hist. Catal. of a Collection of Japanese and Chinese Pictures*, in the B.M. (1886), p. 482.

A. Pattini Devi. Cast brass. Singalese, now in the British Museum. (Probably 12th Cent. A.D.)

(By Courtesy of Dr. A. K. Coomaraswamy.)

B. Siva Nataraja (3 ft.). Copper casting. No. 1, from Polonnaruwa. Colombo Museum (Probably 12th Cent. A.D.)

(By Courtesy of Dr. A. Nell)

PLATE 147

A. Sundara-murti Swami. (Ht. 1 ft. 8 in.). Polonnaruwa (No. 16). (Probably cast in South India, 11th Cent. A.D.).

B. Bodhisattva. Copper casting. Anuradhapura (No. 97), now in the Colombo Museum. (Probaly cast South India. 8th-9th Cent. A.D.).

(By Courtesy of Dr. A. Nell)

A

B

C. Siva Nataraja. Copper casting. Polonnaruwa (No. 15).

D. Siva (1 ft. $10\frac{1}{2}$ in). Polonnaruwa (No. 12). (Probably cast in South India, 11th Cent A.D.).

(By Courtesy of Dr. A. Nell)

PLATE 148

or Greek influence. Buddhist pictures form but a single subdivision of Chinese painting, the subjects of which, according to Professor Giles, may be classified under seven heads, namely—(1) history, (2) religion (including Buddhism and Taoism), (3) landscape, (4) flowers, (5) birds, (6) beasts, and (7) portraiture.[1] Excepting the Buddhist designs under the second head, China learned nothing, and had nothing to learn from 'the land of the Brahmans'. I am disposed to agree with Mr. Binyon, who finds in China 'if not the parent art of Asia, its earliest mature flower in painting'.[2]

Wall-painting of Horiuji temple, Japan.

Mr. Griffiths thought that he could discern marks of Chinese influence in the paintings at Ajanta; and he may be right, although such marks are not very distinct, and may, perhaps, be explained as derived from the common stock of Asiatic art. However that may be, the art of Ajanta certainly produced no effect upon the general development of painting in China; and in Japan the only conspicuous instance of imitation of the Ajanta style is the wall-painting in the temple of Horiuji at Nara, supposed by some critics to date from A.D. 607, but according to others about a century later.[3]

Part II. TIBET AND NEPAL

Tibetan and Nepalese schools.

The art of Tibet is so closely related to that of Nepal that the paintings of both countries may be grouped together. The style is a combination of Indian and Chinese characteristics, traceable back to the earlier style of Turkistan, specimens of which have been cited above. Nepal probably imitated Indian painting before Tibet was sufficiently civilized to do so. According to Taranath, the earliest Nepalese school followed the model of the school of the 'Ancient West' founded by Sringadhara of Marwar in the seventh century, while subsequent Nepalese artists inclined rather to favour the methods of the Bengal 'Eastern' school of the ninth century. The latest Nepalese artists before Taranath's time in A.D. 1600 are said to have had 'no special character'. All the existing specimens of Nepalese painting, with the exception of the miniatures in MSS., apparently are later than the seventeenth century. Most of the extant Tibetan pictures are believed to be not older, but it is not possible to determine exact dates.

Modern Tibetan painting.

Painting is still extensively practised by Tibetan *Lamas* for the purposes of their ritualistic worship and as a source of income. Usually the compositions are depicted on long narrow banners of either silk or cotton. They may be painted either directly on the fabric or on a coat of plaster applied to it. Pictures on paper also exist. The silken banners obtained by Stein from a walled-up temple near the Chinese frontier, and dating from the seventh or eighth century, closely resemble those now made by the *Lamas*, who follow strictly prescribed ritual rules. The *Lamas* also execute frescoes on the temple walls, some of which, according to travellers, are remarkable compositions.

Mechanical methods.

Tibetan painting is generally more a matter of skilled craftsmanship than of fine art. The canonical process of manufacture has been fully described by Godwin Austen, who explains in detail the way in which a figure of Buddha is built up. The draughtsman starts by drawing a long vertical rectangle, within which are inscribed a medial perpendicular line and sundry horizontal parallels at prescribed distances. The different organs of the body are then plotted out for

[1] *An Introduction to the History of Chinese Pictorial Art*, 1905, p. 7.
[2] *Painting in the Far East* (1908), p. 48.
[3] A tracing (No. 148, Anderson's *Catal.*) is in the B. M. Mr. Okakura favours the later date.

insertion at certain intersections of the lines. For example, the face is plotted from the starting-point determined by the intersection of the medial perpendicular with the transverse line No. 17. The remaining parts of the body are worked out in a similar way, and other sacred objects, such as a *stupa* (*chorten*, or *dagaba*), are imaged on like principles.[1] Travellers tell us that the monks of the Greek communities at Mount Athos manufacture the sacred *ikons* in an equally mechanical fashion.

Good colouring and details.

The examination of specimens of Tibetan ritualistic paintings confirms the expectation formed from knowledge of the mechanical process enjoined. The line, however, is truly drawn and full of subtlety. The colouring is often rich and harmonious, shades of indigo blue in particular being combined with black in a very effective manner. The execution of details, too, is often finished with characteristic Indian minuteness.[2]

Banners in British Museum.

The British Museum possesses a considerable collection of Tibetan banner-paintings on silk, mounted on rollers. Most of the pictures are distinctly Chinese in style, with little trace of Indian influence on the art, as distinguished from the subjects. But a few are more Indian than Chinese. One such is No. $\frac{1905}{5.20}$, 63 (measuring 2 feet 3 inches × 20 inches), with an embroidered border. The central figure is a seated Buddha of Indian style in the 'earth-touching' pose. An unpleasant Tantric *Bodhisattva* of little artistic value is depicted on No. $\frac{1905}{5.20}$, 57. The most characteristically Tibetan specimen, combining Indian with Chinese peculiarities, is No. $\frac{1905}{5.20}$, 62, which possesses considerable beauty as a scheme of colour, dark indigo blue predominating. The central figure is a horrible and repulsive *Yama*, or Death, wearing a garland of skulls. The field is mostly occupied by a series of scrolls in dark tints, of distinctively Tibetan form. In the upper section three small figures, a seated Buddha in Chinese costume, with on each side a *Bodhisattva*, or Tibetan *Lama*, wearing a tall, conical head-dress, are tolerably well executed. The painting does not look old.

Cotton pictures at South Kensington.

The Tibetan pictures on cotton exhibited in the Indian Section of the Victoria and Albert Museum, South Kensington, include many of great aesthetic interest, especially No. 2451 from the Schlagintweit collection.

The Hodgson collection.

The considerable collection of Tibetan drawings and paintings, presented by Mr. Brian Hodgson to the Institut de France and still preserved there, has had the good fortune to have been described by two eminent scholars, M. Barthélemy St. Hilaire and M. A. Foucher. M. St. Hilaire, who formed a higher estimate of the artistic quality of a set of ten numbered paintings in the collection than M. Foucher can accept, criticized them generally in the following terms:—

'Mais les monuments de sculpture et de peinture que nous venons de passer en revue sont très loin d'être dénués de mérite; le dessin en est quelquefois très pur, les attitudes des personnages sont élégantes et naturelles. Il y a même, quoique plus rarement, une onction profonde dans la physionomie du Buddha et des principaux Bhikshous. . . . La composition est ordinairement régulière, quelquefois vaste et très bien ordonnée, comme l'atteste la description que j'ai donnée plus haut du troisième tableau tibétain.'

Nos. 3, 9, 10 of Hodgson collection.

No. 3, alluded to in the passage quoted, depicts various Buddhas and a crowd of worshippers. The uppermost scene represents a *Dhyani-Buddha* holding his *Sakti*, or female counterpart, in close embrace, a common subject in these paintings.

[1] 'On the System of outlining the Figures of Deities and other Religious Drawings, as practised at Ladak' (*J.A.S.B.*, Part I, vol. xxxiii (1864), p. 151, with plates). 'Il est de règle, quand il s'agit de personnages, qu'on commence toujours par les yeux, qui, aussitôt terminés, doivent être purifiés au moyen de prières et de formules d'exorcisme de peur que quelque démon ne vienne à en prendre possession; c'est ce qui explique que tous les peintres sont des Lamas' (de Milloué, *Bod-Youl ou Tibet*, p. 295).

[2] *Indian Sculpture and Painting*.

M. St. Hilaire considered No. 9, a large work measuring $1\frac{1}{4}$ metres in length by 70 cm. in breadth, to be 'd'un travail presqu'aussi délicat que celui du numéro 3'. No. 10, which includes representations of devil dances performed by Lamas wearing horrible masks, is also commended.

No. 5 of Hodgson collection.

M. Foucher has kindly selected No. 5 as being one of the best and most suitable for reproduction (Plate 155A). It depicts Buddha in the 'earth-touching' pose surrounded by a host of worshippers on earth and in the clouds, and is framed in a pretty border. The figures of the adoring Lamas are numbered. Similar numbers are inserted in other pictures.

Tibetan and Mongolian pictures of the Ukhtomskij collection.

The valuable collection of objects illustrative of Buddhism formed by Prince E. Ukhtomskij, and once preserved in the Museum of the Emperor Alexander III, St. Petersburg, includes many Tibetan and Mongolian pictures, of which select specimens, including portraits, have been engraved in outline as illustrations of the Catalogue in Russian prepared by Prof. A. Grünwedel.

Nepalese art a variety of Tibetan.

Very little can be recorded concerning the pictorial art of Nepal, which, as known to us, is only a modern variety of the Tibetan school (A 1). The extant specimens are all Buddhist, and seem to possess little aesthetic value. The Hodgson collection in Paris (Plates 155B, 156A), includes ten pictures, two of which have been reproduced by M. Sylvain Lévi in his learned work, 'Nepal'. The first of his plates is a reduced copy of No. 6, a large pen-and-ink drawing, 2 m. 85 cm. long and 1 m. high, believed to have been prepared to the order of Mr. Brian Hodgson. The subject has been identified as a procession in honour of *Padmapani* or *Avalokitesvara*, marching round the walls of a town in the valley. The drawing is carefully executed and shows a knowledge of linear perspective presumably due to European teaching, but as a specimen of Indian art it is of no interest. M. Lévi's second and larger folding plate reproduces in six sections a photograph of the illustrated manuscript giving the sacred legend of Nepal. This work, too, possesses little merit as art.

Magic circles in Hodgson collection.

The Buddhists of the Northern School are fond of constructing magic circles (*mandala*) crowded with figures of Buddhas, worshippers, monks, lotus-plants, and other sacred persons or things, believing that the maker or user of such a picture will have a claim on the protection of all the influential beings and lucky objects depicted. No. 10 of the Hodgson collection is such a magic circle, filled with more than 200 figures. Another magic circle is No. 7 of the Hodgson collection. The silken magic circle in the British Museum (MS. Add. 8898) is accompanied by a description from the competent pen of Col. Waddell. The composition, as a whole, is ugly and barbarous, not worth copying, though the floral border is pretty.

Ancient miniatures in MSS.

The only relics of an ancient school of Nepalese painting are the miniature illustrations of two manuscripts, Add. 1643, Cambridge, and A. 15, Asiatic Society of Bengal, Calcutta, which have been minutely studied and in large part reproduced by M. Foucher.[1] Unfortunately, the age of the manuscripts and miniatures is not quite certain, but probably both date from the eleventh century. The older document, that at Cambridge, cannot be later than A.D. 1015; the Calcutta manuscript may be some fifty years posterior in date. The miniatures, numbering 85 in Add. 1643, and 37 in A. 15, equal in height ($0^{m}\cdot055$) the narrow

[1] Similar miniatures are executed in Tibet (de Milloué, *Bod-Youl ou Tibet*, p. 237), but I am not in a position to cite examples. Good specimens, dating from the seventeenth century, or earlier, are inserted in a manuscript of the *Kahgyur* ('Tibétain 10') in the Bibliothèque Nationale, Paris (Blochet, 'Inventaire,' *Revue des Bibliothèques*, 1899, p. 265).

strip of palm-leaf on which the text is written, and each depicts a holy place, a sacred personage, or an incident in Buddhist legend. Most of them being plainly labelled, they are of high archaeological and historical value, but from the purely aesthetic point of view are not of much account.

Technique and quality.

The technique is simple. The outlines were drawn in red ink and filled in with colour washes, only the five canonical colours being used—white, blue, red, yellow, and green. The designs evidently transmit an ancient tradition, and are the production of an art long stereotyped; but, notwithstanding the mechanical monotony of treatment, M. Foucher holds that these little paintings, although not masterpieces, cannot be regarded as merely vulgar daubs. They have been drawn and coloured by illuminators 'très suffisamment maîtres de leurs moyens'. If they date from the eleventh century, they may represent the 'Eastern' school of Dhiman, which according to Taranath was favoured in Nepal at about that time.

Close relation of Tibetan and Nepalese art.

The plastic art of both Tibet and Nepal is Indian in origin and essentially one. The art of Nepal, apart from wood-carving, is represented by images mostly cast in copper or cut in slate or coarse marbles,[1] all being comparatively recent in date, none, perhaps, being more than three or four centuries old. The castings are made specially for *Lamaist* use in Tibet. They include large and small figures of gilt copper, and many ritualistic instruments, such as candlesticks, thunder-bolts, and daggers. The latter are usually in brass.

M. de Milloué gives a summary account of Tibetan fine-art work in copper:

Tibetan art industry in copper.

'Copper is found both native and in the form of pyrites in Tibet, where it is wrought with uncommon perfection. Several localities are well known for their famous foundries, which supply the whole of the Buddhist East with statuettes of divinities. Lhasa has a special reputation for small figures in gilt copper, which are esteemed the more the smaller they are. Its productions are easily recognized by their graceful and somewhat arch (*mièvre*) style. The statuettes made by the monks and craftsmen of Tashilumpo are equally esteemed. Most of the bronze[2] statuettes come from the workshops of the Tsang and Khams provinces. The bronzes from the region last named are famous for the perfection of their execution in details and their wonderful *patina*, qualities especially noticeable in the examples which go back to the sixteenth or seventeenth century, notwithstanding the impurity of the metal. Tsiamdo, Jaya, Bathang, and Lithang seem to be the principal centres of this art industry, which possesses an eminently religious character.'[3]

Portrait statuettes.

A special characteristic of Tibetan art is the abundance of realistic, highly individualized portrait statuettes of holy Lamas and other Buddhist saints. How far such reputed portraits are actual likenesses and how far merely typical forms it is impossible to say. They may be authentic portraits transmitted by tradition through contemporary paintings. A good example of such a traditional portrait is the seated image of the '*Dalai Lama* of the Third Re-birth', also known as the 'Apostle of the Mongols', whom he converted to Buddhism in the sixteenth century (1543-89). The original is in the large collection formed by Prince E. Ukhtomskij, until lately in the Museum of H.I.M. Alexander III, St. Petersburg, which has been carefully catalogued by Professor Grünwedel.[4] The presentment is thoroughly realistic, and possibly may be from the life. No criterion seems to

[1] E. B. Havell, *Stone Carving in Bengal*, thin quarto, 16 pp., 5 plates (Bengal Secretariat Depot, Calcutta, 1906).

[2] The Indian castings as a whole are copper, with brass coming into use in comparatively modern times. In Burma and Indo-China the castings are of true bronze as are the oldest in Tibet which show strong Chinese influence. Most of these Tibetan 'bronzes' are copper castings, the term being used in a very wide sense.

[3] *Bod-Youl ou Tibet* (Paris, 1906), p. 130. Tsang and Khams lie to the east.

[4] See Prof. Grünwedel's *Mythologie des Buddhismus in Tibet und der Mongolei, Führer durch die Sammlung des Fürsten E. Ukhtomskij* (Leipzig, 1900), cited as *Guide*; and his illustrated *Catalogue* of the collection in Russian (Bibliotheca Buddhica, No. vi, 2 fasc., St. Petersburg, 1905). The Tibetan name of the Apostle is *mK'as-grub-bSod-nams-rgya-mtso*.

A. Surya, the Sun-god. (1 ft. 5½ in.). Polonnaruwa (No. 18.) (Probably cast in South India, 11th Cent. A.D.).

B. Parvati. (1 ft. 8 in.). Polonnaruwa (No. 23)

(By Courtesy of Dr. A. Nell)

C. Parvati. (1 ft. 4½ in.). Polonnaruwa (No. 20). (Probably cast in South India, 11th Cent. A.D.).

COPPER CASTINGS IN THE COLOMBO MUSEUM

PLATE 149

A. Avalokitesvara, or Padmapani. Singalese. Boston Museum. (Probably 8th Cent. A.D.).

B. Jambhala, or Kuvera. Singalese. Boston Museum. (Probably 8th-9th Cent. A.D.).

(By Courtesy of Dr. A. K. Coomaraswamy)

C. Seated Buddha. Copper casting. Colombo Museum. (Probably 5th Cent. A.D.).

PLATE 150

exist by which the age of such images can be determined. The Prince's collection contains many equally good portrait statuettes. One notable portrait is that of the Lama reproduced in *Guide*, Abb. 72. An ancient image in Chinese crackled porcelain vividly represents in Indian pose a follower of the teacher known as *Bhaisajya-guru*, or *Man-la*, the 'Buddha of Medicine' (*Guide*, Abb. 94).

Other portraits.

Other artistic examples of the same portrait class are in the Musée Guimet, among which may be specially noted the bronze images of *Padmasambhava* and *Tsong-kapa*, the founder of 'Yellow Lamaism' (*Petit Guide Illustré*, pp. 143, 144). A reproduction of a statuette of *Tsong-kapa* from an original in the Pitt-Rivers Museum, Oxford, is here given (Plate 157). Portraits of this kind do not come from Nepal, so far as I know.

The effigies of Buddhas and deities (Plate 157B and C), although similar in style to the human portrait statuettes, are necessarily more conventional. They are often gilt and decorated with turquoises. The goddess *Tara* in her various forms is, perhaps, the favourite, but many deities are represented.[1] (A 2). In Plate 157 illustrations are given of three other figures—an unnamed teacher; the *Bodhisattva Manjusri;* and his consort, *Sarasvati*, goddess of music and poetry. The last-named object, which is gracefully and freely modelled, closely resembles the best Nepalese work.

Images of deities.

NOTES TO CHAPTER TWELVE

Today we know much more about Nepalese pictorial art. The paintings are both Buddhist and Brahmanical and some fine work has come to light. A 1

Some beautiful Nepalese images in wood are known. See Plate 156B. A 2

[1] The well-executed nearly black bronze Tara in the Pitt-Rivers Museum holds in her left hand a *phallus* of amethyst-colour glass.

Chapter Thirteen

THE INDO-MUHAMMADAN STYLES OF ARCHITECTURE

Origin of Musalman art.

WITHIN about eighty years after the death of Muhammad in A.D. 632 the followers of his religion reigned supreme over Arabia, Persia, Syria, Western Turkistan, Sind, Egypt, North Africa, and Southern Spain, the marvellously rapid extension of Muhammadan power having been rendered possible by the barbarism and weakness of the subjugated kingdoms in Asia, Africa, and Europe. The first contact of Islam, as M.M. Le Bon and Saladin observe, was stimulating to what remained alive of the older forms of civilization. Muslim armies, recruited in Persia, Syria, and Egypt, carried with them crowds of Asiatic skilled craftsmen, who introduced everywhere the arts of Asia, and modified the various local forms of art so as to suit the needs of the new faith and satisfy the luxurious tastes of magnificent courts. The Arabs, although possessing little art of their own, succeeded in impressing upon the local styles which they utilized for Muslim purposes a general character of uniformity, which we now recognize as that of Musalman art.

Indo-Muhammadan art begins A.D. 1200.

The Muhammadan conquest in A.D. 712 of Sind, which at that time was regarded as distinct from India, did not seriously affect India proper, and the occupation of Kabul in A.D. 870 was equally without appreciable influence on Hindu polity, which continued its isolated course unchanged by external forces, developing on the political side the Rajput kingdoms, and on the aesthetic side the Brahmanical art already described. India did not feel the impact of Muslim ideas until the beginning of the eleventh century, when the repeated fierce raids of Mahmud of Ghazni compelled her to take notice of the new force which had arisen. Before his death in A.D. 1030 the Panjab had become a province of the Muhammadan Sultanate of Ghazni. But, until the closing years of the twelfth century, Islam made no further progress in India. The early Arab conquerors of Sind seem to have left nothing but ruined Hindu temples behind them, nor are there tangible traces of the rule of the Ghaznivide rulers of the Panjab.

The history of Indo-Muhammadan art begins with the year A.D. 1200 in round numbers. Between 1193 and 1236 Muhammad of Ghor, Kutb-ud-din Ibak, and Sultan Altamsh had compelled all Northern India, including Bengal, to submit, more or less completely, to the Muslim government established at Delhi. The earliest Muhammadan monuments in India date from the reigns of the three princes named; the principal works of that time being the mosque at Ajmer, the Kutb mosque and *minar* at Delhi, the gateway of the chief mosque at Budaun (A.D. 1223),[1] and the tomb of the Sultan Altamsh at Delhi.

Essentials of a mosque.

The simple, world-wide worship of Muslims, who adore the One God and hate every kind of idol, can be performed satisfactorily without any building. But it is convenient to have a spacious edifice in which the faithful can assemble on Friday, the Musalman Sabbath, to join in public prayer, and occasionally hear a sermon. During prayer the worshippers should turn towards Mecca, the direction of which is indicated by a niche or niches in the appropriate wall. The Muhammadan mosque, or church, therefore, consists essentially of an enclosure, with a niche in one wall to indicate the direction of Mecca. There should be also a pulpit, and a tank for ablution. All other things, such as cloisters, chambers,

[1] Cunningham, *A. S. Rep.*, vol. xi, p. 5, Pl. III.

1

2

A. Offerings to a Bodhisattva. 1. The Bodhisattva's descent to earth. 2. The story of Prince Sudhana. Relief-panels in the first gallery, Borobudur, Java (Indonesia).

(From van Kinsbergen, *Cudheden van Java*)

B. Sarasvati enthroned; from Jogyokaita, Java (Indonesia).

C. Prajna Paramita. Javanese (Indonesian). (*By Courtesy of Dr. A. K. Coomaraswamy*)

A. Seated Buddha. Javanese.

B. Manjusri. Copper casting. Javanese. British Museum.

(By Courtesy of Dr. A. K. Coomaraswamy)

C. Sculpture. Indonesia. A.D. 1227-1248. Tropenmuseum, Amsterdam.

A. Persian Bodhisattva. Rev. of wooden panel, D. VII, 6, from Dandan-Uiliq.

B. Mounted princes or saints; wooden panel from Dandan-Uiliq.

(From Stein, *Ancient Khotan*)

A. Water-sprite, etc.; fresco from Dandan-Uiliq.

B. Chinese princess; fresco from Dandan-Uiliq.

C. Bactrian camel; Indian ink-drawing on paper from Endere.

(From Stein, *Ancient Khotan*)

and lofty portals are unessential, being needed only for purposes of convenience and dignity. The mosque may be wholly open to the air, or wholly or partially roofed. Examples of wholly roofed mosques are very rare in India, the only one on a large scale being that at Gulbarga in the Deccan. Ordinarily a large open quadrangle is the principal feature of an Indian mosque. The covered portions of the more considerable buildings usually consist of an aisle or aisles (*liwan*), at the western side, with cloisters round the enclosing walls, and often include huge gateways with many chambers, and sundry minor structures. The roofs are invariably domed in some fashion or other, and pointed arches are a prominent feature.[1]

Origin of domes and arches.

The almost universal presence of domes and arches, usually of the pointed kind, in Muhammadan buildings is due to the fact that Muslim architecture is based on the style practised at Baghdad in the time of the great *Abbasid Khalifs* (Caliphs), of whom Harun-ar-rashid (786-809) is the best known. The Baghdad style was derived from the ancient vaulted architecture of Mesopotamia, as transmitted through the modified developments of Sassanian times (A.D. 226-641). The beginnings of the familiar forms of Muhammadan architecture have been recently traced by General de Beylié in the buildings of Samara in Mesopotamia, erected in the early part of the ninth century, and abandoned in 875, when Baghdad became the capital of the *Khalifate*. From Baghdad the style spread rapidly throughout the Muhammadan world, and became to such a degree universal that it is hardly possible to imagine a mosque of brick or stone without domes and arches.[2]

Hindu construction of earliest Indian mosques.

At the beginning of the thirteenth century, when Kutb-ud-din undertook to build mosques and tombs at Delhi and Ajmer, domes and pointed arches were recognized to be essential. But the conquerors were obliged to employ Hindu masons, unaccustomed to turning true radiating arches and domes, and ordinarily used only to make the semblance of such by means of the horizontal corbelled construction familiar to them with which the Muslim architects had to be content. The cloisters were easily made up from the materials of overthrown Hindu temples, and retained a manifest Hindu character without objection.

At the Kutb mosque of Delhi the glory of the building is the screen of eleven pointed arches, eight smaller and three larger, Muslim in form, but Hindu in construction (Plate 160B). The faces of these structures are decorated with 'a lace-work of intricate and delicate carving', considered by Fergusson to be 'the most exquisite specimen of its class known to exist anywhere'. It bears some resemblance to the decorations of the Sassanian palace of Mashita and those of certain parts of Santa Sophia at Constantinople. The similar screen at Ajmer (Plates 158A, 160A), built between A.D. 1200 and 1235, consists of seven arches, the central one being 22 feet 2 inches wide. 'Each arch is surrounded by three lines of writing, the outer in the *Kufic* and the other two in Arabic characters, and divided from each other by bands of Arabesque ornament boldly and clearly cut and still as sharp as when first chiselled.[3] In the centre the screen rises to a

[1] The growth of the mosque was radically affected by the extension of its purely religious function to include education. The great mosques of Asia were universities as well as places of worship.

[2] The exceptional wooden mosques of Kashmir have tall spires, probably derived from Buddhist architecture (Nicholls, 'Muhammadan Architecture in Kashmir', *Ann. Rep. A. S. India* 1906-7 pp. 161-70 with plates; a valuable treatise). My text is based on the article 'Les Origines de l'Art musulman', by M. Louis Bréhier (*La Revue des Idées*, Paris, No. 75, Mars 1910, pp. 189-99), and on Saladin, *Manuel d'Art musulman*, tome i, chap. I (Paris, 1907).

[3] This foliated scroll-work is unmistakably Indian in character.

height of 56 feet' (Plate 158A). The illustration shows clearly the Hindu mode of construction, and the peculiar low conical dome appearing within.

Origin of the name 'Kutb'.

The mosque colloquially known as 'the Kutb' is commonly believed to be named after the Sultan Kutb-ud-din Ibak (1205-10), and it is true that it was completed in its original form in the year A.D. 1198 by him while he was still Viceroy of Delhi and the Indian territory under the Sultan of Ghazni. But the building is really named after a famous saint, Kutb-ud-din of Ush near Baghdad, who lies buried near, and is popularly remembered as Kutb Sahib.

The Kutb Minar.

Muslim usage requires that the faithful should be summoned to prayer at the stated time by a loud call uttered by an official known as *muazzin*. In order to facilitate his duty many mosques, although by no means all, were furnished with a minaret, or two minarets, from which the summons could be proclaimed. Sometimes the minarets were attached to the mosque, sometimes they were detached. The Kutb Minar at Delhi, originally about 250 feet high, and even now not much less, is the most remarkable example of the detached minaret in existence. Like the adjoining mosque, it derives its familiar name from the saint, not the prince. It is, however, some thirty years or more later in date than the mosque, having been erected about A.D. 1232 by the Sultan Altamsh when he made large additions to the mosque. The details of the building are due to its Hindu sculptors. The structure has been so often described at length, that it will be sufficient to give photographs (Plate 159A and B), and to cite Fergusson's authority for the statement that the Minar is 'the most beautiful example of its class known to exist anywhere'. Fine specimens of *minars* of later date will be illustrated presently. The form, a specially Muslim one, offers much scope for variety of treatment. 'The minaret', as Sir George Birdwood observes, 'is the one original feature the Saracens contributed to architecture.'[1]

Gateways of Ala-ud-din Khalji.

The magnificent gateway erected in A.D. 1310 by the Sultan Ala-ud-din Khalji on the south side of the enlarged Kutb Mosque marks an advance in Indo-Muhammadan architecture. Here the true arches with keystones were no longer constrained to execute the designs of their foreign masters by the structurally inferior Hindu methods. The building consists of a rectangular chamber surmounted by a low-spreading dome. The ornament is composed mainly of geometrical designs and artistic Arabic inscriptions, but sundry details show influence of Hindu tradition (Plate 161A).[2]

Tughlak style at Delhi.

The Kings or Sultans of the Tughlak dynasty of Delhi in the fourteenth century introduced a new style of architecture marked by massiveness and extreme simplicity, qualities which have suggested a comparison with the early Norman work in England. The most characteristic example of this severe style is the tomb of Ghiyas-ud-din Tughlak, who was killed by a carefully devised 'accident' in 1324 (Plate 161B). The plan is a square measuring 38½ feet inside and 61½ feet outside, and the height to the top of the dome is 70 feet. The enormously thick walls slope inwards. The exterior decoration is effected in an austere manner by the free use of bands and borders of white marble, varied with a few panels of black marble, showing against the large surfaces of red sandstone.[3] No trace of Hindu tradition is evident. The style is more or less unique.

At the close of the fourteenth century many provinces broke away from the

[1] *J. Roy. Soc. Arts*, Jan. 1911, p. 179.

[2] This building was copied for the gateway of the tomb of Sultan Sikandar Lodi, built in A.D. 1494 at Khairpur near Delhi (Cunningham, *A. S. Rep.*, vol. xx, p. 156).

[3] Cunningham, *A. S. Rep.*, vol. i, p. 123.

A. Buddha with worshippers. Tibet.
('Tibet, N. 5', Institut de France).

B. Portrait of young Lama. Tibet.
(Hodgson Collection, Institut de France).

PLATE 155

A. Portrait of a lama evoking a demon. Tibet.
(Hodgson Collection, Institut de France).

B. Tara. Wood sculpture, Nepalese. 17th Cent. A.D.

suzerainty of the Sultans of Delhi, and set up as independent kingdoms. Among such mushroom states one of the most notable was that known as the Sharki, or Eastern Sultanate, with its capital at Jaunpur, forty miles from Benares. Its independence lasted until 1476. During its short period of glory the local sovereigns occupied themselves by destroying Hindu temples and replacing them by mosques designed on a grand scale, and in a distinctive style. The handsomest of the Jaunpur mosques is the Atala, completed in 1408, of which the main portal is shown in Plate 162A. The gateways and great halls are thoroughly Muslim, with radiating arches and true domes, but in the cloisters and interior galleries, where there was no need to roof large spaces, square pillars often borrowed from Hindu temples, are used, and the construction is Hindu. The style, while it has much of the massiveness of the Tughlak buildings at Delhi, is less severe and more attractive, a curious hybrid of Muslim and Hindu.

The Jaunpur style.

Under the patronage of its independent kings Bengal developed a Muhammadan style of its own.

The Bengal style.

'It is' (Fergusson observes) 'neither like that of Delhi, nor Jaunpur, nor any other style, but one purely local, and not without considerable merit in itself; its principal characteristic being heavy short pillars of stone supporting pointed arches and vaults in brick—whereas, at Jaunpur, for instance, light pillars carried horizontal architraves and flat ceilings.'

The second characteristic of the style is the curvilinear cornice copied from bamboo structures. The best examples are to be seen among the extensive ruins of the cities Gaur and Pandua in the Malda District. The buildings are mostly in brick and possess little beauty. But one mosque, known as the *Small Golden*, or *Eunuch's Mosque* at Gaur, is built wholly of basalt with massive solidity. This elegant building, which has been called 'the gem of Gaur', was erected about A.D. 1500, and is covered inside and out with beautifully chiselled designs, including the Indian lotus. The gateway is shown in Plate 163A. There are fifteen domes.

The buildings at Mandu, the capital of the kingdom of Malwa, which was independent from A.D. 1401 to 1531, are purely Muslim in style, closely related to those of the Sultans of Delhi. They are distinguished from the later Mughal buildings by the absence of groining and by the spreading domes.

The Mandu style.

Unquestionably, the most beautiful of the provincial styles of Muhammadan architecture in Northern and Western India is that of Gujarat. By good fortune it has been studied more carefully than any other Indian style, all the chief examples having been elaborately described and illustrated by Dr. Burgess and his staff in three quarto volumes, fully furnished with plans, sections, elevations, and photographs. The style is that of the late medieval Hindu and Jain temples with such modifications as were necessary for the purposes of Muslim worship, and is characterized by all the richness of ornament distinctive of the temples of Gujarat and Southern Rajputana—a strange contrast to the stern simplicity of the Tughlak buildings contemporary with the earlier examples. Hindu construction, too, is freely used, but the indispensable domes and pointed arches are introduced. The entrance to the chief mosque at Cambay, for instance, erected early in the fourteenth century, is simply a Hindu temple porch, with a low dome, plain on the exterior, put on top of it.[1] The exquisite roofed pulpit of Hilal Khan Kazi's mosque at Dholka, built in A.D. 1333, has a purely Hindu pyramidal roof, and much of

The Gujarat style.

[1] Burgess, *A. S. R.*, *Western India*, vol. vi, Pl. XIX, p. 28.

the panelled ornament with which the whole surface has been covered is equally Hindu.[1]

Ahmadabad.

The finest examples of the style, which, of course, gradually discarded some of its Hindu features, are to be seen at and near Ahmadabad, the ancient provincial capital, to the architecture of which two of Dr. Burgess's volumes are devoted. The name of the city is derived from Ahmad Shah, Sultan of Gujarat from 1411 to 1443, and the earliest Muhammadan buildings date from his time. The domes of his cathedral (*Jam'i*) mosque are constructed in the Hindu fashion. The elaborate traceries and other decorative accessories of the Ahmadabad buildings will be noticed in the next chapter.

Mosque of Mahafiz Khan.

The best preserved mosque in Ahmadabad, and one of the prettiest buildings in the city, is that built by Mahafiz Khan at the close of the fifteenth century. The minarets are adorned with panels of rich floral tracery undercut to such an extent that it is almost detached from the masonry. The architecture still largely retains a Hindu character (Plate 162B).

Tomb of Abu Turab.

The tomb of Abu Turab, about a century later than Mahafiz Khan's mosque, although still preserving the Ahmadabad character, is constructed with arches throughout, and is completely free from Hindu pillars (Plate 163B). The perforated screens which formerly connected the internal columns have disappeared.

Buildings in Persian style.

The buildings designed in the distinctive Ahmadabad style have no specially Persian features, and are thus sharply distinguished from the styles which we are about to notice. But two exceptional edifices at Ahmadabad, the mosque and tomb of Nawab Sardar Khan, built about 1680, are quite Persian in style. The mosque is very elegant.[2]

Styles of the Deccan: Golkonda.

The Bahmani Sultanate of the Deccan, established in 1347 by a successful revolt against the authority of Sultan Muhammad bin Tughlak of Delhi, broke up into five states at the close of the fifteenth century. The rulers of all those kingdoms encouraged architecture, and, consequently, ancient buildings of greater or less importance exist at all the local capitals. The covered mosque of Gulbarga has been already mentioned (*ante*, p. 153), and other notable edifices exist in the same town. Bidar possesses an imposing mosque, several remarkable tombs, and the ruins of a great college. The royal tombs at Golkonda, near the Nizam's capital, Hyderabad, are more or less familiar to tourists. The special peculiarities of the Golkonda style, high clerestories, stucco work in minarets, and domes of peculiar shape with narrow bases, may be illustrated from a tomb built in that style at Bijapur in the seventeenth century (Plate 164A).

The Deccan buildings, except a few of the earliest, are free from Hindu forms and constructions, and are related to the Mughal Indo-Persian style. But each kingdom had fashions of its own.

The Bijapur style.

By far the most important of the Deccan styles is that of Bijapur. The buildings in it date between the years 1557 and 1686. The most ornate is the comparatively small tomb of Ibrahim Adil Shah II (1579-1626), the character of which may be judged from Plate 164B.

Tomb of Muhammad Adil Shah.

The stately tomb of Muhammad Adil Shah (1636-60) is covered with a dome the second largest in the world, 'a wonder of constructive skill',

[1] Ibid, Pl. XXX, p. 31.

[2] Burgess, *A. S. R.*, *Western India*, vol. viii, p. 55, Pls. LX, LXI.

balanced internally by an ingenious arrangement of pendentives, fully explained by Fergusson, and with an internal height of 178 feet.

'The external ordonnance of this building is as beautiful as that of the interior. At each angle stands an octagonal tower eight storeys high, simple and bold in its proportions, and crowned by a dome of great elegance. The lower part of the building is plain and solid, pierced only with such openings as are requisite to admit light and air; at the height of 83 feet a cornice projects to the extent of 12 feet from the wall, or nearly twice as much as the boldest European architect ever attempted. Above this an open gallery gives lightness and finish to the whole, each face being further relieved by two minarets.'

The name of the architect of this wonderful structure, commonly known as the *Gol Gumbaz*, or Circular Dome (Plate 165A), does not seem to be recorded. Foreigners, Asiatic or European, were frequently employed by the Indo-Muhammadan sovereigns, and the Bijapur style is thought to show the influence of Ottoman architects. An expert critic truly observes that 'under Mohammedan influence the dome-builders of India attained a mastery over this form unknown *to* and seemingly unappreciated by the builders of the Western world'.[1]

Tatta Scinde.

At Tatta in Scinde is a fine group of tombs. The earliest of these is the tomb of Jam Nizam-ud-din which was built in 1508. Most of the tombs, however, were built within twenty-five years before or after the year 1600, and in fact are monuments to Moghul officials. The tomb of Sharfa Khan (*c.* 1638) stands on a stone base, but is of brick and tile-work. It is rather Persian in style than Indian.[2]

Sur style: tomb of Sher Shah.

We now pass on to the Indo-Persian styles of the North, the only forms of Muhammadan architecture in India familiar to the world in general. The short-lived and unstable Sur dynasty (1540-55), of which Sher Shah was the most distinguished member, had such a hard fight for existence that it could not have been expected to pay much attention to architecture. Nevertheless, several meritorious buildings are due to the Sur Sultans, and the mausoleum of Sher Shah at Sasaram (Sahasram), built on a lofty plinth in the midst of a lake, is one of the best designed and most beautiful buildings in India, unequalled among the earlier buildings in the northern provinces for grandeur and dignity. Cunningham was half inclined to prefer it even to the Taj. The dome, although not equal in size to the *Gol Gumbaz* of Bijapur, is 13 feet wider than that of the Agra monument.[3] Externally, the architecture is wholly Muhammadan, but Hindu corbelling and horizontal architraves are used in all the inner doorways, as at Jaunpur. The style may be described as intermediate between the austerity of the Tughlak buildings and the feminine grace of Shahjahan's masterpiece. Plate 166A may suffice to give a good notion of the merits of this admirable style. The plan is octagonal, and coloured glazed tiles were used for decoration. Both the octagonal form and the use of glazed tiles were importations from Persia.[4]

Babar's buildings.

Babar, the versatile founder of the Mughal dynasty, was an active builder during his brief and stormy Indian reign of five years (1526-31). Holding a poor opinion of all Indian products, he summoned from Constantinople pupils of the celebrated architect Sinan, an Albanian officer on the staff of the Janis-

[1] R. F. Chisholm, F.R.I.B.A., F.S.A., in *J. Roy. Soc. of Arts*, Jan. 1911, p. 173.

[2] For examples of Tatta tiles see Cousins, *Scinde Tiles*.

[3] Cunningham, *A. S. Rep.*, vol. xi, pp. 133, 137.

[4] Octagonal memorial mosque of the fourteenth century at Sultaniyah in Persia (Saladin, *Manuel d'Art musulman*, tome I, Fig. 267).

saries, who had planned hundreds of important buildings in the Ottoman empire.[1] Out of the numerous edifices erected by these foreigners to Babar's order at Agra, Delhi, Kabul, and other places, only two are now visible, namely, the large mosque in the Kabul Bagh, Panipat, built after the great victory of 1526, and the *Jami Masjid* at Sambhal in Rohilkhand, bearing the same date (A.H. 933). The Panipat building is said to be still in fair condition. The Sambhal mosque has a remarkable ovoid dome.[2] Although the Indian buildings are much more Persian than Ottoman in style, there is some reason for thinking that the grandeur of the proportions of the existing monuments in Northern India and Bijapur may be partly due to the teaching of the school of Sinan.

Humayun's buildings.

Babar's accomplished son and successor, Humayun, the rival and opponent of Sher Shah, found time in the midst of his unceasing wars to do some building. But most of his works have been destroyed, and, as in his father's case, only two are known to have survived, namely, a ruinous mosque near Agra, and one much better preserved at Fathabad in the Hissar District, Panjab, which is decorated in the Persian manner with enamelled tiles.[3] The buildings of Babar and Humayun are purely foreign in decoration.

Akbar's Hindu leaning.

Akbar's strong liking for Hindu ways induced him to revert to Hindu styles of decoration, and many of the buildings erected during his long reign (1556-1605) are more Hindu than Muslim. A conspicuous instance of such reversion is afforded by the well-known palace in the Agra Fort, commonly called the *Jahangiri Mahal*, which really dates from Akbar's time and might have been built for a Hindu Raja.[4] The other buildings of Akbar in the Fort were demolished by Shahjahan.

Tomb of Humayun.

The splendid mausoleum of Humayun, near Delhi, erected early in Akbar's reign, while distinctly Persian in style, is differentiated by the free use of white marble, a material little employed in Persia, and by the abstinence from coloured tile decoration so much favoured by the architects of that country. The building (Plate 165 B) is of special interest as being to some extent the model of the inimitable 'Taj'. The dome is built entirely of white marble, the rest of the masonry being in red sandstone, with inlaid ornaments of white marble. The four corner cupolas and the narrow-necked dome now make their first appearance in India.[5]

The 'Buland Darwaza'.

Space fails to enumerate even in the most summary fashion the architectural marvels of Akbar's palace-city of Fatehpur Sikri, begun in 1569, finished fifteen years later, and practically abandoned after its founder's death in 1605.[6] That wondrous city bears in every part the impress of Akbar's tact

[1] Saladin, *op. cit.*, pp. 509, 561, with reference to Montani, *Architecture ottomane*.

[2] Cunningham, *A. S. Rep.*, vol. xii, p. 26; E. W. Smith, *Akbar's Tomb*, p. 4, editor's note.

[3] The ruinous mosque at Kachpura opposite Agra is described by Carlleyle, in Cunningham, *A. S. Rep.*, vol. iv, p. 100; and by Moin-ud-din, *History of the Taj*, p. 111. It is dated A.H. 937=A.D. 1530-1. The Fathabad mosque is a massive, well-proportioned building with domes rather more than hemispherical, built to the order of Humayun about 1540 or 1541, when he was on his way to Sind (Garrick, in Cunningham, *A. S. Rep.*, vol. xxiii, p. 12, Pls. III, IV).

[4] *Ann. Rep. A. S., India*, 1902-3, p. 62; and 1903-4, p. 170.

[5] Cunningham, *A. S. Rep.*, vol. i, p. 224. Mr. Chisholm points out that in both the Tomb of Humayun and the Taj the small corner domes are much earlier in style than the main dome and façade.

[6] From 1569 to 1584 Fatehpur Sikri was the principal residence of the Court. From 1585 to 1598 Lahore was the capital of Akbar, who moved to Agra in the latter year, but continued to prefer Fatehpur Sikri as a residence until his death. The regular issue of coins from the Fatehpur mint (*Darus-sultanat*) continued only until A.D. 1581 (A.H. 989). No more is heard of the mint until A.D. 1628-9 (A.H. 1038), the first year of Shahjahan, when one coin is known to have been struck there (Wright, *Cat. Coins in I. M.*, vol. iii, p. xlvii).

A. A Teacher. Pitt-Rivers Museum, Oxford.

B. The Bodhisattva Manjusri. Pitt-Rivers Museum.

C. The goddess Sarasvati Ukhtomskij Collection.

D. Tsong-Kapa. Pitt-Rivers Museum.

(By Courtesy of Prof. Grünwedel)

BRONZE IMAGES OF TIBETAN DEITIES AND SAINTS. COPPER CASTINGS. TIBETAN

PLATE 157

A. Great Mosque at Ajmer. (*c.* 1205 A.D.)

B. Sultan Ghari, Delhi. (A.D. 1231)

and genius, and justifies the courtly phrase of his biographer, who declares that 'His Majesty plans splendid edifices, and dresses the work of his mind and heart in the garments of stone and clay'. The fullest possible details will be found in the four well-illustrated quarto volumes devoted to the subject by the late Mr. E. W. Smith, a work not easily to be matched. But a few words must be devoted to the southern gateway of the great mosque, known as the *Buland Darwaza*, or Lofty Portal, a name justified by the fact that it is the highest of Indian gateways, and among the largest in the world. The height to the summit of the finials from the pavement at the top of the stairs is 134 feet, and reckoned from the road at the foot of the stairs is 176 feet. The structure is a magnificent example of the Persian form of gateway, deriving its dignity from the great semi-dome in which the actual doors are inset—an arrangement extolled by Fergusson. The mosque, purporting to be copied from one at Mecca, was built in 1571. The *Buland Darwaza* (Plate 166B) was added in 1601-2 as a triumphal arch to commemorate Akbar's conquest of Khandesh, and probably replaced a more ordinary edifice consonant with the other entrances. It may be taken as typical of the innumerable similar gateways on a smaller scale which characterize the Mughal style. It is the most beautiful specimen of the second type of Indo-Persian architecture, that in which marble is freely intermixed with sandstone, which was used alone in the earlier style exemplified by the Jahangir Mahal.

Jahangir: Mausoleum of Akbar.

The extant contributions of the Emperor Jahangir (1605-27) to[1] Indo-Persian architecture, although important, are not very numerous. The design of the magnificent mausoleum of Akbar at Sikandra near Agra, in which Jahangir personally had an undefined share, is exceptional. The building, completed in 1612 (A.H. 1021), is said by one Muslim writer to have been under construction for twenty years, having been begun, according to custom, by the sovereign whose remains were to find their resting-place within it. But the inscriptions and the *Memoirs* of Jahangir seem to prove that it was wholly erected under his orders between 1605 and 1612.[2] It is composed of five square terraces, diminishing as they ascend, and the only edifice of the period at all resembling it is Akbar's five-storied pavilion, or *Panch-Mahal*, at Fatehpur Sikri. In all oriental houses and palaces the roof plays a part of great importance in daily life. From the earliest times it was used as an additional room, being covered by awnings and screened in. These hangings, which were beautifully dyed and embroidered, are indispensible in Mughal architectural planning, being hung from pillar to pillar or supported on finely worked staffs. The design of Akbar's and Itimad-ud-daula's tombs is a translation into stone of a tent-pavilion on the open roof, altogether in keeping with the Mughal conception of garden-tombs.

Tomb of Itimad-ud-daula.

Another famous building of Jahangir's reign, the tomb of Itimad-ud-daula, near Agra, finished in or about 1628 by that nobleman's daughter, the Empress Nurjahan, is almost equally exceptional in other ways. The material is wholly white marble, enriched with *pietra dura* patterns in semi-precious stones, and equal to or surpassing in splendour the finest work of the kind executed in Shahjahan's reign. Although the architectural design does not wholly satisfy expert critics, there can be no question that the structure

[1] Jahangir died in Oct. 1627, but Shahjahan was not able to ascend the throne formally until Feb. 1628.

[2] *Ann. Rep. A. S., India*, 1903-4, p. 19.

possesses rare beauty (Plate 168A).

The buildings of Shahjahan.

Passing by other notable buildings of Jahangir's reign at Lahore and elsewhere, we come to the reign of his son Shahjahan (1627-58), during which the Indo-Persian style, by universal consent, attained supreme beauty in the Taj Mahal (1632-53) (Plate 167), the Moti Masjid, or *Pearl Mosque* at Agra (1646-53) (Plate 168B), and the palace at Delhi (Plate 169A), begun in 1638.[1] It is possible only to indicate briefly the general character of Shahjahan's modification of Indo-Persian architecture, give a few typical illustrations, and note certain points of special interest.

Characteristics of the style.

The style is essentially Persian, but with an undefinable difference of expression, and sharply distinguished from the fashions of Isfahan as well as those of Constantinople by the lavish use of white marble, carved and fretted, and supplemented by sumptuous decoration in *pietra dura* inlay and other enrichments. Coloured tiles were rarely used. Open-work tracery of incomparable beauty is a marked feature, and spacious grandeur of design is successfully combined with feminine elegance. It is, indeed, impossible to exaggerate descriptions of the magnificence of the Delhi palace, nor is there any need to insist on the unearthly loveliness of the Taj, the noblest monument ever erected to man or woman:—

> 'Not architecture! as all others are,
> But the proud passion of an Emperor's love,
> Wrought into living stone, which gleams and soars
> With body of beauty shrining soul and thought.'[2]

The chaste simplicity of the Moti Masjid commands admiration equally ungrudging. '*Verily*,' says the inscription on its walls, '*it is an exalted palace of Paradise made of a single resplendent pearl, because, since the beginning of the population of this world, no mosque pure and entirely of marble has appeared as its equal, nor since the creation of the universe, any place of worship, wholly bright and polished has come to view to rival it*.' That testimony is true. After many years there is nothing which I remember more distinctly or with greater pleasure than the pearly colonnades of this unequalled mosque.

The Taj group of buildings.

The immense enclosed complex of buildings and gardens familiarly designated as 'the Taj', comprises the central mausoleum, the mosque on the west, a corresponding (*jawab*) edifice on the east, intended as a place of assembly for the congregation of the mosque and the persons invited to the annual commemoration services; huge gateways with many chambers, massive enclosing walls, and various minor structures, some of which have been ruined. The purpose of all was to honour the memory of Shahjahan's well-beloved wife, the Empress Arjumand Banu Begam, whose title *Mumtaz Mahal* ('The Chosen One of the Palace') has been corrupted into *Taj*. Outside the enclosure a considerable town grew up, named Mumtazabad, now represented by Tajganj. The villas and tombs of the great nobles and many other buildings, few of which remain, once crowded the approaches and surrounding space.

Time occupied in construction.

The Empress died in childbirth, on 17 June 1631 N.S. (17 *Zu'l Q'adah*, A.H. 1040), while in camp at Burhanpur in the Deccan, where her remains rested for six months. They were then conveyed to Agra, and the wondrous tomb destined to give her immortal fame was begun early in A.D. 1632, corresponding to the fifth year of Shahjahan's reign. When the plans had been

[1] Ibid., p. 184.

[2] Sir Edwin Arnold.

A. The Kutb Minar, Delhi. (Early 13th Century A.D.)

B. Close-up of the Kutb Minar, Delhi.
(Photo : A. L. Syed)

PLATE 159

A. Arch of the Great Mosque, Ajmer. (A.D. 1200-1235)

B. Arches of the Kutb Mosque, showing the Iron Pillar.

A. Gateway of Ala-ud-din Khalji, Delhi. (A.D. 1310)
(Photo: Indian Museum, Calcutta)

B. Tomb of Tughlak Shah, Tughlakabad, Old Delhi. (A.D. 1325)

A. Main entrance of Ataladevi Mosque, Jaunpur. (A.D. 1408).

(From Führer and Smith, *The Sharqi Architecture of Jaunpur*)

B. Mosque of Mahafiz Khan, Ahmadabad. (*c.* 1492 A.D.).

(From Burgess, *A.S.R. Western India*, Vol. VII)

PLATE 162

settled to the Emperor's satisfaction work was pushed on with eagerness, some 20,000 men being employed daily.[1] On 6 February 1643 N.S. (17 *Zu'l Q'adah*, A.H. 1052), the anniversary of the death of the Empress, the annual funeral ceremony was celebrated by the bereaved husband at the new mausoleum which was then regarded as complete. But the construction of the subsidiary buildings continued for many years longer. The latest inscription, one on the entrance gateway, was set up in A.D. 1647 (A.H. 1057). We know, however, from Tavernier, who witnessed both the commencement and completion of the buildings, that operations did not cease finally until 1653, nearly twenty-two years after they had begun. The general superintendence was entrusted to Mukramat Khan and Mir Abdul Karim.

Cost.

The statements of cost recorded by writers in Persian vary enormously. The *Badshah namah* gives Rs. 50,00,000 (50 lakhs) as the cost of the mausoleum itself. The highest estimate of the cost of the whole amounts to the huge sum of Rs. 411,48,826: 7: 6 (411 lakhs, 48 thousand, 826 rupees, seven annas, six pies), as stated with curious minuteness, equivalent, at the rate of 2*s.* 3*d.* to the rupee, in round numbers to four and a half million pounds sterling. Intermediate estimates put the expense at three millions sterling, said to have been about the sum which Shahjahan resolved to spend. If the full value of materials be included, the highest figure is not excessive, and may be considered as approximately correct. Tavernier notes that the expense was increased enormously by the necessity of using brick scaffolding and centring. Such lavish expenditure on a single monument and its adjuncts is not likely to be repeated anywhere in the world. Shahjahan planned for himself a mausoleum of equal magnificence to be erected on the opposite side of the river and united with the Taj by a marble bridge, but his family troubles prevented the realization of this gigantic conception, and so he sleeps beside the 'Lady of the Taj'. 'They were lovely and pleasant in their lives and in their death they were not divided.'[2]

Question as to identity of the architect.

The foregoing details, rarely to be found stated with accuracy, help us to realize the grandiose scale on which the whole composition known collectively as 'the Taj' was designed, and the absolute disregard of cost in realizing the design. Much of the credit for the vastness of the scale must be given to Shahjahan himself, who, of course, is solely responsible for sanctioning the unparalleled expense. But nobody supposes that the Emperor was his own architect, and much interest attaches to the question, 'Who was the architect by whom this noblest of monuments was designed, and to what nation did he belong?' The controversy on the subject, lately revived, excites some heat in the disputants. I approach it simply as a case in which evidence should be weighed and appraised impartially. Sleeman's notion that Austin de

[1] The number rests on Tavernier's excellent authority. According to Manrique the staff of 'maestros, officiales, y obreros (workman)' numbered only about 1,000 in 1640 (*Itinerario*, ed. 1649, chap. lx, p. 352). No doubt the numbers varied much from time to time.

[2] Correct dates have been kindly supplied by Wm. Irvine, Esq., I. C. S. Ret. Those in the books are usually wrong. For the value of the rupee see Tavernier, *Travels in India*, transl. V. Ball, vol. i, 413, and Manrique (chap. lx) 'una rupia medio peso Español'; and for time of completion, Tavernier, p. 110. The explanation of the practical purpose of the *jawab* building is due to S. Muhammad Latif, *Agra, Historical and Descriptive*, p. 113. From the artistic point of view, the structure was essential to the perfect symmetry aimed at by the architect. The highest estimate of the cost is given in Anderson's translation of one of the Persian MSS., now No. II in Or. 2030, B. M. Much of the more costly material was presented by tributary princes, and its value probably was excluded from the lower estimates. Mr. Chisholm is mistaken in believing that 'these domes seem to have been built without centres' (*J. Roy. Soc. Arts*, Jan. 1911, p. 173). He overlooked Tavernier's statement.

Bordeaux, a skilled French engineer and craftsman employed by Shahjahan, was the architect, and identical with the *Master* (*Ustad*) *Isa* (*Jesus*), also called, more correctly, *Muhammad Isa Effendi*, certainly is erroneous,[1] and his statement, first published in 1844, seems to be the sole foundation for the current assertions about the connexion of Austin with the Taj. Balfour's *Cyclopaedia of India* (3rd ed., 1885) boldly asserts that 'Austin de Bourdeaux [was] an artist who erected the Taj at Agra'. For that assertion I believe that Sleeman's loose guessing is the only authority. The note recently printed by Dr. Burgess stating that the Taj was 'most probably designed by Ali Mardan Khan, a Persian refugee', is opposed to the evidence of the Persian *History of The Taj*, and I do not know on what grounds it is based.[2]

Ustad Isa the architect according to Persian authorities.

The Persian MSS. purporting to give the history of the Taj, the names of the chief artists and artificers, and the cost of the buildings, appear to exhibit many discrepancies in details, but to agree in stating that the chief designer and draughtsman was 'Ustad (or Master) Isa', otherwise called Muhammad Isa Effendi, who drew a salary of Rs. 1,000 a month, and was assisted by his son, Muhammad Sharif. The Agra copy, in the possession of the hereditary custodians of the monument, says that he came from 'Rum', interpreted to mean Turkey or Constantinople, and that his son came from Samarkand. Other copies are alleged to assert that the Ustad came from Shiraz in Persia. The title 'Effendi' sometimes given to him is an Ottoman one. No details of his life seem to be on record.

Geronimo Veroneo the architect according to Manrique.

The rival statement is the categorical assertion made by Father Sebastian Manrique, a Spanish Augustinian friar, Visitor of his order in the East, that the architect was a Venetian named Geronimo Veroneo, who drew a large salary from Shahjahan. Manrique's words, as translated by Father Hosten, S.J., are:

> 'The architect of those structures was a Venetian, named Jerome Veroneo, who went to those parts in the ships from Portugal, and died in the city of Laor [Lahore] shortly before my arrival. Emperor Corrombo [=*Khurram*=*Shahjahan*] gave him large salaries; but it is thought that he profited so badly by them that when he died, they say Father Joseph de Castro, of the [Jesuit] Society, a Lombard by birth, found on him much less than was imagined.'

The author then proceeds to give merely as current gossip (*fama velocissima*) the story of Geronimo Veroneo's supposed interview with Shahjahan. The positive assertion quoted above seems to be made of his own knowledge, and not as hearsay.[3] I attach little importance to the hearsay gossip, but much to the categorical allegation of fact.

[1] Sleeman, *Rambles and Recollections*, ed. V. A. Smith, vol. i, p. 385. The MS. used by Anderson (*Calcutta Rev.*, 1873, p. 237) alleges that artist No. 1, unnamed, 'a rare plan-drawer and artist', was a Christian, as was also Muhammad Sharif. Sleeman appears to have used a similar document, and agrees with the custodian's MS. in stating that Muhammad Sharif was the son of No. 1, whom Sleeman names as Ustad Isa. The name Isa may have suggested the notion that the Ustad was a Christian (*Isahi*). If 'Ustad Isa' and Muhammad Sharif really were Christians, one of the objections urged against Father Manrique's statement is removed.

[2] Fergusson, *Hist. of Indian and E. Archit.*, 2nd ed., p. 306 note. Ali Mardan Khan, a famous engineer in Shahjahan's service, constructed or repaired canals, and laid out the Shalamar gardens at Lahore (see Index, s.v. 'Ali Mardan Khan', *Imp. Gaz.* 1908).

[3] The Spanish text is: 'El Architeto destas fabricas fue un Veneciano por nombre Geronimo Veroneo que passò a aquellas partes en las naves de Portugal, y murio en la Ciudad de Laòr poco tiempo antes de mia llegada. A este dava el Corrombo Emperador grandes salarios: mas supose aprovechar tan mal dellos, que quando murio, dizan que le hallara el Padre Joseph de Castro de la Compañia, y de nacion Lombardo, muy menos de lo que si imaginava' (*Itinerario de las Missiones que hizo el Padre F. Sebastian Manrique*, p. 352; ed. Roma, 1649). A reprint with an altered title-page appeared at Rome in 1653. Both impressions are in the British Museum. The Bodleian possesses only the earlier one, which alone I have consulted,

A. Gateway of Small Golden (Eunuch's) Mosque, Gaur. (A.D. 1493 - 1519).
(From Ravenshaw, *Gaur, Its Ruins and Inscriptions*)

B. Tomb of Abu Turab, Ahmadabad.
(From Burgess, *A. S. R. Western India*, Vol. VIII)

PLATE 163

A. Tomb in Golkonda style at Bijapur.
(From Fergusson and Taylor, *Architecture of Bijapoor*)

B. Ibrahim Rauza, Bijapur ; front view.
(*c.* 1615 A.D.)

PLATE 164

The credibility of Father Manrique.

Father Manrique spent about a month at Agra in December 1640 and January 1641, and thence travelled to Lahore where he met Father de Castro. He thus had ample opportunities of learning facts as well as gossip, and, moreover, he was on friendly terms with the greatest of the Muhammadan nobles Asaf Khan, 'the ancient and only protector of the priests', and father of the Lady of the Taj, who gave him 'a goodly alms'. Geronimo Veroneo died at Lahore as stated, but was buried at Agra, some four hundred miles distant, where his tomb, dated A.D. 1640, still exists. Before his death he had spent money, presumably a considerable sum, to ransom Christians from prison. Father Manrique's accuracy is thus confirmed on several points, and the fact that Veroneo's body was removed to Agra for burial indicates that he must have been a person of considerable importance and specially connected with Agra.

I have no doubt that the good Father's positive assertion that Veroneo was the architect of the Taj was made in perfect good faith, and, indeed, nobody impugns his personal veracity. But it is argued that he must have been misinformed. The most weighty objection raised is that the Taj unquestionably is Asiatic in style, a development from the tomb of Humayun, and that even in the decoration, except perhaps the technique, as distinguished from the designs of the *pietra dura* inlay, there is little trace of European influence. The objection, although deserving of attention, is not conclusive, because, so far as I can see, there is no reason why a seventeenth-century Venetian of genius, aided by skilled Asiatic technical advisers, should have been unwilling or unable to design a group of buildings on Asiatic lines, in accordance with a general idea prescribed by Shahjahan, who must have known and declared what he wanted. M. Saladin, writing without reference to or apparent knowledge of the documentary evidence, simply in his capacity of architectural expert, expresses the opinion that 'the hand of a European architect has traced the exact symmetries and the outlines, perhaps too regular, of the monument'; adding that the decoration combines Florentine elegance with Oriental richness, while the breadth and symmetry of the composition give the design the appearance almost of a classical conception.[1]

Conclusion.

On the whole, after considering all the arguments, including that drawn from the silence of other authors, I do not see any reason sufficient to discredit the positive assertion of Father Manrique, published in 1649 before the work on the Taj buildings was completed. It is not inconsistent with the Persian authorities. I accept their evidence as proving that *Ustad Isa*,[2] whether he was a Turk or a Persian, was the chief architect during the later stages of the construction; and it is easy to understand that when the history of the monument was being put on record no Muhammadan writer would have cared to recall the leading part taken by a long-deceased Christian European in framing the original design. Thus the matter stands. I abide by the opinion expressed by me in 1893 that 'the incomparable Taj is the product of a combination of European and Asiatic genius'. It should be observed that no authority ascribes the design to an Indian

[1] '*Le Tadj-Mahal à Agra.*—Il semble que la main d'un architecte européen a tracé les symétries exactes et les profils peut-être trop réguliers de ce monument . . . cet art qui, en effet, allie l'élégance florentine à la richesse orientale' (*Manuel d'Art Musulman*, tome i, p. 571). 'Le Tadj n'est que le centre de la composition . . . On voit donc que, par l'ampleur de la composition et par la symétrie, ce plan est presque de conception classique' (Ibid., p. 575). M. Saladin's wide experience of Muslim art in countries where it comes in contact with that of Europe entitles his critical opinions to respectful consideration.

[2] The name Ustad Isa commonly used is incorrect. The fuller form, Muhammad Isa, really means 'Muhammad the son of Isa', as Professor Margoliouth points out.

architect. The credit for it belongs to either or both of two foreigners, one a Venetian, the other most probably a Turk (A 1). The lively interest felt in the question of the authorship of the building, which may fairly claim to be the most beautiful in the world, will, I trust, be considered justification sufficient for this long, although much condensed, disquisition on the subject.[1]

Architecture of Aurangzeb's reign; and afterwards.

The long and unhappy reign of Aurangzeb Alamgir (1659–1707)[2] was marked by a rapid decline in art, including architecture. The emperor was more eager to throw down Hindu temples than to construct great edifices of his own. Some few buildings of his time, however, are not without merit ; for instance, the tall minarets of the mosque which he caused to be erected at Benares on the site of the holiest temple are graceful objects well known to all travellers in India. The principal mosque at Lahore (1674), almost a copy of the great mosque at Delhi, but inferior to that noble building, is described by Fergusson as being 'the latest specimen of the Mughal architectural style'. The emperor's own tomb at Khuldabad near Aurangabad in the Deccan is insignificant. The buildings in Persian style of Aurangzeb's age, being merely examples of growing deterioration, are not worth detailed study or illustration. The tomb of Nawab Safdar Jang of Oudh near Delhi (1756), a passable copy of the mausoleum of Humayun, is marred by wretched plaster decoration in the interior. The shoddy buildings of the Nawab Vazirs at Lucknow are pretentious abominations.

Composite style.

In many places modern architects have effected a graceful compromise between the Hindu and Muhammadan styles by combining Persian domes with Bengali bent cornices and Hindu or half-Hindu columns. Excellent examples of this pretty though feeble style, as used for both civil and religious buildings, are to be seen at Mathura and in hundreds of other localities. It is quite impossible to tell merely from inspection of the architecture whether a building is intended for Muslim or Hindu use. The modern part of the ancient shrine of Sayyid Salar in Northern Oudh (Plate 169B) is a good example of the style in its more Muhammadan form.

Thus the story of Indo-Muhammadan architecture ends, as it began, with the subjection of foreign innovations to the irresistible pressure of native taste and methods.

[1] The principal Persian authorities, as enumerated by by Mr. Wm. Irvine, are (1) the contemporary *Badshah namah* by Abd-ul-hamid, Lahori (*Bibl. Ind.*, 2 vols., Calcutta, 1868; vol. ii, pp. 322-31); (2) *Aml-i-Salih*, by Muhammad Salih, Lahore (A.H. 1052), perhaps copied from No. 1; (3) a group of MSS., mostly anonymous, purporting to give the history of the Taj. One copy at least is in the hands of the custodians at Agra, and another is in the Imperial Library, Calcutta. The MSS. in the B. M. with similar contents are Addl. 8910 (62 foll.), Or. 194 (94 foll.), Or. 195 (55 foll.)—all in Rieu, *Catal.*, p. 430: Or. 2030, containing two MSS., viz. (1) by Manik Chand, foll. 1-30, and (2) notice of the Taj Mahall, foll. 32-81, nearly identical with Addl. 8910. This is the version partly translated by Capt. Anderson in *Calc. Review*, vol. lvii (1873), pp. 233-7. The above are on p. 958*b* of Rieu, *Catal.* Or. 2031 (Rieu, p. 1044*a*), No. IV, foll. 148-226 is another copy of Manik Chand's account.

The Agra version, used and parly translated by Sleeman, S. Muhammad Latif (*Agra, Historical and Descriptive*, Calcutta, 1896) and Muhammad Moin-ud-din (*History of the Taj*, Agra, 1905) seems to exist in more than one form. F. Manrique's account is discredited by the two Muhammadan writers named, as well as by Mr. E. B. Havell, 'The Taj and its Designers' (*Nineteenth Century and After*, June 1903; reprinted in *Essays on Indian Art, Etc.*, Madras, n. d.), and by Sir J. Marshall in *Ann. Rep. Arch. S., India*, 1904-5, pp. 1-3. Father Hosten, S.J., stoutly defends Manrique in his article, 'Who Planned the Taj?' (*J. and Proc. A. S. B.*, N. S. vol. vi (1910), pp. 281-8). Mr. Keene also accepted his statement (*Turks in India*, pp. 251-5). Mr. Havell erroneously denounces the positive, contemporary evidence of the Spaniard Father Manrique as 'the old Anglo-Indian legend' (*J. Roy. Soc. Arts*, Jan. 1911, p. 180).

The question has not been thoroughly threshed out yet, the Persian MSS. especially requiring careful examination and comparison. Mr. Irvine has made a beginning at my request by examining the Manik Chand MSS., Or. 2030 and 2031. They are of no independent value as authorities, and the text of Manik Chand's late compilation in Or. 2031 is merely a copy of that in Or. 2030, made for the use of Sir H. Elliot.

[2] Shahjahan was deposed in 1658. Aurangzeb's formal accession took place in 1659.

NOTE TO CHAPTER THIRTEEN

Today no one seriously considers the claim of Geronimo Veroneo to be considered as the architect of the Taj. The concensus of opinion favours the theory that the architect was a Central Asian, Ustad Isa. But another claimant to this honour is the builder of the Red Fort. Whatever the truth be, on stylistic grounds a Central Asian architect would appear to be the most likely designer of this Mausoleum. There is no gainsaying the fact that it is a peerless monument. Certain intellectual foreign visitors regard it as fashionable to decry the Taj, while another idiosyncracy peculiar to this group is to regard Humayun's tomb as a much greater architectural achievement. It may be observed that despite the vehemence with which such opinions have been expressed the supreme beauty of the Taj has remained unimpaired. A 1

Chapter Fourteen

INDO-MUHAMMADAN DECORATIVE AND MINOR ARTS

Part I. COINS, GEMS, AND SEALS

Limitations of Musalman art.

MUHAMMADAN architecture, excluding the styles most deeply affected by Hindu influence, and in spite of infinite variety in detail, presents, as we have seen in the last chapter, a character of general uniformity throughout the Muslim world, partly due to the practically universal use of pointed arches and domes, and partly to the free interchange of architects between different countries, resulting in the frequent imitation of foreign models. Muhammadan decorative art presents a similarly uniform character by reason chiefly of the Koranic prohibition of images, which, although not universally respected, was observed in all ages and countries sufficiently to impose narrow limits on the field open to the creative artist. The orthodox Muslim decorator has found himself in practice constrained to restrict his invention to the dexterous use of calligraphy, geometrical patterns, and floral devices. However varied in detail the application of those elements may be, the effect is necessarily flat and somewhat monotonous.

Elements of Musalman decoration.

Scope of this chapter.

In this chapter a few pages will be devoted to the art of calligraphy as displayed in coinage, to the rare figure types on coins and gems, and to the exceptional attempts at stone sculpture in the round or in high relief. They will be followed by a condensed account of the leading forms of Musalman architectural decoration arranged under the heads of *Calligraphy* and *Decorative Reliefs*, *Lattices*, *Inlay* and *Mosaic* and *Enamelled Tiles*. No attempt will be made to follow the Muhammadan decorator in his treatment of minor objects of luxury, which is essentially the same as that of architectural ornament. Even in his floral designs the tendency of the Muslim artist is in favour of a formal, over-symmetrical conventionalism, calculated to harmonize with his favourite geometrical patterns. Akbar's taste inclined to a more interesting naturalism, as displayed in the exquisite ornament on his cenotaph executed a few years after his death, and designed in his spirit. The art of painting, in the exercise of which greater liberty was assumed, will be discussed at considerable length in the concluding chapter.

Transitional Musalman coins with figure types.

It is a common error to suppose that the ancient Semitic prohibition of images, repeated in the Koran, invariably prevented Muhammadan artists from representing the forms of living creatures, real or imaginary. As a matter of fact, the prohibition, although respected as a rule, has been disregarded frequently in almost every Musalman country from the earliest ages of Islam to the present day, and especially in those countries, like Persia, where the *Shia* sect prevails. The introduction of figure types in many ancient Muhammadan coinages was due to the business necessity of maintaining for a time the forms of currency to which people had become accustomed. For example, when the Sassanian dynasty of Persia fell in the seventh century the newly appointed Arab governors continued to issue coins in the familiar national form with the king's head, distinguished from the native issues merely by the insertion of Arabic legends in minute characters. In India Muhammad of Ghor was obliged to accept a similar compromise and even to issue coins bearing the image of a Hindu goddess.

Orthodox calligraphic coinage.

In most Muhammadan kingdoms such numismatic compromises with idolatry were only temporary, and the die-cutters of the Muslim sovereigns were ordinarily obliged to content themselves with calligraphic devices, on which much skill was

A. Gol Gumbaz, or tomb of Muhammad Adil Shah, Bijapur. (dec. A.D. 1660)

B. Tomb of Humayun, Delhi. *c.* 1560 A.D.

PLATE 165

A. Tomb of Sher Shah. Sahasram. Shahabad District, Bengal.

(*Copyright by Department of Archaeology, Government of India*)

B. The "Buland Darwaja" of Jam'i Mosque, Fatehpur Sikri. (A.D. 1601-2).

PLATE 166

lavished. The coins issued by Sultan Muhammad bin Tughlak of Delhi (A.D. 1324-51), who has been called 'the prince of moneyers', are exceptionally brilliant examples of calligraphic art. A specimen is shown in Plate 170, Fig. 1, and may be taken as a typical illustration of well-executed Muhamadan orthodox coinage.

Peculiar issues of Akbar.

Akbar, notwithstanding his scant respect for orthodoxy, submitted as a rule to Koranic restrictions in the types of his coinage, which exhibits many varieties of artistic ornamental writing. A highly elaborated specimen, a rupee struck at Agra, is shown in Plate 170, Fig. 5. On three occasions only did he permit himself the luxury of figure types, and the pieces struck on those three occasions are medals rather than ordinary current coins. A falcon (ibid., Fig. 2) commemorates the capture of Asirgarh, the strong fortress commanding the road to the Deccan. The *Brahmini* goose appears on an Agra coin (ibid., Fig. 4). Both birds are well designed and surrounded by pretty floral scrolls. A curious piece, exhibiting the figures of a crowned archer and a veiled lady (ibid., Fig. 3), is a memorial of the submission in A.H. 1013 (A.D. 1604-5) of the King of Bijapur, who gave his daughter in marriage to Prince Daniyal, Akbar's youngest son.

The freaks of Jahangir.

Jahangir, although officially a better Musalman than his father, was less orthodox in his coinage. He alone of all the Muhammadan sovereigns of India dared to put his own portrait on coins intended for circulation. He habitually disregarded the Prophet's prohibition of strong drink, and was not ashamed to show himself on the coinage holding a goblet of wine (ibid., Figs. 7, 8). He also indulged in the freak of issuing a coinage, both gold and silver, on which the months were indicated by pictorial symbols of the zodiacal signs, instead of by words or numbers (ibid., Figs. 9, 10). The figure of *Virgo* is a Europeanized angel.[1] The great bulk, however, of Jahangir's coinage is perfectly orthodox in form. His five-mohur piece (ibid., Fig. 6) is an excellent example of first-class calligraphy. Many of the coins of the later Mughal emperors are well executed, but the specimens given are enough to illustrate the general character of calligraphic dies.

Cameo with exploit of Shahjahan.

Muhammadan gems and seals with artistic devices other than calligraphic are necessarily extremely scarce. Mr. King, after referring to the rarity of cameos in purely Oriental style, mentions one conspicuous Muhammadan specimen:

> 'The most remarkable example of all in the Oriental class,' he writes, 'although of modern origin, came to my knowledge among the Webb gems (when sold by Christie and Manson in 1854), the subject being the feat performed by Shahjahan in cleaving asunder a lion which was mauling a courtier. The inscription consists of two parts [namely], "The portrait of the Second Sahib-Qiran, Shahjahan the victorious emperor", and the artist's signature "Made by Kan Atem" [*sic*, the reading is impossible]. The gem probably must be dated early in his reign, for it shows Shahjahan with a moustache but no beard. He wears a long double row of big pearls round his neck, and, as a pendant, a great convex gem, perhaps the Kohinoor.'[2]

The actual feat commemorated here was performed by Shahjahan, as Prince Khurram, when he rescued Anup Rai from the jaws of a tiger.[3]

Elephant cameo.

Another notable Indo-Muhammadan artistic gem which has come to my notice is the beautiful sardonyx cameo of the Mughal period, bought by Sir John Marshall some years ago and now in the Lahore Museum, which is 3.6 inches

[1] 'Mais les beaux chefs-d'oeuvre numismatiques sont les délicieuses monnaies d'or de Djehangir (1605-1628) frappées d'animaux et de personnages d'un dessin si parfait et d'un relief si précis et si vif' (Migeon, *Manuel d'art musulman*, tome ii, p. 164).

[2] *Ancient Gems and Rings*, London, 1872, pp. 314-16.

[3] *Memoirs of Jahangir*, transl. Rogers and Beveridge (1909), pp. 185-8.

broad and 3.3 high. It represents two elephants with riders, locking their tusks and trunks together apparently in combat.[1]

Part II SCULPTURE

Musalman sculpture in other countries.

Musalman representations of living forms in stone or stucco of various ages from Egypt, Mesopotamia, Asia Minor, and Spain have been published, and although rare in any one country, amount in the aggregate to a considerable number. A few bronze figures of a ruder kind, mostly dating from the time of the Fatimite sovereigns of Egypt and Syria (A.D. 969-1171), are also known.[2]

Indian examples, almost confined to elephants and riders.

In India the examples of sculpture in the round or in high relief, executed to the order of Muhammadan princes, but probably by the hands of Hindu artists, are extremely few; the most notable of which any remains exist being the elephants, sometimes with riders, set up at the gateways of fortresses, in continuance of Hindu custom. Nearly every stronghold of importance had its Elephant Gate (*Hathipol*). The portal of that name at Akbar's city of Fatehpur Sikri is still guarded by the mutilated figures of two colossal elephants, perched on supports 12½ feet high, whose trunks originally were interlocked across the entrance. Aurangzeb caused the heads to be knocked off. The elephants, being clumsily made up of large blocks of hewn stone laid in mortar and joined by iron cramps, are of no account as works of art.[3] Other statues, presumably of Hindu origin, which once guarded the Elephant Gates of Gwalior, Mandu, and other fortresses have been destroyed.

Elephants and riders at Agra Fort.

William Finch, the English traveller, who visited Agra early in the reign of Jahangir (1610), there saw 'a second gate, over which are two Rajaws in stone, who were slain in the King's Derbar before the King's eyes, for being overbold in speech, they selling their lives bravely, in remembrance of which they are heere placed'. From a note appended by Purchas, it would seem that the two 'Rajaws' were mounted on elephants. The note states :—

> 'It is said that they were two Brothers, Resboots, Tutors to a Prince, their nephew, whom the King demanded of them. They refused, and were committed ; but drew on the Officers, slew twelve, and at last, by multitudes oppressing, were slain, and here have Elephants of stone and themselves figured.'[4]

Mr. Keene is of opinion that 'the allusion probably is to the three sons of Akhiraj, son of Akbar's brother-in-law, Raja Bhagwan Das of Jaipur, killed in a fight arising out of a tumult caused by themselves in the Palace'.[5] Whoever the originals may have been, Finch's testimony is clear that two statues of men over one of the gates of the Agra Fort were erected by order of either Akbar or Jahangir, and Purchas's note indicates that they were mounted on elephants.

Current errors about Delhi statues.

The similar, but wholly distinct, statues of elephants with riders which formerly stood at the Delhi Gate of the Delhi Fort, and of which fragments still exist, have been the subject of so much discussion and misunderstanding that it is desirable to state the facts as recently elucidated by the officers of the Archaeological Survey. The statements in all the ordinary books of reference are erroneous. The Delhi groups certainly possessed considerable merit as works of art,

[1] *Ann. Rep. A. S., India*, 1905-6, p. 40, Fig. 1.

[2] Catalogued by Migeon, *Manuel d'art musulman*, tome ii, chaps. ii, vii.

[3] E. W. Smith, *Fathpur-Sikri*, Part III, p. 33, Pl. LV. Small elephants, poorly modelled, occur among the decorative sculptures of various Mughal buildings.

[4] *Hakluytus Posthumus or Purchas His Pilgrims*, in 20 volumes, MacLehose, Glasgow, MCMV, vol. iv, p. 72. Purchas does not cite any authority for his note.

[5] The incident, which occurred 28 Dec.1605, is described by Jahangir (*Memoirs of Jahangir*, transl. Rogers and Beveridge (1909), p. 29).

The Taj Mahal, Agra. (A.D. 1632-53)

PLATE 167

A. Tomb of Itimad-ud-daula, near Agra. (A.D. (1628).

B. The Moti Masjid, Agra. (A.D. 1646-53).

A. Diwan-i-Khas of Delhi Palace. (Begun A.D. 1638).

B. Shrine of Sayyid Salar, Bahraich.

PLATE 169

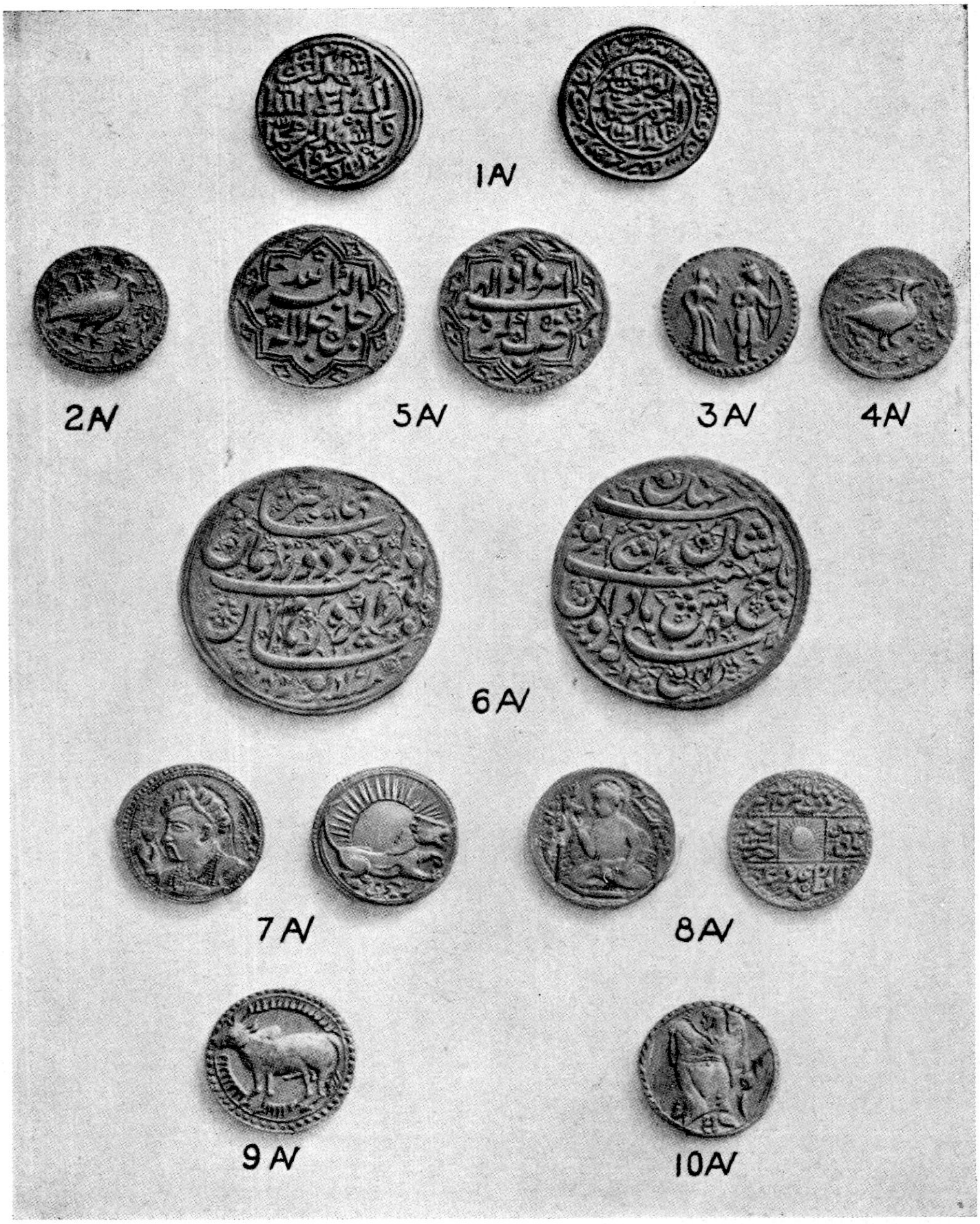

Indo-Muhammadan Coins. Fig. 1, Muhammad b. Tughlak. Fig. 2-5, Akbar. Fig. 6-10, Jahangir.
(From *British Museum Catalogue of Coins of Sultans of Delhi*)

and the riders at least must be counted as examples of sculpture executed to Musalman order.

But before going into the history of the much debated Delhi statues it is well to note that Jahangir, in the eleventh year of his reign, had caused life-size figures of the Rana of Chitor (Amar Singh) and his son Karan to be carved in marble and set up in the palace garden at Agra, below the window (*darshan jharokha*) where the Emperor made his daily public appearance.[1] This undoubted fact, recorded by Jahangir himself, is clear proof that the early Mughal emperors had no objection to life-size statues of men, and sometimes had them made. No trace has been found of the garden effigies, which appear to have been carved at Ajmer and thence sent to Agra.

Life-size statues in Agra palace garden.

The history of the Delhi groups may be summarized as follows:

In 1663, early in Aurangzeb's reign, Bernier saw and warmly admired the effigies of two elephants with riders which then stood at the Delhi Gate of the Delhi Fort. A few years later they were seen still in position by Thévenot. Subsequently they were broken up by order of Aurangzeb, and the fragments cast away. In 1863 the buried fragments were found, and after an interval some of them were pieced together and made into an absurd monster, which was set up in the Queen's Gardens, with a false inscription based on an erroneous guess of Alexander Cunningham. Lord Curzon expressed a desire to reconstruct the groups from the broken pieces, but it proved impossible to carry out his wishes. A skilled European artist, Mr. R. D. Mackenzie, was commissioned to make a new model. He did so, and his work is preserved in the Delhi Museum. Native sculptors were then instructed to make two elephants without riders from that model. They carried out their orders as well as they could, and their productions have been erected on the old pedestals.

History of the Delhi elephant groups.

The original elephants were made of black stone (? *marble*), and according to Sir John Marshall, who has examined the fragments carefully, were 'moulded with masterly skill and care' and 'true to nature'. They are believed to be of Hindu origin. The riders were carved in red sandstone, and 'their material, style, and technique establish beyond a doubt', according to the same authority, that they were 'carved by Mughal sculptors', a phrase presumably to be interpreted as meaning 'sculptors of the Mughal period'. The actual artists are more likely to have been Hindus than Musalmans. Whoever wrought them, the statues of the riders also seem to have been good, well-finished work.

Material.

Bernier was told that the riders represented the brothers Jaimall and Palta, the brave heroes of the defence of Chitor in 1568, who 'with their still braver mother, immortalized their names by the extraordinary resistance which they opposed to the celebrated Ecbar.... It is owing to this extraordinary devotion on their part that their enemies have thought them deserving of the statues here erected to their memory.' I see no reason to doubt the truth of this explanation, which is confirmed by the fact already noticed that Jahangir erected statues of two other chiefs of Chitor in the palace garden at Agra. But if the statues of the riders date from the time of either Akbar or Jahangir, they must have been placed originally somewhere else, and subsequently shifted by Shahjahan who built the Delhi (*Shahjahanabad*) Fort. There is, however, nothing in Bernier's statement to indicate that the statues were not ordered by Shahjahan, who

Identity of the riders.

[1] Beveridge, *J. R. A. S.*, 1909, p. 743; *Memoirs of Jahangir*, transl. Rogers and Beveridge (1909), p. 332.

may have been influenced by the precedent set at Agra by his father.[1]

Statue of a horse.

A life-size statue of a horse in red sandstone standing on the left-hand side of the Sikandra road about two miles from Agra, near the garden of Suraj Bhan, and opposite a masonry Muhammadan tomb, may be a work of Mughal age, but nothing definite about it is known, and no photograph is available. Mr. Beglar's conjecture that it may date from the time of Sikandar Lodi, the idol-breaking Sultan in the fifteenth century, is extremely improbable.[2]

Part III. CALLIGRAPHY AND DECORATIVE RELIEFS

Calligraphic decoration; Ajmer.

The Arabic alphabet in its various forms, as used for writing both the Arabic and Persian languages, is so well adapted for decorative purposes, that almost every Muhammadan building of importance is freely adorned with texts from

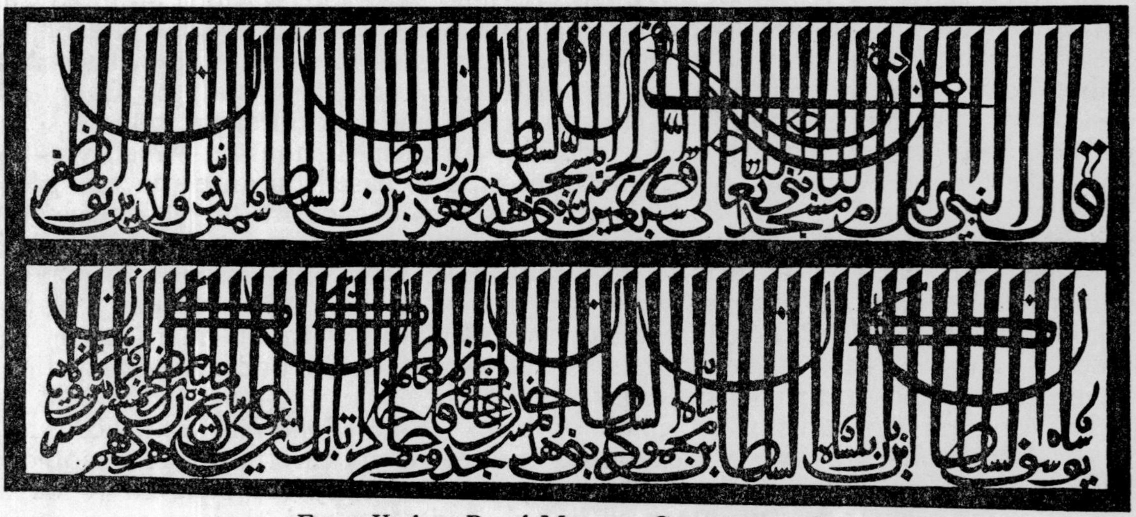

From Kadam Rasul Mosque, Gaur, A.D. 1480.

the Koran or other inscriptions arranged decoratively to form part of the architectural design, and often signed as the work of famous calligraphists. A good early Indian example of such calligraphic decoration is afforded by the great arch of the Ajmer mosque, where the outer line of writing is in the angular *Kufic* script, while the other lines are in a more rounded *Arabic* character. Later examples from Indo-Muhammadan buildings of all styles and ages might be multiplied indefinitely.

Relief decoration.

Musalman figure sculpture in the round has, as we have seen, slight artistic value and is interesting chiefly as a curiosity. But Musalman decorative sculpture in bas-relief applied to architecture may fairly claim on its merits to take at least equal rank with first-rate Italian work of the kind (Plate 171A, B and C).

'L'on ne saurait,' writes M. Migeon, 'trop recommander l'étude des arts de l'Islam aux artistes décorateurs et aux ouvriers d'art. Par la puissante beauté de ses formules, par sa fantaisie toujours régie par les lois les plus rigoureousement logiques, par le rayonnant éclat de la couleur, il n'est pas d'art qui offre plus de richesse décorative et plus de souveraine harmonie. Il renferme des germes féconds qui transplantés doivent fructifier à l'infini.'[3]

[1] For fuller details see *Ann. Rep. A. S., India*, 1905-6, pp. 33-42.

[2] Cunningham and Beglar, *A. S. Rep.*, vol. iv, p. 183; Latif, *Agra, Descriptive and Historical*, p. 183.

[3] *Manuel d'art musulman*, tome ii, p. 454.

A. From Jam'i Masjid, Fatehpur Sikri.

B. South end (*jalla jalalahu*) of Akbar's cenotaph.
(A, B, from E. W. Smith, *Fathpur Sikri*)

C. Panel in dado of "false Mosque" (*Jawab*) at the Taj, Agra.
(From Burgess, *Ann. Rep. A. S. India 1903-4*)

MUGHAL RELIEFS

PLATE 171

A.

B.

Panels from Sarangpur Mosque, Ahmadabad. *Cir.* A.D. 1500.
(From *A. S. Rep. Western India*)

PLATE 172

The validity of the concluding proposition may be doubted, and it seems to me by no means certain that the teaching of Musalman art to European craftsmen would produce satisfactory results. But, however that may be, M. Migeon's enthusiastic praise of the decorative quality of Muslim art generally may be accepted. The best Indian specimens, with which alone we are concerned at present, could not be surpassed as pure decoration. Among all the many varieties of Muhammadan decorative designs none are more agreeable than the best of those carved in relief on the Mughal buildings, from the time of Akbar to that of Shahjahan. The work of Akbar's time being more naturalistic, is more interesting than that of the later period, which is formally conventional, with a tendency to monotony.

Akbar's cenotaph.

The choicest Italian work does not surpass, if it equals, the superb carving on the white marble cenotaph of Akbar, which occupies the centre of the topmost story of his mausoleum at Sikandra.

'The two oblong sides and the top are adorned with the ninety-nine titles of the Creator in alto-relievo, set in delicate Arabic tracery (Plates XI and XV of *Akbar's Tomb*). The words *Allahu Akbar jalla jalalahu* are inscribed on the head and foot, set in panels surrounded by most beautiful and delicate floral ornamentation (ibid., Plates XVI, XVII ; *ante*, Plate XCIX, Fig. C). The carving, which is most exquisitely done, is in very low relief, and savours of Chinese workmanship. Amongst other flowers and plants portrayed one recognizes the lily, the almond, and the dahlia, all of which are found carved or painted upon Akbar's palace at Fatehpur-Sikri. In the left-hand corner of each of the panels, cloud-forms carved after a most distinctive Chinese type are noticeable. Similar cloud-forms are met with upon the dado panels in the Turkish Sultanah's house at Fatehpur-Sikri, and it is generally supposed that they were executed by Chinese workmen.'

But forms of a like kind so often appear in Persian art that it is unnecessary to assume the employment of Chinese craftsmen by Akbar.

'Small butterflies and insects flitting from flower to flower are carved upon the panels. Upon the top of the cenotaph a *qalam-dan* or pen-box is sculptured, signifying that the tomb is a man's, in distinction from a woman's, which is generally provided with the *takhti* or slate.'[1]

Relief at Taj.

Shahjahan's architects relied on inlay rather than relief sculpture for decoration; but at the Taj dados are very effectively adorned by conventional flowers cut on red sandstone in low relief (Plate 171C).

Ahmadabad reliefs.

Plate 172 illustrates the totally different style adopted in the much earlier Sarangpur mosque at Ahmadabad, erected about A.D. 1500. The tree motive is characteristic of Ahmadabad. The whole design is far more Hindu than Muhammadan.

Part IV. LATTICES

Hindu lattices.

Pierced stone screens or lattices used as windows were not unknown to Hindu architects, and were especially favoured by the builders of the highly decorated temples in the Mysore, Deccan, or Chalukyan style. At Pattadkal and in the Kailasa at Ellora beautiful lattices are to be found. At Belur there are twenty-eight such windows, all different. Some of these are pierced with merely conventional patterns, generally star-shaped, with bands of foliage between; others are interspersed with figures and mythological subjects.[2]

Musalman.

But the Musalman architects, who were more restricted than the Hindus in their liberty of decoration, developed the art of designing and executing stone lattices to a degree of perfection unknown to other schools. Endless variations

[1] *Akbar's Tomb, Sikandarah*, p. 15.

[2] Fergusson, *Hist. of Ind. and E. Archit.*, ed. 1910, vol. i, p. 440, with a bad illustration.

Inscribed principal *Mihrab*, Jam'i Mosque, Fatehpur-Sikri.

Vase motive panel, east false gate of Akbar's tomb.

of geometrical patterns, generally pleasing, although wearisome when examined in large numbers, are the most characteristic forms of Muhammadan lattice-work, which is seen at its best in the Gujarat (Ahmadabad) and Mughal buildings. The designs both in Gujarat and the earlier Mughal work have been often influenced by Hindu tradition. The Muslim artists used the lattice, not only for windows, but also for the panels of doors and for screens or railings round tombs with excellent effect.

Ahmadabad. The most beautiful traceries at Ahmadabad are to be seen in ten nearly semi-circular windows of Sidi Sayyad's mosque built about A.D. 1500, which may be fairly described as the most artistic stone lattice-work to be found anywhere in the world. I give two examples—one with geometrical patterns, and the other with the tree motive of Hindu origin, which should be compared with the modern carving in the Mysore Palace.

'It would be dificult,' Fergusson observes, 'to excel the skill with which the vegetable forms are conventionalized just to the extent required for the purpose. The equal spacing also of the subject by the three ordinary trees and four palms takes it out of the category of direct imitation of nature, and renders it sufficiently structural for its situation ; but perhaps the greatest skill is shown in the even manner in which the pattern is spread over the whole surface. There are some exquisite specimens of tracery in precious marbles at Agra and Delhi, but none quite equal to this.'[1]

The material of the Ahmadabad windows is Gujarat sandstone. (Plate 173.)

Mughal. The examples of well-designed and well-executed open-work tracery, chiefly in marble, at Agra and Delhi are so numerous that it is difficult to select typical specimens. But it is impossible to do better than to illustrate the style of Akbar's time from the tomb of Salim Chishti at Fatehpur-Sikri, built A.D. 1571. Plate 174A reproduces some of the marble screen-work enclosing the verandah, exhibiting an elegant and effective combination of a geometrical pattern with a conventionalized plant design.

The well-known railing round the cenotaph in the Taj may be taken as an unsurpassed example of the art in Shahjahan's time (Plate 175). The lines of the repeating pattern in this case are more like Italian renaissance than Asiatic work. According to Sir John Marshall this is the only case in which Italian influence can be discerned in the decorations of the Taj. However, it suggests a textile design translated into relief in stone, and considered as such is purely eastern.

Part V. INLAY AND MOSAIC

Marble inlay and mosaic. The device for breaking the monotony of a wide wall surface by inserting broad bands of white marble, as employed in the fourteenth century on the tomb of Tughlak Shah, and a few years earlier on Ala-ud-din's gateway, was commonly used in the Musalman art of Central Asia, Syria, and Egypt, and was freely adopted for Christian buildings in Italy. In Akbar's time this early severe form of decoration was supplemented by mosaics made up after the Roman and Byzantine fashion from small *tesserae*, which were combined in Persian geometrical patterns. The great mosque at Fatehpur-Sikri offers many examples. Sometimes the effect was enhanced by the insertion of little bits of blue or green enamel.

[1] *Hist. Ind. and E. Archit.*, ed. 1910, vol. ii, p. 236. The companion window (Pl. IV of Burgess) represents more distinctly 'the phenomenon, not unfamiliar to the Indian traveller, of a banyan-tree growing out of and around a palm, until in its snake-like entanglements of root and branch the banyan strangles its foster parent' (*Indian Art at Delhi*, p. 122, Pl. XXVII).

A.

B. Windows of Sidi Sayyid's Mosque, Ahmadabad. *Cir.* A.D. 1500.
(From *Arch. S. Western India*)

PLATE 173

A. Marble verandah screen, tomb of Salim Chisti, Fatehpur Sikri. A.D. 1571.
(From E. W. Smith, *Fathpur-Sikri*)

B. *Pietra dura* inlay on the cenotaph of the Taj.
(From *J. Indian Art*, Vol. I)

PLATE 174

Pietra dura.

A great innovation was effected by the introduction of the form of inlay known technically by the Italian name of *pietra dura*, which is composed of hard precious or semi-precious stones, such as onyx, jasper, carnelian, etc., cut into thin slices and neatly bedded in sockets prepared in the marble. This process, of which the best comparatively small specimens are to be seen at Florence, is capable of producing charming decorative effects when executed by capable workmen. In India, where expense was disregarded, it was applied to buildings on an enormous scale. The bold floral mosaics made of marble or red sandstone which appear on the south gateway of Akbar's tomb (1605-12) are nearly equivalent in effect to *pietra dura* work, but are not identical with it.[1] The Mughal kings evidently loved flowers, which are admirably treated in all forms of art patronized by them. The motives, are borrowed from Persian art. Nowhere else are the assimilating, transforming powers of the Indian genius more evident, both in the colour and the perfect freedom of the lines.

Earliest example.

The earliest Indian example of true *pietra dura*, according to Major Cole, is said to be that in the *Gol Mandal*, a domed pavilion in the small Jagmandir palace, at Udaipur in Rajputana, built in or about 1623 for Prince Khurram, afterwards the Emperor Shahjahan, while he was an exile from his father's court. The process is very extensively employed on the approximately contemporary mausoleum of Itimad-ud-daula near Agra, erected by his daughter Nurjahan after her father's death in A.D. 1621. The general effect of the *pietra dura* decoration is well shown (so far as it can be without colour) in Plate 176A, which represents one of the white marble turrets at the corners of the tomb. The older style of marble mosaic is seen in the lower panels.

Shahjahan's buildings.

Shahjahan (1627-58) wholly abandoned mosaic in favour of *pietra dura*, which probably he learned to admire while residing in the Jagmandir palace at Udaipur before his accession. The decoration is applied so lavishly in the Taj and the palaces of Agra and Delhi that volumes might be filled with reproductions of the designs, which are familiar to most people from modern copies. One plate will be enough to show their character (Plate 174B). They are remarkable for their restraint and good taste, and are superior to the similar work in the Delhi palace.

Origin of *pietra dura* work.

The Florentine *pietra dura* inlay, a revival of the ancient Roman *opus sectile*, first appears, according to Major Cole, in the Fabbrica Ducale built by Ferdinand I, Grand Duke of Tuscany, in 1558. The earliest certain Indian examples being considerably later in date and identical in technique, a strong presumption arises that the art must have been introduced into India from Italy. There is no doubt that the Mughal sovereigns freely entertained artists from Europe as well as from most parts of Asia. The presumption is not rebutted by the obvious fact that the designs of the Mughal work are essentially Asiatic, and in the main Persian, because the ordinary Indian practice is to transpose foreign importations, so to speak, into an Indian key. Persian designs were readily assimilated, but in the seventeenth century nobody in India cared much for outlandish European forms, or wanted to have them. Now, of course, things are different, and European forms are fashionable because the government is English. If Sir John Marshall was correctly informed when he wrote some years ago that '*pietra dura* work in a rougher and earlier stage than was hitherto known' had been discovered in the ruins of the Khalji mausoleum at Mandu in Central India, the presumption of Italian origin

[1] E. W. Smith, *Akbar's Tomb*, Pls. XLI, XLII.

would no longer hold good, because Mahmud Khalji, in whose honour the mausoleum seems to have been erected, died in 1475.[1] But the details given in an earlier report suggest that the remains found were those of marble mosaic, not of *pietra dura* inlay.

Modern *pietra dura* inlay.

The decline and fall of the Mughal empire during the eighteenth century necessarily involved the rapid decay of the arts which had ministered to the splendour of the imperial court. Among other arts that of producing *pietra dura* inlay had been almost forgotten until about 1830, when Dr. Murray, Inspector-General of Hospitals, induced the craftsmen to revive it for commercial purposes. Since that time it has been practised sufficiently to provide a constant supply of pretty trifles for European tourists and visitors, but nobody dreams of decorating a building in the fashion which appealed to Shahjahan the Magnificent. The plaques and other inlaid objects now made at Agra are too familiar to need illustration. A selection of first-class specimens is figured in *Indian Art at Delhi*, Plate 17–A.

Glass mosaics.

Inlay with mother-of-pearl occurs at Salim Chishti's tomb, Fatehpur Sikri, and elsewhere. Glass mosaics are to be seen in several *Shish Mahals*, or 'glass chambers', at Udaipur, Amber, Agra, Lahore, and other places. Those in the ceiling of the *Shish Mahal*, Lahore, are said to be particularly well done. But such meretricious bedizenment certainly is not fine art, and need not be further discussed.

Part VI. TILES

Ancient Persian tiles.

The practice of decorating wall surface with coloured enamelled bricks or tiles was of very ancient date in Persia, and derived ultimately from Babylonia. The Lion and Archer friezes from Susa now in the Louvre, and well reproduced by Perrot and Chipiez, are the best examples of the art as practised in Achaemenian times.[2] But the style of those friezes is not imitated in any extant Indian work. The Indo-Muhammadan enamelled or glazed tiles were copied from a much later development of the art in Persia, where the ancient technique apparently was never wholly forgotten. This later Persian work shows traces of Chinese influence.

Persian tiles of Timurid age.

M. Migeon believes that the Muhammadan use of enamelled tiles in numerous Persian buildings of the fourteenth and fifteenth centuries was derived from Khorasan. From that province it seems to have spread to Samarkand, where we find coloured tile facings on the tomb of Timur at the beginning of the fifteenth century. Coloured tiles had become known in India at an earlier date, certainly in the first quarter of the fourteenth and possibly in the thirteenth century, but the Timurid tradition of the Mughal emperors made them still more fashionable. The Indian work, although sometimes very good, is not admitted by experts to equal the best Persian in either the beauty of the colours or the brilliancy of the enamel.[3]

Early tile-work at Multan.

The Tomb of Baha-ul-hakk at Multan, built between A.D. 1264 and 1286, still retains, or retained in 1882 when Cunningham wrote, 'some fairly preserved specimens of diaper ornament in glazed tiles', which may or may not be contemporaneous with the building in its original form. The tomb was extensively

[1] *Ann. Rep. A. S., India*, 1904-5, p. 5.

[2] Perrot and Chipiez, *Hist. of Art in Persia*, London, 1892, p. 420 and plates. Persian and Indian tiles are not strong enough for use in pavements.

[3] Migeon, *Manuel d'art musulman*, tome ii, pp. 295, 296.

Marble screen around the cenotaph of the Taj.

A. Upper part of a corner turret, Itmad-ud-Daula's tomb, Agra, showing *pietra dura* inlay and marble mosaic.

(From E. W. Smith, *Moghul Colour Decoration of Agra*)

B. Minaret of Wazir Khan's Mosque, Lahore.

(From *J. Indian Art*, Vol. X)

B. Glazed earthenware tile from Panjab.
17th Century.

A. Chini-ka-Rauza, Agra.
(From E. W. Smith, *Moghul Colour Decoration of Agra*)

C. Enamelled earthenware tile from Delhi.
16th Century.

D. Enamelled earthenware tile from Lahore.
17th Century.

MUGHAL TILES IN THE VICTORIA AND ALBERT MUSEUM

A

B

C

ENAMELLED EARTHENWARE TILES FROM LAHORE, IN THE VICTORIA AND ALBERT MUSEUM, SOUTH KENSINGTON. 17TH CENTURY

rebuilt in the seventeenth century, and Sir John Marshall is of opinion that most of the tile-work belongs to that age. The tomb of Baha-ul-hakk's grandson, Rukn-ud-din (A.D. 1320), a well-designed octagonal domed building of brick, in the same city, has its whole exterior

'elaborately ornamented with glazed tile panels and string courses and battlements. The only colours used are dark blue, azure, and white ; but these are contrasted with the deep red of the finely polished bricks, and the result is both effective and pleasing. These mosaics are not, like those of later days, mere plain surfaces, but the patterns are raised from half an inch to two inches above the background. This mode of construction must have been very troublesome, but its increased effect is undeniable, as it unites all the beauty of variety of colour with the light and shade of a raised pattern.'

The tile from Baha-ul-hakk's tomb figured by Cunningham exhibits the 'key pattern' in white on a dark blue ground; that from Rukn-ud-din's tomb has a white ground with interlacing circles in dark blue, the interspaces being partly filled by six-petalled stars and polygonal blocks in pale azure.[1]

Two of the mosques at Gaur in Bengal, the Tantipara and Lotan (*Lattan*), erected between A.D. 1475 and 1480, are decorated with true encaustic tiles. Those of the Lotan mosque are the best preserved. A collection of earlier glazed tiles from Gaur in the Victoria and Albert Museum, South Kensington, is described as having 'a marked Hindu character, quite distinct from the blue, and diapered, and banded tiles which are distinctive of Mahommadan manufacture elsewhere in India, before the florid designs of the Mogul period came into vogue.'[2] It is possible that the art, however introduced originally, may have been known to the Hindus of Bengal in an imperfect form before the Muhammadan conquest. Gaur tiles.

The palace of Raja Man Singh at Gwalior, built at the beginning of the sixteenth century, 'was once profusely decorated with glazed tiles of various colours', as noticed by Babar, who recorded in his *Memoirs*: 'The outside of the walls they have inlaid with green painted tiles. All around they have inlaid the walls with figures of plantain trees made of painted tiles.' Cunningham, writing in 1871, states that Gwalior tiles.

'the plaintain [i.e. banana] trees mentioned by Babar still exist. They are of the natural size, but the leaves made of bright green glazed tiles are very regularly disposed on each side of the yellow stems, and the effect is consequently too stiff and formal. The diamond patterns in blue tile, and the long narrow lines of the same colour are, however, both effective and pleasing.'[3]

We now pass on to the more highly developed and artistic use of glazed tiles after the Persian manner on the walls and domes of Mughal buildings. Most of the Mughal tiling is of the kind called *Kashi* or *Chini*, composed of pieces cut out from a painted sheet and laid as mosaic. The larger part dates from the seventeenth century, with a range of colours considerably more extensive than that employed on the early Panjab tiles already noticed.[4] Such *Kashi* tile casing, sparingly employed on the tomb of Sher Shah and Humayun, came largely into Tile-work of Mughal period.

[1] Cunningham, *A. S. Rep.*, vol. v, pp. 131-3, Pl. XXXIX. At Sitpur in the Muzaffargarh District, where similar tile decoration occurs, the colours include yellow. The Sitpur tombs date from the fifteenth century.

[2] Birdwood, *Industrial Arts of India*, p. 322. These objects are rather enamelled bricks or terra-cotta than tiles. The body is similar to that of red bricks, moulded on the edges or sides into relief patterns, which are covered with a poor vitreous dip, forming a ground of opaque dark blue, upon which patterns in opaque white—either enamel or clay—have been laid. The patterns include Muhammadan (Saracenic) and Hindu forms, and may be referred to the eleventh or twelfth century (Furnival, *Leadless Decorative Tiles*, p. 118, Figs. 72-5).

[3] Cunningham, *A. S. Rep.*, vol. i, pp. 347-9.

[4] Opinions differ as to the mode of manufacture. Mr. J. L. Kipling thought that the designs were painted on large sheets, which were cut up into tiles *before* firing (*J. Ind. Art*, vol. ii, pp. 17, 18); but Mr. F. H. Andrews, after making experiments, believes that the shaped pieces were cut *after* glazing and firing (*Ibid.*, vol. x, pp. 27-30).

favour in the reigns of Jahangir and Shahjahan (1605-58), and continued to be used in Aurangzeb's time. The art is now extinct.

Tile pictures on wall of Lahore Fort.

The most remarkable series of tile pictures in the world is the huge band on the walls of the Lahore Fort, extending from the Elephant Gate (*Hathi Pol*) to the north-eastern tower of Jahangir's quadrangle for a length of 497 yards, with a height of 17 yards. Nearly the whole of this enormous surface is faced with painted tiles representing elephant fights, a game of polo, and other scenes. Dr. Vogel has obtained tracings of 116 panels, of which many select examples have been reproduced on a reduced scale in colour.[1]

Mosque of Wazir Khan.

The most beautiful example of *Kashi* tile-work on a large scale is universally recognized to be the mosque built in 1634 at Lahore by the governor, Wazir Khan. The building is a well-designed domed structure with four handsome minarets, constructed of small thin bricks. The exterior is panelled, the panels and minarets being veneered with *Kashi* tile-work of great brilliancy, still in fairly good preservation (Plate 176B).

Chini-ka-Rauza.

Passing by several interesting buildings exhibiting more or less decoration in coloured tiles, we come next to the tomb near Agra known as the *Chini-ka-Rauza*, which has had the advantage of being exhaustively described and illustrated by the late Mr. E. W. Smith in a volume mainly devoted to it. The building, a large octagonal domed tomb of uncertain date, supposed to have been built early in the reign of Aurangzeb, in memory of Afzal Khan, a poet who died in 1639, was originally covered on the outside from top to bottom with mosaic in *Kashi* tiling of various colours, worked up into numerous patterns so as to form one unbroken flat surface. It is now much dilapidated. The tiles, $\frac{5}{8}$ of an inch thick, are bedded in a layer of fine plaster an inch thick, which was laid on a stratum of coarser plaster two inches in thickness. The principal colours include blues, greens, orange, vermilion, lake, etc., in a variety of delicate shades with a metallic lustre, the unavoidable slight irregularities of the surface producing wonderful play of light. One illustration may be given to show the style (Plate 177A). The tomb also exhibits some painted internal decoration in excellent taste.

Eighteenth-century square tiles.

Sir John Marshall describes as follows a third type of Indian tile decoration:

'A third kind of tiles is found on buildings of the eighteenth century, such as the mosque of Muhammad Amin at Lahore (beginning eighteenth century) and the mosque of Zakariya Khan near Lahore. The founder of the latter was a viceroy of the Punjab from A.D. 1717 to 1738. It is strange to find the same type combined with *Kashi* work on the tomb of Asaf Khan at Shahdara as early as A.D. 1634. The tiles of this class are square. They form, consequently, not a tile-mosaic as the two earlier types, in which each separate piece has its own shape and colour, but are similar to the tiles known in Europe, from where presumably they were introduced into India. The colours are faint as compared to [*sic*] those of the *Kashi* tiles, pale green, blue and yellow being the most prominent. In one case, the tomb of Sharf-un-nissa, known as the cypress tomb (*Sarvvali maqbara*), not far from Begampura near Lahore, we find, besides *Kashi* work on the lower part of the walls, square blue and white tiles of a type well known in the west of Europe. This building also would seem to belong to the eighteenth century.'[2]

In Plates 177 and 178 reproductions are given from photographs specially taken of six artistic square tiles in the Victoria and Albert Museum, Indian Section, all believed to date from either the sixteenth or seventeenth century. Plate 177B, showing the complete figure of a young woman seated on her heels, with part of

[1] *Progress Rep. A. S., Panjab Circle*, 1901–2, par. 13; *J. I. A. I.*, 1911.

[2] For a long list of Indian buildings decorated with tiles, prepared by Mr. C. Stanley Clarke, see Furnival, *Leadless Decorative Tiles*, pp. 121–6 and Appendix C.

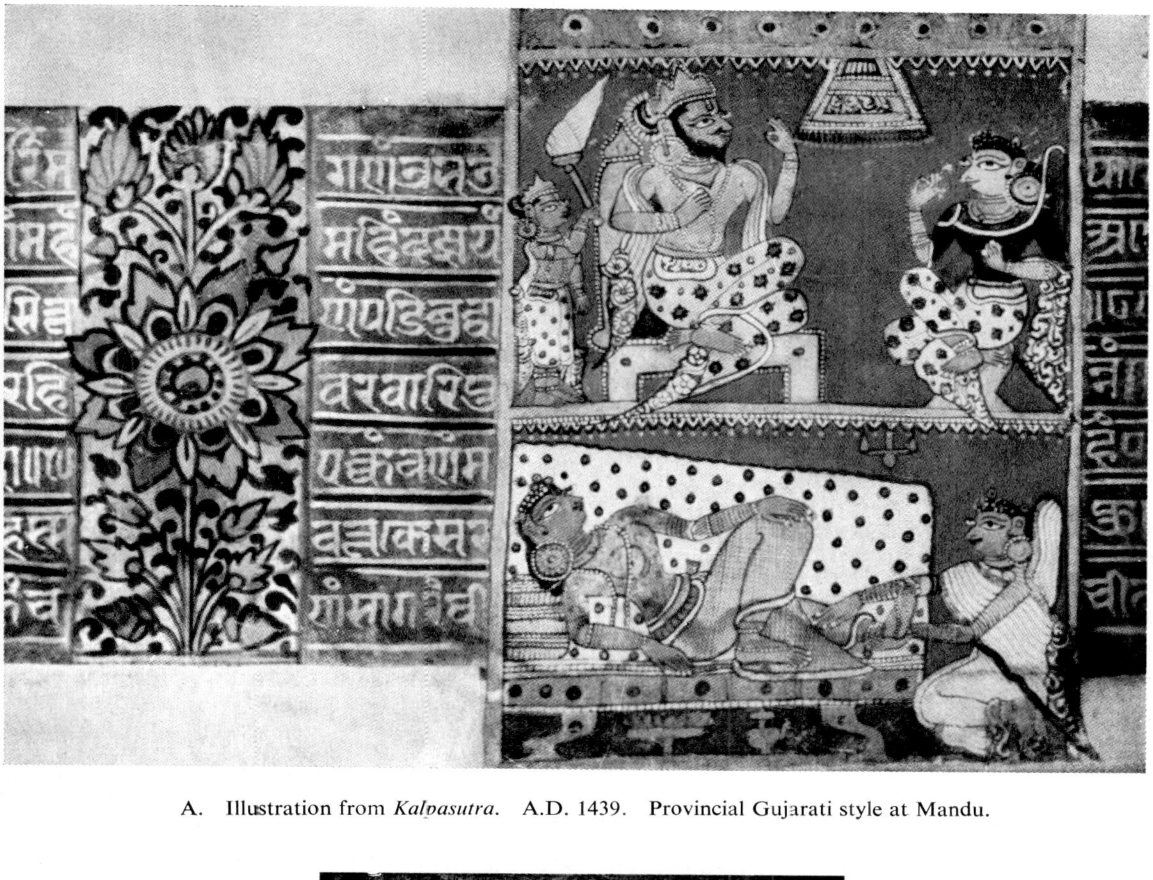

A. Illustration from *Kalpasutra*. A.D. 1439. Provincial Gujarati style at Mandu.

B. *Kalpasutra* (Jain) MS. Gujarati School, A.D. 1464. Or 5149. British Museum.

PLATE 179

Painting on cotton cloth. Illustration of the *Amir Hamzah* (A.D. 1550-75). Victoria and Albert Museum, Indian Section, South Kensington.

(A.D. 1567-1582 during the reign of Akbar).

another woman offering her a fruit, appears to be unique, and is supposed to date from the seventeenth century. The drawing is good, and the general aspect suggests European influence, of which there was plenty in those times. The broken tile from Delhi (Plate 177C) presents a humped bull and flowers in brilliant colours. The fragments of a hunting scene on two perfect tiles (Plate 177D, and Plate 178A) from Lahore are vividly designed and, I think, rightly referred to the seventeenth century, when such pictures of Persian origin were much in fashion. The floral devices on the Lahore tiles (Plates 178B and C) are pretty and well coloured.

Sind tiles.

The modern tile-work of Sind and Multan is described in various books dealing with the industrial arts. The oldest Sind tiles on the Dabgir mosque and Mirza Jani Beg's mosque at Tatta, dating from about A.D. 1509, exhibit only two colours, a deep rich blue and a pale turquoise blue, on a white ground, and so resemble the early Multan tiles.[1] Multan used to be reckoned as in Sind, not in the Panjab, as it is now.

[1] Cousens, H., *Portfolio of Sind Tiles*, Griggs, 1906.

Chapter Fifteen

PAINTING

Part I. THE GUJARATI SCHOOL

THE study of Indian painting has of late been greatly advanced by the work of Goetz, Mehta, and Percy Brown, [and many other recent writers]. However, a great deal [still] remains to be done, before an acceptable classification of the various schools is arrived at. Dr. Coomaraswamy was among the first investigators of Indian painting. It is therefore only right to outline his pioneer views at the head of this chapter. To him, above all else, Indian miniature-painting is divided into two, the foreign Muhammadan school which rose under Persian tuition during the reigns of the Mughal emperors, and in contradistinction, an ancient, indigenous, wholly Indian school, which he designates 'Rajput', and treats of as persisting 'in Rajputana and the Himalayas . . . up to the end of the eighteenth century, comparatively little affected by the Persian and European influences which enter so largely into the art of the Mughal Court'.[1] '. . . Rajput painting', he writes, 'has none of the characteristics of a new art. It is, on the contrary, related to the classic art of Ajanta, as the Hindu language and literature are related to the older Prakrits and to Sanskrit. . . . The Rajput paintings, indeed, show a remarkable combination of folk idioms with ancient hieratic design.'[2] Mughal art, on the other hand, is a purely miniature art, unrelated to the ancient Indian frescoes. It is courtly not popular, secular not religious, material not spiritual.

Modern trend of research.

Several objections may be made to this radical division. For one thing, it is perfectly evident that both schools share a common technique, seemingly derived from Persian painting. Furthermore, a closer study of 'Rajput Painting', shows it also to be a 'courtly' art, associated with the capitals of various ruling dynasties. It is also evident that on the one hand, the Hindu *Krishna* and *Ragmala* subjects of the 'Rajput' schools are often embodied in purely 'Mughal' renderings, although they are of course commoner in Hindu Jaipur and Garwhal than in Delhi; on the other hand, it is equally evident that magnificent examples of 'Rajput' portraiture exist, fulfilling the same demand as 'Mughal' portraiture. Lastly, Goetz' study of costume and, still more conclusively, various dated examples of 'Rajput' paintings, prove without a shadow of doubt that the bulk of 'Rajput' painting is posterior to, rather than contemporary with the great 'Mughal' work of the court artists of Akbar and Jahangir.

Jain paintings.

This criticism of Coomaraswamy's primary classification is reinforced by a study of the few examples of pre-Mughal Indian miniature-paintings known to us. These are mostly illustrations to Jain palm-leaf manuscripts, and the school has therefore become generally known as 'Jain'.[3] This is unfortunate for the art was not confined to religious subjects. It appears likely that many purely secular examples exist, such as is the MS. of *Vasanta Vilasa* described and illustrated by Mehta.[4] This was written during the reign of Ahmad Shah Kutb-ud-din of Gujarat in A.D. 1451; only two older examples of the school are known. The MS. in question is written on a long roll of prepared cotton, 35 feet 6 inches long

[1] *Museum of Fine Arts Bulletin*, Boston, xvi. 49.

[2] *Burlington Mag.*, 1912, p. 315.

[3] See Coomaraswamy's pioneer work on Jain Painting, Part IV of the catalogue of the Indian Collection, Museum of Fine Arts, Boston: also his 'Jaina Art', *Jour. Ind. Art.*, vol. xvi, p. 82.

[4] *loc. cit.*, p. 15.

Plate A.

Illustration to the *Gita Govinda*. Provenance uncertain. Probably A.D. 1570-80. Kulahdar group.
(By Courtesy of Prince of Wales Museum, Bombay)

and just over 9 inches wide. The colours are laid on flat and there is a preponderance of red and yellow, the body-ground being yellow. Features are usually rendered half-face, but occasionally side-face, the long almond-shaped eye of the Indian canon of beauty being greatly exaggerated. Trees are portrayed formally as lozenges containing branch and foliage; this treatment is usual in Indian art but is not found in the frescoes at Ajanta and Ellora, where foliage, blossom, and fruit are luxuriously reproduced. Here, except in the case of banana trees and mangoes, the treatment is strictly formal in a rather slovenly way; only here and there does any attempt at design lighten the arid convention. The figure-drawing is weak, but fortunately the costume with its detail of jewellery and floating scarf and waist-cloth is faithfully and delightfully set down. On the whole one is impressed by the candour of this naive art, the purpose of which is frankly book-illustration, as indeed was the primary purpose of the masters whose work still glows on the dark walls of Ajanta and Ellora.

Indian costume.

Indian costume as shown in these paintings is proven conservative. The men wear the waist-cloth (*dhoti*), long or short, with a scarf for the shoulders. Jewelled head-dresses of various kinds are worn, but more commonly the hair was dressed with flowers. The pyjama and the women's veil do not appear. It is evident that the costume of fifteenth-century Gujarat must be treated of as being akin to that of Ajanta, not of Delhi and Agra. The subsequent change speaks clearly of a far deeper penetration of Mughal influence than has hitherto been allowed for.

Examples of Jain painting.

As has been said the bulk of the known illustrated MSS. of this school are Jain. Of these the earliest appears to be the *Kalpa Sutra* in the Patan library dated in the year A.D. 1237. Two representative MSS. are the *Kalpa Sutras* respectively in the India Office Library (A.D. 1427), and the British Museum (A.D. 1464). The MSS. in the Boston Museum, illustrated in volume iv of the *Catalogue of the Indian Collections*, form perhaps the best group for comparative study. There are also several excellent examples in the Ghose collection in Calcutta, including one dated in A.D. 1480. The illustrations (Plates 179B, C and D) are from a MS. in the British Museum.

Origin of the School.

Since all these fifteenth-century paintings seem to belong to Gujarat, 'Gujarati' would be a preferable title to 'Jain'. As a local school they are closely comparable with the few examples of medieval Nepalese paintings in existence.

Part II. MUGHAL PAINTING

Islam and Art.

It is undeniable that Indian miniature-painting is largely derived from Persia, although the essential 'Indianess' of the work is also undeniable. Persian painting is divided chronologically into three periods, the Mongol, the Timurid, and the Safavid. As a branch of Islamic art, it exists as the result of a direct breach of the *Law*, for it is written that whosoever makes a representation of a figure, human or animal, shall give it his soul at the Day of Judgement and so come to perdition. Until the collapse of the Caliphate of Baghdad it seems that the Law was upheld, for no illuminated Arab manuscripts are known to exist before the end of the thirteenth century. It seems that Islamic painting came into existence under the somewhat heterodox Aiyubite sultans, whose coins bear on the reverse the head of the Byzantine Christ. The most important early MS. is the Schafer *Makamat of Hariri* (Bibliothèque Nationale: Arabe, No. 5847), made in the year A.D. 1237. In these pictures one sees a vital pictorial sense struggling to embody itself in foreign and decadent forms. Byzantine influence is obvious, the nimbus, vestments, drapery, and the architectural setting being borrowed *en bloc*. One is also reminded of the art of the Persian potters and of the older tradition that lies at the root of Sassanian art. . . . Islamic art was created in a land that had witnessed the rise, modification, and decay of many schools of art. Assyrian and Greek influences are blended in the colonnades of the Apadana of Xerxes, and East and West, Bactria and India, Sassanian and Chinese met in the markets of the Taklamakan trade-routes, long before the coming of the Mongols released Persian art from its religious bonds. As has been said, foreign influence is paramount in these early pictures, but the drawing is full of interest, and when displaying familiar things, horses and horsemen, and their furniture and arms, has a native vigour of its own.

The Mongol invasion.

Under the Abbasids Arab painting flourished in the great cities of the Tigris valley, Baghdad, Wasit, and Basrah. Its development and very existence was cut short with everything else that represented the Caliphate at its greatest, in the year A.D. 1258, the date of the Mongol invasion. The flood of destruction passed away and good arose out of evil. Under Mongol rule China was in direct contact with Persia. Byzantine influence and whatever remnants of decadent classicism that still lingered on, died away before a steady current of influence from the East. It has been pointed out that Hulagu had Christian wives and that the Mongols favoured Christianity in the face of Islam. It has also been stressed that Central Asia and especially the Tarim Basin was a polyglot meeting-place of foreign cultures, western, Chinese, and Indian. However, from the point of view of Persian painting, Chinese art was the dominant art of the period. China was the source of Persian technique and inspiration, not only indirectly by the importation of Chinese wares, but, it is said, directly by the introduction of Chinese craftsmen, potters and embroiderers, as well as painters. So arose in the Mongol cities of Maraghan, Sultania, and Tabriz, a well established art destined to a long and illustrious history.[1]

The house of Timur.

The Mongol period (1258-1335) drew to its turbulent close, and out of chaos emerged the house of Timur under whom civilization and art awoke to new life in the cities of the Oxus, Bokhara, and Samarqand. Of this house came Babar, the founder of the Mughal Empire of India. In Timurid Persia architecture flourished. Shah Rukh of Herat, son of Timur, himself a poet, maintained court-painters, one of whom journeyed to China with an embassy. At the end of the fifteenth century Sultan Husain Mirza gathered at his court the most famous artists of his time, among them Bihzad, the painter.

The Safavids.

After the death of Husain Mirza in 1506 Bihzad was employed at the court of the Safavid Shah Ismail. Under the new dynasty Persian painting entered upon its period of romanticism. Timurid clarity and restraint were cast aside and design and colour are lavishly conceived. At its best under Shah Abbas at the end of the sixteenth century, this period inevitably led to decadence.

Mughal painting.

The history of Mughal painting begins with the name of Mir Sayyid Ali. In the year 1525 Babar set out upon the conquest of India, a land, however, of which he did not conceive highly. Five years later he was dead. In 1546 Humayun, his son, was deprived of his empire by the Afghan, Sher Shah, and until his final

[1] For minor influences in Persian painting, especially Manichean, see Arnold, *Some Survivals in Persian Painting*. But the survival of a few motives does not postulate the survival of stylistic influence.

A. Wall-painting : eight men in a boat ; from Fatehpur Sikri.
(From E. W. Smith, *The Moghul Architecture of Fathpur-Sikri*)

B. Illustration of the *Darabnamah* ; by Bihzad and Abdus Samad.
[B.N. Or. 4615]. (Early Mughal School. 16th Century A.D.).

Illustration from the Akbarnama, painted by Basawan and Chatar. Subject : Akbar in an elephant fight on a boat bridge across the Jhelum ; Victoria and Albert Museum, Indian Section, South Kensington. (Mughal School, Akbar period. *c.* 1600 A.D.).

PLATE 182

victory in 1555 existed as a landless refugee. One year of this period was spent at the Safavid court at Tabriz, where Shah Tahmasp now ruled. Bihzad was dead, but the work of a young painter, Mir Sayyid Ali, was already attracting attention. His father, Mir Mansur of Badakshan, who was also a painter, was a contemporary of Bihzad's. Another painter of growing reputation also attracted the notice of the exiled emperor; this was Abdus Samad.

In 1550 both these artists joined Humayun's court at Kabul. It was here that Mir Sayyid Ali was commissioned to supervise the illustration of the romance of Amir Hamzah (*Dastan-i-Amir Hamzah*) in twelve volumes of a hundred folios each. Sixty of these illustrations painted in tempera colours on prepared cotton cloth are in Vienna, and twenty-five of them in the Indian Museum, South Kensington (Plate 180). They must probably be attributed to the artists of the imperial court working under Mir Sayyid Ali, rather than to that painter himself. After Humayun's death Mir Sayyid Ali continued to work at the court of Akbar, and also performed the pilgrimage to Mecca. The style of these early Mughal paintings is, of course, largely Safavid, but it is evident that modification and developments have already taken place. It is said that Bihzad added skill in portraiture to the art of painting; portraiture is further developed in Mughal painting. Also a greater use is made of relief and the range of colours is larger and more striking. There is something, too, about the use of flower and foliage that is un-Persian and wholly Indian. A certain simplicity and breadth of design dominates the wealth of detail; the microscopic rendering of costume and accoutrements, textile hangings and architectural details is doubly delightful in so much as it is never obtrusive.

Amir Hamzah paintings.

Such paintings on prepared fabric are common in India. It appears that paper itself was rare, or at any rate that large sheets were hard to obtain.

Summing up the technique and quality of early Mughal painting, it may be said that it was an offshoot of the Safavid school, the handiwork of artists trained in the school of Bihzad.[1] However, as has been said, the local character of the detail as shown in the portrayal of the Indian countryside and of its flowers and foliage is proof of complete acclimatization, promising vigorous development.

Early Mughal painting.

Akbar succeeded to the insecure throne of his father when still a boy with this distinction: that whereas Babar and Humayun were rulers in a foreign land, he was native born. The culture of his court did not merely reflect at a distance the splendour of Bukhara and Samarqand. The building of Fatehpur Sikri in 1569 heralded a new era of Indian rule. And after the architects, masons, and sculptors had done their work, painters were called in to decorate the walls of the public halls and private apartments. The art of these paintings, as far as may be judged from what remains of them (Plate 181A), was closely allied to that of the Mughal miniatures, the colours being applied upon a ground of white pigment laid directly upon the sandstone. Some of the paintings are purely Persian in style; others are Indian. It is evident that many artists were employed, each working in his own style. As the result of this co-operation under royal patronage, a school of court-painters was set up under the Emperor's direct control, the Persian artists, Mir Sayyid Ali and Abdus Samad being, of course, prominent. The latter rose to be master of the mint at Fatehpur, and afterwards Divan or Controller of the Revenues of Multan.[2]

Painting under Akbar.

[1] Percy Brown, *Indian Painting*, p. 56.
[2] His son attained the dignity of Amir-ul-Umara under Jahangir.

Wall-paintings. The wall-paintings of Fatehpur are fully described in E. W. Smith's book, *The Mughal Architecture of Fathpur-Sikri*, from which Plate 181A is taken. The treatment is flat, no shading being made use of. One scene in which winged figures play a part is called 'The Annunciation' by the local guides. Chinese motives such as dragon-clouds appear as an inheritance from the parent Persian school. That the arts of painting and sculpture were closely united is proved by many of the bas-relief panels where flowering trees and animal forms are represented in a very naturalistic manner.[1] It has been said that Mughal miniature-painting are wall-paintings in little, a statement which tends to be confusing, since neither branch of Mughal painting has anything in common with the ancient Indian schools of painting of Ajanta and Gujarat, except certain inclinations to bright colouring and fine line-drawing which seem temperamentally inherent in Indian artists.

Calligraphy. In Persia and India, as in China, calligraphy was regarded as a fine art worthy of the most serious study, and masters of it enjoyed fame throughout Asia like that of great painters in Europe. They were careful to sign and date their works, which were eagerly collected by connoisseurs. Abul Fazl gives a list of calligraphic experts, among whom in Akbar's time the most eminent was Muhammad Husain of Kashmir, who survived the emperor for six years. Many of the albums in the London collections containing 'miniatures' include hundreds of specimens of beautiful writing in various styles and of different periods, which often seem to have been more valued than the drawings and paintings associated with them. Abul Fazl enumerates eight calligraphical systems as current during the sixteenth century in Iran (Persia), Turan (Turkistan), India, and Turkey, distinguished one from the other by differences in the relative proportion of straight and curved lines, ranging from the *Kufic* with five-sixths of straight lines to the *Nastalik*, Akbar's favourite script, with nothing but curved strokes. The forms of the Arabic alphabet used for writing Persian, although not distinctly reminiscent of pictorial hieroglyphs, as the Chinese characters are, lend themselves readily to artistic treatment, and even Europeans may understand to some extent the high technical skill of the masters of the calligraphic art, and admire the beauty of their productions. But full enjoyment and appreciation are possible only to persons familiar with the character from infancy and sensitive to all the associated ideas.[2]

Close connexion of calligraphy and painting. 'Among the general characteristics of Chinese painting the most striking, and the one which has prevailed most strongly throughout its long historical evolution, is the graphic quality of the painting; Chinese painters are, first of all, draughtsmen and calligraphists . . . The different legends all carry out the leading idea of the common origin and essential unity of writing and painting, and this unity is constantly insisted upon by Chinese critics of the two arts.'[3]

The same idea dominated the Persian artists and their Indian imitators at Akbar's court. Abul Fazl, accordingly, devotes Ain 34 of his *Institutes of Akbar* to the discussion of the 'Arts of Writing and Painting', passing naturally from the account of calligraphic systems summarized above to the invaluable notice of the early history of Indo-Persian painting, which forms our only source of knowledge of the subject other than the information to be gleaned laboriously by minute

[1] See casts of the panels from the Turkish Sultana's house in the Indian Museum, South Kensington.

[2] The technicalities of the art are explained by Huart in *Les Calligraphes et les Miniaturistes de l'Orient Musulman*, Paris, 1908. He gives (p. 256) a list of Indian calligraphists in the eighteenth century, and also mentions Jawahir Raqam, Aurangzeb's librarian, who died in 1683. The Department of Design, &c., at South Kensington, possesses specimens of the work of Roshan Raqam, one of the artists named.

[3] Bushell, *Chinese Art*, ii. 207.

A. Portraits of Sher Muhammad Nawal, Jahangir, and Shahjahan, by Muhammad Nadir of Samarkand. [B.M. Add. 18801, No. 40]. (Only the main portrait is by Nadir. Mughal School, Jahangir period. 2nd. decade of the 17th Century A. D.).

B. Picture of a Plane Tree. [*cir.* A.D. 1610]. Johnson Collection, vol. I, fol. 30. (Mughal School, Jahangir period. Early 17th Century A.D.).

(India Office Library, London)

PLATE 183

A. Faqirs resting under trees. [*cir.* A. D. 1650]. Collection of Baron Maurice Rothschild, Paris. (Mughal School, Shahjahan period).

B. Portrait of Suleiman Shiko, son of Dara Shiko. Mughal School, Shahjahan period. Mid–17th. Century A. D. Collection of the late A. C. Ardeshir of Poona.

PLATE 184

A.

B.

C.

A. Illustration from *Laur Chanda* story. School and provenance uncertain. *c.* 1570-80 A.D. Bharat Kala Bhawan, Banaras.

B. Ragini Vibhasa. Popular Mughal School. *c.* 1630 A.D. National Museum, New Delhi.

C. Sketch portrait of Emperor Jahangir [*cir.* A.D. 1625]. Collection of M. Cartier, Paris. (Popular Mughal School, 2nd quarter of 17th Century A.D. Now in the Prince of Wales Museum, Bombay).

A. Ragini. Malwa idiom of Rajasthani School. 3rd quarter of the 17th Century A.D. National Museum, New Delhi.

B. Princess with attendants in a garden. Bundi School of Rajasthani painting. Last quarter of the 17th Century A.D. Prince of Wales Museum, Bombay.

PLATE 186

study in detail of individual works. M. Huart sums up the close relations between calligraphy and Asiatic painting in the phrase: 'En Orient la miniature n'est que la servante de la calligraphie.' The phrase, however, is not applicable to the ancient Hindu schools of painting, which, except in so far as they may have been influenced by Chinese and Persian ideas, were independent of the scribe's art. None of the many varieties of the square Brahmi or Sanskrit script ever tempted the calligraphist to regard his manuscript as a picture, nor did anybody dream of collecting specimens of writing in that script merely for the sake of their beauty.

Daswanth Kahar.

The rapidity with which the teaching of Abdus Samad and his Musalman colleagues was assimilated and then modified by scores of Hindu artists of various castes is in itself sufficient proof that the foreign teachers must have found trained indigenous scholars with whom to work. Men accustomed to draw and paint could easily learn new methods and a foreign style, but not even the despotic power of Akbar would have been able to create a numerous school of Hindu artists out of nothing.

This inference, inevitable from a general survey of the facts, is established with certainty by the positive testimony of Abul Fazl that Daswanth, who disputed with Basawan the first place among the Hindu painters of Akbar's court, had 'devoted his whole life to the art, and used, from love to his profession, to draw and paint figures even on walls'. He was the son of a poor man, a member of the Kahar or palanquin-bearer caste; and when such a man, in spite of all social disadvantages, could become a professional artist, many others more favourably situated must have done the same. Daswanth's genius was rescued from obscurity by the royal favour. 'One day,' writes the courtly historian, 'the eye of His Majesty fell on him; his talent was discovered, and he himself handed over to the Khajah (*scil. Abdus Samad*). In a short time he surpassed all painters and became the first master of the age. Unfortunately the light of his talents was dimmed by the shadow of madness; he committed suicide. He has left many masterpieces.' Abul Fazl goes on to say that the work of Basawan is so excellent that many connoisseurs preferred him to Daswanth.

Disregard of prohibition of images.

As has been said the Koran, following the Semitic principle formulated in the Mosaic Second Commandment, absolutely forbids Muslims to make the likeness of anything in heaven or on earth; and the prohibition has been and is strictly obeyed, with rare exceptions, in all countries and at all times, so far as the decoration of mosques and other buildings devoted to religious purposes is concerned.[1] In book illustrations, however, such liberty is commonly assumed. The Persians, adherents of the *Shia* sect of Islam, always have been especially lax in their open disregard of the Koranic prohibition. The Mughal emperors of India looked to Iran for the graces of civilization, and it was natural that Akbar should desire to add the charms of Persian pictorial art to the amenities of his court. Regarding himself as Head of the Church and pontiff of a new religion, he cared little about the Prophet, and at a private party was heard by his Boswell to observe:

'There are many that hate painting, but such men I dislike. It appears to me as if a painter had quite peculiar means of recognizing God; for a painter in sketching anything that has life, and in

[1] Two exceptional cases are cited by Migeon. The Khalif Abd-ul-Malik (A.D. 685-705) erected a mosque at Jerusalem decorated with images of the Prophet and paintings of heaven and hell. The Jumai Mosque at Isfahan exhibits on the walls two paintings, one of Ali, son-in-law of the Prophet, and another, perhaps representing Fatima veiled (*Manuel d'art musulman*, tome ii, pp. 1, 56).

devising its limbs one after the other, must come to feel that he cannot bestow individuality upon his work, and is thus forced to think of God, the Giver of life, and will thus increase in knowledge.'

Akbar's liberal patronage.

He found no difficulty in gratifying his taste. Liberal pay and abundant honour drew crowds of artists, both foreigners and Indians, Muslims, and Hindus, to his magnificent court, where the more distinguished were enrolled as *mansabdars*, or members of the official nobility, and assigned ample salaries. His system of government making no distinction between civil and military employ, or rather giving military titles to all official rank, the successful artists ranked as army officers of good standing, while their assistants and allies, gilders, binders, and the like, were enrolled either as members of the imperial bodyguard (*ahadi*), or as private soldiers, with pay ranging from fifteen to thirty rupees a month, sufficient for comfortable subsistence. The industry of all grades was stimulated by weekly inspections, at which His Majesty generously rewarded merit.

Imperial libraries.

Imperial libraries of large extent were formed at Agra, Delhi, and other places, stored with all that was best in Asiatic literature, both originals and Persian translations, the volumes being enshrined in the richest bindings, and adorned with miniatures regardless of expense.

For example, the *Razmnamah*, or Persian abridged translation of the *Mahabharata*, with preface dated A.D. 1588, now at Jaipur, is said to have cost £40,000 sterling; and Colonel Hanna estimates that his copy of the *Ramayana*, now at Washington, must have cost quite half that sum.[1] The *Akbarnamah*, from which 117 large paintings are preserved at South Kensington, was a similar work, and Abul Fazl mentions many others.[2] According to the Spanish priest, Father Sebastian Manrique, who was at Agra in 1641, the imperial library at that city contained 24,000 volumes, valued by him at the astounding figure of 6,463,731 rupees, or £720,000 sterling, an average per volume of almost 270 rupees, equivalent then to about £30.[3]

Destruction of the libraries.

The libraries thus formed were maintained and increased by Jahangir, Shahjahan, and Aurangzeb (1605-1707); and even the weak successors of the last Great Mogul were not indifferent to the delights of choice books and dainty pictures.[4] But the political convulsions of the eighteenth and nineteenth centuries destroyed the imperial libraries, with most of the similar collections formed by subordinate potentates like the Rohilla chief and the Nawab-Vazir of Oudh.[5] Fragments of these wonderful accumulations are now scattered over the world in private and public collections, and although constituting but a small fraction of the great mass once in existence, supply ample material for the history of Indo-Persian calligraphy and the sister art of the miniaturist. Many of these paintings have had adventurous histories.

[1] Vol. iv. of Hendley, *Memorials of the Jeypore Exhibition*, 1883, 4to, is solely devoted to reproductions from the *Razmnamah*, of which two are in colour.

[2] The *Ain-i-Akbari*, usually regarded as a separate work, was really part of the *Akbarnamah*, or 'History of Akbar'.

[3] Manrique, *Itinerario de las missiones que hizo el padre F. Sebastian Manrique*, Roma, 1649, p. 417. See *ante*, chap. xii, p. 417. Some of Manrique's observations are summarized in English in Murray, *Historical Account of Discoveries and Travels in Asia*, 1820, vol. ii, pp. 96-119, and again, more briefly, in Oaten, *European Travellers in India*, 1909, pp. 97-102.

[4] For instance, the splendid B.M. MS. Add. 20734 (*Pers. Catal.*, p. 259) was given to an English officer by Akbar II in 1815 as an official present. Mir Muhammad, the artist from whom Manucci obtained the portraits of the imperial family which he brought to Venice before 1712, was in the service of Shah Alam (Irvine, *Storia do Mogor*, vol. i, pp. liii-lvi).

[5] B.M. MS. Add. 22470 belonged to Hafiz Rahmat of Rohilkhand, and came into the possession of an English officer after Hastings's Rohilla war, in the course of which the Bareilly library was plundered. Asaf-ud-daulah, Nawab-Vazir of Oudh, secured most of the books for Lucknow, where they were again plundered and scattered in 1858. B.M. MS. Add. 18579 was illustrated for the last king of Bijapur in the Deccan, whose capital was sacked by Aurangzeb in 1686. Most princes probably owned libraries of considerable value. See paragraphs on Rajput painting.

A. Illustration to the *Bhagavata Purana*. Gajendra Moksha episode. Mewar School of Rajasthani painting. Artist, Shabbudin. A.D. 1648. Bhandarkar Oriental Institute, Poona.

B. Krishna and Gopis. Rajasthani painting, probably from a Thikana. 18th Century A.D. National Museum, New Delhi.

PLATE 187

Portrait of Raja Kirpal Pal of Basohli (A.D. 1678-1694). Basohli School, *c.* 1693-94 A.D. Formerly in the Samarendranath Gupta Collection.

B. Illustration from Bhanu Datta's *Rasamanjari*. Basohli School. A.D. 1694. Artist, Devidas. National Museum, New Delhi.

PLATE 188

When Shahjahan began to grow old, his four sons, each eager to secure for himself the succession to the throne, engaged in bitter, internecine strife. Aurangzeb, the third son, a master of craft and guile, won the prize, imprisoned his father, and assumed power in 1658. Dara Shikoh, his eldest brother, doubly hateful as a rival and a heretic, was pursued to the death with unrelenting rigour. Driven into the deserts of Sind, he was foully betrayed, and, to augment his affliction, before reaching the house of his betrayer,

'received by a foot messenger the sad intelligence of the death of that one of his wives whom he loved most, and who had accompanied him always during his misfortunes. He learnt that she had died of heat and thirst, not being able to find a drop of water in the country to assuage her thirst. The Prince was so affected by the news that he fell as though he were dead.'[1]

The memory of this sad tale is recalled by a beautiful little album now preserved in the India Office Library, which bears the unhappy prince's autograph inscription written across a splash of gold smeared over the delicately decorated fly-leaf: 'This album was presented to his nearest and dearest friend, the Lady Nadirah Begam, by Prince Muhammad Dara Shikoh, son of the Emperor Shahjahan, in the year 1051 (=A.D. 1641-2).'

Albums.

The illustration of manuscripts was only one form of Indo-Persian art, and that, as M. Blochet truly observes, was not always the most successful. The highest achievements of the Indian draughtsmen and colourists were often attained in separate pictures of varying sizes, which were frequently bound in albums, like that given by Dara Shikoh to his beloved wife. The British Museum collection includes many such albums, some of which, such as Hafiz Rahmat's volume, constitute historical portrait galleries of the deepest interest. The fashion set by the court of Delhi and followed by all the feudatory courts and many individual nobles, was passed on to the wealthy English 'Nabobs' in the latter part of the eighteenth century, who gladly seized opportunities of procuring specimens and bringing them home. Certain pictures in B.M. MS. Add. 18801 were much admired by Sir Joshua Reynolds in July 1777.

Prices.

Occasional memoranda of prices give some notion of the pecuniary value of such pictures. One of those specially noticed by Sir Joshua—a large sketch of Shahjahan holding court—is marked Rupees 200, equivalent in those days to at least £25 sterling. In the Johnson Collection at the India Office formed by Warren Hasting's banker, Richard Johnson, a drawing of Nawab Shayista Khan, a great noble of Aurangzeb's time (vol. xxii, fol. 5), is priced Rupees 170, and in another volume a number of more ordinary small portraits are priced at 25 rupees each. During the nineteenth century the taste for the work of the school was lost by both Europeans and Indians, and very few persons seemed to care what happened to the pictures, which were then procurable for nominal sums. Interest in them has now been revived, chiefly by reason of Mr. Havell's efforts and the publications of French scholars. According to Badaoni, Akbar's hostile critic, the courtiers' taste for illuminated books had been stimulated in his time by a certain amount of compulsion, and it was natural that, during the 'great anarchy' of the Maratha period, when the influence of the Delhi court sank to nothing, the amount of liberal patronage by the minor native courts should diminish. Nevertheless, even during those stormy times much meritorious portrait work was produced, and some good portraiture was executed as late as the nineteenth century.

[1] Tavernier, *Travels*, transl. V. Ball, i. 350.

Position of artists in 1669.

When Bernier was writing to Colbert in 1669, early in the reign of Aurangzeb, who had the Puritan dislike for art, the position of artists had become much less favourable than that enjoyed by them in the days of Akbar, Jahangir, and Shahjahan. The observant French physician, a thoroughly trustworthy witness, described as follows the relations between artists and their patrons, or rather taskmasters, as seen by him:

'Can it excite wonder that under these circumstances [*of general misery*] the arts do not flourish here as they would do under better government, or as they flourish in our happier France? No artist can be expected to give his mind to his calling in the midst of a people who are either wretchedly poor, or who, if rich, assume an appearance of poverty, and who regard not the beauty and excellence, but the cheapness of an article; a people whose grandees pay for a work of art considerably under its value, and according to their own caprice, and who do not hesitate to punish an importunate artist or tradesman with the *korrah*, that long and terrible whip hanging at every Omrah's [*nobleman's*] gate. Is it not enough to damp the ardour of any artist when he feels that he can never hope to attain to any distinction? . . . The arts in the Indies would long ago have lost their beauty and delicacy if the monarch and principal Omrahs did not keep in their pay a number of artists who work in their houses, teach the children, and are stimulated to exertion by the hope of reward and the fear of the *korrah*. The protection afforded by powerful patrons to rich merchants and tradesmen who pay the workmen rather higher wages tends also to preserve the arts. I say, "rather higher wages", for it should not be inferred from the goodness of the manufactures that the workman is held in esteem, or arrives at a state of independence. Nothing but sheer necessity of blows from a cudgel keeps him employed.'

In a subsequent passage the author describes the workshops attached to great houses:

'In one hall embroiderers are busily employed, superintended by a master. In another you see the goldsmiths, in a third, painters, &c.'[1]

Bernier's description of the servile position of artists, while applicable specially to the experts in the industrial arts, must have been generally true also for that of the professors of the fine art of painting. A tyrannical 'Omrah' and his henchmen would not have drawn nice distinctions between the artist who painted the miniatures and the embroiderers or carvers who executed the binding of a sumptuous manuscript. Indeed the binding is sometimes as much a work of art as the pictures are.[2]

Technique.

Excepting the modern Delhi miniatures in ivory, the frescoes, the early paintings on cotton, and a few pictures on vellum, the Indo-Persian paintings are all executed on paper.[3] I do not know any Indian examples of painting on silk in the Chinese manner. The Indo-Persian, like other Asiatic artists, conceived every object as being bounded by firm lines, and consequently, his first step was the drawing of an outline. For the illustration of ordinary Persian books, according to M. Blochet, the outline drawn directly on the page in red or black chalk was filled in with colours at once. For more costly and elaborate volumes the process was more complicated, the illustrations being executed upon a separate sheet subsequently applied to the blank space left in the manuscript. That sheet was first covered with a layer of very fine plaster, mixed in a solution of gum arabic. The outline was then drawn upon the perfectly smooth surface thus obtained, and opaque body-colours, mixed with water, were laid on in successive layers, just as in oil-painting, but with the difference that mistakes could not be rectified.

[1] Bernier, *Travels*, transl. Constable, pp. 228, 258.

[2] B.M. MS. Add. 18579, a copy of the *Anwar-i-Suhaili* in a beautiful minute script, has a handsome stamped gilt binding, and there are other examples of rich early bindings in the Museum collection. See *Indian Art at Delhi*, p. 203, several papers in *J.I.A.I.*, and Migeon, *Manuel d'art musulman*, tome ii. p. 59.

[3] Col. Hanna's Collection, now at Washington, U. S. A., included three examples on vellum, namely, No. 28, Jahangir standing on globe; No. 52, a Sultan of Turkey; and No. 86, Babar.

Plate B
The House of Sheikh Fūl, painted by Bishandas. (Mughal school. *Circa* A.D. 1625).

Jewels and ornaments were indicated by needle prickings in sheets of gold-leaf, or even by the insertion of pearls or diamond chips.[1] The work was all done by the Indian artists with fine squirrel-hair brushes, the most delicate strokes being executed with a brush of a single hair, an instrument requiring the utmost correctness of eye and steadiness of hand. The collections in London contain many examples of unfinished drawings and paintings, which, if examined critically by experts, would reveal fully the Indian methods of work, and show how far they agreed with or differed from the Persian methods described by M. Blochet. It must be pointed out that portraits often exist in duplicate and triplicate.

Pigments.

The blue was ordinarily obtained from powdered lapis lazuli, imported from Badakshan, but indigo blues appear in early book illustrations of Hindu subjects. The reds used were cinnabar, vermilion, or cochineal.[2] The yellow was chrome, and other colours were made up by mixing these. Gold was freely used in the form of gold-leaf, and also as a wash of which the Indians had the secret.[3] The Persians applied an admirably transparent varnish made of sandarac and linseed-oil, mixed as a paste and dissolved in either petroleum or highly rectified spirits of wine.[4] Probably the Indians used all the Persian appliances with some additions and modifications, but the ascertainment of full details would require special expert study and hardly repay the trouble.[5]

Collaboration.

The practice of beginning a picture by laying down a firmly drawn outline led to a curious division of labour, the outline often being drawn by one man and the painting done by another. For example, in the Clarke MS. of the *Akbarnamah* at South Kensington the picture (No. $\frac{89}{117}$) of the execution of Adham Khan was drawn by Miskin and painted by Shankar. Sometimes three artists collaborated in one work, and I have noticed one instance in which the collaborators numbered four, namely, the audience scene ($\frac{1}{117}$) in the Clarke MS. The outlines in that picture were drawn by Miskin, the painting was done by Sarwan, the faces (*chihra-nami*) by an artist whose name is indistinct, and the figures (*surat*) by Madho. It is not clear how such a complicated arrangement was worked. The method, whether only two artists or four collaborated, necessarily tended to reduce their art to the level of a skilled mechanical craft; and, as a matter of fact, the mechanical nature of much of the fine Indo-Persian work is its greatest defect.[6]

The early Indian book illustrations.

The early Indo-Persian book illustrations, such as those in the Clarke MS. of the *Akbarnamah*, are wrought in excessively brilliant colours, chiefly red, yellow, and blue. As has been said they are avowed imitations or, rather, developments of Persian work.

Change of character in Persian art.

In Persia, at the close of the fifteenth century, the character of Timurid art began to change, passing into the more delicate and sentimental style of the

[1] Blochet, 'Musalman MSS. and Miniatures as illustrated in the Recent Exhibition at Paris,' *Burlington Magazine*, vol. ii, June to Aug. 1903.

[2] C. Stanley Clarke's introduction to the Wantage Paintings (Victoria and Albert Museum).

[3] Before the discovery of cochineal in 1518, *kermes*, a pigment obtained from *Coccus Indicus*, an insect found in Persia, must have been used (*Burlington Magazine*, vol. iv, p. 144). Other authorities call the species *Coccus ilicis*.

[4] Recipe in Ozias Humphrey MSS. in B.M., No. 15962, first leaf. See also Moor, *Hindu Pantheon* (ed. 1810), p. 63 *n*.

[5] Blochet, *Burlington Magazine*, vol. ii, *ut supra*.

[6] The word طرح, *tarh*, or *tarrah*, primarily means 'foundation'; e.g. *tarh afgandan*, 'to lay a foundation,' *tarh-kash*, a 'plan-drawer' (Steingass, *Pers. Dict.*). The transition to the meaning 'outline' was easy, and the word always has that meaning in the signatures to the Indo-Persian drawings, as M. Blochet rightly perceived. Blochmann's erroneous rendering 'back-grounding' in his translation of the *Ain-i-Akbari* made the signatures unintelligible. 'Painting' or 'colouring', as distinguished from 'outline', is expressed by either the Arabic word عمل, *a'mal*, 'execution', or the Persian term *rang-amezi*, 'colouring'. When *a'mal* stands alone, it implies execution of the picture by a single artist. The term *rang-amezi*, to signify 'colouring', is preferred in the Jaipur *Razmnamah*.

Safavid period in the sixteenth century. During the seventeenth century the refined Safavid style, with its lowered scale of colour, became familiar in India, where further local modifications were effected under the influence of Hindu tradition. The Indian artists 'had a truer feeling for colour and more sober tonality' than their Persian teachers, according to M. Blochet, who is disposed to think that the Indians sometimes carried the policy of softening colour to an undue extreme. They were wonderfully successful in their *grisaille* drawings of a single colour, frequently a pale sepia, with delicate gradations of tint, very pleasing to my eye. At the same time they developed a mastery over individual characteristic portraiture never equalled, I think, by the Persians. The best Indian work dates from the first half of the seventeenth century, but good portraits are to be found executed as late as the early years of the nineteenth century.

Indian modifications.

During Akbar's reign (1556-1605) and a portion of Jahangir's (1605-27) the standing portrait figures are usually represented in profile in a formal, conventional manner, with the right hand holding up a flower or jewel, and the feet placed one in front of the other. Gradually this stiff formalism was dropped, and men and women were drawn in natural attitudes. The more ancient Indo-Persian works, like their Persian models, follow unreservedly a style marked by the total lack of roundness, depth of tone, and aerial perspective, every object being represented as absolutely flat. During the later years of Jahangir's reign and subsequently, this flat style was modified by the Indian artists, who frequently introduced slight line shading with admirable effect, so contriving to give their figures a sufficient degree of roundness with wonderfully few strokes. The change adds much to the attractiveness of seventeenth-century Indian work in European eyes, and was due to foreign influence. But chiaroscuro was imported to the detriment of colouring and line drawing. Delicacy and subtlety are bought at the cost of strength and vitality. Highly developed skill in portraiture seems to have swamped the sense of design and decoration. Foreign influence is also particularly noticeable in the treatment of clouds and foliage : such influence is often of a late eighteenth-century kind.

Christian subjects.

This improvement, if it may be so called, was the result of European influence, which certainly became a potent factor in Persian and Indian art at that time. Most of the albums show it plainly. For instance, Dara Shikoh's album includes two wood engravings (fol. 42*b*, 43), one of S. Caterina di Siena, dated 1585, and the other of S. Margarita of about the same period, while the picture on folio 74 exhibits a lady and gentleman in European costume. Biblical subjects were frequently treated by the artists, and were specially favoured by the royal family, who used them for palace decorations at both Fatehpur-Sikri and Lahore. The treatment at times seems very quaint, as when we see the *Good Shepherd* depicted in the form of a stout middle-aged man with a black beard, wearing a Muslim's robe and a twisted turban of gold brocade. A Good Shepherd in vol. xvi, fol. 1 of the Johnson Collection is signed by Ustad Miskin, probably to be identified with Muhammad Miskin, the author of a lady's portrait in vol. xxi, fol. 1 of the same collection, and with Miskin, Akbar's artist, who signed some of the pictures in the Clarke MS of the *Akbarnamah.* Many other biblical subjects will be found in the collections, and it must be confessed that the pictures are not usually equal to those devoted to topics more congenial to the artists.

One subject, frequently treated with variations, has been mistakenly identified as Christian, and dubbed *Angels ministering to Christ*, although all the composi-

A. Basohli School. 18th. Century A.D. Ghose Collection. (Illustration from a *Gitā Govindā* series. An inscription states that it was painted for the Lady Manaku, the patroness of the series, in A.D. 1730. This inscription has often been mis-read as referring to an artist named Manaku).

B. A princess listening to the singer Vasistu. Pre-Kangra phase of Pahari Painting. *c.* 1760 A.D. Formerly in the Sir Dorab Tata Collection.

PLATE 189

A. Illustration to the *Gita Govinda*. Kangra School of Pahari painting. *c*. 1790 A.D. Probably painted at the Court of the great Sansar Chand of Kangra. Collection of the Maharaja of Garhwal.

B. Pahari School. Late 18th Century. Victoria and Albert Museum. (Kangra School of Pahari painting probably at the Court of the great Sansar Chand of Kangra)

PLATE 190

tions dealing with it are purely Muslim. The main motive is the miraculous supply of food to a hermit saint dwelling in the wilderness by angels, who vary in number in different replicas, and are generally, if not always, provided with wings in the conventional fashion borrowed by Christian art from the Greek figure of Victory. Most of the pictures show a second figure, a discontented darvish sitting sulking in a corner or at the mouth of a cave. As is proved in several instances by the labels, the principal figure undoubtedly is that of Ibrahim, son of Adham, who resigned the kingdom of Balkh, and withdrew as a hermit into the wilderness already haunted by a darvish, whose food had been provided regularly by the angels. When the ex-king appeared on the scene, the angels, while continuing to supply their old client the darvish with a single daily dish as a bare subsistence, liberally brought ten dishes to the retired monarch, in recognition of the sacrifice made by him. The darvish naturally was annoyed, and whenever he is introduced into the picture his feelings are indicated by the artist.[1] The so-called *Angels ministering to Christ.*

Many of the attempts to combine the methods of the West with those of the East are decided failures, as similar attempts in China have failed, but some few attain a high level of executive excellence.

The origin of such influence is not far to seek. The Persian kings admired European art, and deliberately sought to introduce its methods into their country. During the residence of Sir Robert Sherley at the Persian court, sometime about A.D. 1606, Shah Abbas I (1587-1629) sent to Rome a party of students, one of whom became a Christian and published a book under the name of Don John of Persia. Shah Abbas II (1642-67) repeated the experiment and dispatched a second party. One of these, by name Muhammad Zaman, also was converted, and returned to Persia as a Christian under the name of Paolo Zaman. Having been obliged to quit his native land, he obtained in India the protection of Shahjahan, who granted him, with other exiled Persians, allowances as a *mansabdar* in Kashmir. Early in Aurangzeb's reign all the Persian refugee *mansabdars* were summoned to court for the verification of their grants, and on that occasion, about A.D. 1660, Manucci made the acquaintance of Muhammad or Paolo Zaman, who avowed his Christian profession, while continuing to live in the ordinary Musalman manner. The three Europeanized pictures in B. M. Or. 2265 evidently are from his brush. Persian art students in Rome.

To this day the painters and illuminators of Isfahan, the earlier, and Teheran, the later, capital of Persia, cherish as their ideal the ambition to 'paint like Raphael', and pride themselves on their descent from certain of the students sent long ago to Rome who survived to return to the home of their fathers.[2]

The attempt to weld Asiatic ideals and methods with those of Europe, although responsible for some pretty pictures, was not a permanent success in either Persia or India. It is now being renewed by the clever Bengali artists of Abanindro Nath Tagore's school in a different form, and with considerable ability, but I fear, without much prospect of producing any really important results. Modern combination of Eastern and Western art.

The Indo-Persian or Mughal school of drawing and painting having lived in considerable vigour from about A.D. 1570 to 1820 or 1830—a period, roughly Enormous output.

[1] *J. R. A. S.*, 1909, p. 751; 1910, p. 167.

[2] The strange story of the Persian missions to Rome is pieced together from Irvine, *Storia do Mogor*, ii. 17; and Sir C. Purdon Clarke's article 'A Tradition of Raphael in Persia', *J. Ind. Art*, vol. vii (1897), pp. 25, 26, Pls. XLII-XLVI. The author of that article heard the tradition of the artists when he was visiting Persia in 1874-6. It is said that Muhammad Zaman, who was converted, had been sent abroad to learn how to confute the Christian missionaries. The adventurous lives of the Sherley (Shirley) brothers may be read in the *Dict. of Nat. Biography*.

speaking, of two centuries and a half—and not being quite dead even now, naturally produced an enormous output. The extant works, notwithstanding all the mishaps to which Indian art has been exposed, still can be numbered by thousands. Almost at the very beginning of the operations of the school, about the year 1590, when Abul Fazl, the minister of Akbar, wrote his memorable description of his sovereign's administration, a hundred artists were reckoned to be masters of their craft, while tolerable practitioners were past counting. During the reigns of Akbar's son and grandson, in the first half of the seventeenth century, when the new form of art grafted upon the stock of ancient Indian tradition attained its highest development, the number of proficients must have increased. Although the long-continued political and social agony which accompanied the decline and fall of the Mughal empire necessarily limited the opportunities for the practice of art and diminished its rewards, art did not die; a synthesis between Hindu tradition and Persian technique produced a new variety of Indian pictorial art possessing high merits. It is plain, therefore, that even when the eighteenth-century mythological painting is placed on one side for separate treatment, the mass of material to be dealt with by the historian is enormous, and that it is not possible within reasonable limits to do more than select a small number of typical examples.

100-200 artists recorded.

Many, perhaps most, of the extant Indo-Persian compositions are anonymous, but hundreds are signed, and it would not be difficult to compile a list of the names of from one hundred to two hundred artists. Abul Fazl's list of those considered by him to be the most eminent numbers seventeen persons, all of whom, with possibly one exception, are represented by extant works. In one manuscript, the *Waqiat-i-Babari*, or history of Babar, written and illustrated about A. D. 1600, towards the close of Akbar's reign (B.M. Or. 3714), I noted the names of twenty-two artists, and probably overlooked several. Unfortunately, a great many of the names thus freely recorded are mere names, nothing being known concerning the men who bore them, so that the perusal of nominal lists offers little of interest.

Hindu names predominate.

Perhaps the most fruitful general observation arising from such perusal is that of the predominance of Hindu names. For instance, in the *Waqiat-i-Babari* above mentioned, out of twenty-two names, nineteen are Hindu, and only three Muslim. Similarly, in Abul Fazl's catalogue of seventeen artists, only four are Muhammadan, while thirteen are Hindu.

Muhammadan artists in Abul Fazl's list.

The four Muhammadans named are:—(1) Mir Sayyid Ali, the illustrator of the story of *Amir Hamzah*, whose work probably is represented by the two large pictures in B.M. Or. 3600 (*ante*, *p.* 468); (2) Khwajah Abdus Samad (*ante*, p. 452); (3) Farrukh the Qalmak (Calmuck); and (4) Miskin (*ante*, p. 464). Farrukh certainly deserves high praise. He contributed good work to the Clarke MS. of the *Akbarnamah*, and was the author of a remarkable painting in three scenes occupying a full page on the reverse of folio 13 of B.M. Or. 3714. Miskin, who drew the outlines of two pictures ($\frac{1}{117}$, $\frac{89}{117}$) in the Clarke MS., seems to be identical with the Ustad (*scil.* 'Master') Miskin who painted the Good Shepherd in the Johnson Collection and the Muhammad Miskin, author of a lady's portrait in the same collection (LVIII, 15). Both those works are early in style.

Hindu artists in same.

The thirteen Hindu names in Abul Fazl's list are:—(5) Daswanth; (6) Basawan; (7) Kesu (Kesava); (8) Lal; (9) Mukund; (10) Madho; (11) Jagan [nath]; (12) Mahesh; (13) Khemkaran; (14) Tara; (15) Sanwlan; (16) Haribans; and (17) Ram. The signatures of all the seventeen artists named by Abul Fazl appear

A. Pahari School. Late 18th Century. Victoria and Albert Museum. (Kangra School of Pahari painting. *c.* 1800 A.D.)

B. Illustration to the *Bhagavata Purana*. Gopis lamenting the disappearance of Krishna. Kangra School of Pahari painting. *c.* 1790 A.D. Probably painted at the Court of the great Sansar Chand of Kangra. F. D. Wadia Collection, Poona.

PLATE 191

Portrait of Nizam Burhan Shah II of Ahmadnagar (?) Decanni School. Late 17th Century A.D.
Bibliothèque Nationale, Paris.

PLATE 192

in the Clarke MS., except Haribans, No. 16; and reappear in the Jaipur *Razmnamah*, excepting Nos. 1, 2, and 16. I do not remember seeing any picture signed by Haribans. There were two Madhos, the Elder (*Kalan*) and the Younger (*Khurd*). Kesu (Kesava) and some other artists are similarly duplicated in the signatures. Abul Fazl probably referred to the elder persons bearing the names. In the *Razmnamah* I have noted twenty-eight names, of whom twenty or twenty-one are Hindu.

Daswanth.

The sad story of Daswanth has been told already. Good specimens of his work as draughtsman are to be seen in Plates XII and XV of Col. Hendley's reproduction of the Jaipur *Razmnamah*, both of which were drawn in outline by him, and coloured respectively by Madho the Elder and Kanha. The subjects are Hindu legends, treated in the Persian manner, but with differences. The principal figures are distinctively Indian in feature and form, and even in the minor figures, where the chubby cheeks characteristic of the Persian style are preserved, the bodies are much less elongated than in Persian pictures. The scheme of colour too is lowered in brilliancy, and indigo blue is introduced for the bodies of deities.

Basawan.

Basawan, whom some critics preferred to Daswanth, is represented by Plate XXI of the *Razmnamah*, illustrating the story of the Raja who married the daughter of the King of Frogs. The lady, divesting herself of her fine clothes, returned to the water and resumed her froggy form, whereupon the angry husband proceeded to kill all the frogs he could find, until the lady was restored to him. The prevailing colour is green in various shades. The birds, frogs, trees, and flowers are drawn and painted with the utmost delicacy, but the general effect is marred by the intrusion of blocks of manuscript. The perspective convention is the same as that of the ancient bas-reliefs. If the spectator imagines that all the persons, trees, etc., are on hinges and can be raised to their feet, they will then all fall into their proper relative positions. The artist saw with his mind's eye all the figures standing up, but in order to paint them, conceived them all to be laid down on one side. The subject seems to be regarded and viewed from above, all the parts being equally bathed in light, which is not represented as coming from any particular direction. Consequently, there are no shadows, and there is hardly any shading. Strong sunlight is indicated by a wash of gold behind the big tree. The drawing is by Basawan, the colouring by Bhawani. I am inclined to prefer Basawan to Daswanth.

Kesu, etc.

The two Kesus, or Kesavas, like Daswanth, were members of the lowly Kahar or palanquin-bearer caste. The elder (Kesava-dasa) dedicated a collection of pictures, including copies and imitations of Christian works, to Akbar in A.D. 1588 (Sam. 1646).[1]

Animals.

The Indo-Persian artists excelled in the delineation of animals, both quadrupeds and birds, and a delightful album might be composed of their pictures of animal life. The celebrated artist Mansur, who enjoyed the special favour of Jahangir, and was honoured by him with a title of nobility, began his career in Akbar's reign. Two hunting scenes ($\frac{11}{117}$ and $\frac{62}{117}$) in the Clark MS. of the *Akbarnamah* are his work. The *Waqiat-i-Babari*, B.M. Or. 3714, contains a series of eight exquisite little miniatures from his brush (Persian, Nos. 110–17, on folios 387–9). Mansur, however, excelled as an animal and bird painter. His work is further represented in the India section of the Victoria and Albert

[1] 'Assess. 9278, 9360' in Royal Library, Berlin; cited by Weber, *Ind. Ant.*, vi. 353.

Museum by Nos. 21, 22, and 23 of the Wantage Bequest, paintings of a pheasant, a turkey-cock, and a blue-throated barbet. Mr. Havell has reproduced successfully a beautiful white crane by Mansur in the Calcutta Art Gallery (*Indian Sculpture and Painting*, Plate LXI).

Date of Dara Shikoh's Album.

In Dara Shikoh's album (*ante*, p. 457) only three pictures (folios 25, 27, and 21*b*) are dated—the dates being A.H. 1014 = A.D. 1605-6; A.H. 1018 = A.D. 1609-10; and A.H. 1043 = 1633-4. The first of those years was that in which the sceptre passed from the hands of Akbar to those of Jahangir ; the third falls in the reign of Shahjahan. Six of the paintings (folios 17*b*, 18, 19*b*, 33*b*, 35*b*, and 45*b*) seem to include portraits of Jahangir (Prince Salim) in his youth and early manhood. The collection, as a whole, therefore, may be ascribed to the time of Jahangir and the earlier part of Shahjahan's reign, or in other words, to the first forty years of the seventeenth century.

Muhammad Khan.

The only signed composition is that on folio 21*b*, dated 1633-4, which bears the name of Muhammad Khan. The picture is characteristic of Jahangir's bibulous court. It represents a young man clad in a bright yellow robe and large green turban, kneeling before a vase of flowers and a golden dish containing four earthenware jars, and engaged in pouring red wine from a jewelled goglet into a cup held in his left hand. No shading is used.

Beautiful birds.

The birds in this album, exquisitely drawn and coloured, are worthy of Mansur and may possibly be from his brush. I admire particularly the picture on folio 8 of a long-legged, brown bird standing by the side of a pool fringed with grass, flowers, and bamboos in tolerably good perspective. The blue sky, unfortunately, is rather crude. Another remarkable bird study is that on folio 10 representing admirably a wild duck standing by the side of a pool at the foot of a hillock. The sunlight on the face of the hillock is boldly indicated by a wash of gold, with surprisingly fine effect. No Chinese work could surpass the picture of the turkey-cock, ordered specially by Jahangir, and now in the Calcutta Art Gallery, reproduced by Mr. Havell in Plate LXII of *Indian Sculpture and Painting*.[1]

Historical portraits.

The works of the Indo-Persian draughtsmen and painters furnish a gallery of historical portraits, lifelike and perfectly authentic, which enable the historian to realize the personal appearance of all the Mughal emperors and of almost every public man of note in India for more than two centuries.[2] It may be doubted if any other country in the world possesses a better series of portraits of the men who made history. Pictures of this class are so numerous, and so many of such excellence, that it is difficult to make a representative selection.

Portraits of Akbar and his friends.

Portraits of Akbar are too many for specification in detail. One (B.M. Add. 18801, fol. 10) shows him standing with Prince Salim (Jahangir) as a child beside him; and another (B.M. Add. 22470, fol. 4) exhibits him as the enthroned monarch hearing a woman's petition. The principal courtiers in this latter scene are all represented by careful likenesses with the names attached in minute script. Volume lvii of the Johnson Collection in the India Office Library, presented in 1816 by Dr. Buchanan (Hamilton), contains fifty-three rather rough sketches of princes and nobles, including Akbar's friends, Abul Fazl, Birbal, and Raja Man Singh. Volume lviii of the same collection is mostly filled with similar

[1] See *Memoirs of Jahangir*, transl. Rogers and Beveridge (1909), p. 215.

[2] They are, as stated, perfectly authentic for the men, but I share Manucci's doubts about the authenticity of the numerous supposed likenesses of Nurjahan and other ladies. The rigid seclusion of females prescribed by Muslim usage seems to preclude the possibility of real portraits of ladies of rank.

Plate C
Jahangir as Prince Salim, anonymous. Fol. 18 of Dara Shikoh's album. ("Prince and Preceptor." Mughal school, Shah Jehan period. Mid-17th. Century).

sketches of better quality and some unfinished portraits. No. 18, a finished work by Miskin, may be the earliest in the set.

All critics, presumably, would admit that Indo-Persian art attained its highest achievements during the reign of the magnificent Shahjahan (A.D. 1627-58), when the land enjoyed comparative peace, and a luxurious court offered liberal encouragement to all artists capable of ministering to its pleasure. The fierce scenes of bloodshed in which the earlier artists delighted were replaced by pageants of peaceful courtly splendour, the old aggressive colouring was toned down or dispensed with, and a general refinement of style and execution was cultivated. In the portraits of men and favourite animals a little shading executed by a few delicate strokes was dexterously introduced, sufficient to suggest solidity and roundness, and yet managed with such reserve that the Asiatic reliance on the power of line was not interfered with. Art in reign of Shahjahan.

The compositions of this period comprise a variety of subjects and are the work of many artists. The names of a few whose productions have attracted my special attention may be mentioned:—Chitarman, *alias* Kalyan Das; Anupchhatar; Rai Anup (possibly the same person), court painter to Prince Dara Shikoh; Manohar; Muhammad Nadir of Samarkand; Mir Hashim; and Muhammad Fakirullah Khan. Some of the artists.

One of the richest albums in the British Museum is the manuscript Add. 18801, inscribed with a note stating that the volume was dedicated as a pious donation in A.H. 1072 = A.D. 1661-2. Sir Joshua Reynolds examined the collection in July 1777, and expressed his particular admiration for the following six works: Pictures selected by Sir Joshua Reynolds.

No. 20. Pencil sketch of an officer of Shahjahan, by Chitarman, who was also called Kalyan Das;

No. 21. Similar sketch of Azam Khan Koka, by Muhammad Nadir of Samarkand;

No. 27. Similar sketch of Asaf Khan, anonymous;

No. 28. Large anonymous sketch of Shahjahan holding court, surrounded by nobles whose portraits are named. The price is marked as 200 rupees, equivalent at that time to £25 or more;

No. 30. Sketch of head of Hakim Masih-uz-zaman, a noble who had lived in Akbar's time, by Mir Hashim, very small and very good; and

No. 40. Three portraits. The principal one is a sketch of Sher Muhammad Nawal, by Muhammad Nadir of Samarkand. The minor ones are small coloured miniatures of Jahangir and Shahjahan by the same artist.

No. 41. A delicate little head of Mirza Nauzar, a noble of Shahjahan's court, by Mir Hashim, is worthy to rank with Sir Joshua's selections.

Turning to animals, we find in the Johnson Collection (vol. iii, fol. 1) a life-like portrait of Dilpasand, or 'Heart's Delight', a favourite charger of Dara Shikoh, by an artist named Manohar. An equestrian portrait of the same prince mounted on another charger is also notable (ibid., vol. iv, fol. 9) and of unusually large size, about 11 inches by 9. Charger by Manohar.

The tiny cat sitting up, in vol. liii, fol. 5, of the same collection, is excellent. This is not the only example of pictures of cats. One appears at the feet of the Emperor Farrukhsiyar in volume No. 5 of Exhibition Case B in the King's Library, British Museum, and a few others occur in other compositions. Cats.

Perfectly drawn elephants are numerous. Indian artists, whether sculptors Elephants.

or painters, rarely failed to produce good representations of the huge quadruped, the nature of which they understood thoroughly. Volume lxvii in the Johnson Collection is specially devoted to elephants, several of which are admirable. One of the best is that on folio 7, by Nadir-uz-zaman (Abul Hasan).[1] Another fine picture is that on folio 15. The main subject is a magnificent elephant standing in a palace courtyard, with other elephants, a bullock, &c., as accessories. The drawing is *grisaille* in a brownish sepia tint, no other colour being used, except that the golden ornaments of the elephant are yellow.

Miscellaneous subjects.

The many charming pictures treating of miscellaneous subjects including illustrations of popular stories, offer a wide field for description and selection, far too large to be treated exhaustively.

Baz Bahadur and Rupmati.

A favourite subject was the story of Baz Bahadur, king of Malwa, and his lady-love, Princess Rupmati, who are represented in several pictures as riding together by torchlight. A good example in the Calcutta Art Gallery has been reproduced in Plate LXIV of Mr. Havell's *Indian Sculpture and Painting;* another, from the Hercules Read's rich collection, is of special value because of the label indicating the subject; and a third is on folio 22 of B.M. Add. 21928. Other romances frequently illustrated are the tales of Laila and Majnun, Khusru and Shirin, and Kamrup and Kamta.

Contrast between light and darkness.

Mr. Havell has rightly drawn attention to the skill with which the Indian artists treated the contrast between the pitchy darkness of night and the flare of artificial light. Several pictures are extant which exhibit this contrast in scenes of hunting by night, flaming torches being used to dazzle and hypnotize the deer. Colonel Hanna's Collection, now in Washington, includes two such scenes, Nos. 42 and 102, of which the latter excited the warm admiration of the late Sir Frederick Burton. A more modern specimen in the Calcutta Art Gallery is reproduced in Mr. Havell's Plate LXV.

The same motive, which also attracted Rembrandt, inspires the pictures representing a lady standing on a balcony watching the effect of fireworks over the dark waters of the Jumna. Sometimes she is shown in the act of discharging a squib herself.[2] In folio 4 of vol. xv of the Johnson Collection, the lady, clad in bright scarlet and standing against a background of inky darkness, produces a very impressive effect. A picture by Muhammad Fakirullah Khan (folio 7 of the same volume) depicting the nocturnal pursuit of a warrior is equally successful in bringing out the opposition of light and darkness. Other compositions exhibitng people grouped round a camp-fire aim at like effects.

Pictures of holy men.

Many artists took great delight in depicting holy men and ascetics of all sorts, Musulman and Hindu, singly or in groups. Two of the most exquisite works dealing with this class of subject, and no doubt executed in the reign of Shahjahan, are the companion pictures, folios 11 *b* and 12, Dara Shikoh's album, representing an old fakir in two positions, holding a book in the one case, and a rosary in the other. The outline of the figure is drawn with less than the usual sharpness, and shading with fine lines is employed sufficiently to give an impression of roundness. In the old man's beard the delicacy and accuracy with which individual hairs are drawn displays a wonderful mastery over that most difficult instrument, the single-hair brush. The colouring is subdued, and the perspective fairly correct.

[1] Nadir-uz-zaman was the official title of Abul Hasan, a favourite artist of Jahangir. He seems to have continued to work in the following reign.

[2] Dr. Coomaraswamy possesses a good picture of girls discharging fireworks, signed by Muhammad Afzal, with a Persian verse on the back, dated A.H. 1069 = A.D. 1658-9, commendatory of the painter. Another of his works is in volume xi of the Johnson Collection.

A. Syama Gujari Ragini from the Laud *Ragamala*. Deccani School with Mughal influence. *c.* 1625 A.D. Bodlein Library, Oxford.

B. The exiled Yaksha, by Abanindro Nath Tagore. (*By Courtesy of Dr. A. K. Coomaraswamy*)

C. The Bride's Toilet, by Amrita Sher Gil. Died A.D. 1941. National Gallery of Modern Art, New Delhi.

PLATE 193

A. Mother and child. Early Deccani School. 1st quarter of 17th Century. Salar Jung Museum, Hyderabad.

B. Yogini. Deccani School. Mid-17th Century. Salar Jung Museum, Hyderabad.

PLATE 194

Another drawing in the same volume, in similar style, and probably by the same artist, is that on folio 60. The subject is the reading by a young *mullah* (Muhammadan teacher) from a Koran resting on a stand. Two of his companions are listening attentively, while the third, in the foreground, is engaged in pouring water over the toes of his left foot held up in his hand. The drawing of the difficult position of this figure is extremely clever. The reader of the Koran.

Most of the albums contain examples of gorgeous court scenes elaborated with infinite patience and minuteness of detail, harmoniously coloured, and often enriched with gold. It would be next to impossible to reproduce the most splendid of these pictures in colours with success, and I think it better not to make the attempt. The composition being the weak point in these works, photographs do them an injustice. Colonel Hanna possessed two of the richest specimens in existence, Nos. 1 and 2 in his volume marked *Persian Drawings*. No. 2 is the largest Indo-Persian picture known to me, excepting the early illustrations of the *Story of Amir Hamzah*, the measurements being 23 inches by 17½ inches. The subject is a review of cavalry on the bank of the Jumna by Shahjahan mounted on an elephant. The portraits of the principal chiefs and officers in the crowd have their names attached. Court scenes.

The manuscript B.M. Add. 20734, an official present given by the titular Emperor of Delhi in 1815, contains nine pictures in the most highly finished style, of which two may be specified. One representing the infant Shahjahan (Prince Khurram) lying in his mother's lap, surrounded by admiring attendants, is wrought with colouring so rich and decorative details so elaborate that an attempt to copy it would certainly fail. Another picture, extending across two pages (fol. 689, 690), and depicting Shahjahan seated on the peacock throne in all his glory, while Asaf Khan offers a present of costly pearls, gives a vivid notion of the extravagant magnificence of the Mughal court in its prime. Court of Shahjahan.

Volumes ix, x, xi of the Johnson Collection may be noticed as being specially devoted to the ladies, some of whom are represented half nude in the bath or at their toilet. The pictures in volume xi are particularly good, the most noticeable being a charming portrait of a lady wearing a high conical head-dress, and admirably shaded. From an inferior replica (B.M. Add. 11747, fol. 52) we learn that the lady's name or title was Malkah Zamaniya. The ladies.

Passing on to the reigns of Aurangzeb (1658-1707) and his decadent successors during the eighteenth century, we find the artists still numerous and specimens of their work abundant. Although Aurangzeb was too zealous a puritan to care for art himself, the fashion set by his predecessors had not died out, and princes and nobles still kept court painters. Portraiture continued to be practised with great success, although the execution rarely attains the perfection of the first half of the seventeenth century. The art of this period and subsequent periods can only be justly treated of as the product of artists who gained a living at minor courts, Hindu or Muhammadan, and whose style and choice of subject are modified by the local demand. Certain of these local styles, spoken of collectively as 'Rajput', are distinct, but much of the later work remains true to the decadent Mughal tradition. Later art.

RAJPUT PAINTING

To Dr. Coomaraswamy must be given the credit of the primary study and

'Rajput' painting.

classification of non-Mughal Indian paintings. He begins his survey[1] with a quotation from Abul Fazl who says of the Hindu painters at the Mughal court that 'their pictures surpass our conception of things. Few, indeed, in the world are equal to them.' As has been said, his classification is based upon a dual conception of two schools of Indian painting, Mughal and Rajput, which are 'utterly diverse' in temper, the Rajput school dating from the fifteenth and sixteenth centuries and therefore preceding the Mughal school. He acknowledges that in latter days the schools tended to converge and blend, but at all times the subject-matter was different. With regard to his early dating of Rajput painting, he supports his views by a direct comparison with Ajanta and Sigiriya. The well-known 'Death of Bishma' is therefore 'unmistakably . . . reminiscent of the great Buddhist *Parinirvanas*'. It is evident that much of his argument is based on the subject-matter. Rajput painting is Hindu, popular, spiritual. . . . Mughal painting is Muhammadan, courtly, material. The primary fact that is overlooked is that the technique of the two schools is identical, and Persian in origin.

Classification.

Dr. Coomaraswamy's classification of Rajput painting is a geographical one, which invites chronological inexactitude. There is a *Rajasthani* (lowland) school and a *Pahari* (Himalayan) school. Though these subdivisions are absolutely acceptable in themselves, it must be acknowledged that there are numerous local schools and certain period differences to be distinguished. Roughly speaking, the Kangra paintings with their flowing line and westernized drawing of foliage and landscape are typical of the *Pahari* schools, while the Jaipur paintings with their concentration on jewellery treated in relief and formal drapery are typical of the *Rajasthani* schools. Both of these lesser schools show Mughal, if not foreign influence, especially with regard to their architectural settings. Certain *Rajasthani* paintings, however, exist which are clearly earlier than the eighteenth and nineteenth century Kangra and Jaipur work. Most of these are *Ragini* subjects, but their technique and the details of costume and architecture will not allow of them being dated pre-seventeenth century.

Origin of Rajput painting.

These Rajput paintings seem to have been the work of the court painters of the petty Rajput courts of the seventeenth and eighteenth centuries. As with the parent Mughal school, portraits are plentiful, especially of the Jaipur, Bijapur, and Hyderabad schools, and a survey of them would provide accurate chronological data. Nineteenth century work is plentiful, being chiefly of the copyist order. The colouring tends to be crude and the drawing slovenly. Moreover, certain painters are still at work, turning out the old subjects usually on old paper—to the great confusion of students.

Bazaar painting.

Apart from the work of the court painters, much work exists which is the product of 'bazaar schools'. Of these the Calcutta brush drawings in colour of the *Patua* caste are especially notable for their vigorous line. At Trichinopoly also there flourished a bazaar-school during the last century, working in tempera colours on paper or talc. It may be taken for granted that most of the large cities have produced 'bazaar-work' of a kind, very little of which has been preserved. The subjects depicted in this type of work are usually purely iconographical.

The Modern Schools

Pictures at the Delhi exhibition.

At the Delhi Exhibition of 1902-3 many examples were shown of the oil-paintings

[1] *Burlington Magazine*, March 1912, quoting Blochmann's *Ain-i-Akbari*, i. 107.

Plate D.

Marble building, etc., by Muhammad Fakirullah Khan. Johnson Collection Vol. XVII, fol. 3.
(Worship in a Pavilion, Mughal school. Late 17th Century).

and water-colours produced in considerable quantities of late years by students trained in European methods, chiefly at the Government Schools of Art in Calcutta, Bombay, Madras, and Lahore. In Sir George Watt's book Mr. Percy Brown, late Principal of the Calcutta School of Art, criticizes the Delhi exhibits as follows:—

'Until its introduction from Europe, there was no oil painting of any kind practised throughout the country, but the number of pictures executed in the medium shown in the Exhibition reveals the fact that oil picture painting as a branch of study, as well as a means of livelihood, is being taken up seriously by a rapidly increasing class. Some of the work displayed in the Eastern Hall of the Exhibition was remarkably good; in the life studies the modelling and feeling of living flesh being well reproduced, and one or two landscapes showed an atmosphere and a consideration for composition which is [*sic*] worthy of remark. Much, however, of the work shown was of a very ordinary character, the drawing being decidedly defective, and the technique and colouring in most cases crude.'[1]

Raja Ravi-varma.

The most prominent representative of the Europeanized school of Indian artists was the late Raja Ravi-varma of Travancore, a connexion of the Maharaja of that State. His works, which are extremely numerous, achieved wide popularity, and have been freely vulgarized by oleographs and other cheap modes of reproduction. The Raja practised both portrait and landscape painting, and four of the portraits in the Banqueting Hall, Madras, are from his brush.[2] He was assisted by his relative, Raja Raja-varma, and other members of his family. He had received instruction from Theodore Jensen and other European artists who visited Southern India, as well as from Alagri Naidu, a native of Madura, in the Madras Presidency, who was patronized by Swati Tirumal, Maharaja of Travancore from 1829 to 1847, and was considered in his day to be the best painter in India after the European fashion. Ravi-varma had a formidable rival in Ramaswamy Naidu, a member of the clan of Naiks at Madura, who was considered to excel in portrait painting.

Stimulated by the active encouragement of the royal family of Travancore, the Gaikwar of Baroda, and other wealthy patrons, Ravi-varma turned his attention to the illustration of the Hindu legends and epics.

Criticism of Ravi-varma's works.

In his own country his works in that kind are regarded as masterpieces and adequate expressions of Indian feeling. At the hands of recent critics in Europe they have met with a different reception.

'The art', writes Mr. Havell, 'which truly reflects the fictitious culture of Indian universities and the teaching of Anglo-Indian art schools, is exhibited in the paintings of Ravi-varma, who is the fashionable painter of modern India for those Indians who do not ignore Indian art altogether. . . . Certain it is that his pictures invariably manifest a most painful lack of the poetic faculty in illustrating the most imaginative Indian poetry and allegory; and this cardinal sin is not to be atoned for by any kind of technical skill in the execution.'[3]

Dr. Coomaraswamy, a fellow mystic, is still more severe, and declares that

'theatrical conceptions, want of imagination, and lack of Indian feeling in the treatment of sacred and epic Indian subjects are Ravi-varma's fatal faults . . . . His pictures are such as any European student could paint, after perusal of the necessary literature and a superficial study of Indian life.[4]

In a more recent publication the same author gives his opinion with greater brevity and somewhat less severity to the effect that

'the late Raja Ravi-varma was the best known of these painters in a purely European style, but neither he nor any other workers of the pseudo-European school attained to excellence. His work at the best reached a second-rate standard.'

[1] *Indian Art at Delhi*, p. 457.

[2] The four portraits are those of the Duke of Buckingham and Chandos, Sir Arthur Havelock, and the Ladies Mary and Caroline Grenville (Col. H. D. Love, R.E., *Descriptive List of Pictures in Government House and the Banqueting Hall, Madras* (Government Press, Madras, 1903), p. 132).

[3] *Indian Sculpture and Painting*, p. 251.

[4] *Modern Review* (Allahabad), vol. ii. p. 107.

Probably this last quoted judgement is not far wrong.[1]

The Bengali Nationalist School.

'The work of the modern school of Indian painters in Calcutta', Dr. Coomaraswamy writes, 'is a phase of the National reawakening. Whereas the ambition of the nineteenth-century reformers had been to make India like England, that of the later workers has been to bring back or create a state of society in which the ideals expressed and implied in Indian culture shall be more nearly realized.'

This new movement on the art side has been enthusiastically supported by Mr. E. B. Havell, late Principal of the Calcutta School of Art, who felt keenly the futility of training Bengali students on purely foreign methods, alien to their nature, and sought to turn their attention to the productions of the Indo-Persian and eighteenth-century Hindu schools as being more expressive of Indian ideals. With some difficulty Mr. Havell persuaded the authorities to let him have his way, and replace a collection of poor European works by a choice selection of Indian paintings. He found in Mr. Abanindro Nath Tagore, now Vice-Principal of the School of Art, a willing coadjutor, and a painter of considerable power. Mr. Havell recognized in his colleague a real artist 'who has come to pick up the broken threads of Indian pictorial tradition', and credited him with 'giving us a true interpretation of Indian spirituality, and an insight into that higher world, the fairy land of Eastern poetry and romance, which Eastern thought has suggested'.[2]

The critic proceeds to say that

'if neither Mr. Tagore nor his pupils have yet altogether attained to the splendid technique of the old Indian painters, they have certainly revived the spirit of Indian art, and besides, as every true artist will, invested their work with a charm distinctively their own. For their work is an indication of that happy blending of Eastern and Western thought, from the full realization of which humanity has so much to gain.'

These rather large claims are founded on a series of small works described in the *Studio* as 'water-colour drawings', and very far indeed from having 'attained to the splendid technique of the old Indian painters', which they do not attempt to rival. The more sober criticism of Dr. Coomaraswamy is more closely in accordance with the facts.

'The subjects chosen by the Calcutta painters', he observes, 'are taken from Indian history, romance, and epic, and from the mythology and religious literature and legends, as well as from the life of the people around them. Their significance lies in their distinctive "Indianness". They are, however, by no means free from European and Japanese influence. The work is full of refinement and subtlety in colour, and of a deep love of all things Indian; but, contrasted with the Ajanta and Mughal and Rajput paintings which have in part inspired it, it is frequently lacking in strength. The work should be considered as a promise rather than a fulfilment. So regarded, it has very great significance for the future of Indian Art.'[3]

Mr. Roger Fry holds a poor opinion of the work of the modern artists. 'Such pictures as that of "The Siddhas of the Upper Air",' he observes, 'show that, however anxiously these artists strive to adopt the formulae of their ancestors, the spirit that comes to expression is that of the American magazine illustrator. Nothing, indeed, could provide a stronger proof of the profound corruption which contact with European ideas has created in Oriental taste than these well-intentioned but regrettable drawings.'[4]

The leader of the school, Mr. Abanindro Nath Tagore, began as a painter in oils, after the European fashion, but soon abandoned the oils medium, and

[1] Thirty-five of Ravi-varma's pictures are reproduced in an illustrated collection of Hindi poems, entitled *Kavita Kalap* (Allahabad, 1909), edited by Mr. Mahavira Prasada Dirvedi, and shown to me by Dr. Grierson. That book also contains prints of pictures in a similar style by Braj Bhushan Rai Chaudhri, Babu Vamapad Bandhopadhvaya, and Sriyut M. V. Dhurandhar. The prints are too rough for reproduction, courteously permitted by the editor. A list of Ravi-varma's works and an enthusiastic appreciation of his art will be found in V. Nazam Aiya, *Travancore Manual*, vol. iii, p. 263, a compilation which is a rich mine of information.

[2] *Indian Sculpture and Painting*, pp. 256, 257.

[3] *Catalogue of the Indian Court, Festival of Empire*, 1911, p. 106.

[4] *Quart. Rev.*, 1910, p. 237.

Plate E

Night Scene. Krishna and Radha on the banks of the Jumna. Illustration to the *Gita Govinda*. (Kangra School. Probably painted at the court of the great Sansar Chand of Kangra).

devoted himself to the 'water-colour drawings'. Many works by him and his pupils have been exhibited at meetings of Societies in London, and reproduced in Mr. Havell's book or in periodicals. One specimen, therefore, may suffice—the picture of the 'Exiled Yaksha', or demigod, an illustration of a passage in Kalidasa's poem, the *Meghaduta*, or 'Cloud Messenger', by Mr. Tagore. Another good picture is 'The Flight of Lakshman Sen' by the late Mr. Surendra Nath Gangooly (Mr. Havell's Pl. LXXVIII). Other pupils of Mr. Tagore deserving mention are Nanda Lal Bose, Ishwari Parshad, a descendant of hereditary painters at Patna, Gogonendra Nath Tagore, brother of Abanindro Nath, Asit Kumar Haldar, and Hakim Muhammad Khan.[1] (A 1).

All well-wishers to India will join in the hope that the promise shown by this new Bengali school may lead to something more important than the works hitherto produced. Probably all critics will agree that nothing of high worth can be created by men who merely seek to imitate foreign models. If modern India is to evolve a new art of her own, it must have its roots in the Indian past and appeal to Indian sentiment. 'L'art dans l'Inde sera indien, ou il ne sera pas'[2]: but 'to be, or not to be, that is the question' which at present no man can answer. The future

NOTES TO CHAPTER FIFTEEN

Though the Bengal school brought about a renaissance in Indian painting it suffered from certain inherent shortcomings, such as, revivalism of India's past heritage which soon degenerated into mannered imitation; a medley of oriental motifs and designs all laid on without much comprehension as to their import and purport; weak draughtsmanship and dull murky colour tonalities which it was erroneously thought created an atmosphere of spiritual mystery. A major revolt against this school was led by the most remarkable Indian painter of the century, Amrita Sher Gil, a half-Sikh, half-Hungarian girl who died in 1941 at the age of 29. She left behind a body of work which is in no way inferior to the masterpieces of the great exponents of the modern movement in Europe. She was influenced in her early period by Gaugin but developed an individuality all her own and an outlook so essentially Indian that her work can never be labelled as imitation. She was influenced by Ajanta and also by Rajasthani and Basohli painting, but she possessed the rare gift of being able to assimilate the works of the great periods of Indian art and then distil their principles so that her style was free of all superficial resemblances. Much of her work (Plate 193C) has now been acquired for the nation and some of it can be seen in the National Gallery of Modern Art at New Delhi. Neglected in her lifetime, to-day she has become a legend. A 1

INDIAN PAINTING

The history of Indian painting requires reconsideration in view of much new material that has come to light. The earliest paintings at Ajanta, namely, certain scenes in Caves 9 and 10, belong to 1st century A.D. or thereabouts. They are examples of Satavahana art and we may infer that other Buddhist monastic establishments in the Deccan may have also been embellished with such paintings though no traces of them now exist. Painting, at least in the Deccan, followed a parallel course to that of sculpture. Just as the late Satavahana and Ikshavaku sculpture at Amaravati, Goli and Nagarjunakonda is the basis and inspiration of the Vakataka sculpture of Ajanta, so also Vakataka paintings, such as those in Caves 16 and 17 at Ajanta, are the outcome of the same inspiration with a leavening of Gupta idioms. It must be apparent to any student of style that the Vakataka artists of the late 5th century A.D. were considerably indebted to the artists and artisans who had conceived and executed the great masterpieces of the Satavahana period, namely, the carved stupa railings and carved encasings. Even though there is a considerable gap between the latest Ikshavaku sculptures of Nagarjunakonda and the Vakataka art of the late 5th century A.D. at Ajanta, there is no sharp break in stylistic continuity though a new development is discernible. The art of the Vakatakas, both in sculpture and painting, is a blend of the influence of Gupta art and the late art of the Sata-

[1] See *Studio* for 1902, 1905, 1908; *Modern Review* (Allahabad), May, 1907; Havell, *Indian Sculpture and Painting*, Pls. LXXIII-LXXVIII.

[2] M. le comte Goblet d'Alviella, *Ce que l'Inde doit à la Grèce* (Paris, 1897), p. 94.

vahanas. In Northern India the great school of Kushan sculpture at Mathura had passed through a period of transition in the 3rd century A.D. and was being transformed into the fully fledged Gupta idiom at the end of the 4th century A.D. But the Gupta idiom was not confined to Northern and Central India. The relations between the Guptas and the Vakatakas, as a result of matrimonial ties, are well known to every student of Indian history and in the circumstances it is not surprising that the Gupta idiom began to play an important role in the development of sculpture and painting in the Deccan during the 5th, 6th and 7th centuries A.D. Its impact on the late Satavahana-Ikshavaku style is so pronounced that despite the attempts of certain critics to confine the Gupta style to Northern and Central India there is no escape from the conclusion that a distinctive Deccan-Gupta style must be recognized. As far as painting is concerned, we see the style in the 5th century Vakataka Caves Nos. 16 and 17 at Ajanta and in the 6th century Vaishnava cave fragments at Badami (Plate 89A) under Chalukyan patronage. Further south at Sittanavasal (Plate 89B) the Jain frescoes, also fragmentary, appear to belong to the same tradition and have been ascribed to the 7th century though an attempt not quite unconvincing, has been made to suggest a 9th century date for them.

It was generally thought that the art of wall painting ceased with the latest work at Ajanta such as that seen in Caves 1 and 2 in which the Deccan-Gupta idiom remains strong. But that belief is long outdated. Work of very considerable interest is to be seen in the 9th century Jain caves of Ellora as also in Kailasnath Temple itself at Ellora. The importance of this phase will be dealt with later on. But even after the 9th century paintings at Ellora the art of wall painting did not die out altogether. It received a set-back no doubt, but work of sufficient merit to warrant attention was produced at Tanjore in the Chola period frescoes of the great Brihadesvara Temple. They are ascribed to the 11th century and that may well be the date of some of them while some might be of the 12th century. They are unequal in workmanship, but in parts it is apparent that the heritage of Ajanta was not completely a thing of the past. Yet, barring a glimmer here and there, the 7th century saw the end of the great fresco period. The ever increasing desire for more and more intricate and elaborate sculpture and the pre-eminence accorded to such sculptural representations in the scheme of temple building appears to be one of the causes that caused a decline in the patronage to the painter guilds and consequent stagnation. Of course, having regard to the trends of medieval sculpture mentioned above it is most doubtful whether the excellence of the great fresco period would have continued to manifest itself even if it had been accorded adequate patronage. We know that as a general rule both sculpture and painting followed the prevailing trend of the times at all periods in the development of Indian art. In South India, during the rule of the Vijayanagar dynasty in the 16th century, we have frescoes at various sites such as Leepakshi and we also have frescoes of more than ordinary interest at Cochin and Padmanabhapuram and elsewhere in Kerala State which belong to the 17th century or thereabouts. There can also be little doubt that in Central and Northern India palaces and temples were painted in the 16th, 17th and 18th centuries and even earlier, the style varying from that of the Gujerati M.S. illustrations in the earlier period to a mixed Mughal-Rajasthani idiom in the 17th and 18th centuries. Such 17th century examples in the mixed idiom can be seen in a Chhatri at Amber and in the garden palace at Bairat.

With regard to forms of painting other than wall painting we have literary references which indicate that even in early times portraits and other subjects were painted on wooden boards, cloth and other material. But nothing has survived which is earlier than the illustrated palm leaf manuscripts from Gujerat and Bengal of the 11th and 12th centuries A.D. In Gujerat these manuscript illustrations are highly stylized with sharp noses, pointed double chins, farther projecting eye and a set formula for illustrating the subject matter which is mostly related to the Jain canon. But these illustrations do possess a naive charm which to some extent relieves the monotony of this style which persisted right up to the late 16th century. The illustrated palm leaf manuscripts of Bengal and Bihar during Pala rule are also stylized though not quite so hidebound in their conventions being more naturalistic in their representation of the human figure. With the introduction of paper these manuscript illustrations (Plate 179A and B) began to receive more expansive treatment than was possible on the narrow palm leaves. Thus from about 1375 A.D. onwards we enter into what may be called the 'paper period' of the Gujerati style of manuscript illustration. The Pala style died out in Bengal when the Muslim invaders overran this province in 1299 A.D., but refugee immigrants and Buddhist monks carried this style to Nepal where it was extensively practised on palm leaf and later on paper. In fact the style had reached Nepal even prior to 1299 A.D. These Pala palm leaf illustrations are mostly related to the Buddhist canon.

But though this art of book illustration, particularly in the Gujerati style, was prolific right through the 14th, 15th and 16th centuries A.D., it was not an art of miniature painting in the sense in which the Persians understood this term. A little Persian influence limited to certain motifs and certain categories of the *dramatis personnae* of the Kalaka story, namely the Sahis, is found in these MSS. while we possess one famous example at the Ahmedabad Devasano Pada Bhandar where the Timurid period influence is quite marked in the border panels. The patronage which was responsible for the illustrated MSS. of the Jain style came largely from the merchant classes. Tradition, with its usual exaggerations has it that King Kumarpala of Gujerat who ruled in the 12th century was responsible for the distribution of thousands of such illustrated MSS, to the Jain monastic orders.

This Jain or Gujerati style spread to centres in Central and Northern India such as Mandu (Plate 179A), Delhi and Jaunpur. Of course, it was natural that in its spread it should be affected by local influences such as costumes and local perferences. The result was that the Gujerati style when practised away from its home of origin always evidenced local variations. But basically it always remained the same style. Here again the patronage was from the merchant classes. The 14th, 15th and 16th centuries is the period of the most prolific production of the Gujerati style MSS. including the local variations of this style. During this period Muslim Sultans ruled over Gujerat, Malwa, Jaunpur and Delhi. The question naturally arises whether they patronized the art of miniature painting or book illustration in India. Most of these Sultans had strong leanings towards Persian culture and none of them seems to have been interested in the rather stereotyped indigenous Gujerati school illustrations which must have appeared very crude to them as compared to Persian paintings. Nor do they seem to have been interested in creating a new school of book illustration by taking Indian artists in their employ under the guidance of Persian masters. We have a few stray works which seem to have been commissioned by one or the other of these Sultans and in them we discern a mixture of Persian and Gujerati MS. style influences. But it seems that such productions were few and far between and there was no royal patronage worth the name to the art of book illustration in pre-Mughal India during the Sultanate period. The Sultans probably preferred to import illustrated Persian MSS. rather than attempt to create a local school by employing Persian masters. Whatever the truth be, painting under the Sultans is so scanty that it does not warrant any far reaching conclusions. The picture may become clearer when more material comes to light. It is therefore erroneous in our present state of knowledge to talk of the existence of regular pre-Mughal Sultanate schools of book illustration as existing side by side with the Gujerati style. The only conclusion which is at present permissible is that the Gujerati style and its local variations in Central and Northern India persisted from the 11th to the late 16th century A.D. largely unaffected by Persian miniature painting save in certain limited respects as stated above. Even the pronounced Timurid influence seen in the border panels and in the *Kalakacharya* section of the *Kalpasutra* of the Devasano Pada at Ahmedabad is absent in the principal illustrations which retain their stereotype conventions. But one notices a tendency in the late 15th and first half of the 16th century for these Gujerati MS. illustrations to become more elaborate, being often enclosed along with the text, by borders of floral decoration and geometrical patterns evidencing some direct or indirect Persian influence. This period of elaborate production is known as the period of the 'opulent style'. The writing was often in gold on coloured backgrounds, and gold was freely used in the illustrations which sometimes extended over the whole page. Usually these illustrations occupy only one section of the page.

But after the advent of the Mughals and with the accession of the great Akbar to the throne (1556-1605 A.D.), the outlook underwent a complete change. His great atelier consisted of scores of Indian artists from all over the country who worked under Persian masters and thus with constant and intensive royal patronage there grew up a style now famous as the Mughal school of miniature painting. In its turn the growth of Mughal painting exerted a strong influence on the indigenous Gujerati style and its variations in Central and Northern India. The result was that there grew up a mixed style in Rajasthan and nearby areas which is known as the early Rajasthani style. A related style, though with certain distinctive features of its own, appears to have flourished in Northern India, most probably at Jaunpur (Plate 185A) and another related style existed probably in Central India or thereabouts (Colour Pl. A) One marked characterstic of this style is the small turban with *kulah* often worn by male characters (Colour Pl. A) and which is not seen in Mughal painting. This group is therefore at times called the *Kulahdar* group though the style may have flourished in different parts of the country. Several variations in this style can be discerned. But these developments do not appear to be pre-Mughal so far as the available evidence indicates. There has been much confusion of thought on this problem which has been aggravated by the use of loose phraseology. The available evidence goes to show that the book illustration style up to the time when Akbar's great atelier began to function on vast projects, such as the *Hamza Namah* (Plate 180), was the Gujerati style with its local variations in Central India and Northern India. It was the influence exerted by Mughal painting on all these indigenous centres of MS. production in the Gujerati style which brought into being the early Rajasthani school as well as related productions typified by illustrated MSS. such as the *Laur Chanda* of the Bharat Kala Bhawan (Plate 185A), the *Gita Govinda* of the Prince of Wales Museum (Colour Pl. A) and a few similar MSS. They all appear to be post-Mughal and whether or not they be closer to *circa* 1580 A.D. than to *circa* 1600 A.D., they disclose features which suggest the influence of Mughal painting. Whatever may prove to be the truth it is certain that it was Mughal painting by far and large that provided the powerful impetus so essential to make the stereotype Gujerati style adopt a new outlook and approach.

There has also been much loose thinking about the relationship of the frescoes of the great period of Ajanta in the 5th and 6th centuries A.D. to the Gujerati style MS. illustrations and the 17th century early Rajasthani and early Pahari schools. Some writers affect to see a development and continuity of the Ajanta tradition through all this period of time. This viewpoint may be dismissed as a flight of fancy. That there is an obvious relationship between the early Rajasthani style and the earlier Gujerati MS. style cannot be gainsaid, but the art of the great frescoes is in an entirely different tradition. It is a fundamental error to think that the Gujerati MS. illustrations, or more particularly Rajasthani or Pahari paintings, are frescoes in miniature and show the ancestry of Ajanta when they are enlarged. First and foremost, it is a perversion of taste for any one to want to destroy the essentials of a miniature by trying to enlarge it, and secondly the enlarged miniature is in any event a bad fresco, very different from the great frescoes of Ajanta. The approach of the true fresco painter and of the true miniaturist are poles apart, and there is nothing more futile than to compare these forms of art in an attempt to attribute a non-existent ancestry to Rajasthani miniature painting.

The beginnings of the Mughal school are to be found in the work of Akbar's great atelier. The general belief that the school really started with Humayun is based on the fact that he had in his employ two persian artists, Mir Sayyid Ali and Abdus Samad. But the great *Hamza Namah* series (Plate 180) said to have been commenced in his reign was really commenced in about 1567 A.D. under Akbar and completed about 1582 A.D. The testimony of the historian Badaoni on this point is quite clear and is to be preferred to the general speculation that this important series, comprising more than 1400 paintings on linen, was planned and initiated in Humayun's reign. The series was of vital importance in the development of the Mughal school. This undertaking, commenced under the Persian masters whom Humayun had brought to India, required extensive planning and a large number of artists for its execution. Artists were recruited from all parts of the country. It was but natural that those painters who belonged to the guilds which had illustrated the Gujerati style MSS. in Gujerat, Rajasthan, Malwa, Jaunpur, Delhi and other centres should be drawn into Akbar's atelier. Their natural skill was soon given another direction by the Persian masters under whom they worked, but the transformation could not be carried out overnight. The result was that a new style began to be formulated. The mental approach of the Indian artists, despite the guidance of Persian masters, was bound to affect the output in various ways, so that it was not a mere imitation of Persian models. Akbar himself was not slow to recognise this fact and no doubt his eclectic mind welcomed the new style. When Akbar began to have the Indian epics and other Indian works illustrated, the outlook of the Indian artists in his atelier made itself felt more strongly than ever before and the Mughal school became firmly established as possessing distinctive qualities of its own. The old term 'Indo-Persian' used for the work of this period is not altogether inappropriate, but it is far better to refer to the products of the Mughal school of this period (Plate 181B), namely, 1580 A.D.-1590 A.D., as well as prior thereto, as the early Akbar school. Apart from portraiture the emphasis of the Akbar school was largely on illustrated MSS. dealing with Persian and Indian subjects and the copies made for the imperial library are truly magnificent. In the reign of Jehangir (1605-1628) the fondness for portraits is even greater and the art of portraiture is carried to such heights that one notices a touch of genius in these technically splendid characterizations (Plates 183A, 184B) which mark the reign of Jehangir as also the reign of Shah Jahan (1628-1658). Apart from the usual court scenes which characterize all periods of Mughal art, the Jehangir period specializes in marvellous bird and animal studies (Plate 183B). In the reign of Shah Jahan studies of saints and dervishes (Plate 184A) became more frequent than before, while portraits in the *siyahi kalam*, i.e., line drawings with slight touches of colour, achieved a vogue. This type of portrait study in the *siyahi kalam* appears to have had its origin in the work of one of Jehangir's painters, Muhammad Nadir of Samarkand (Plate 183A). The reign of Shah Jahan brings to a close the great period of Mughal painting. It is necessary to realize this fact in arriving at any estimate of the achievements of the Mughal school. Though it is a court art, it possesses such a high degree of excellence in characterization, design, composition, drawing and colour values, that Mughal miniatures of the great period have attracted many connoisseurs and dealers in Europe and America and have fetched considerable prices. On the other hand, it has to be observed that these very connoisseurs and dealers have shown little or no interest in the products of the Rajasthani and Pahari schools. These have a much better market in India itself than abroad where the taste for the products of these schools is only now being developed.

When Aurangzeb (1658-1707) came to the throne he gave little patronage to the art of painting and a decline set in. His bigotry and austerity were a damper to all artistic activities, though portraits, court and hunting scenes continued to be produced. This dull period for Mughal painting, which had in fact commenced from the later part of Shah Jahan's reign, had however one notable consequence. Artists trained in the Mughal capitals in the Mughal style began to drift to the courts of Rajasthani rajas and the Hill States of the Punjab. Here they were not circumscribed by the limited requirements of the Mughal court and the Mughal aristocracy. In fact, their new Hindu patrons delighted in the Epics, the Krishna legend, the *Braj Bhasa* poems, bardic lore and romance, the *Gita Govinda* and many other such literary masterpices. To illustrate such themes the Mughal manner of painting was not adequate to a vigorous mind. Many of these painters at the Rajasthani and Hill courts appear to have been inventive, imbued with an urge to experiment and very much alive to the sheer delight of large flat areas of glowing colours, such as strong lacquer reds, intense blues, rich ochre yellows, olive greens, deep blacks, etc. In addition, their sense of design was something unique. The early Akbar period painting with its extraordinary compositional effects (Plate 182) had left a strong impress on the Indian miniaturists. It taught them the lesson that where the primary object was pictorial narration, the subject matter could be fitted into the composition in any attractive design quite regardless of perspective or naturalism. Such an attitude to composition was very easy for any Indian artist to grasp. It was the familiar method of the Gujerati style MS. illustrations given a new and more elaborate orientation. In early Rajasthani as well as early Pahari painting we can sense that artists trained in the Mughal school have made a deliberate departure from the Mughal method and have attempted to combine certain aspects of their training with an outlook widely different to that of the true Mughal artist. The marked Mughal influence can be seen particularly in the treatment of figures, costumes, accessories, architecture and sometimes in composition, but the colour tonality is widely different as also the treatment of trees and landscape in general. Above all, Rajasthani and Pahari miniatures are in the main the result of an intense emotional complex created by the great Vaishnava renaissance in song, dance, music and painting, which swept over all Central and Northern India in the 15th to the 18th centuries and dominated the life of the people. No such emotional complex affected Mughal painting.

With the death of Aurangzeb in 1707 A.D., Mughal painting entered on a new phase. As a reaction against the austerity of Aurangzeb's bigoted rule, the court life of the Mughals from about 1712 A.D. became one of soft ease and constant pleasure, degenerating into debauchery. Musicians and dancing girls held sway at the Imperial capital. Royal and aristocratic patronage was once more extended to the art of miniature painting, but now the productions centred mainly round music and dance parties, love scenes, zenana pastimes, courtesans, singing girls and such other subjects. Some of this work is quite skilful and the colour is often effective, but it is not to be compared to the output of the great period of Akbar, Jehangir, and Shah Jahan. This rather effete art remained the norm throughout the 18th century at the Mughal court and later degenerated into the bazar work known as Delhi ivory miniatures once popular with Indian and foreign visitors to Delhi.

The beginnings of Rajasthani painting can be placed round about 1600 A.D. Prior thereto there was a transition period about 1580 A.D. to 1600 A.D. in which the Gujerati MS. style began to change under the impact of Mughal painting. This impact largely came through what has been termed the Popular Mughal school in contradistinction to the output of the court ateliers. The taste for miniature painting created by Akbar led to the employment of artists by Rajasthani Rajas, the nobles of the Imperial court and even by the well-to-do merchant classes for illustrating a variety of literary themes (Plate 185B) and also for making portrait studies (Plate 185C). These were naturally painted in the Mughal idiom, though not by the great court artists and thus a Popular Mughal style, attractive in content and manner, came into being. A certain amount of coarse Bazar style Mughal painting also came into existance at the same time being the work of inferior artists.

The early Rajasthani school appears to have had its main centre at Mewar (Plate 187A), but local styles also grew up during the 17th century in Marwar, Bundi (Plate 186B), the Thikanas in the Ajmer area, Narsingarh in Malwa (Plate 186A) and other districts. In Bikaner, during the second half of the 17th century, a very strong Mughal influence prevailed and accordingly the work there, some of it very fine, is markedly in the Mughal manner. It must accordingly be differentiated from the early Rajasthani idiom proper. The 17th century is the vital period of the Rajasthani school.

In the 18th century much good work was done but there was an ever increasing tendency towards the the norms of 18th century Mughal painting. The work at Mewar, which centre was the leader of the early movement, suffered a very considerable decline, but Bundi continued to produce a variety of interesting styles right up to *circa* 1760-1770 A.D. A remarkable phenomenon during this period was the exceptional brilliance of the atelier of a small Rajput State called Kishangarh from about 1735 to 1755 A.D. During this period the Kishangarh atelier, which had hitherto produced the general run of 18th century Rajasthani work, was inspired by the poet prince Savant Singh of Kishangarh, known to all lovers of *Braj Bhasa* literature as the famous poet Nagari Das. Under the guidance of a master artist named Nihal Chand and the inspiration of Nagari Das, the Kishangarh atelier produced a small body of work which is regarded as one of the noblest achievements of Rajasthani art.

The second half of the 18th and the first half of the 19th century is also characterized by an unprecedented outburst of painting throughout Rajasthan. Not only every Rajput court but also every Rajput Thikana (feudal estate) had its atelier of artists. Some of these Thikanas, such as that of Ghanerao, employed quite a number of artists in their ateliers. The general quality of this Thikana painting, which consists largely of portraits, court scenes, hunting scenes, studies of favourite horses and dogs, music parties and such like subjects pertaining to the daily life of the Rajput aristocracy, is very mediocre indeed, yet sometimes paintings of considerable interest (Plate 187B) were produced. But by far and large the prolific output of this period is apt to become tedious. Even in the 19th century when the art of painting all over Rajasthan had become decadent, some very vigorous drawings of elephants were made at Bundi, a state which always seemed to maintain a praiseworthy standard in the output of its ateliers.

Just as Mughal painting was the mainspring behind the Rajasthani schools, so also it was the same influence which led to the creation of Pahari painting, the art of the Rajput Hill States of the Punjab. In contrast to the position in Gujerat and Rajasthan in pre-Mughal times, no form of book illustration appears to have flourished in these Hill States. The Gujerati style had not penetrated the hill fastnesses. Moreover, the Hill States were poor and their rulers lacked a taste for such cultural refinements as miniature painting. Besides, the maintenance of ateliers would cost money and the none too well-off Hill Chieftains no doubt preferred to spend their limited resources on other more obvious forms of entertainment, such as the maintenance of singers and dancers, and the purchase of excellent falcons for hawking. But it must not be forgotten that their traditional background was one of bardic lore, of knightly warfare and bold and ardent romance. Here was fertile soil for the growth of a vigorous school of painting. When the Mughal overlords introduced the system of hostages those Hill Princes who had perforce to reside for several years at the Mughal court began to assimilate various aspects of Mughal culture and develop a taste for Mughal type architecture, costume, etc. It was also but natural that they should have seen the work of Akbar's and Jehangir's numerous painters for both these sovereigns had a great love for miniature painting. When these hostages returned to their states they began to introduce various aspects of Mughal court life at their own courts. The first result of this new impact was the adoption of Mughal type architecture and costume. This change came into being in the Hill States not only through the hostages but also by reason of the fact that several Hill Rajas and their close relations served in the Mughal army and became accustomed to the life and manners of the Imperial capitals. Though we cannot be quite certain as to when the art of miniature painting was first practised in the Hill States, yet it seems that the first Hill chief to maintain a regular atelier and evince a real interest in book illustration was Raja Kirpal Pal of Basohli (1678-1694) (Plate 188A), a small Hill State with its capital on the Ravi. Today it is but a village with the ruins of the great fortress palace, once known as one of the wonders of the Hills. The style of painting which developed in Kirpal Pal's atelier and which soon became the norm all over the Hill States is known as the Basohli Kalam. It is characterized by its glowing hot tonality, large areas of background in a single colour such as red, yellow, orange, green, etc., and its passionate, almost savage, male and female types with their large staring eyes and sloping foreheads (Plates 188B and 189A). When this style of painting became the norm in all the Hill States many of the Rajas appear to have emulated Kirpal Pal's example and maintained ateliers of their own. Though the Basohli school was only indirectly influenced by early Rajasthani painting it was born of the same inspiration and inventiveness on the part of artists trained in the Mughal ateliers of the Aurangzeb period who had migrated to the Basohli court and were alive to the new movements which had taken place in Rajasthan and which we refer to as early Rajasthani painting. Thus Basohli painting is a complete synthesis, which did not develop from any earlier primitive style in the Hills. Those who have not carefully analyzed the elements of the Mughal school in Basohli painting have fallen into the error of regarding this school as having an ancestry in the Hills. But to date there is no evidence on which to base such a conclusion. Basohli painting in its great period, namely, *circa* 1675 to 1740 A.D. is as vital and as colourful as the best products of early Rajasthani painting. Its passionate intensity and excellent sense of design impart to it a quality which some find more captivating than the products of the Rajasthani school. But such preferences are after all a matter of individual taste. As already stated the Basohli Kalam was the norm in the Hills till *circa* 1740 A.D. Thereafter a major change in outlook took place. In 1739 A.D. Nadir Shah of Persia invaded Northern India and sacked Delhi. The insecurity of the decaying Mughal Empire thus became very evident and the first of the migrations to places where life could be secure and less troubled began to take place. There was a not inconsiderable exodus to the Punjab Hill States, including artists and artisans. Amongst such emigrants were artist families who had been trained in the Mughal school of the 18th century and accordingly their drawing and brushwork was of considerable merit. They were soon absorbed in the Hill courts where their work achieved immediate popularity. Their approach was more towards naturalism and softer and quieter colouring than the hot palette of the Basohli School.

This new phase of Pahari painting from about 1740 A.D. to 1765 A.D., when artists trained in the Mughal school of the first half of the 18th century dominated the ateliers of the Hill Rajas, is known as the "Pre-Kangra" phase (Plate 189B). It was not confined to any particular Hill State but became the accepted style all over the Hills. In Jammu its great patron was Balwant Singh, brother of the ruler Ranjit Dev. Balwant Singh used to have himself painted at work, at play, at leisure, and even when he was being shaved!

At Guler, Raja Govardhan Singh (1744-1770) also maintained an atelier where good work was produced. So also painters trained in the Mughal school worked at Jasrota, Suket, Kangra, Chamba and other States. The work of these artists trained in the Mughal school underwent a great change when they migrated to the Hills. At the Mughal capitals it was a period of decadence. The depiction of love scenes, music parties, zenana pastimes, and such frivolities were largely in vogue. It was the art of an effete over-ripe culture lacking in virility though not wanting in the graces which one could associate with songstresses and dancing girls. But when these artists came to the Hills, in an entirely different fresh atmosphere, to work for Rajas who loved the stories of the Krishna legend, the epics, bardic lore and the famous romances of old, their outlook changed so rapidly that they soon began to develop a style which, though based on Mughal painting of that period, had a charm which 18th century Mughal painting lacked (Pl. 189B). The "Pre-Kangra" phase led the way to what is known as the Kangra school of painting. This again is a generic name like the Basohli Kalam. It was not confined to the State of Kangra though the style may have originated in that State. It was a logical development from the "Pre-Kangra" phase. It is characterized by two main female facial types. One with straight nose in line with the forehead, pointed chin, flat mass of hair and narrow slanting eyes. It is known as the "Standard Type" (Plates 190B, 191A). The other known as the "Bhagavata Type" (Plates 190A, 191B), because it appears in a famous series illustrating the *Bhagavata Purana*, has a small round face of porcelain-like delicacy, small nose, finely painted hair and rounded chin. These Kangra school women are exquisite creatures who seem to live in a world of eternal romance no matter whether they be village milk maidens or princesses of royal estate. The fame of the Kangra school is closely associated with the greatest Raja of the Hills, Sansar Chand of Kangra (1774-1823 A.D.). He became overlord of almost the entire Hill territory till his downfall at the hands of Ranjit Singh of Lahore. He was a great patron of painting and had the largest and most varied atelier of artists ever known in the Hills. It is primarily the fame of his atelier that is responsible for the nomenclature "Kangra Kalam" being applied to almost all Hill painting during the period, *circa* 1770-1820 A.D. The famous *Bhagavata* series (Pl. 191B) was in all likelihood painted or supervised by his favourite artist Kaushala also known as Kushanlal.

The Kangra Kalam is in marked contrast to the Basohli Kalam. It is characterized by elegance, delicacy and a soft ethereal quality which imparts to it an air of great refinement and distinction. It is not passionate or intense like Basohli art, but is not wanting in an atmosphere of romance which is often cast in surroundings of natural beauty.

We have noted that it was the influence of the Mughal school which brought Rajasthani and Pahari painting into being. The first phase was the impact of the Mughal style on the Gujerati style and its variations in Central and Northern India. But the position in the Deccan in the 16th century was different. With the break up of the Bahamani Empire and the formation of five separate sultanates it seems that the art of miniature painting began to receive some encouragement. The Bahamanis, it appears, had not patronized this art at all, but there is good reason to believe that the Bijapur Sultans and also the Golconda Sultans had painters from Persia and Turkey at their courts. Such painting must have been in the Persian and Turkish manner though it is not difficult to conclude that foreign painters on Indian soil were bound in course of time to modify their original style under local influences. The great Hindu kingdom in the South during this period was the mighty and prosperous Vijayanagar Empire. Of the art of wall painting under Vijayanagar rule we have frescoes at several sites, but we are not aware whether any art of book illustration was in vogue at the Vijayanagar court. It is difficult to believe that a centre so famed for its cultural activities did not have some form of book illustration even though no examples have come to light. But after the downfall and destruction of Vijayanagar at the hands of the confederate sultanates at the battle of Talikota, if not before, artists and artisans from Vijayanagar must have sought employment at the courts of the sultans. Thus there arose a mixed style in which the indigenous influences from Vijayanagar intermingled with the style derived from Persia and Turkey. This mixed style may have come into being even before the battle of Talikota. One illustrated manuscript called the *Nujum-ul-Ulum* in the Chester Beatty Collection, which appears to have been painted in 1570, evidences this mixed style; while we have a somewhat later manuscript called the *Tarif-i-Husein Shahi* also in this mixed style, which deals with the battle of Talikota (1565 A.D.)as well as with the leisure moments of Hussain Nizam Shah of Ahmadnagar. It is however, not easy to distinguish any school of Ahmadnagar (Pl. 192) as distinct from that of Bijapur. Bijapur was perhaps the main centre of early Deccani painting and here the mixed style may have first developed. But in this connection Golconda may also have to be considered. This mixed style shows Persian, Turkish and indigenous features, the last named being derived from Vijayanagar. In this mixed style were *Ragamala* paintings which could have been painted for that great lover of music Ibrahim Adil Shah II of Bijapur, but here again Golconda may have to be considered. They can be ascribed to *circa* 1590 A.D. There is also a body of painting which can be ascribed to the period 1590 - 1620 in which we see Persian and Turkish characteristics prevailing, with some influence from the Mughal school which must have become quite well known in the Deccan during that period. This early group of paintings contains some fine portrait studies including portraits of Ibrahim Adil Shah II who must be regarded as the foremost patron of Deccani painting. The early Deccani school has to be distinguished from the Mughal school. Its initial inspiration was not via the Imperial capital of Delhi, but via Persia and Turkey from which countries artists came and worked in the Deccan.

The later phases of the Deccan school from about 1620 onwards show increased Mughal influences (Pl. 193A) though the school still maintains distinctive features which enables one to recognize its provenance. The main centres of Deccani painting were Bijapur, Golconda, Hyderabad, Ahmadnagar and Aurangabad, though it seems that certain families of artists had also settled at several less important centres. Most of the work of the 18th Century calls for no particular attention though quite competent in execution.

NOTES TO COLOUR PLATES

Frontispiece. Wild duck, anonymous. (Fol. 10, Dara Shikoh's album). Mughal School, Shah Jahan period. Mid-17th century or earlier.

Plate A. Illustration to the *Gita Govinda.* Provenance uncertain. Probably A.D. 1570-80. *Kulahdar* group. Prince of Wales Museum, Bombay.

Plate B. The House of Sheikh Fūl, painted by Bishandas. Mughal School. *Circa* A.D. 1625.

Plate C. Jahangir as Prince Salim, anonymous. (Fol. 18 of Dara Shikoh's album). "Prince and Preceptor". Mughal School, Shah Jahan period. Mid-17th century.

Plate D. Marble building, etc., by Muhammad Fakirullah Khan. (Johnson Collection, vol. xvii, fol. 3). Worship in a Pavilion. Mughal School. Late 17th century.

Plate E. Night scene. Krishna and Radha on the banks of the Jumna. Illustration to the *Gita Govinda.* Kangra school. Probably painted at the court of the great Sansar Chand of Kangra.

SHORT BIBLIOGRAPHY

GENERAL

L. D. Barnett, *The Antiquities of India*. Medici Society, 1913: 'Handbooks to Ancient Civilizations'.
Sir G. Birdwood, *The Industrial Arts of India*. 1880.
Cambridge History of India: Vol. i, *Ancient India*. Edited by E. J. Rapson. Cambridge University Press, 1922.
A. K. Coomaraswamy, *A History of Indian and Indonesian Art*. Goldston, 1927.
Vincent Smith, *Oxford History of India*. Edited by S. M. Edwardes. Clarendon Press, 1923.
Sir G. Watt, *Indian Art at Delhi*. 1904.

ARCHITECTURE AND SCULPTURE

J. Burgess, *Archaeological Survey of India Reports*, Vols. i-v. For Cave Temples, &c.
K. de B. Codrington, *Ancient India* (Benn, 1926); *Medieval India*.
Sir A. Cunningham, *Archaeological Survey of India Reports*, Vols. i-xxiii.
——, *The Stupa at Bharhut*. London, 1879.
——, *Bhilsa Topes*. London, 1854.
J. Fergusson and J. Burgess, *A History of Indian and Eastern Architecture*. Murray, 1910.
A Foucher, *L'Art Gréco-Bouddhique du Ghandhara*. Paris, 1905 and 1923.
——, *Étude sur l'Iconographie bouddhique de l'Inde*. Paris, 1905.
O. C. Gangoly, *South Indian Bronzes*. Calcutta, 1914.
G. Jouveau-Dubreuil, *Iconographie du Sud de l'Inde*. Paris, 1914.
Archaeological Survey of India *Reports* and *Memoirs*.
Sir J. H. Marshall, *Guide to Sanchi*. Calcutta, 1918.
——, *Guide to Taxila*. Calcutta, 1918.
Sir A. Stein, *Serindia*. Clarendon Press, 1921.

PAINTING

P. Brown, *Indian Painting*. Oxford University Press, 1918.
A. K. Coomaraswamy, *Indian Drawings*. London, 1910 and 1912.
——, *Rajput Painting*. Oxford University Press, 1916.
V. Goloubew, *Peintures bouddhiques aux Indes;* in *Annales du Musée Guimet*, xl. Paris.
J. Griffiths, *The Paintings....of Ajanta*. London, 1896-7.
E. Kuhnel and H. Goetz, *Indische Buchmalereien*.
N. C. Mehta, *Studies in Indian Painting*. Bombay, 1927.

ADDITIONAL BOOKS

(*Not listed in the previous Edition*)

V. S. Agrawala, *Sculptures in the Curzon Museum of Archaeology*. Mathura, 1933.
——, *Guide to the Archaeological Sections of the Provincial Museum, Lucknow*. Lucknow, 1940.
Sir T. W. Arnold and J. V. S. Wilkinson, *The Library of A. Chester Beatty*, 3 vols. Oxford, 1936.
L. Bachoffer, *Early Indian Sculpture*, 2 vols. Paris, 1929.
Douglas Barret, *Painting of the Deccan, XVI-XVII Century*. London, n.d.
Binyon and Arnold, *The Court Painters of the Grand Moguls*. Oxford, 1921.
Percy Brown, *Indian Architecture*, 2 vols. Bombay, 1959.
——, *Indian Painting under the Mughals*. London, 1924.
Moti Chandra, *Mewar Painting*. Lalit Kala Akademi, New Delhi, 1957.
——, *Jain Miniature Paintings from Western India*. Ahmedabad, 1949.
Pramod Chandra, *Bundi Painting*. Lalit Kala Akademi, New Delhi, 1959.
A. K. Coomaraswamy, *Catalogue of the Indian Collections in the Museum of Fine Arts, Boston*, 5 vols. 1923-24.
Rai Krishnadasa, *Mughal Miniatures*. Lalit Kala Akademi, New Delhi, 1955.
E. Dickinson and Karl Khandalavala, *Kisangarh Painting*. Lalit Kala Akademi, New Delhi, 1959.
Hermann Goetz, *India*, Five Thousand Years of Indian Art. 1960.
——, *Art and Architecture of Bikaner*. Oxford, 1950.
F. Graveley and T. N. Ramachandra, *Catalogue of the South Indian Hindu Images in the Madras Government Museum*. Madras, 1932.

Karl Khandalavala, *Indian Sculpture and Painting*. Bombay, 1938.
——, *Pahari Miniature Painting*. Bombay, 1958.
Karl Khandalavala, Moti Chandra and Pramod Chandra, *Miniature Paintings from the Khajanchi Collection*. Lalit Kala Akademi, New Delhi, 1960..
Stella Kramrisch, *Indian Sculpture*. Calcutta, 1933.
——, *The Art of India Through the Ages*. London, 1954.
——, *A Survey of Painting in the Deccan*. London, 1937.
E. Mackay, *The Indus Civilization*. London, 1935.
Sir. J. Marshall, *Mohenjo-daro and the Indus Civilization*. London, 1931.
——, *The Buddhist Art of Gandhara*. Cambridge, 1960.
Benjamin Rowland, *The Art and Architecture of India*. London, 1959.
C. Sivaramamurti, *Amaravati Sculptures in the Madras Government Museum*. Madras, 1942.
Ivan Stchoukine, *La Peinture Indienne, à l'Epoque des Grand Moghols*. Paris, 1929.
Sir R. E. M. Wheeler, *The Indus Civilization*. Cambridge, 1953.
H. Zimmer, *The Art of Indian Asia*. New York, 1955.

Journals and Reports

Marg.
Lalit-Kala.
Ancient India.
Indian Antiquary.
Archaeological Survey of India, Annual Reports.
Archaeological Survey of India, Memoirs.
Indian Archaeology, Annual Reports.

INDEX